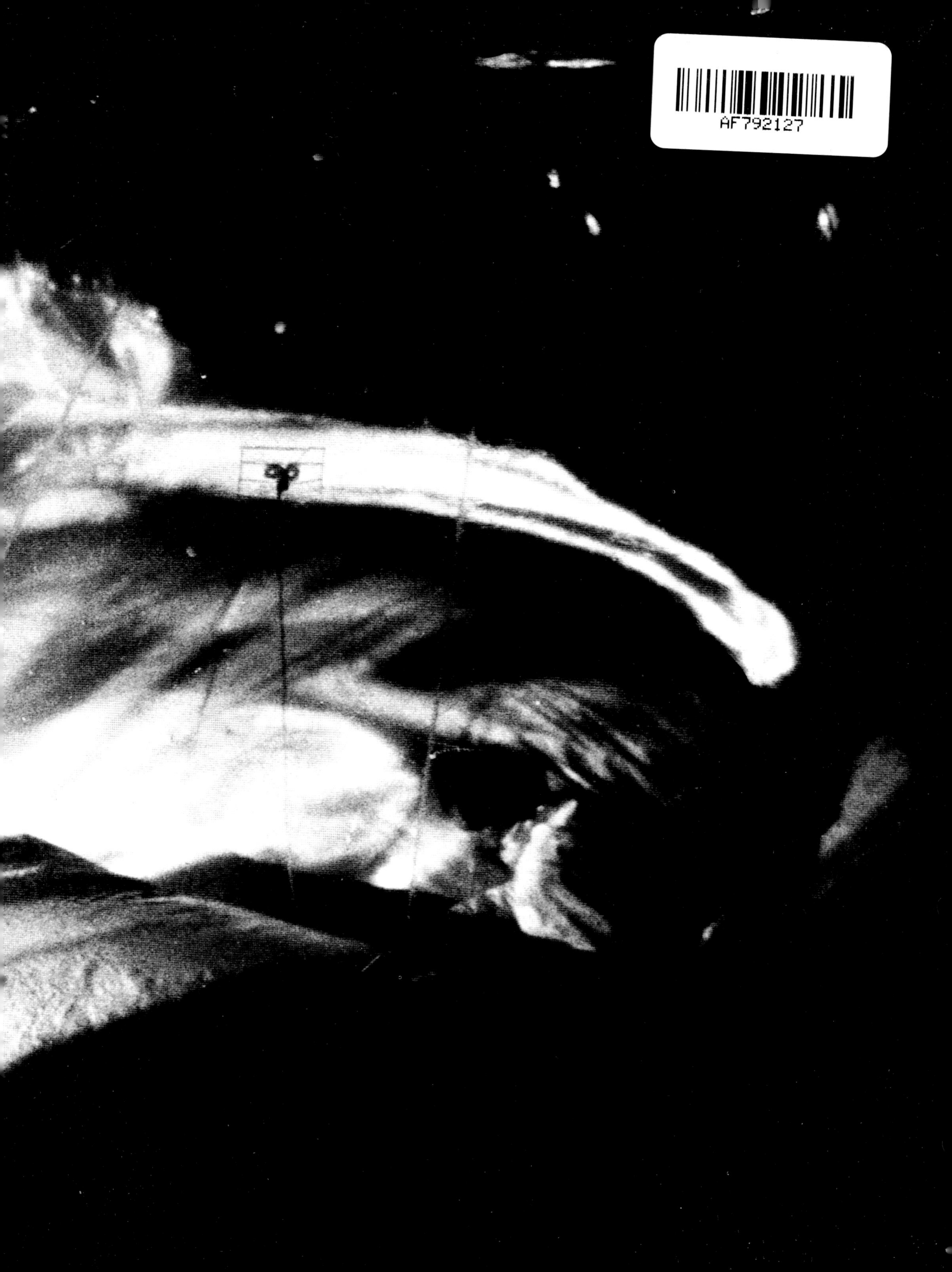

Jeffrey Shaw – a user's manual

From Expanded Cinema to Virtual Reality

Jeffrey Shaw – eine Gebrauchsanweisung

Vom Expanded Cinema zur Virtuellen Realität

Edition ZKM Cantz

Edition ZKM
Publisher: ZKM/Zentrum für Kunst und Medientechnologie Karlsruhe, Heinrich Klotz

Jeffrey Shaw – a user's manual. From Expanded Cinema to Virtual Reality
Publishers: ZKM/Zentrum für Kunst und Medientechnologie Karlsruhe, Heinrich Klotz and Neue Galerie am Landesmuseum Joanneum Graz, Peter Weibel

Editor: Manuela Abel

Translators: Manuela Abel, Agnes Choma, Deke Dusinberre, Thomas Morrison, Florian Rötzer, Astrid Sommer

English-language proofreading: Thomas Morrison

German-language proofreading: Astrid Sommer

Graphic design: Holger Jost

Printed by Dr. Cantz'sche Druckerei, Ostfildern, Germany

Published by Cantz Verlag
Senefelderstraße 9
73760 Ostfildern-Ruit
Tel. (0) 7 11 / 44 99 30
Fax (0) 7 11 / 4 41 45 79

Distribution in the USA:
DAP Distributed Art Publishers
155 Avenue of the Americas, 2nd Floor
New York, N.Y. 10013
Tel. (001) 2 12 - 6 27 19 99
Fax (001) 2 12 - 6 27 84 94

ISBN 3-89322-882-9

Printed in Germany

Edition ZKM
Herausgeber: ZKM/Zentrum für Kunst und Medientechnologie Karlsruhe, Heinrich Klotz

Jeffrey Shaw – eine Gebrauchsanweisung. Vom Expanded Cinema zur Virtuellen Realität
Herausgeber: ZKM/Zentrum für Kunst und Medientechnologie Karlsruhe, Heinrich Klotz und Neue Galerie am Landesmuseum Joanneum Graz, Peter Weibel

Redaktion: Manuela Abel

Übersetzungen: Manuela Abel, Agnes Choma, Deke Dusinberre, Thomas Morrison, Florian Rötzer, Astrid Sommer

Englisches Lektorat: Thomas Morrison

Deutsches Lektorat: Astrid Sommer

Grafik-Design: Holger Jost

Gesamtherstellung: Dr. Cantz'sche Druckerei, Ostfildern bei Stuttgart

Erschienen im Cantz Verlag
Senefelderstraße 9
73760 Ostfildern-Ruit
Tel. (0) 7 11 / 44 99 30
Fax (0) 7 11 / 4 41 45 79

ISBN 3-89322-882-9

Contents

Inhalt

Participation and Interaction

By Heinrich Klotz

Jeffrey Shaw belongs to that small, international group of media artists representing a new type of artist for whom electronic technologies are everyday tools and any trepidation regarding the computer has long been overcome. Since 1991 he has been director of the Institute for Visual Media at the ZKM/Center for Art and Media Karlsruhe. The media artists from all over the world who spend a term of residence there profit not only from the stipends and technical facilities the Institute places at their disposal, but also from the capabilities of its director. This combination of artistic imagination with organizational talent and technical expertise willing to experiment with and discover the reach of a new creative potential is what characterizes Jeffrey Shaw – and with him a new type of artist.

In this jointly published monograph on Jeffrey Shaw's work, the ZKM/Center for Art and Media Karlsruhe and the Neue Galerie am Landesmuseum Joanneum Graz present a first-ever survey of the œuvre of a media artist. It is an attempt to convey with the classical means of still pictures works of art based on moving images.

Jeffrey Shaw's outstanding achievement lies in the development of 'interactive art', which his early works brought into being and explored even before it was possible to incorporate electronic devices. In countermanding the purely spectatorial role of the public, interaction also overruled the traditional conception of art. Active intervention took the place of passive absorption and contemplation. Those who mount Jeffrey Shaw's bicycle in *The Legible City* (1989) and ride at will through the capital letters rendering the architectural landscapes of Manhattan, Amsterdam and Karlsruhe, switching cities as they please, moving the handlebars to re-align the perspective opening up in front of them, pedalling harder or softer to vary the speed, have become actors rather than 'observers'. The huge image projected before their eyes is the model that guides them; yet it can be re-modelled by their actions.

Other works by Shaw corroborate this principle of intervention and modulation producing new relationships between work and spectator, between aesthetic object and responsive and impressionable subject; the leitmotiv is no longer the 'disinterested perception' on which aesthetic theory was once founded. Schopenhauer's philosophical theory of the 'world as will and idea', which extols the status of disinterested contemplation as the first and highest aesthetic knowledge, and the concomitant silencing of the interest-governed will as a form of detachment from the world, might today be expounded somewhat differently. The contemplative mode of aesthetic reception is no longer the matter of interactive art.

Instead, the new work of art allows us to apprehend the world in a different mode of abstraction from human aims and anxieties: in

Partizipation und Interaktion

Von Heinrich Klotz

Jeffrey Shaw gehört zu jener kleinen Gruppe internationaler Medienkünstler mit der ein neuer Künstlertypus geboren wurde, der die elektronischen Techniken als alltägliches Werkzeug zu gebrauchen weiß und der die Scheu vor dem Computer schon frühzeitig überwunden hat. Seit 1991 leitet Jeffrey Shaw das Institut für Bildmedien am ZKM/Zentrum für Kunst und Medientechnologie Karlsruhe. Es sind dort Medienkünstler aus aller Welt zu Gast; sie profitieren nicht nur von den Stipendien und den technischen Einrichtungen des Zentrums, sondern zugleich auch von den Fähigkeiten seines Leiters. Die Verbindung von künstlerischer Phantasie mit Organisationstalent und technischem Wissen, das sich experimentierend auf ein noch unbekanntes Gestaltungspotential einläßt, charakterisiert Jeffrey Shaw – und mit ihm den neuen Typus des Künstlers.

Das ZKM Karlsruhe und die Neue Galerie am Landesmuseum Joanneum Graz legen mit der Werkmonographie von Jeffrey Shaw zum ersten Mal einen Gesamtüberblick über das Werk eines Medienkünstlers vor. Es ist der Versuch, mit den klassischen Mitteln des stehenden Bildes die Werke der bewegten Bilder wiederzugeben.

Die besondere Leistung Jeffrey Shaws besteht in der Entwicklung des sogenannten interaktiven Kunstwerks, das er bereits frühzeitig mit seinen ersten Arbeiten – noch vor der Einführung der elektronischen Techniken – auf den Weg gebracht hat. Mit der Interaktion wurde die bloße Betrachterrolle des Publikums und damit auch der traditionelle Kunstbegriff außer Kraft gesetzt. An die Stelle passiver Versenkung und Kontemplation trat der aktive Eingriff. Wer sich auf das Fahrrad von Jeffrey Shaws *The Legible City* (1989) setzt und nach seiner Wahl – schaltbar – durch die in Buchstaben umgesetzten Stadtlandschaften von Manhattan, Amsterdam und Karlsruhe fährt, die Lenkstange betätigt und damit die vor ihm sich öffnenden Perspektiven neu ausrichtet, auch das Tempo über das Tretpedal variiert, ist nicht mehr ein ›Betrachter‹, sondern ein Handelnder. Er verändert mit seinem Tun das große Projektionsbild, das er vor Augen hat und das sowohl ihn leitet als auch von ihm verwandelt wird.

Andere Arbeiten Shaws bestätigen dieses Prinzip des Eingreifens und Veränderns, mit dem ein neues Verhältnis zwischen Werk und Betrachter, zwischen ästhetischem Objekt und reagierendem und beeindruckbarem Subjekt entsteht; das ›interesselose Wahrnehmen‹, das einmal die Grundlage der ästhetischen Theorie bildete, ist nicht länger das Leitmotiv. Schopenhauers Philosophie der ›Welt als Wille und Vorstellung‹, die den Status der interesselosen Anschauung als höchste ästhetische Erkenntnisstufe und des Verlöschens des interessensgebundenen Willens als eine Form des Weltvergessens preist, könnte so nicht mehr geschrieben werden. Die Kontemplation als eine Weise ästhetischer Rezeption ist nicht mehr Sache des interaktiven Kunstwerks.

the mode of the player. More earthly now by far, we operate the mechanism that transports us, the experimentalists, into alien-but-benevolent worlds. *Homo ludens* is the closest relation of the aesthetic observer, and attains by comparable means the respite from the world achieved by absorption into artistic experience – namely, the liberation from the utilitarian goals of the functionalized practice of life. This experience of a moment of freedom is also central to the definition of a work of art.

Participation was the forerunner of interaction. The spectator involvement solicited by the emergent participative environments of the 1960s had already wrought fundamental changes in the mode of dealings with art, had transformed the recipient into actor. The expanded cinema events staged by Shaw and his collaborators in the Netherlands were an early inducement to leave the world of pure illusionism. Putting inflatable tubes into a screen to metamorphize the projection surface, they issued a call for interaction. It is significant that Shaw chose moving pictures as a means of design in these early expanded cinema experiments. His attempt to extend art into life was based on the film medium – the vehicle possessing the strongest illusionary powers and the most persuasive ability to distract the viewers from the world around them – which he used to shatter the alchemy of illusion in order to make the spectator a participant whose actions produced an effect. The spirit of the 1960s, with its ardour for enlightenment, had begun to permeate the arts. And, in spite of changing times, this zeal to remove the frontiers in creations that are no longer purely illusionist has remained central to Jeffrey Shaw's work.

Shaw repeatedly varied this scenario by presenting works made solely to be contemplated; *Heavens Gate* (1986), for instance, in which cascading abstract forms fall down from the opening Baroque heavens onto the mirrored floor space of the viewer. This time, the classical work of art changes into a stream of animated images, minor miracles of fulfilled expectations. For one had never stopped hoping that one day the heavenly Baroque portal really would open.

Translated from the German by Thomas Morrison.

Stattdessen begegnen wir dem neuen Kunstwerk auf eine andere Art der Selbstvergessenheit, als spielende. Weitaus irdischer betätigen wir den Mechanismus, der uns – experimentierend – in fremdfreundliche Welten entführt. Der *homo ludens* ist der engste Verwandte des ästhetisch Genießenden – und er dringt auf vergleichbaren Wegen zu jener Befindlichkeit vor, die der sich in das Kunstwerk Versenkende ebenso zu erfahren vermag: dem Status des Befreitseins von den nützlichen Zielen der funktionalisierten Lebenspraxis. Die Erfahrung eines Moments der Freiheit ist auch der Kern einer Definition des Kunstwerks.

Die Interaktion hatte ihre Vorläufer in der Partizipation. Die während der sechziger Jahre aufkommenden partizipativen, zum Spiel einladenden Environments haben bereits den Umgang mit dem Kunstwerk grundsätzlich verändert und den Rezipienten in einen Agierenden verwandelt. Shaw und seine niederländischen Kollegen haben schon mit dem ›Expanded Cinema‹ dazu aufgefordert, die Welt der reinen Illusion zu verlassen. Die aufblasbaren Schläuche, die in eine Leinwand eingenäht waren und die Projektionsfläche veränderten, haben bereits zur Interaktion herausgefordert. Es ist bezeichnend, daß Shaw mit diesen frühen Arbeiten des ›Expanded Cinema‹ zu den bewegten Bildern als Gestaltungsmaterial griff. Mit dem illusionistisch am stärksten wirkenden Medium, dem Film, der den Betrachter am intensivsten fortlenkt von seiner Lebensumwelt, hat Shaw die Erweiterung in das Leben hinein versucht, also die Hermetik der Illusion gesprengt, um den Betrachter in einen aktiv Beteiligten zu verwandeln und ihn in die Rolle des wirkungsvoll Handelnden zu versetzen. Der Geist der sechziger Jahre mit seinem Aufklärungspathos mischte sich in die Künste hinein. Das Entgrenzungspathos des nicht mehr nur illusionistischen Kunstwerks ist den Arbeiten Jeffrey Shaws trotz der sich ändernden Zeiten geblieben.

Mitten hinein in die Szenerie dieser neuen Kunst stellt Shaw die zu reiner Anschauung gemachten Werke wie *Heavens Gate* (1986): Aus einem sich öffnenden Barockhimmel fallen die Formenkaskaden der Abstraktion auf die spiegelnde Standfläche des Betrachters herab. Hier verwandelt sich das klassische Kunstwerk in einen Strom bewegter Bilder, kleine Wunder der Verwirklichung vergangener Erwartungen. Denn schon immer hatte man gehofft, daß sich dereinst das barocke Himmelstor wirklich öffnen würde.

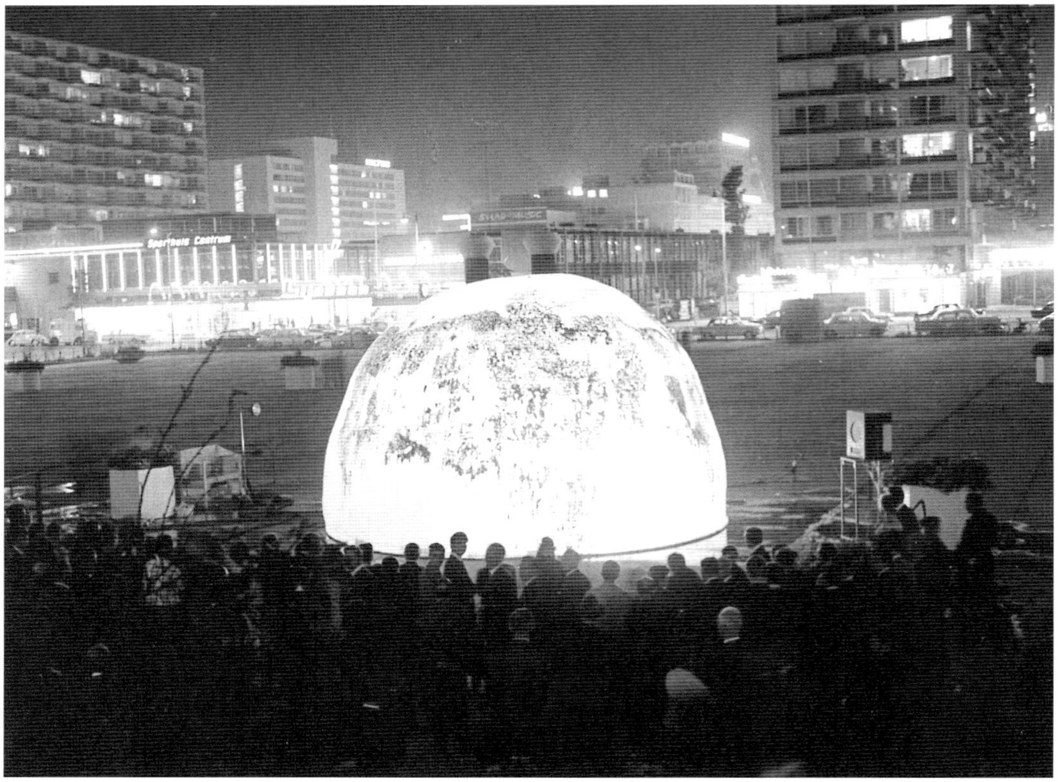

Corpocinema, Amsterdam, Netherlands, 1967. Photo: Pieter Boersma.

Jeffrey Shaw: A User's Manual
By Peter Weibel

I. From Expanded Cinema to Virtual Reality

The Experimental Film Festival in Knokke-le-Zoute, Belgium, a festival now legendary for its radical commitment to pure film art and from the 1950s up to the early '70s a unique forum – whose disappearance from the cultural landscape was an irretrievable loss – for innovative exploration of the cinematographic code, was the venue of a performance by Theo Botschuijver, Jeffrey Shaw, Tjebbe van Tijen and Sean Wellesley-Miller in 1967. *MovieMovie* was an early film environment whose combination of several aspects of avant-garde cinema evoked an accordingly enthusiastic response from the audience. A large plastic skin had been inflated to produce a balloon-shaped structure made up of two cones. The surface of the inner cone was white, that of the larger outer cone transparent. While spotlights and film projectors beamed coloured light and moving pictures (including excerpts from narrative and abstract films) onto the structure, various activities went on inside the free space between the two cones: white balloons were inflated and the space filled with smoke in order to add a sense of space and depth to the images being projected; performers wearing white overalls moved around inside large white tubes. Soon the performers were joined by members of the audience, who shed their clothes and jumped into the inflatable structure, the motion of their bodies bringing about further changes in the shape of the pneumatic architecture and in this way distorting the projected images. The mixed-media event was intensified by strobe light effects as well as electronic sounds (by the Musica Elettronica Viva) that were partially modulated by the movement of performers and public in their acoustic space.

MovieMovie was the public climax in a series of expanded cinema experiments which began in 1966 with the film *Continuous Sound and Image Moments* (with Tjebbe van Tijen) and continued until 1971. A number of formal and material factors figured throughout the actions, installations, performances, happenings, situations and environments associated with the experiments:

1. Mobile screens: semi-transparent projection screens set up behind each other in a row to achieve the effect of spatial depth; plastic projection surfaces whose shapes could be changed (by spectator interaction).

2. Audience participation: balloon-shaped screens could be inflated and deformed by the spectators; the audience could move around inside the projected images; the viewers' bodies served as projection screens; incipient interactivity between image and viewer, between image and sound.

3. New materials: pyrotechnic experiments, inflatable structures, air, water, fire, confetti, steam, gelatine, etc.

4. Mobile projections.

These four conditions brought into being a new equation be-

Jeffrey Shaw: Eine Gebrauchsanweisung
Von Peter Weibel

I. Vom Expanded Cinema zur Virtuellen Realität

Beim Experimentalfilm-Festival in Knokke-le-Zoute (Belgien), das von den fünfziger Jahren bis Anfang der Siebziger ein einzigartiges Forum für die innovative Erforschung des kinematographischen Codes war und wegen seines radikalen Engagements für die reine Filmkunst einen legendären Status erlangt hat und dessen Verschwinden von der kulturellen Landkarte ein unwiederbringlicher Verlust ist, gab es 1967 eine Vorführung, in der mehrere Aspekte des Avantgardefilms kumulierten und deren Resonanz beim Publikum daher entsprechend groß war: *MovieMovie* war der Titel dieser frühen Environment-Aktion mit Film von Theo Botschuijver, Jeffrey Shaw, Tjebbe van Tijen und Sean Wellesley-Miller. Eine große Plastikhülle war mit Preßluft aufgeblasen worden, so daß ein ballonförmiges Gebilde aus zwei Kegeln entstand, wovon der innere eine weiße und der größere äußere eine transparente Oberfläche besaß. Im Raum dazwischen fanden verschiedene Aktionen statt: weiße Ballons wurden aufgeblasen und Rauch wurde erzeugt, um den Bildern eine räumliche Wirkung zu geben; Performer in weißen Overalls bewegten sich in großen weißen Röhren. Scheinwerfer und Filmprojektoren warfen von oben farbiges Licht bzw. Filme (Ausschnitte aus Spielfilmen, abstrakte Filme u.a.) auf den Raumkörper. Bald mischten sich auch die Zuschauer unter die Performer, warfen ihre Kleider weg und veränderten durch ihre Bewegungen die Form der pneumatischen Architektur, wobei sie auch die projizierten Bilder deformierten. Dieses multimediale Ereignis wurde durch elektronische Geräuschmusik (von Musica Elettronica Viva), welche zum Teil von den Bewegungen der Performer moduliert wurde, und durch stroboskopische Lichteffekte verstärkt.

MovieMovie war der öffentliche Höhepunkt einer Reihe von ›Expanded Cinema‹-Experimenten, die 1966 mit dem Film *Continuous Sound and Image Moments* (mit Tjebbe van Tijen) begann und bis 1971 fortgeführt wurde. Bei all diesen Aktionen, Installationen, Performances, Ereignissen, Situationen und Environments gab es einige formale und materiale Konstanten:

1. Mobile Leinwände: semitransparente Projektionsleinwände wurden hintereinander gehängt, um eine räumliche Tiefenwirkung zu erreichen; (durch das Publikum) veränderbare Gestalt der Projektionsflächen aus Plastik.

2. Publikumspartizipation: ballonförmige Leinwände konnten vom Publikum aufgeblasen und verformt werden; das Publikum konnte sich in den projizierten Bildern bewegen; die Körper der Zuschauer dienten als Leinwand; Anfänge von Interaktivität zwischen Bild und Betrachter, zwischen Bild und Ton.

3. Neue Materialien: pyrotechnische Experimente, aufblasbare Strukturen, Luft, Wasser, Feuer, Konfetti, Dampf, Gelatine etc.

4. Mobile Projektionen.

Durch diese vier Bedingungen entstand eine neue Gleichung zwischen Bild und Raum, zwischen Bild und Betrachter. Die Kinetik des Körpers des Betrachters und des dreidimensionalen Körpers

tween image and space, between image and spectator. A dynamic architectonic space for visual events was created by the kinesis of the viewers bodies and three-dimensional screen structures. Body, architecture and image fused together in the course of a multi-media event in which the historical boundaries between these three elements evaporated – hence the title *Corpocinema* given to an expanded cinema environment produced (by the same team as *MovieMovie*) in 1967. Architecture and body served as projection screen, the spectators were integrated in the image because they were denizens of the architecture, and the image could be entered because it was integrated in the architecture. The viewer moved about in this visual space, plunged into the expanded visual area. A moving projector sent the image wandering over a physically mobile plastic screen to be deformed and transformed. Body, image and space were synchronized in a new way, treated as a dynamic field of variables. Everything that digital technology would some years later make possible to a intensified degree – the immersion of the viewer in the image and the reciprocally synchronized motion of viewer and image – was anticipated by the analog technology used in the expanded cinema events. *Corpocinema*, for instance, consisted of a huge, inflated, transparent PVC dome (7 m in diameter and 4.5 m high) onto which various films and slides were projected. Structured events and actions – the inflation of balloons, the filling of the dome interior with smoke and steam – created conditions allowing a temporal materialization of the immaterial images being projected. Incidentally, most of these expanded cinema environments were presented in a context outside that of institutional art.

In the years (from c. 1970) that followed the expanded cinema experiments, Jeffrey Shaw continued, as a member of the Eventstructure Research Group (1967–79, Botschuijver, Shaw, Wellesley-Miller), to add to the vocabulary of soft, reactive, inflatable architectures: *Waterwalk* (1969), *Waterquake* (1970), *Cloud* (1970, where images of daytime clouds were projected at night onto an inflated sculpture suspended from the roof of the Stedelijk Museum, Amsterdam), *Inflatable Creatures, Artificial Landscapes, Airgrounds*, the huge *Three Pavilions* (1971). The pneumatic domes built between 1968 and 1973 by the Eventstructure Research Group clearly reflect the influence of Richard Buckminster Fuller's dome structures and their visionary, utopian aspects. The title of his book 'Operating Manual for Spaceship Earth' (1969) has exercised an equally lasting influence on the Expanded Cinema movement up to the present-day. Stan VanDerBeek, who coined the term 'expanded cinema' (some time around 1965), also built a dome-shaped structure for multiple cinematic projections. The inflatable dome re-appears in later work, for instance in Shaw's *EVE* (*Extended Virtual Environment*, 1993). Right down to the choice of words – from 'expanded cinema environment' to 'extended virtual environment' – a striking continuity runs through the thirty years of

der Leinwand schufen einen dynamischen architektonischen Raum für visuelle Ereignisse. Der Körper, die Architektur und das Bild verschmolzen im multimedialen Ereignis, indem sich ihre historischen Grenzen auflösten. Deshalb hieß auch ein ›Expanded Cinema‹-Environment von 1967 *Corpocinema* (mit der gleichen Mannschaft wie bei *MovieMovie*). Architektur und Körper dienten als Leinwand, der Betrachter als Bewohner der Architektur wurde zu einem Teil des Bildes, das Bild als Teil der Architektur wurde begehbar. Der Betrachter bewegte sich im Bildraum, er tauchte in die erweiterte Bildfläche ein. Das Bild konnte mittels eines beweglichen Projektors wandern und sich aufgrund der mobilen Leinwand aus Plastik verformen und verändern. Körper, Bild und Raum wurden auf neue Weise, nämlich als dynamisches Feld von Variablen, synchronisiert. All das, was später durch die digitale Technologie erhöht möglich wurde, nämlich die Immersion des Betrachters in das Bild und die wechselseitige Synchronisation der Bewegung des Betrachters und des Bildes, war in der analogen Technologie der ›Expanded Cinema‹-Aktionen vorgezeichnet. *Corpocinema* beispielsweise bestand aus einer riesigen aufgeblasenen Kuppel aus transparenter PVC-Folie (mit einem Durchmesser von 7 m und einer Höhe von 4,5 m), auf die verschiedene Filme und Dias projiziert wurden. Durch strukturierte Ereignisse und Aktionen – Ballons wurden aufgeblasen, der Innenraum der Kuppel mit Rauch und Dampf gefüllt – wurden die Bedingungen für die zeitliche Materialisation der projizierten immateriellen Bilder geschaffen. Im übrigen fanden die meisten dieser ›Expanded Cinema‹-Environments außerhalb des institutionellen Kunstkontextes statt.

In den Jahren nach den ›Expanded Cinema‹-Experimenten, ab ca. 1970, baute Jeffrey Shaw im Rahmen der Eventstructure Research Group (1967–79, Botschuijver, Shaw, Wellesley-Miller) das Vokabular der weichen, reaktiven, aufblasbaren Architektur aus: *Waterwalk* (1969), *Waterquake* (1970), *Cloud* (1970, wo des nachts auf eine aufgeblasene Skulptur, die vom Dach des Stedelijk Museums Amsterdam hing, Aufnahmen von Wolken zur Tageszeit projiziert wurden), *Inflatable Creatures, Artificial Landscapes, Airgrounds, Three Pavilions* (1971) von gigantischer Größe. Die pneumatischen Kuppeln, die zwischen 1968 und 1973 von der Eventstructure Research Group erbaut wurden, reflektieren klar den Einfluß der Kuppelbauten von Richard Buckminster Fuller und deren visionäre utopischen Aspekte. Auch der Titel von Fullers Buch ›Bedienungsanleitung für das Raumschiff Erde‹ (1969) hat bis heute einen bleibenden Einfluß auf die ›Expanded-Cinema‹-Bewegung ausgeübt. Stan VanDerBeek, von dem der Ausdruck ›Expanded Cinema‹ (um 1965) stammt, hat ebenfalls eine Kuppel für kinematographische Mehrfachprojektionen gebaut. Diese Kuppel taucht z.B. 1993 wieder auf in Shaws *EVE* (*Extended Virtual Environment*/Erweiterte Virtuelle Umgebung). Bis in die Wortwahl hinein, von ›Expanded Cinema Environment‹ zu ›Extended Virtual Environment‹, ist die Kontinuität der dreißigjährigen kinematographischen Recherche von Jeffrey Shaw erkennbar, die ganz offensichtlich um die Beziehung Bild und Betrachter, Bild und

cinematographic research Jeffrey Shaw conducted into the relationship between image and viewer, image and space. What makes his work distinctive from comparable explorations such as those Gene Youngblood describes in his book 'Expanded Cinema' (1970) is the emphasis on architecture and space rather than the image. Clearly, the reason Shaw passed over the expanded cinesemiotic possibilities presented by video technology in the 1970s was that he wasn't interested in expanding the visual code. With the aid of other technologies such as slide projection, mirroring techniques and anamorphosis, he attempted to establish a new interactive relationship between image and viewer. In this process he never deployed the image as an autonomous world in the way of modern painting, however, but mainly as a component of the architecture and three-dimensional space in a manner similar to that of, for example, the Baroque. A video installation like *Heavens Gate* (1986), which uses Baroque ceiling paintings, is therefore significant, and likewise *Anamorphoses of Memory* and *Going to the Heart of the Center of The Garden of Delights*, two other works made in the same year.

The mid-1960s saw the creation of film environments in which the film medium was spatially expanded in the course of a dialectic confrontation not involving the screening of actual films. Expanded cinema was the attempt to exceed the boundaries of established film syntax in order to restore to film its original value as a medium. Claes Oldenburg, for one, staged a film-less cinema happening with *Moviehouse* (1965). Peter Weibel similarly showed a 'film-less film' in 1966 by beaming pure projector light onto a wall in front of which he stood calmly holding up in his outstretched hands a big blue ball advertising Nivea, the hum of a running camera audible in the background. These film-less films – whereby 'film-less' generally denoted the absence of celluloid – were the first attempts to abandon classical cinema and its traditional conception of reality. Film was seen as a technological medium that had been arrested at some point in its historical development, and therefore needed to be expanded and exceeded. These staged expansions of the customary film form that broke through the conventional order of commercial filmmaking marked the beginnings of a search for new technologies able to facilitate an expanded notion of reality corresponding to the expanded – and sometimes drug-induced – state of consciousness of the period. Expanded cinema opened up the path away from cinematography towards video and digital technology. The classical celluloid film and its standard configuration was seen as merely one among many possible linkages of specific elements. It was the multitude of alternative linkages of cinematographic elements that expanded cinema wished to explore. With its stock figures and set rules – projector, projection surface, projection booth, motion-picture house, audience, projectionist, film strip, sound track, director, camera, camera movement, cutting equipment, montage, camera

Raum konzentriert ist. Kennzeichnend als Differenz zu anderen vergleichbaren Recherchen – wie sie in Gene Youngbloods Buch ›Expanded Cinema‹ (1970) nachzulesen sind – ist die Zentrierung auf die Architektur, auf den Raum und weniger auf das Bild. Shaw hat die Erweiterung des kinematographischen Codes in den siebziger Jahren durch die Videotechnologie offensichtlich deswegen ausgelassen, weil er an der Erweiterung des Bildcodes nicht interessiert war. Er hat mit Hilfe anderer Technologien wie Diaprojektion, Spiegeltechniken, Anamorphose etc. versucht, eine neue interaktive Beziehung zwischen Bild und Betrachter herzustellen. Dabei ist das Bild aber niemals als autonome Welt wie in der modernen Malerei eingesetzt worden, sondern vorwiegend als Teil der Architektur und des Raumes wie z.B. im Barock. Eine Video-Installation wie *Heavens Gate* (1986), die Deckenfresken aus dem Barock verwendet, ist daher bezeichnend; desgleichen die aus demselben Jahr stammenden Arbeiten *Anamorphoses of Memory* und *Going to the Heart of the Center of The Garden of Delights*.

Mitte der sechziger Jahre entstanden Film-Environments, die in einer dialektischen Auseinandersetzung mit dem Medium Film zu dessen räumlicher Erweiterung führten, ohne daß dabei Filme vorgeführt worden wären. ›Erweitertes Kino‹ oder ›Expanded Cinema‹ bildete den Versuch, die Grenzen der etablierten Syntax des Films zu überschreiten, um den Film wieder auf seinen ursprünglichen Wert als Medium zurückzuführen. So inszenierte Claes Oldenburg 1965 mit dem Happening *Moviehouse* eine Kinovorstellung ohne Film. Peter Weibel zeigte 1966 ebenfalls einen Film ohne Film, indem er reines Projektorlicht an eine Wand strahlte, vor der er mit einem Nivea-Ball in den erhobenen Händen ruhig stand. Dazu war das Geräusch einer laufenden Kamera zu hören. Diese Filme ohne Film, wobei ›ohne Film‹ zumeist das Fehlen von Zelluloid bedeutete, waren die ersten Versuche, das klassische Kino und dessen klassische Wirklichkeitsauffassung zu desavouieren. Film wurde als ein technologisches Medium gesehen, das historisch eingefroren war und deswegen erweitert und überschritten werden mußte. Diese Erweiterungen der gewohnten Filmform auf der Bühne, welche die konventionelle Reihenfolge des kommerziellen Filmemachens durchbrachen, waren die Anfänge auf der Suche nach neuen Technologien, die einen erweiterten Wirklichkeitsbegriff ermöglichten, der dem erweiterten und zum Teil drogeninduzierten Bewußtseinszustand der damaligen Zeit entsprach. Durch das ›Expanded Cinema‹ wurde der Weg geöffnet weg von der Kinematographie hin zu Video und digitaler Technologie. Der klassische Film mit Zelluloid und seiner üblichen Konfiguration wurde als nur eine besondere Verknüpfung bestimmter Elemente unter vielen möglichen Verknüpfungen aufgefaßt. Das erweiterte Kino wollte diese Vielzahl der anderen möglichen Verknüpfungen der kinematographischen Elemente erforschen. Das klassische Filmsystem mit den Grundfiguren und Grundregeln – Projektor, Projektionsfläche, Projektionsraum, Kinosaal, Zuschauer, Vorführer, Filmstreifen, Tonstreifen, Regisseur, Kamera, Kamerabewegung, Schneide-

position, curtain in front of the screen and so forth – the traditional cinematic system was seen as a convention that could be changed at any time, as a system of variables. Celluloid could be replaced by a length of thread, the projector by a mirror, a ray of light by a piece of string, the screen by a human torso, light reactions by chemical reactions – cinema was possible inside or outside a theatre, with a flexible or rigid screen or without one at all, with a camera serving as projector, people acting as the reflective surface, and so on.

These permutations of the prevailing film forms also altered the character of filmic representation. A film is usually expected to supply a picture of the world, to reproduce the world. Expanded cinema aimed no longer to reproduce reality but to construct its own reality in the filmic play. The expansion of the technological medium brought with it an expansion of the reality able to be grasped by the senses. A mobile projector was deployed not just to suspend habitual modes of perceiving and of experiencing reality but also to make reality itself more mobile. The true goal of expanded cinema was the expansion of reality and the way it is experienced. Altered media produce a changed world, and a world pressing for change calls for altered media. Expanded cinema was aimed at changing and constructing – not reproducing – the world. In this respect, expanded cinema was the first step to virtual reality (not just artistically and conceptually, but technologically, too), since the notion of reality cemented ontologically by classical cinema was the core around which this mode orbited as a critique of representation.

MovieMovie featured a mobile projector and flexible, three-dimensional screen as well as, most importantly, visually integrated viewers who constituted a part of the screen onto which pictures were projected. A short-lived but heady period of success was enjoyed in the mid-1960s (among architects especially) by pneumatic structures, air-inflated housings in the form of capsules, cells, balls, tubes and bubbles. These architectural explorations of pneumatic structures were experiments with variable, dynamic space. A body-centred definition of architecture – in line with the classical architectonic metaphor equating the skin, as the protective sleeve for the body, with the first form of architecture, followed by clothing and buildings as second and third forms respectively – had led to architecture being viewed as an extension of the physical body. The pneumatic dwelling cells produced in experiments by Hausrucker & Co. to Coop Himmelblau must be viewed with hindsight as the first technical costumes, as interface technology allowing a controlled alteration of how the world is perceived. These body-encapsulating pneumatic structures enabling the viewers to move about inside a closed world were the first data suits, the means by which their wearers, in conjunction with sensor technology and keypads, could communicate with the environment. In this respect, the evolution from body-related cinema ('corpocinema') to body-related pneumatic architecture was logical.

maschine, Montage, Kameraposition, Kinovorhang etc.– wurde als jederzeit veränderbare Konvention, als ein System von Variablen aufgefaßt. Man kann statt Zelluloid einen Zwirnsfaden nehmen, statt des Projektors einen Spiegel, statt eines Lichtstrahls eine Schnur, statt einer Leinwand einen Brustkorb, statt elektrischem Licht Feuer, statt Lichtreaktionen chemische Reaktionen, man kann mit oder ohne Zelluloid arbeiten, im Kinosaal oder außerhalb, mit oder ohne Leinwand, mit beweglicher oder stabiler Leinwand, mit der Kamera als Projektor, mit dem Menschen als Leinwand etc.

Mit diesen Veränderungen der gewohnten Filmformen wurde auch der Charakter der filmischen Repräsentation verändert. Der Film soll normalerweise ein Bild der Welt liefern, die Welt abbilden. Die erweiterte Filmform wollte die Wirklichkeit nicht mehr abbilden, sondern im filmischen Spiel selbst Wirklichkeit konstruieren. Die Erweiterung des technologischen Mediums bedeutete auch die Erweiterung der sinnlich erfaßbaren Realität. Ein mobiler Projektor sollte nicht nur Gewohnheiten der Wahrnehmung und der Wirklichkeitserfahrung außer Kraft setzen, sondern die Wirklichkeit selbst mobiler machen. Die Erweiterung der Wirklichkeit und der Wirklichkeitserfahrung war also das eigentliche Ziel des erweiterten Kinos. Veränderte Medien produzieren eine veränderte Welt, und eine auf Veränderung drängende Welt drängt nach veränderten Medien. Das erweiterte Kino soll die Welt nicht abbilden, sondern sie verändern und konstruieren. Insofern begann mit dem ›Expanded Cinema‹ nicht nur künstlerisch und konzeptuell, sondern auch technologisch der Schritt zur virtuellen Realität, da der eigentliche Kern, um den das ›Expanded Cinema‹ als Kritik der Repräsentation kreiste, der Wirklichkeitsbegriff war, der durch das klassische Kino ontologisch festgeschrieben wurde.

In *MovieMovie* gab es einen beweglichen Projektor, eine bewegliche dreidimensionale Leinwand, und vor allem waren die Betrachter selbst im Bild, da sie Teil der Leinwand waren, auf die viele Bilder projiziert wurden. Pneumatische Strukturen – mit Luft aufgeblasene Gehäuse in Form von Kapseln, Zellen, Kugeln, Röhren, Blasen – haben ab Mitte der sechziger Jahre besonders in der Architekturszene kurzfristig einen euphorischen Erfolg gehabt. Die architektonischen Experimente mit pneumatischen Strukturen waren Experimente mit einem veränderbaren, dynamischen Raum. Die klassische architektonische Gleichung, daß die Haut als Schutzhülle des Körpers die erste Form der Architektur ist, die Kleidung die zweite und das Gebäude die dritte Stufe der Architektur, diese körperzentrierte Definition der Architektur hat dazu geführt, Architektur als Extension des Leibes zu verstehen. Die pneumatischen Wohnzellen der architektonischen Experimente von Hausrucker & Co. bis Coop Himmelblau sind daher rückwirkend als erste technische Anzüge zu verstehen, als Schnittstellentechnologie, mit der die Wahrnehmung der Welt kontrolliert verändert werden konnte. Die den Körper umhüllenden pneumatischen Strukturen, in denen der Zuschauer sich in einer abgeschlossenen Welt bewegen konnte, waren die ersten Datenanzüge, mittels derer der Bewohner über Sensorentechnologie und Tastaturenfelder mit der

This development makes it clear that Jeffrey Shaw's interest shifted from the composition of the image to the composition of space and/or visual space, and it also makes visible a second major aspect of the technological evolution initiated by expanded cinema. Whereas classical cinema was devoted to the theatrical and operatic tradition of verbal and visual language, non-commercial, experimental cinema moved further and further away from the classical, formal criteria, abandoned the pictorial arts in favour of the spatial arts. Digital technology has placed on a new, more intense footing the closeness between visual art and architecture originally so triumphantly established in the Baroque and Rococo. Jeffrey Shaw's path from expanded cinema to temporary architecture is rooted in the same tradition, and therefore consistent.

From the late 1970s Jeffrey Shaw drew on his experience with pneumatic architecture and the light shows and laser installations created for rock groups (Genesis/Peter Gabriel world tour 1975-78) to develop permanent installations for buildings. Discernible in these works is a marked increase in the impetus of interaction between the public (or other external parameters) and the artistic structure, as can be seen in *Neon Wave Sculpture* (1979), *Bubble Wall* (1979), *Video Ball Sculpture* (1980), all jointly produced with Theo Botschuijver. In these installations, walls and facades were treated as surfaces of intersection whose character was controlled by the viewer. These were veritable interactive sculptures, therefore – interactive public architecture-related art.

The decisive phase began however with works that placed the viewer's vantage point in the centre of the piece. This becomes especially clear in two projection performances dating from the mid-1970s: *Diadrama* (1974, with Theo Botschuijver), a 60-minute audio-visual performance in which six projectors showed more than 2,000 slides on a 12 x 3 m panoramic screen, strikingly demonstrates an initial attempt to immerse the viewer in the picture that would fully succeed in the later computer installation *Place – a user's manual* (1995). As a formal medium, the panorama was deployed to render space as a surface the viewer could manipulate. *Viewpoint* (1975) used an optical viewing system and large-format photographic slide projection which precisely incorporated fictional virtual events in the real museum situation. The viewer looking at the real room through the optical apparatus saw events apparently taking place there which were invisible to visitors not looking through the apparatus, since the photographed, projected room and the real room were absolutely congruent, or isomorphous. In the 1980s and 1990s, Jeffrey Shaw was to intensify his explorations of this technique of isomorphous superimposition of virtual images and real spaces, for instance in *The Golden Calf* (1994).

In contrast to the expanded cinema experiments of the Eventstructure Research Group, where image and space had remained clearly separated or else met together only on the surface of intersection provided by the screen, or to the interactive sculptures,

Umwelt kommunizierte. Insofern war die Weiterentwicklung vom körperbezogenen Kino (›corpocinema‹) zur körperbezogenen pneumatischen Architektur logisch. Durch diese Entwicklung ist klar, daß Jeffrey Shaw sein Interesse von der Gestaltung des Bildes zur Gestaltung des Raumes bzw. Bildraumes lenkte. Hier wird ein zweiter wichtiger Punkt für die vom ›Expanded Cinema‹ eingeleitete technologische Entwicklung sichtbar. Während das klassische Kino sich der Tradition von Theater, von Oper, der gesprochenen Sprache und der Bildsprache verschrieb, hat sich das eigentliche künstlerische Kino immer mehr von den klassischen, formalen Kriterien entfernt, sich von den Bildkünsten ab- und den Raumkünsten zugewandt. Die schon im Barock und Rokoko triumphal etablierte Nähe zwischen Bildkunst und Baukunst hat durch die digitale Technologie eine neue Steigerung erfahren. Der Weg Jeffrey Shaws vom erweiterten Kino zur temporären Architektur fußt in dieser Tradition und ist daher nur konsequent.

Von den Erfahrungen mit der pneumatischen Architektur und seinen Lightshows und Laserinstallationen für Rockgruppen (Genesis/Peter Gabriel Welttournee 1975-78) ausgehend, entwickelte Jeffrey Shaw ab Ende der siebziger Jahre permanente Installationen für Gebäude, in denen das Moment der Interaktivität bzw. der Wechselwirkung zwischen Publikum bzw. anderen Parametern der Außenwelt und den künstlerischen Gebilden stark zunahm: *Neon Wave Sculpture* (1979), *Bubble Wall* (1979), *Video Ball Sculpture* (1980), alle mit Theo Botschuijver. Hier wurden Wände und Fassaden als ›Surfaces‹, als Schnittflächen behandelt, deren Beschaffenheit vom Betrachter gesteuert wurde. Es handelt sich also um veritable interaktive Skulpturen bzw. um interaktive öffentliche Kunst am Bau.

Die entscheidende Phase begann jedoch mit Arbeiten, die den Standpunkt des Betrachters zum Zentrum der Arbeit machten. Zwei Diaprojektionen, die Mitte der siebziger Jahre entstanden, machen dies besonders deutlich: *Diadrama* (1974, mit Theo Botschuijver), eine sechzigminütige, audiovisuelle Performance mit über 2 000 Dias, die mit sechs Projektoren auf eine panoramische Leinwand (12 x 3 m) projiziert wurden, zeigt eindringlich den Versuch, den Beobachter in das Bild zu plazieren, wie dies später mit der interaktiven Computerinstallation *Place – a user's manual* (1995) gelang. Das Panorama als formales Medium sollte den Raum als vom Betrachter manipulierbare Oberfläche darstellen. *Viewpoint* (1975) verwendete ein optisches Betrachtersystem und eine fotografische Großprojektion, die fiktive virtuelle Ereignisse präzise in eine reale aktuelle Raumsituation des Museums einfügte, so daß der Betrachter beim Blick durch die optische Apparatur im realen Raum Ereignisse wahrnahm, die dort scheinbar stattfanden, aber im realen Raum ohne die optische Apparatur nicht wahrgenommen werden konnten, weil der fotografierte projizierte Raum und der reale Raum absolut kongruent bzw. isomorph waren. Diese Technik der isomorphen Überblendung von virtuellen Bildern und realen Räumen explorierte Shaw insbesondere in den achtziger und neunziger Jahren, beispielsweise in *The Golden Calf* (1994).

where viewer and surface of intersection had remained visibly separate even if the relationship between them was reciprocal, virtual images were almost indivisibly joined with real space in the mid-1970s' projection experiments using devices such as mirror machines and stereoscopic images. Visual and physical space, pictorial and spatial art now fused together. The difference from painting lay in a mobility of the image mechanism that set in motion not only the viewpoint but also the visual events in real space, thus making narration possible. A logical continuation of the foregoing work with mobility of projection/viewpoint, of the image, was to investigate possibilities of mobilizing space. And this mobilization of visual space came about in the mid-1980s as a sequel to the previously accomplished mobilization and virtualization of visual events. Now, virtual images not only fused with real space, but virtual visual events took place in virtual spaces. Virtual images co-operated in virtual space. Jeffrey Shaw's architectural research had never lain in the tradition of a classical sculptural practice concerned with the formal design of the image (he was not content merely to create beautiful pictures), but strove to explore the framework – view, viewer, perspective, projection surface, plane of intersection – within which images are perceived. The first phase of Shaw's research brought him to the virtualized image, the second phase to virtualized space. Digital technology enabled him to fuse together both aspects on an interactive basis. The beginning of this interaction between a mobile viewpoint and movement in virtual space was marked by *Points of View* (1983). One of the earliest interactive computer installations and probably the first work of art to deploy flight simulation techniques, it was also a prototype anticipating the interactivity between mobile vantage point and movement in virtual space that would characterize Shaw's famous later works *The Legible City* (1989) and *The Virtual Museum* (1991). Thanks to this new interactive equation between viewer, visual space and real space, however, Shaw was ultimately able to liberate his works from the shackles of locality by subjecting all three components to a process of virtualization (virtual viewpoint, virtual images, virtual spaces), and in the 1990s proceeded to design televirtual artificial environments in which communication was wholly detached from local conditions and spaces (*Televirtual Chit Chat*, 1993). By creating a televirtual architecture, Shaw virtualized even the remote.

If the relationship between image and space is a constant subject running through the different stages and phases of development in Jeffrey Shaw's œuvre, it is accompanied by the basic method of isomorphism. The term 'isomorphous' denotes a similarity between unrelated forms and indicates the existence of a formal similarity, or sameness, between virtual and real signs, virtual and real images, virtual and real spaces. Even in a dynamic interactive environment, the virtual form imperceptibly joins on from the real form (*The Golden Calf*, 1994). Behind this isomorphism lies a fun-

Im Unterschied zu den ›Expanded Cinema‹-Experimenten der Eventstructure Research Group, wo Bild und Raum noch klar separiert waren bzw. sich bloß auf der Schnittfläche der Leinwand begegneten, und den interaktiven Skulpturen, wo zwar Betrachter und Schnittfläche in einer Wechselbeziehung standen, aber dennoch klar erkennbar getrennt waren, verbinden sich bei diesen Projektionsexperimenten mit Spiegelmaschinen, Stereobildern etc. Mitte der siebziger Jahre virtuelle Bilder fast untrennbar mit dem realen Raum. Bildraum und physikalischer Raum, Bildkunst und Raumkunst verschmelzen miteinander. Der Unterschied zur Malerei besteht darin, daß durch die Mobilität der Bildmaschine nicht nur der Blick in Bewegung gerät, sondern auch die Bildereignisse im realen Raum beweglich werden, eine Narration ermöglichen. Nach der Beweglichkeit der Projektion bzw. des Blicks, nach der Beweglichkeit des Bildes, war es nur konsequent, auch nach Möglichkeiten der Beweglichkeit des Raumes, genauer gesagt des Bildraumes, zu forschen. Nach der Mobilisierung und Virtualisierung der Bildereignisse folgte Mitte der achtziger Jahre die Mobilisierung des Bildraumes. Nicht nur virtuelle Bilder verschmolzen mit dem realen Raum, sondern virtuelle visuelle Ereignisse fanden in einem virtuellen Raum statt. Virtuelle Bilder kooperierten in virtuellen Räumen. Die architektonische Recherche Jeffrey Shaws, die von Anfang an nicht in der Tradition der klassischen bildnerischen Praxis, in der formalen Gestaltung des Bildes, stand (Shaw gab sich nicht damit ab, schöne Bilder zu schaffen), sondern danach trachtete, die Rahmenbedingungen der Wahrnehmung von Bildern wie Blick, Beobachter, Perspektive, Projektionsfläche, Schnittfläche zu explorieren, führte ihn in der ersten Phase zur Virtualisierung des Bildes und in einer zweiten Phase zur Virtualisierung des Raumes. Die digitale Technologie ermöglichte ihm die Verschmelzung beider auf der Grundlage der Interaktivität. Die Arbeit *Points of View* (1983), eine der ersten interaktiven Computerinstallationen und wahrscheinlich das erste Kunstwerk überhaupt, das die Technik der Flugsimulation verwendete, ist prototypisch für den Beginn dieser Interaktivität zwischen mobilem Betrachterstandpunkt und Bewegung im virtuellen Raum, wie sie denn auch später für Shaws berühmte Arbeiten *The Legible City* (1989) und *The Virtual Museum* (1991) kennzeichnend sein wird. Shaw hat sich aber schließlich durch diese neue interaktive Gleichung zwischen Betrachter, Bildraum und Realraum aus dem Gefängnis der Lokalität befreit, indem er sie alle dem Prozeß der Virtualisierung unterwarf (virtueller Betrachterstandpunkt, virtuelle Bilder, virtuelle Räume) und in den neunziger Jahren televirtuelle künstliche Environments entworfen, wo die Kommunikation jenseits lokaler Bedingungen und lokaler Räume stattfand (*Televirtual Chit Chat*, 1993). Shaw hat also auch die Ferne virtualisiert, indem er eine televirtuelle Architektur schuf.

In den verschiedenen Stufen und Phasen in der Entwicklung des künstlerischen Œuvres von Jeffrey Shaw ist die Beziehung von Bild und Raum als Sujet eine grundlegende Konstante und die Isomorphie eine grundlegende Methode. Isomorphie bedeutet soviel wie

damental axiom of Conceptual art, namely the tautology known from the work of Joseph Kosuth. Other structures of Conceptual art – such as self-reference and self-resemblance, loop formations or the circular observer situations based on mirrors and semi-transparent glass walls observable in the architectural sculptures of Dan Graham – are carried on in Shaw's work. But whereas these analog works remain largely in real space, Shaw's works go beyond reality in their contextualization of the perceptual situation, and make accessible the two other poles in the Lacanian triple of real, symbolic and imaginary. Shaw's expansion of the cinematographic code not only changed the notion of the image and our concept of space by virtualizing, mobilizing and interactively synchronizing image and space; in his cyberspace and virtual-reality installations we also find further consistent embranchments and elaborations of various aesthetic programmes of the 1960s – the abandonment of the traditional image for new artistic realities, the renunciation of standard establishment reality in favour of an individual, made-to-measure, constructible reality. Shaw's installations aim at expanded states of consciousness and reality. He used the means of digital technology to pursue the contextualization of perceptual procedures to an extent which surpassed the results of Op art and Kinetic art, at the same time acting on the insights communicated by Conceptual art and Action art. With the narrative presentation of perceptual procedures he so singularly integrated in media art, Shaw offered art possible ways of breaking out of the traditional impasses and opening up unexplored horizons.

II. Cyber Art and Architecture

The new problems facing architects and urban planners in the age of information highways, cyberspace and telematic media are conveyed in the headings 'digital city', 'media architecture', 'telepolis' and 'networked world'. The most perceptible response to the changed spatial conditions brought about by the new technologies has so far come from the school of architecture labelled as 'Deconstructivist'. But just as architects have begun to approach the complex of new media (by consideration of variable electronic facade designs, with theories defining architecture as an algorithm and dynamic, self-regulating system), conversely artists are approaching the new digital media from the angle of architectural issues. A new equation is evolving between visual art and the art of designing and constructing buildings.

By dedicating the autumn festival 'Trigon-Personale des Steirischen Herbstes 1995' to Jeffrey Shaw, the Neue Galerie in Graz launched a similar advance into the new territory of digital technology and architecture, the field where architectonic visual spaces meet digital three-dimensional images. The exhibition was the first ever to be devoted to a world-class artist working exclusively with digital technology, to a representative of Cyber art, one of the

gleichgestaltig und meint, daß zwischen virtuellen und realen Zeichen, virtuellen und realen Bildern, virtuellen und realen Räumen eine formale Gleichheit bzw. Ähnlichkeit besteht. Die virtuelle Form setzt die reale Form fort – auch in einem dynamischen interaktiven Environment (*The Golden Calf*, 1994). Hinter dieser Isomorphie verbirgt sich ein grundlegendes Axiom der Konzeptkunst, nämlich die Tautologie, wie wir sie aus der Arbeit von Joseph Kosuth kennen. Auch andere Strukturen der Konzeptkunst, wie Selbstreferenz und Selbstähnlichkeit, Schleifenbildungen, zirkuläre Beobachtersituationen mit Hilfe von Spiegeln und semitransparenten Glaswänden, wie wir sie von den architektonischen Skulpturen Dan Grahams kennen, finden in Shaws Arbeit ihre Fortsetzung. Verharren diese analogen Arbeiten jedoch *grosso modo* noch im Realraum, gehen die Arbeiten von Shaw bei der Kontextualisierung der Wahrnehmungssituation über das Reale hinaus und erschließen die beiden anderen Pole des Lacanschen Tripels: real, symbolisch, imaginär. Shaw hat bei seiner Ausdehnung des kinematographischen Codes nicht nur den Begriff des Bildes und unsere Vorstellung vom Raum verändert, indem er sie virtualisierte, mobilisierte und zueinander interaktiv synchronisierte, sondern in seinen Cyberspace- und Virtual-Reality-Installationen finden wir weiter konsequente Verzweigungen und Ausformulierungen verschiedener ästhetischer Programme der sechziger Jahre wie Ausstieg aus dem traditionellen Bild und Einstieg in neue künstliche Wirklichkeiten, Ausstieg aus der staatlich normierten Realität und Einstieg in eine individuell maßgeschneiderte, konstruierbare Realität. Shaws Installationen zielen auf Erweiterungen des Bewußtseins und der Wirklichkeit. Die Kontextualisierung von Wahrnehmungsvorgängen hat er mittels der digitalen Technologie weit über die Ergebnisse der Op-art und Kinetik hinaus verfolgt und dabei die Einsichten der Konzeptkunst und Aktionskunst befolgt. Mit der narrativen Inszenierung von Wahrnehmungsvorgängen, die er singulär in die Medienkunst eingeführt hat, bot er der Kunst Möglichkeiten, aus den traditionellen Impasses auszubrechen und ungeschaute Horizonte zu eröffnen.

II. Cyber Art und Architektur

Unter den Begriffen ›digitale Stadt‹, ›Media-Architecture‹, ›Telepolis‹, ›vernetzte Welt‹ werden jene neuen Problemstellungen rubriziert, welche auf die Architektur wie auch auf die Stadtplanung im Zeitalter der Datenautobahnen, des Cyberspace und der telematischen Medien zukommen. Auf die veränderten Raumbedingungen durch die neuen Technologien hat bislang vor allem jene Schule der Architektur reagiert, die unter dem Titel Dekonstruktivismus bekannt geworden ist. Aber nicht nur die Architekten nähern sich dem Komplex der neuen Medien (durch Überlegungen zu variablen elektronischen Fassadengestaltungen, durch Theorien, welche die Architektur als Algorithmus und als dynamisches selbstregulierendes System definieren), sondern auch umgekehrt nähern sich die Künstler den neuen digitalen Medien mit architektonischen Fragestellungen. Zwischen Bildkunst und Baukunst entsteht eine neue Gleichung.

present decade's key positions. A selection of five pieces produced between 1985 and 1995 offered an exemplary demonstration of the new relationship between visual art and architecture, a relationship consisting in the televirtual architecture made possible by digital interfacing techniques and based on interaction between image and spectator. In collaboration with the Graz-based architect Manfred Wolff-Plottegg, whose work is characterized by architectural algorithms, Shaw created environments – ranging from the light trap to startling projection realms – in which these interactive virtual worlds of simulated architectural spaces were particularly effective.

The masterpiece of the Graz show was indubitably the new work *Place – a user's manual*, on public view for the first time. A camera, three projectors and a spectator stand on a turntable in the centre of a panoramic landscape. The spectator controls the projection with the camera; if the camera turns, the turntable rotates too, causing the projected section of the image to wander, like a telescope scanning a landscape. The scenery consists of an infinite number of panoramic views which the viewer can penetrate with the aid of the camera zoom lens. Any noises made by the viewer trigger programmed texts that drift across the landscape.

The Narrative Landscape (1985/95) demonstrates the exploration of visual layers (three levels with nine visual units respectively) by means of joystick zoom control. The optical strata are composed of satellite pictures of the earth, architectural images and abstract symbols. To create spatial illusions that forge imaginary links between 'real-life' and 'virtual' architecture, scaling is deployed in conjunction with unusual tilted image projection that gives the viewer a feeling of looking down at the image from a balcony.

Another virtual journey – through Amsterdam, Manhattan, Karlsruhe – is offered by *The Legible City*, a work in which letters the size of real buildings are imposed, row-by-row and street-for-street, on the ground plan of these cities. The letters join together to form coherent sentences legible to the visitor riding round on a bicycle. This form of presentation consummates an idea hinted at in the Middle Ages and Baroque, namely that a relationship exists between syntax and structural design, between the grammar of building and language, between architecture and alphabet. It should be pointed out that the computer-assisted simulations of cyberspace are a sequel to the Baroque trompe-l'œil painting which once enriched the real-life architecture of churches and palaces by adding imaginary virtual spatiality, and now takes on contemporary relevance for the advancement of our architectural vocabulary. The role of pictorial illusionism becomes strikingly clear in *Heavens Gate*, a work in which a mirror inset in the floor causes the image projected onto the ceiling to simultaneously open up a chasm in which satellite views of the earth fuse with Baroque church paintings looking up to the heavens.

Einen Vorstoß in dieses neue Territorium von digitaler Technologie und Architektur, in dieses neue Feld von architektonischen Bildräumen und digitalen Raumbildern, machte die Neue Galerie Graz mit ihrer Trigon-Personale im Rahmen des Festivals Steirischer Herbst 1995, die Jeffrey Shaw gewidmet war. Die Ausstellung war die erste Retrospektive weltweit, die einen Künstler von Weltrang vorstellte, der nur mit digitaler Technologie arbeitet, der also ein Vertreter der Cyber art ist, einer grundlegenden Position der neunziger Jahre. In fünf ausgewählten Arbeiten aus der Zeit von 1985 bis 1995 wurde exemplarisch die neue Beziehung zwischen Bildkunst und Baukunst gezeigt, die eben eine auf der Interaktivität zwischen Bild und Beobachter aufbauende, durch die digitale Schnittstellentechnologie ermöglichte televirtuelle Architektur ist. In Zusammenarbeit mit dem Grazer Architekten Manfred Wolff-Plottegg, dessen Programm Architektur-Algorithmen kennzeichnen, wurde im Grazer Künstlerhaus ein Ambiente konstruiert – von der Lichtschleuse bis zu ungewöhnlichen Projektionsräumen – in denen diese interaktiven virtuellen Welten simulierter Architekturräume besonders gut zur Geltung kamen.

Das Meisterwerk dieser Ausstellung war zweifelsohne die in Graz uraufgeführte Arbeit *Place – a user's manual*. Eine Kamera, drei Projektoren und ein Betrachter stehen auf einer Drehscheibe in der Mitte eines Panoramas. Mit der Kamera steuert der Betrachter die Projektion des Bildes. Dreht sich die Kamera, dreht sich auch die Scheibe, und der projizierte Bildausschnitt wandert, wie ein Fernrohr, das eine Landschaft abtastet. Die Landschaft selbst besteht wiederum aus unendlich vielen Panoramen, in die der Betrachter mit Hilfe des Zooms der Kamera eindringen kann. Geräusche der Betrachter lösen vorprogrammierte Texte aus, die durch die Panoramalandschaft wandern.

In der Arbeit *The Narrative Landscape* (1985/95) wird die Durchdringung von Bildschichten (drei Ebenen mit jeweils neun visuellen Einheiten) mittels eines Zooms, ausgeführt durch einen Joystick, vorgestellt. Die Bildschichten bestehen aus Satellitenaufnahmen der Erde, Architekturaufnahmen und abstrakten Zeichen. Die Skalierung dient hier, zusammen mit der ungewöhnlichen vertikalen Bildprojektion – der Betrachter blickt wie von einem Balkon nach unten auf das Bild – der Aufgabe, Raumillusionen zu realisieren, die ›real architecture‹ und ›virtual architecture‹ auf imaginäre Weise verknüpfen.

Die Arbeit *The Legible City* erlaubt eine virtuelle Reise durch die Städte Amsterdam, Manhattan, Karlsruhe, wobei auf die Grundrisse dieser Städte – Zeile für Zeile, Straße für Straße – Buchstaben in der Größe der realen Häuser gesetzt wurden, die beim Durchwandern mit Hilfe eines realen Fahrrads sinnvolle Sätze ergeben. Der Zusammenhang von Satzbau und Bausatz, von der Grammatik des Bauens und der Sprache, von Architektur und Alphabet – im Mittelalter und Barock schon skizziert – wird hier vollendet dargestellt. An dieser Stelle sei auch darauf hingewiesen, daß die Trompe-l'œil-Malerei des Barock, welche bereits die reale Architektur der Kirchen und Paläste um imaginäre virtuelle Räumlichkeiten bereicherte, in den computergestützten Simulatio-

The dialectic of presence and absence is also expressed in *The Golden Calf*. When picked up by the visitor, a blank, flat monitor lying on a pedestal instantly displays the picture of a calf. Holding the monitor up to his eyes, the visitor can stroll round the vacant white pedestal and watch a screen on which the same pedestal is adorned by a golden calf. Since the view of the calf rotates according to the viewer's position, it can be viewed from the front, the rear, the side. Recalling standard architectural themes which – particularly in the 1960s – led to a radicalization of the art, this interplay of imagination, presence and absence, on the one hand, and the austerity of the real site and function on the other hand, is picked up once again in the 1990s by the new media and the architecture influenced by their virtual-reality technology.

III. Art as a User's Manual for the World

The work of Jeffrey Shaw undoubtedly occupies a central position in the electronic media art of the 1990s. Moreover, his works co-created, co-constructed the genre, gave it initial contours. Without Shaw's output we would be unaware of the full range of electronic media art, would be ignorant of an essential aspect. The way digital technology can be used to transform spaces into images, images into texts, would still be a secret; likewise the insight that spaces, images and texts are nothing other than diverse codes for experiencing the world and instructions for using the world. Shaw demonstrates the world to us not as an a priori, Kantian one, but as a user's manual. For some thirty years now, his work has been developing and revealing the deeper sense of the world's technological transformation, stringently and coherently, unaffected by changing fashions in art. Shaw has exposed and given play to the contours of a new art and artistic practice. Consequently, the position he has attained is less decisive than the way he reached it, than the path he took to get there. On the one hand, a large component of his art consisted in developing an apparatus that enabled us to identify and use the world as a user's manual.

The ingenious techniques Shaw engineered with the aid of a team of experts should not be disparaged – as an obsolete understanding of art might dictate – as the functional product of applied art, but seen as a component of the artistic work, especially in an art that calls itself technological. The world can be used and read as a user's manual only by virtue of this transparency of the tools, of this usage of the technological resources. The more the complex of apparatus is developed, the more accessible becomes the world as a user's manual. The technical implementation of the philosophical ideas is therefore decisive and constitutes the actual artistic agent. Without a manual there can be no usage of the world, without an agenda there can be no technological art. Shaw designs his artistic terrain in the complex technical relationship developed and implemented as interface between space, image and viewer in all his works, in the synchronized motion of the interface apparatus (camera, bicycle, joystick, etc.). From the outset,

nen des Cyberspace ihre Fortsetzung findet und deswegen für die Weiterentwicklung des architektonischen Vokabulars von Bedeutung ist. In der Arbeit *Heavens Gate* wird dies besonders deutlich, weil dort eine Projektion an den Plafond durch einen Bodenspiegel eine Tiefe nach unten schafft, in welcher Satellitenaufnahmen auf die Erde herab und barocke Kirchengemälde mit dem Blick zum Himmel hinauf verschmelzen.

Auch bei *The Golden Calf*, wo auf einem Podest ein flacher Monitor mit leerem Bildschirm liegt, der sich, sobald er aufgehoben wird, mit dem Abbild eines Kalbes belebt, kommt die Dialektik von Präsenz und Absenz zum Ausdruck. Hält der Betrachter den Monitor vor seine Augen und wandert dabei um das leere weiße Podest herum, sieht er im Bildschirm ein goldenes Kalb auf dem Podest, das sich, je nach Position des Betrachters, mit ihm dreht und daher sowohl von vorne als auch von hinten oder von der Seite zu sehen ist. Dieses Wechselspiel von Imagination, Präsenz und Absenz einerseits und Kahlheit der realen Funktion und des realen Ortes andererseits, alte Topoi der Architektur, die insbesondere in den sechziger Jahren zu einer Radikalisierung der Architektur führten, wird in den Neunzigern durch die neuen Medien und die von ihr beeinflußte Architektur wieder aufgenommen.

III. Die Kunst als Bedienungsanleitung zum Gebrauch der Welt

In der elektronischen Medienkunst der neunziger Jahre nimmt das künstlerische Werk Jeffrey Shaws zweifelsohne eine zentrale Position ein. Aber darüberhinaus hat sein Werk diese Kunstrichtung mitgeschaffen, mitkonstruiert, ihr erst ihre Konturen verliehen. Ohne Shaws Werk wüßten wir nicht, was elektronische Medienkunst alles sein kann, ein wesentlicher Aspekt bliebe uns verborgen. Die Verwandlung von Räumen in Bilder und die Verwandlung von Bildern in Texte als Optionen der digitalen Technologie blieben uns ebenso unzugänglich wie die Einsicht, daß Räume, Bilder und Texte nichts anderes sind als diverse Codes der Welterfahrung und Anweisungen für den Gebrauch der Welt. Shaw zeigt uns die Welt nicht als ein Kantsches *a priori*, sondern als eine Gebrauchsanweisung. Dieser tiefere Sinn der Technotransformation der Welt wird in seinem Werk seit dreißig Jahren stringent und kohärent, unbeeinflußt von den Moden der Kunstgeschichte, entwickelt und sichtbar. Shaw hat Konturen einer neuen Kunst und künstlerischen Praxis freigelegt und freigesetzt. Daher ist weniger entscheidend, welche Position er einnimmt, sondern wichtiger, wie er zu dieser Position gelangt ist, welchen Weg er zurückgelegt hat. Seine Kunst bestand im wesentlichen darin, eine Apparatur zu entwickeln, welche uns die Welt als Gebrauchsanweisung erkennbar und benutzbar machte.

Die ingeniöse Technik, die Shaw mit Hilfe eines Teams von hochkarätigen Experten entwickelte, ist nicht pejorativ dem Kunsthandwerk zuzuordnen, wie es obsolete künstlerische Positionen vornehmen, sondern ist Teil der künstlerischen Arbeit selbst, zumal in einer Kunst, die sich selbst apparative Kunst nennt. Erst die Transparenz der Apparatur, die Arbeit an der Apparatur, macht einen Gebrauch und eine Lesbarkeit der Umwelt als Gebrauchsan-

the viewer was in the picture, controlled and deformed the image, the spatial image, and in doing so altered by tendency space itself. The possibilities of interaction between viewer and (artificial) environment were pursued with a degree of intensity bordering on obsession. Shaw's objective is not, has never been, the image, not the classical artistic notion of composing an image. His objective is the relationship between viewer and image, whereby the image is always seen as an image of space, as an image of the environment.

One might say, then, that Shaw's real goal is the relationship between viewer and environment, and this relationship is one established by images and text in the real and virtual worlds alike. Shaw's art defines language and image as the interface between subject and environment. The world is encountered not directly but in the mediatized form of narrative landscapes, Baroque visual realms. Text and images are always interposed as media between the viewer and the world; they are the interfaces establishing the relationship of human to world. Characterized by a deep longing for freedom – a central source that fuelled the art of the 1960s – Shaw wants to make this relationship between subject and environment individually shapeable. The idea of art as a blueprint for a socially changed world, one of the premises on which revolutionary art rests, centres in his work on an individually changed relationship between subject and world. That is why he attaches so much importance to the development of interface technologies, to the improvement of text and image mechanisms – in order to make the relationship between subject and environment one the subject can shape. Shaw cures art of a certain naivety. In his technologically complex œuvre there is no direct meeting between subject and world, only a meeting by the agency of media. If he wants to make the world more free, then, his art can do this only by heightening the freedom of conveyance. The more variable, designable, changeable the interface between the observer and the world – the technological mediation between world and subject – the more free the world is for the subject. Within the premises of his art, therefore, Shaw is obliged to place excessive value on heightened of degrees of freedom in the electronic interface between observer and environment. He does not create free images of the world or images of a free world, but frees up the access to and usage of the pictures of the world. A modest programme on the one hand, but one that is less naive than that of his fellow-artists. In Shaw's work the freedom of art becomes the qualified freedom enjoyed by the observer in dealing with the images of an artificial world, images over which the subject has command. Thus, his art takes leave of historical notions of freedom in art and by means of participatorial practices introduces a radical democracy in which pretensions to absoluteness have been eradicated.

Shaw's composition of the interfacing technology between observer and world is becoming increasingly complex and variable,

weisung möglich. Je mehr der Apparaturkomplex entwickelt wird, umso mehr wird die Welt als Gebrauchsanweisung zugänglich. Die technische Implementierung der philosophischen Ideen ist daher ausschlaggebend und das eigentliche künstlerische Agens. Ohne Bedienungsanleitung kein Gebrauch der Welt, ohne Agenda keine apparative Kunst. In der komplexen technischen Beziehung, der Schnittstellentechnologie, die Shaw zwischen Raum, Bild und Betrachter in all seinen Arbeiten entwickelt, in der Synchronisierung der Bewegung der Schnittstellenapparatur (Kamera, Fahrrad, Joystick etc.), des Betrachters und des Bildes gestaltet Shaw sein künstlerisches Terrain. Von Anfang an war der Betrachter im Bild, steuerte und verformte das Bild, die Abbildung des Raumes und damit tendenziell den Raum selbst. Intensivst, fast obsessiv wurden Möglichkeiten der Interaktion zwischen Betrachter und (künstlicher) Umwelt gesucht. Nicht das Bild, nicht die klassische Kunstvorstellung von Bildgestaltung war und ist Shaws Ziel, sondern die Beziehung zwischen Betrachter und Bild, wobei das Bild stets als Raumbild, als Bild der Umgebung verstanden wird.

Also könnte man sagen, daß das eigentliche Ziel die Beziehung zwischen Betrachter und Umwelt ist, eine Beziehung, die durch Bilder und Texte hergestellt wird – sowohl in der Wirklichkeit als auch in der virtuellen Welt. Shaw definiert in seiner Kunst Sprache und Bilder als Schnittstellen zwischen Subjekt und Umwelt. In Shaws Kunst begegnet man der Welt nicht unvermittelt, sondern mediatisiert als narrative Landschaften, als barocke Bildwelten. Stets stehen Texte und Bilder als Medien zwischen dem Betrachter und der Welt; sie sind die Schnittstellen, welche die Beziehung zwischen Mensch und Welt herstellen. Von einer tiefen Sehnsucht nach Freiheit geprägt, eine zentrale Quelle, aus der die Kunst der sechziger Jahre gespeist wird, will Shaw diese Beziehung zwischen Subjekt und Umwelt individuell gestaltbar machen. Kunst als Entwurf einer sozialen Veränderung der Welt, eine der Prämissen der revolutionären Kunst, konzentriert sich bei Shaw auf die individuelle Veränderung der Beziehung zwischen Subjekt und Welt. Um die Beziehung zwischen Subjekt und Umwelt eben für dieses Subjekt gestaltbar machen zu können, legt Shaw so großen Wert auf die Entwicklung der Schnittstellentechnologie, der Text- und Bild-Apparatur. Shaw treibt der Kunst eine gewisse Naivität aus. In seiner technisch komplexen Kunst gibt es keine direkte Begegnung von Subjekt und Welt, sondern nur eine medial vermittelte. Wenn er also die Welt freier machen will, kann dies seine Kunst nur leisten, wenn sie die Freiheitsgrade der Vermittlung erhöht. Je variabler, gestaltbarer, veränderbarer die Schnittstelle zwischen Beobachter und Welt, die technologische Vermittlung zwischen Welt und Subjekt wird, desto freier wird die Welt für das Subjekt. Shaw muß daher innerhalb der Prämissen seiner Kunst exzessiven Wert auf die Entwicklung der Freiheitsgrade in der technischen Schnittstelle zwischen Beobachter und Umwelt legen. Shaw macht keine freien Bilder der Welt oder Bilder einer freien Welt, sondern er macht den Zugang, den Gebrauch der Bilder der Welt freier. Einerseits ein bescheidenes Programm, andererseits nicht so naiv wie das der Kollegen. Die Freiheit der Kunst

because only such complexity and variation can comprehend the necessary degree of freedom in establishing and shaping the world as a user's manual. In developing implementations of image and space relationships, of image and viewer relationships, his concern is not to enhance the technology, then, but to add to our understanding that these relationships are characterized by the model of the user manual. If the world is a relationship between the images of the world and the viewer of these images, then some of the central questions must be: what does the relationship look like? How is it designed? It is not the pictures that are (artistically) composed by Shaw but the relationship of viewer to images. Relational rather than representational, his art is interface art. Since art using technological tools will set up this interface by technical means, then his art is technical relational art. The arrangement of the technology is simultaneously the shaping of the relationship between image and viewer. Once the relationship between the image of the world and the viewer of the world has been defined as one which is technological, then it can be expanded and changed solely by technical means. Greater degrees of freedom in the relationship to the world and increased possibilities of using the 'world', or at least its images, according to one's own notions are dependent on this development of a controllable technical relation between images of the world and viewers of the world. To see the world (of images) as a user's manual ultimately implies a heightened ability to view and use the world according to one's own notions, more individually, more subjectively. The world is no longer only imperative, *a priori,* unchangeable, objective, normative. Shaw's art shows the world as a possible construction, as something changeable, something usable in accordance with human models, dimensions, specifications and notions. The world as a user's manual is a world of modality. The greater the degree of interactivity between the human and the world – and the aim of a world modelled as user's manual is to increase this degree – the more free this world is. Shaw's art shows the world from a radically constructive point of view.

Translated from the German by Thomas Morrison.

wird bei ihm zur bedingten Freiheit der Beobachter im Umgang mit den Bildern einer künstlichen Welt, die vom Subjekt souverän steuerbar sind. Shaws Kunst verabschiedet sich also von historischen Vorstellungen der Freiheit in der Kunst und führt mit partizipatorischen Praktiken eine radikale Demokratie ein, in der Absolutheitsansprüche getilgt sind.

Shaw gestaltet die Technologie der Schnittstelle zwischen Beobachter und Welt immer komplexer und variabler, denn nur in diesem Maße ist die Beziehung des Menschen zur Welt als eine Gebrauchsanweisung herstellbar und frei gestaltbar. Es geht also nicht um die technische Steigerung bei der Entwicklung der technischen Implementierungen von Bild- und Raum-Beziehungen, von Bild- und Betrachter-Beziehungen, sondern es geht um die Steigerung der Einsicht, daß diese Beziehungen durch das Modell der Gebrauchsanweisungen gekennzeichnet sind. Wenn die Welt eine Beziehung zwischen Bildern der Welt und dem Betrachter dieser Bilder ist, dann lauten einige zentrale Fragen: Wie sieht diese Beziehung aus? Wie ist sie gestaltet? Shaw gestaltet also nicht (künstlerisch) die Bilder, sondern (künstlerisch) die Beziehung des Betrachters zu den Bildern. Seine Kunst ist nicht Bildkunst, sondern Beziehungskunst, Schnittstellenkunst. Da diese Beziehung in der apparativen Kunst technisch hergestellt wird, ist seine Kunst technische Beziehungskunst. Die Ausgestaltung der Technik ist gleichzeitig die Gestaltung der Beziehung zwischen Bild und Betrachter. Ist die Beziehung zwischen dem Bild der Welt und dem Betrachter der Welt einmal als apparative, technische definiert, ist sie auch nur technisch erweiterbar und veränderbar. In der Entwicklung der Steuerbarkeit der technischen Beziehung zwischen Bildern der Welt und Betrachtern der Welt liegt die Steigerung der Freiheitsgrade in der Beziehung zur Welt und der Möglichkeit, die ›Welt‹, zumindest ihre Bilder, nach eigenen Vorstellungen zu gebrauchen. Die Welt (der Bilder) als Gebrauchsanweisung zu sehen, heißt schließlich, die Welt selbst in erhöhter Weise gemäß eigenen Vorstellungen individueller, subjektiver sehen und gebrauchen zu können. Die Welt ist nicht mehr nur notwendig, *a priori*, unveränderbar, objektiv, normativ. Shaws Kunst zeigt die Welt als mögliche Konstruktion, als veränderbar, als nach menschlichen Modellen, Maßen, Vorgaben, Vorstellungen gebrauchbar. Die Welt als Gebrauchsanweisung ist eine Welt der Modalität. Je höher die Grade der Interaktivität zwischen Mensch und Welt – was das Ziel einer Welt, modelliert als Gebrauchsanweisung, ist – desto freier ist diese Welt. Shaws Kunst zeigt die Welt aus einem radikal konstruktiven Standpunkt.

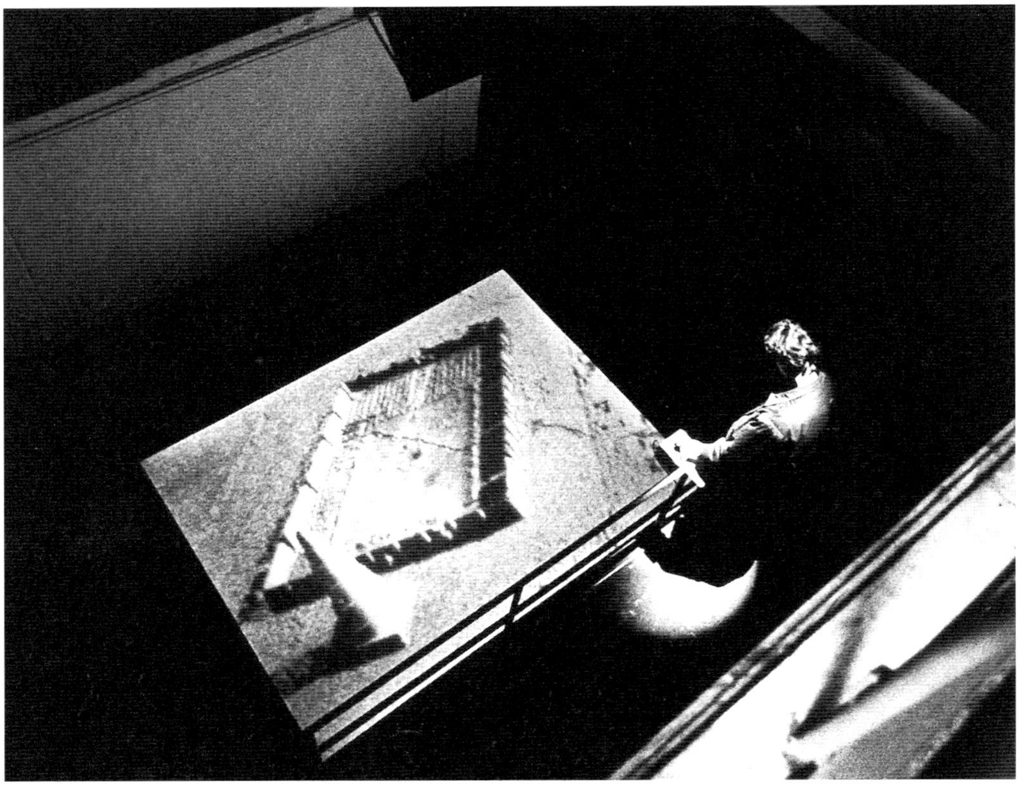

The Narrative Landscape, Aorta, Amsterdam, Netherlands, 1985. Photo: Sjoerd Holsbergen.

Jeffrey Shaw: From Expanded Cinema to Virtual Reality

By Anne-Marie Duguet

A Few Salient Principles

Artistic experimentation of the 1960s and '70s challenged a whole set of hierarchies and limits governing the identity and nature of a work of art, as well as its function, its relationship to the public, and its official site of presentation. Yet stress should be placed not so much on the diversity of interests and activities – from thermodynamics to 'philosophical investigations', from cut-ups to light shows – as on the resonances and the interactions between various spheres and concerns. It would be pointless – or simply contradictory – to attempt to classify each of Jeffrey Shaw's pieces according one of the many trends of the day more or less felicitously designated by labels such as Cybernetic art, Happenings, Fluxus, Performance art, Land art, Conceptual art, and so on. Shaw's artistic propositions belong, in one aspect or another, to all these categories at the same time. They embody the main issues and concepts forged in a context of intellectual, cultural, and political effervescence. They thereby help to define such issues, when comprehended in that climate of interrogation and experimentation.

Time-Based Work

The question of time heavily impinged on artistic theory and practice in those days; qualitative adjectives such as fragile, ephemeral, risky, unstable, and transitory became increasingly dominant. Time emerged not only as a recurrent theme but also as a constituent parameter of the very nature of an art-work. The gap between traditional art objects and performances, environments, events, and installations was produced above all by the special temporal dimension of the latter. As Gérard Genette has pointed out, unlike a material object that endures through time, a performance (or event) has a 'procedural duration', that is to say it unfolds (with a beginning and an end, more or less recognizable depending on the approach) in a continuum that cannot be broken without damaging that very process.[1] As to environments and installations, they have what might be called an exploratory duration – one determined by the visitor, the length of that visitor's experience. Since an event is by nature always in flux, it remains unique and unreproducible. Such works are eminently contingent, closely tied to the specificity of a site or a context, and often dependent on the direct intervention of the audience. They necessarily incorporate chance and accident.

Right from the start, Shaw's work involved installations and environments as well as performances and events. The installations usually hosted performances, as do his current interactive installations (where, however, the main performer is no longer the

Jeffrey Shaw: Vom Expanded Cinema zur Virtuellen Realität

Von Anne-Marie Duguet

Einige Grundprinzipien

Die künstlerischen Experimente der sechziger und siebziger Jahre stellen jene Gesamtheit von Hierarchien und Abgrenzungen in Frage, die die Identität und Natur des Kunstwerks, seine Funktion, seine Beziehung zum Publikum und zu den öffentlichen Ausstellungsstätten bestimmen. Ob Thermodynamik oder ›philosophische Abhandlungen‹, Cut-ups oder Lightshows – im Vordergrund steht nicht die Vielfalt der Interessen und Aktivitäten, sondern die Resonanzen und Wechselwirkungen zwischen verschiedenen Bereichen und Fragestellungen. Es wäre wohl vergeblich – oder gar widersprüchlich – Arbeiten von Jeffrey Shaw einer der vielen Strömungen jener Tage zuordnen zu wollen, unter einem mehr oder minder zutreffenden Etikett wie Happening, Fluxus, Performance, Land-art, kinetische Kunst, Konzeptkunst oder ähnlichem. Durch den einen oder anderen Aspekt gehören Shaws künstlerische Äußerungen all diesen Kategorien zugleich an. Sie sind Ausdruck der wichtigsten Themen und Konzepte, erhärtet in einem Umfeld intellektueller, kultureller und politischer Umbrüche. Und sie sind Beitrag zu ihrer Definition, eingebunden in eben diese Atmosphäre von Infragestellung und Experiment.

Die zeitliche Dimension des Kunstwerks

Die Frage der Zeit beeinflußte in hohem Maße Theorie und Praxis der Kunst jener Tage; qualitative Eigenschaften wie Zerbrechlichkeit, Vergänglichkeit, Zufall, Unbeständigkeit und Flüchtigkeit rückten immer stärker in den Vordergrund. Zeit war nicht nur wiederkehrendes Thema, sie war auch der Parameter, der die Natur des Kunstwerks selbst bestimmte. Die Kluft zwischen traditionellen Kunstformen und den Performances, Environments, Happenings und Installationen entstand in erster Linie durch deren spezielle zeitliche Dimension. Wie Gérard Genette zeigt, ist die Performance (oder das Event) im Unterschied zum materiellen Objekt, welches in der Zeit Bestand hat, von ›prozessualer Dauer‹: Sie entfaltet sich (zwischen einem je nach Auffassung mehr oder weniger erkennbaren Anfang und Ende) in einem Kontinuum, welches nicht unterbrochen werden kann, ohne in den Prozeß als Ganzes einzugreifen.[1] Environments und Installationen haben, so könnte man sagen, eine explorative Dauer – bestimmt durch den Zuschauer, durch die Dauer seiner Erfahrung. Da ein Ereignis aufgrund der ihm eigenen Natur immer im Fluß ist, bleibt es einzigartig und nicht wiederholbar. Solche Arbeiten unterliegen bestimmten Abhängigkeiten; eng gebunden an die Eigenheiten eines Ortes oder Kontextes und oftmals an den direkten Eingriff des Publikums, schließen sie notwendig den Zufall, das Ungewisse mit ein.

Schon die ersten Arbeiten Jeffrey Shaws sind Installationen und Environments, Performances und Ereignisse. Die Installationen integrieren zumeist Performances, wie auch seine jüngsten

artist but the visitor). Ephemeral by nature, most performances – especially those of the 1970s – were recorded on photographs or video, and this mediatization was often incorporated into the performance itself. Shaw, however, contented himself with the fleeting nature of events and kept few traces of the many performances he produced in the late 1960s. They reportedly reflected the ritualistic, provocative character of performances of that period, influenced by Fluxus and the Viennese Actionists, employing a highly diverse range of techniques and materials. The human body became the focus of experiential concerns, just as it later became a key issue in the conception of interfaces with virtual worlds.

These early actions also spurred Shaw to begin to conceive of an art-work as a field of complex interactions composed of simultaneous events, each having its own duration (a performance act, the running time of a film, various physical phenomena). John Latham's work was then developing the notion of 'event structure', along with a theory of time that viewed worldly phenomena, in Margarethe Jochimsen's words, 'as simultaneous and successive events that are all elements of different event structures, each event structure having its own temporal base, its own "score", its own driving force'[2]. That was just one aesthetic reaction among many to the discovery of internal time, a different conception of space-time derived from research into physics, as Ilya Prigogine and Serge Pahaut made clear: 'Under the influence of irreversible phenomena, the geometries of homogeneous and isotropic space-time have given way to a differentiated space-time'.[3] Several artists then explored the concept of entropy at the end of the 1960s, including some like Robert Smithson who produced what he called 'visible analogs for the Second Law of Thermodynamics'[4].

Materialization, not Material

Like several artists at the time, Shaw reacted sharply to the supposed dematerialization of art that was postulated in the late 1960s on the basis of a number of conceptual propositions (which, for that matter, were always concretized in one way or another). The two concepts pointing in that direction, as formulated by Lucy Lippard and John Chandler, were 'art as idea' in which 'matter is denied', and 'art as action' in which 'matter has been transformed into energy and time-motion'.[5] Shaw could claim to adhere to both of them, insofar as this transformation and its very visibleness was the driving concept behind most of his actions (which might be paraphrased as 'art as idea as matter'). The fact that Shaw stopped making objects does not mean that he lost interest in the physical reality of materials. It was simply that the ones he used had no value or reason other than their ability to demonstrate a process – namely, the process of materialization.

Starting in the 1950s, materials previously alien to the artistic context were unleashed on the art scene, from the 'most perishable' (favoured by Allan Kaprow), to the most commonplace or quotidian (Arte Povera), to industrial or natural (Minimal and Land

interakt ven Installationen (in denen jedoch nicht mehr der Künstler selbst, sondern der Zuschauer der wichtigste Akteur ist). An sich vergänglich, sind die meisten Performances, vor allem in den siebziger Jahren, auf Fotos festgehalten oder auf Video aufgezeichnet worden; diese Übertragung in ein anderes Medium wurde wiederum häufig in den Ablauf der Performances integriert. Jeffrey Shaw hat sich jedoch an ihren Ereignischarakter gehalten und nur wenige Spuren seiner zahlreichen Performances Ende der sechziger Jahre aufbewahrt. Sie reflektieren die rituellen und provokativen Charakteristika der Performances jener Zeit, die – beeinflußt von der Fluxus-Bewegung und den Wiener Aktionisten – eine Vielzahl unterschiedlichster Techniken und Materialien einsetzten. Der menschliche Körper rückte in das Zentrum erfahrungsbezogener Reflexion und sollte später ein wesentliches Element für die Konzeption der Schnittstellen zu virtuellen Welten werden.

Diese frühen Aktionen waren Anregung für Jeffrey Shaw, das Kunstwerk als ein Feld komplexer Interaktionen zu konzipieren, das sich zusammensetzt aus gleichzeitigen Ereignissen, die sich über verschiedene Zeitspannen (die Handlung einer Performance, die Spielzeit eines Films, verschiedene physikalische Phänomene) erstrecken. Zu jener Zeit entwickelte John Latham mit seiner künstlerischen Arbeit den Begriff der ›ereignishaften Struktur‹ (›event structure‹), die in enger Verbindung steht mit einer Theorie der Zeit, die weltliche Phänomene interpretiert als – wie es Margarathe Jochimsen formuliert – ›gleichzeitige und aufeinanderfolgende Ereignisse, die jeweils Elemente verschiedenartiger Ereignisstrukturen sind, wobei jede Ereignisstruktur ihre Zeitbasis, ihre »Partitur« und Triebkraft aufweist‹[2]. Dies war nur eine der Reaktionen auf die Entdeckung der inneren Zeit, einer neuen Raum-Zeit-Konzeption, die, wie Ilya Prigogine und Serge Pahaut zeigen, auf physikalische Untersuchungen zurückzuführen ist: ›Unter dem Einfluß irreversibler Phänomene weichen die Geometrien der homogenen und isotropen Raum-Zeit einer differenzierten und von nun an grundlegenden Raum-Zeit.‹[3] Verschiedene Künstler beschäftigten sich Ende der sechziger Jahre mit der Entropie, darunter auch Robert Smithson, der seine Arbeiten als ›visuelle Analogien des zweiten Gesetzes der Thermodynamik‹[4] bezeichnete.

Materialisierung, nicht Material

Wie andere Künstler jener Jahre reagierte auch Jeffrey Shaw heftig auf die Forderung nach einer Entmaterialisierung der Kunst, die Ende der sechziger Jahre auf der Grundlage verschiedener konzeptueller Ansätze (die immer wieder auf die eine oder andere Art konkretisiert wurden) formuliert wurde. Hieraus entwickelten sich nach Lucy Lippard und John Chandler zwei richtungsweisende Konzepte: ›Kunst als Idee‹, die die Materie negiert und ›Kunst als Handlung‹, die die Materie in Energie und Bewegung in der Zeit umwandelt.[5] Shaw könnte für sich in Anspruch nehmen, beide realisiert zu haben: die Transformation und deren gleichzeitige Sichtbarmachung bildeten das Grundkonzept (das man mit ›Kunst als Idee als Materie‹ umschreiben könnte) für die meisten seiner Arbeiten. Daß Shaw keine Objekte mehr schuf, bedeutete jedoch

art). Shaw appropriated highly diverse elements: water, fire, air, neon, polyethylene, pneumatic devices, pyrotechnics, films, photos, lasers, computer data, etc. These were not just substances preferably fluid, light, evanescent, malleable, and in-consistent, they also constituted systems liable to induce immateriality: light, sound, computation, and various artifices. What counted was their ability 'to physically embody the immaterial' (which still remains an issue and above all an interrogation at the heart of Shaw's research). Such transmutations can, however, be effected only through specific tensions and collisions between several poles, through a confrontation of materials. One element alone cannot show how the visible comes into being while simultaneously offering the spectacle of its own disintegration. Indeed, isn't it the property of the virtual to resist the phenomenal?

On Non-Architecture

Noting a radical shift in the logic and scope of sculpture in the 1960s, as well as in the exigencies of the works themselves, Rosalind Krauss theoretically situated sculpture in a four-cornered field, a set of opposing poles labelled landscape, architecture, non-architecture, and non-landscape. Several of Shaw's works, then, could be located between architecture and non-architecture. 'Whatever the medium employed,' claimed Krauss, 'the possibility explored in this category is a process of mapping the axiomatic features of the architectural experience – abstract conditions of openness and closure – onto the reality of a given space'.[6] Here, the reality of that space is essentially urban architecture, while the axiomatic features under consideration relate more to the use and the permanence of materials.

It was by adopting the principle of inflatable structures that Shaw exceeded the limits of architecture, with its formal conventions of stability and permanence, its functions of power and shelter. 'One of the main features of the present environmental design programme is a monumental rigidity which precludes any significant role or identity of the user' noted Shaw.[7] The alternative he proposed was a soft architecture that is transformable, mobile, ephemeral and receptive to intermediate states. The critical and highly provocative approach of the Eventstructure Research Group (with whom Shaw produced these pieces) entailed not only conceiving architecture as spatially fluid but also making it practicable. Krauss's field, then, should be enlarged to include another term – event. Time becomes an active element in an architecture that displays the basic property of malleability and is therefore liable to constant metamorphosis depending on the interests of those practicing it. Pyramids, pavilions, and domes lose their normal functions and are assigned other roles, becoming playful spaces able to produce surprising sensations.

The idea of light architecture had also subtended some new concepts advocated in the 1920s by architects who sought to free architecture from the ground, for example by hoisting it on pilings.

nicht, daß er sich für die physikalische Realität von Materialien nicht mehr interessierte. Vielmehr hatten die von ihm verwendeten Materialien keinen anderen Wert oder Sinn als den, daß sie geeignet waren, einen Vorgang – nämlich den der Materialisierung – darzustellen.

Seit den fünfziger Jahren begann man, in der Kunst Materialien zu verwenden, die in diesem Kontext bis dahin völlig fremd waren: von der ›verderblichsten‹ Art (wie sie Allan Kaprow bevorzugte), banal und alltäglich (Arte Povera), industriell oder natürlich (Minimal art und Land-art). Shaw arbeitete mit einer Vielzahl unterschiedlichster Elemente: Wasser, Feuer, Luft, Neon, Polyäthylen, pneumatische Techniken, Pyrotechnik, Film, Foto, Laser, Computerdaten etc. Er nutzte dabei nicht nur Substanzen, die vorzugsweise flüssig, leicht, vergänglich, formbar und unbeständig waren, sondern auch ganze Systeme, mit Hilfe derer sich das Immaterielle darstellen ließ: Licht, Ton, Rechenoperationen und verschiedene Kunstgriffe. Worauf es ankam, war die Möglichkeit, ›das Immaterielle zu materialisieren‹, dem Virtuellen einen Körper zu geben (bis heute ein wesentliches Thema und vor allem eine wichtige Fragestellung im Zentrum der künstlerischen Forschung Shaws). Solche Transmutationen können jedoch nur durch besondere Spannungen und Kollisionen zwischen verschiedenen Polen und durch die Konfrontation verschiedener Materialien herbeigeführt werden. Ein Element allein kann nicht zeigen, wie etwas sichtbar wird und gleichzeitig das Schauspiel seiner eigenen Auflösung bietet. Denn ist es nicht die Eigenschaft des Virtuellen, dem Phänomenalen zu widerstehen?

Über Nicht-Architektur

Ausgehend von der in den sechziger Jahren stattfindenden radikalen Veränderung in Logik und Spannweite des Skulpturbegriffs und den Erfordernissen der Werke selbst, siedelt Rosalind Krauss die Skulptur in einem Raum mit vier gegensätzlichen Polen an: Landschaft, Architektur, Nicht-Architektur und Nicht-Landschaft. Mehrere Arbeiten Shaws könnten in den Bereich zwischen Architektur und Nicht-Architektur eingeordnet werden; so heißt es bei Krauss: ›Ungeachtet des verwendeten Mediums ist die Möglichkeit, die in dieser Kategorie ausgelotet wird, ein Prozeß, um die axiomatischen Eigenheiten der architektonischen Erfahrung – die abstrakten Grundbedingungen von Offenheit und Geschlossenheit – auf die Wirklichkeit eines realen Raumes zu übertragen.‹[6] Mit der Wirklichkeit des Raumes ist hier in erster Linie die urbane Architektur gemeint, während die axiomatischen Eigenschaften sich eher auf die Verwendung und die Beständigkeit von Materialien beziehen.

Indem Shaw aufblasbare Strukturen wählte, konnte er die Grenzen der Architektur – ihre formalen Konventionen von Stabilität und Dauerhaftigkeit sowie ihre Funktionalisierung als Schutz- und Machtobjekt – erweitern. So heißt es bei Shaw: ›Einer der wichtigsten Punkte des gegenwärtigen Programms zur Gestaltung der Umwelt ist seine monumentale Starrheit, die dem Benutzer sowohl eine bedeutende Rolle als auch jegliche Form von Identität

The architectural metaphor of transatlantic liner also dates from that period, and the idea of navigating is still a pregnant one today, heralding the concept of a fluid architecture that is no longer constructed but can be transmitted and shared across remote computer networks.[8]

Architecture has also acquired other qualities: it is permeable, and can be traversed by sound (*Sonus Lux*, 1987) or by text, as exemplified by *Architext* (1992), which Shaw described as making 'the building porous for a visual transposition of information from interior to exterior'.[9]

Semi-Legitimate Sites and Practice

Right from the start, Shaw's artistic practice addressed a broad audience, not merely that of art galleries. Given the scale and materials used in his works, their deployment demanded spaces quite different from buildings designed for traditional exhibitions. Moreover, the desire to avoid making art a separate activity, to connect it to everyday life, an interest in heterogeneous idioms and references, and the determination to solicit the participation of spectators, all prompted Shaw to seek out new exhibition contexts. He received support for this type of experiment in Great Britain and the Netherlands, and henceforth took over streets, squares canals, fields, and building facades, producing multifarious events up till the early 1970s. Shaw's events were characterized by a provocative humour, a taste for spectacle and artifice, and a wealth of surprises and paradoxes – a street blocked to traffic by an inflatable cushion (*Cushion,* 1969), the facade of Swansea University hidden behind a smoke-screen (*Smokescreen,* 1969), a canal in Assen invaded by inflatable tubes that spilled into the streets and advanced on spectators (*Waterquake,* 1970).

Shaw also collaborated on various other projects, producing an inflatable dragon (*Dragon,* 1969) for William Klein's film *Mr. Freedom*, and the helium pig which famously floated over the English countryside for a Pink Floyd album (*Pig*, 1976). Pop and rock concerts gave him the opportunity to test new techniques and technology in shows that freely combined music, performance, and projections. Working with groups like Pink Floyd, Soft Machine, and Genesis (between 1975 and 1978) enabled Shaw to produce, for example, a spectacle involving simultaneous three-screen projection of hundreds of slides (*The Lamb Lies Down on Broadway,* 1975) during a Peter Gabriel concert.

Kinetics

It was during such shows that Shaw also explored laser technology and kinetic light projections (*Kinetic Light and Mirror Sculpture*, 1977). He developed several principles that would be important in later works, like the simultaneous combination of several movements – luminous rotating beams were bounced off mirrors that also pivoted on two axes in order to sweep an entire space.

In England at that time, as in the rest of Europe, Pop art and

verweigert.‹[7] Als Alternative schlägt er eine weiche Architektur vor, die formbar, mobil und vergänglich ist und Zwischenzustände darstellen kann. Die kritische und höchst provokative Haltung der Eventstructure Research Group, mit der Shaw diese Arbeiten realisierte, umfaßte nicht nur die Konzeption einer räumlich schwebenden Architektur, sondern auch deren praktische Umsetzung. Der von Krauss definierte Raum müßte somit um folgenden Begriff erweitert werden: das Event. Zeit wird aktives Element in einer Architektur, die auf Verformbarkeit beruht und sich entsprechend der Einwirkungen ihrer Nutzer ständig verändert: Pyramiden, Pavillons und Kuppeln verlieren so ihren üblichen Zweck, erhalten andere Funktionen und werden zu Spielräumen, die überraschende Effekte erzeugen.

Bereits in den zwanziger Jahren hatten einige Architekten die Idee einer ›leichten Architektur‹ vertreten, die – etwa mithilfe von Pfeilern – vom Boden gelöst werden sollte. Die architektonische Metapher des Ozeandampfers stammt aus dieser Zeit, und bis heute ist die Idee der Navigation Leitmotiv für den Entwurf einer fließenden Architektur, die nicht mehr gebaut, sondern über ausgedehnte Computernetzwerke vermittelt und gemeinsam genutzt werden kann.[8]

Architektur erhält auch noch andere Eigenschaften: sie wird durchlässig für Töne (*Sonus Lux,* 1987) oder Texte, wie dies in der Arbeit *Architext* (1992) veranschaulicht wird, die – wie Shaw es beschreibt – ›das Gebäude durchlässig werden [läßt] für eine visuelle Transposition von Informationen von innen nach außen‹.[9]

Schauplätze und Handlungen am Rande der Legalität

Von Anfang an richtete sich Shaws künstlerische Praxis an ein breites Publikum, das nicht nur auf die Klientel der Kunstgalerien beschränkt war. Das Ausmaß, die verwendeten Materialien und die Entfaltung seiner Arbeiten verlangten andere Räume als die der traditionellen Ausstellungsorte. Überdies wollte Shaw keine Kunst machen, die sich absonderte, sondern er wollte sie mit dem Alltagsleben verbinden. Sein Interesse konzentrierte sich auf heterogene Ausdrucksformen und Beziehungen, die den Zuschauer zur Partizipation aufforderten – all dies veranlaßte Shaw, nach neuen Ausstellungskontexten zu suchen. In Großbritannien und den Niederlanden fand er Unterstützung für seine Experimente, wo er bis in die frühen siebziger Jahre Straßen, Plätze, Kanäle, Flächen und Hausfassaden für verschiedenste Events nutzte. Kennzeichnend für diese Events war ihr provokativer Humor, ihr Sinn für das Spektakuläre und Künstliche, verbunden mit einer Fülle von Überraschungen und Paradoxien: Eine Straße wurde mit einem aufgeblasenen Kissen blockiert, so daß sich der Verkehr staute (*Cushion,* 1969); die Fassade der Swansea Universität verschwand hinter einer Rauchwand (*Smokescreen,* 1969); ein Kanal in Assen wurde mit aufblasbaren Polyäthylenschläuchen gefüllt, die sich in die Straßen ausbreiteten und die Zuschauer abdrängten (*Waterquake,* 1970).

Darüberhinaus arbeitete Shaw an verschiedenen anderen Projekten: So entwarf er einen aufblasbaren Drachen (*Dragon,* 1968) für William Kleins Film *Mr. Freedom* sowie das berühmte helium-

Cybernetic art were assuming greater importance, providing one of the most obvious links between art and technology.[10]

Neon Wave Sculpture (1979) was a kinetic light sculpture that Shaw placed high on the side wall of a building. A luminous wave travelled through the neon tubes, describing one of the eight different programmed patterns that was determined according to the speed and direction of the wind. The art work was thus rendered 'sensitive' to natural phenomena and was open to chance factors (a key parameter in Cage-influenced experimentation of the day) including public intervention.

One key aspect of such pieces is the often collective nature of their production. The early 1960s saw increasing collaboration between artists from different fields, notably crystallizing in the U.S. around the New Dance and Happening movements, as well as through projects involving new technology in various ways. The Experiments in Art and Technology group (EAT), for instance, was designed to spur encounters between artists, technicians and scientists: Robert Rauschenberg produced an interactive piece with engineer Billy Klüver, while Nam June Paik built his synthesizer with Shuya Abe. Such cooperation stemmed not only from the very nature of pieces that entailed complex technical and computational systems requiring specific skills, but also from a conception of artistic practice as ongoing work, activity, process and experimentation that escape the control of a single artist. Art was no longer a question of a sole creator's subjectivity. This attitude has been a driving force behind Jeffrey Shaw's output; in addition to his work with the Eventstructure Research Group, founded in December 1967 with Theo Botschuijver and Sean Wellesley-Miller, he has collaborated with several programmers – Larry Abel, Gideon May, Adolf Mathias – as well as with writer Dirk Groeneveld, composer Harry de Wit, and artist Tjebbe van Tijen.

Ignoring frontiers and little concerned with the artistic legitimacy of his activities during that period, Shaw worked not only in the sphere of contemporary art (9th Biennale de Paris, 1975) but also in show business and architecture. It was Walter Benjamin who suggested that 'a set of new attitudes' in the appreciation of art-works might belie the 'commonplace' that entertainment is opposed to meditation, for he pointed out that 'architecture has always presented us with models of an art-work that can be received only as entertainment and in a collective fashion. The laws of that reception are most instructive.'[11]

Expanded Cinema

Jeffrey Shaw abandoned painting when he made an animated film with Tjebbe van Tijen in 1966. Composed of a thousand black-and-white drawings, *Continuous Sound and Image Moments* was related to the structural films of the day in the way it employed flicker effects, animation, flipped images, and a rapid pace spurred by specially composed music. It was conceived above all as part of

gefüllte Schwein, das für ein Pink-Floyd-Album über englischer Landschaft schwebte (*Pig,* 1976). Pop- und Rock-Konzerte gaben ihm Gelegenheit, mit neuen Techniken und Technologien zu experimentieren, wobei eine offene Verbindung von Musik, Performance und Projektionen entstand. Seine Zusammenarbeit mit Gruppen wie Pink Floyd, Soft Machine und Genesis (von 1975 bis 1978) ermöglichte ihm die Realisierung von Projekten wie beispielsweise einer Show – bei einer Konzerttournee von Peter Gabriel – in der Hunderte von Dias gleichzeitig auf drei Leinwände projiziert wurden (*The Lamb Lies Down on Broadway*, 1975).

Kinetik

In diesen Shows experimentierte Shaw auch mit der Lasertechnologie und mit kinetischen Lichtprojektionen (*Kinetic Light and Mirror Sculpture,* 1977). Er entwickelte mehrere Prinzipien, die in seinen späteren Arbeiten bedeutsam werden sollten, wie die Kombination mehrerer gleichzeitiger Bewegungen: Zirkulierende Lichtstrahlen wurden von Spiegeln reflektiert, die sich ihrerseits um zwei Achsen drehten und so die Strahlen durch den ganzen Raum lenkten.

Zu dieser Zeit gewannen in England, ähnlich wie auf dem Kontinent, die Pop Art und die kinetische Kunst immer mehr an Bedeutung; sie stellten eine deutliche Verbindung zwischen Kunst und Technologie her.[10]

Neon Wave Sculpture (1979) ist eine kinetische Lichtskulptur, die Shaw hoch oben an der seitlichen Außenwand eines Gebäudes anbrachte. Eine Welle aus Licht wandert durch die Neonröhren und beschreibt eines von acht vorprogrammierten Mustern, die entsprechend der Windrichtung und -stärke bestimmt werden. Das Kunstwerk wird dadurch ›sensibel‹ für natürliche Außeneinflüsse und offen für Zufallselemente (ein fundamentaler Parameter der damaligen, von John Cage beeinflußten Experimente) und integriert die Intervention des Zuschauers.

Ein Schlüsselaspekt jener Werke ist ihre oftmals kollektive Entstehungsweise. In den frühen Sechzigern verstärkte sich die Zusammenarbeit von Künstlern aus verschiedenen Bereichen – insbesondere im Umfeld der New Dance- und Happening-Bewegungen in den USA – sowie auch bei Projekten, die neue Technologien auf unterschiedliche Weise einbezogen. Die Gruppe Experiments in Art and Technology (EAT) z.B. wurde gegründet, um Begegnungen zwischen Künstlern, Technikern und Wissenschaftlern zu fördern: Robert Rauschenberg entwickelte eine interaktive Arbeit mit dem Ingenieur Billy Klüver, Nam June Paik baute seinen Synthesizer zusammen mit Shuya Abe. Diese Zusammenarbeit beruhte nicht nur auf der Struktur der Werke, die komplexes technisches Wissen und Computerkenntnisse erforderten, sondern auch auf einer Vorstellung von künstlerischer Praxis, die Arbeit, Aktivität und Experiment als fortlaufenden Prozeß versteht, der sich der Kontrolle eines einzelnen Künstlers entzieht. Kunst war nicht länger auf die Subjektivität eines einzelnen Schöpfers beschränkt. Diese Auffassung ist eine treibende Kraft im Schaffen Jeffrey Shaws; neben der Eventstructure Research Group, die er

a gallery installation, and in a subsequent version was projected as a loop onto a receding series of semi-transparent screens, one of which could be modified by the audience (*Emergences of Continuous Forms*, 1966). Shaw described this piece at the time as an 'expanded cinema environment'.

The concept of 'expanded cinema'[12] referred to a group of experimental works with varying and sometimes contradictory aims, ranging from critiques of the standard mechanisms behind the cinematic apparatus to efforts to heighten sensory stimulation 'expanding our apprehension of reality' and thereby attaining new levels of consciousness.[13]

For Dominique Noguez, 'any spectacle that goes beyond or modifies [. . .] the cinematic ritual' belongs to the sphere of expanded cinema which, he argued, resulted from the convergence of 'five motivations, trends, and themes', namely:[14]

1. 'the conviction that the traditional screen is inadequate, and a determination to *expand* and *multiply* screen space'. Such schemes date back to the origins of the movies, as witnessed by the Lumière brothers' Cinematograph, Abel Gance's three-screen *Napoléon*[15], and Moholy-Nagy's concept of 'polycinema'[16], to mention just a few;

2. 'the Futurist idea of "polyexpressivity"' that extended the notion of *Gesamtkunstwerk* ('total art-work') to incorporate a diverse range of expressive means, materials, and techniques, breaking down the barriers between the arts;[17]

3. a convergence of cinema with the theatrical arts, tending toward 'a return to the body or, more generally, to the organic (as opposed to mechanical), characterized by actual presence (implying three-dimensionality), contact, and unreproducibility';

4. the work of 'deconstruction' that makes the process of producing a film its very goal. Light beam, projection screen, the advance of the film strip, and the ritual of movie-watching all served as experimental points of departure;[18]

5. an ultimate focus that occasionally led expanded cinema to concentrate on 'a single one of its features: that of being an art of light'.

All of these principles of spatialization, multiplicity, analysis and process were already present in Shaw's first effort at expanding cinematic projection. He repeated the experiment on several occasions, combining the original film with performance, as in *Disillusion of a Fish Pond* (1967), where the images were projected onto an indoor pond full of yellow gelatine, in which a woman covered with cotton-wool dangled her feet. The jelly slowly rose as tubes within it were inflated, pushed into the audience and finally burst, releasing white smoke. The distorted image thus expanded along with the projection surface.

The question of the screen – here, three-dimensional and borderless – has been central to Shaw's thinking, and he has subjected it to a multitude of trials, steadily challenging its specific qualities: paper screens are torn, smoke screens dissipate, and an

im Dezember 1967 mit Theo Botschuijver und Sean Wellesley-Miller gründete, arbeitete er auch mit verschiedenen Programmierern wie Larry Abel, Gideon May oder Adolf Mathias zusammen, oder auch mit dem Schriftsteller Dirk Groeneveld, dem Komponisten Harry de Wit und dem Künstler Tjebbe van Tijen.

Shaw kümmerte sich wenig um die Grenzen oder die künstlerische Legitimierung seiner Aktivitäten in jener Zeit: Er arbeitete sowohl im Bereich der zeitgenössischen Kunst (9. Biennale von Paris, 1975) als auch im Showbusiness und im Bereich der Architektur. Walter Benjamin spricht von ›einer Gesamtheit neuer Anschauungen‹ in der Betrachtung des Kunstwerks, die den ›Gemeinplatz‹, ›Zerstreuung und Sammlung stehen in einem Gegensatz‹, widerlegt: ›Die Architektur bot von jeher den Prototyp eines Kunstwerks, dessen Rezeption in der Zerstreuung und durch das Kollektivum erfolgt. Die Gesetze ihrer Rezeption sind die lehrreichsten.‹[11]

Expanded Cinema

1966 kehrte Jeffrey Shaw der Malerei den Rücken und produzierte mit Tjebbe van Tijen einen animierten Film. *Continuous Sound and Image Moments* besteht aus tausenden Schwarzweißzeichnungen; die Verwendung von Flimmereffekten und Animation sowie die in schnellem Rhythmus aufeinanderfolgenden Bilder, die von einer eigens komponierten Musik vorangetrieben werden, nehmen Bezug auf den zeitgenössischen strukturellen Film. Der Film wurde u.a. im Rahmen einer Installation in einer Galerie gezeigt und als Endlosschleife auf eine hintereinander gestaffelte Reihe halbdurchlässiger Leinwände projiziert; eine der Leinwände konnte von den Zuschauern manipuliert werden (*Emergences of Continuous Forms*, 1966). Jeffrey Shaw bezeichnete diese Arbeit damals als ein ›Expanded Cinema Environment‹.

Der Begriff des ›Expanded Cinema‹[12] bezieht sich auf eine Reihe experimenteller Arbeiten mit verschiedenen, teilweise widersprüchlichen Zielsetzungen, die von der Kritik an den standardisierenden Mechanismen des Kinoapparates bis hin zur stärkeren Stimulierung der Sinne reichen, um so ›unsere Wahrnehmung der Wirklichkeit zu erweitern‹[13] und neue Bewußtseinsstufen zu erreichen.

Nach Dominique Noguez gehört ›jedes Spektaktel, welches das filmische Ritual [...] erweitert oder verändert‹ zum ›Expanded Cinema‹, das sich aus dem Zusammentreffen von folgenden ›fünf Motivationen, Strömungen und Themen‹ entwickelte:[14]

1. ›Die Überzeugung, daß die traditionelle Leinwand nicht ausreicht und das Bestreben, die Projektionsfläche zu *erweitern* und zu *multiplizieren*.‹ Diese Ansätze gehen auf die Anfänge des Kinos zurück wie den Kinematographen der Gebrüder Lumière, Abel Gance' Projektion auf drei Leinwände für seinen Film *Napoléon*[15] oder Moholy-Nagys Entwurf des ›Simultankinos‹[16], um nur einige zu nennen.

2. ›Das futuristische Konzept der »Vielgestaltigkeit«‹, das die Idee des Gesamtkunstwerks erweiterte und eine breite Palette von

absorbent screen is slowly swallowed by the black ink in which it is dipped.

The image printed on the film strip is no longer the main centre of interest; rather, it is the uncertain status of the projected image, the image-in-formation. Film projection itself thus becomes a performance.

Two 'performance events' that Shaw produced in the Netherlands in 1967, *Corpocinema* and *MovieMovie*, sum up his exploration of the notion of expansion.

Corpocinema employed an inflatable transparent dome, set up outdoors, onto which cartoons, feature films, documentaries, and slides of abstract imagery were projected, all organized according to a specific theme each evening.[19] Given its transparency, the dome could not operate as projection screen. It was therefore thrust back onto its architectural function, becoming a protective screen that sheltered not the installation of other reflective surfaces, but rather the generation of events which acted as screen – combinations of unstable phenomena and shapeless substances of varying densities. The visibleness of the projected images thus depended on zones of relative, fleeting opacity produced by physical actions like spraying coloured powder and liquids onto the inner surface of the dome, or triggering smoke, fire-fighting foam, pyrotechnics. The dome might also collapse on what it contained, taking the form of tubes and balloons being inflated to give the projection surface surprising shape. Shaw thereby created a three-dimensional 'volume of particles on which the projected images were attenuated'[20]. Hence the very existence of the cinematic image was at stake, was seriously undermined, as was the very possibility of cinema itself.

This raises the question as to what, exactly, the image is screening. And how can that be ascertained when what it screens is precisely that which subtends its existence? By setting matter against matter, and by intercept ng light with a whole arsenal of processes alien to cinema, Shaw has revealed the function (or, rather, the functioning) of the screen.

In so doing, Shaw demonstrated a type of representation beyond all fiction, creating a field of interaction, a theatre of constant collision between matter and beam, a site of exchange and transformation of energy. The very movement of matter was awarded centre stage. The appearance/disappearance of images inversely corresponded to the appearance/disappearance of actions inside the dome. What was seen depended on the specific action performed – images resulted from a chance encounter between the thickness of smoke and the luminosity of a given scene. Furthermore, this inte-dependence of heterogeneous agents and multiple events constituted a complex layering of time. Live actions by several performers in the space of the dome merged with those recorded on the film strip; the specific duration of the projected imagery confronted the random duration of the

Ausdrucksmitteln, Materialien und Techniken integrierte, die die Grenzen zwischen den verschiedenen Kunstformen aufhoben.[17]

3. Die Annäherung des Kinos an das Theater, die ›Rückkehr zur Körperlichkeit oder allgemeiner zum Organischen (im Gegensatz zum Mechanischen), charakterisiert durch tatsächliche Präsenz (die die Dreidimensionalität impliziert), Kontakt und Nicht-Reproduzierbarkeit‹.

4. Der Vorgang der ›Dekonstruktion‹, die den Prozeß der Re-Produktion des Films zum Thema macht: Projektionsstrahl und Leinwand, das Laufen des Filmstreifens und das Ritual der Filmvorführung selbst wurden zu Experimentierfeldern.[18]

5. Ein grundlegender Aspekt, der in manchen Fällen dazu führte, daß sich die Ausweitung des Kinos auf nur eines seiner charakteristischen Merkmale konzentrierte, war der Anspruch, ein ›Kunstwerk aus Licht‹ zu schaffen.

Bereits Shaws erster Versuch zur Erweiterung der filmischen Projektion umfaßte sämtliche Prinzipien des Raumes, der Multiplizität, der Prozeßhaftigkeit und der Analyse. Er wiederholte dieses Experiment mehrmals, wobei er den ursprünglichen Film mit Performances koppelte: In *Disillusion of a Fish Pond* (1967) wurde der Film auf einen Teich projiziert, der mit gelber Gelatine gefüllt war, in der eine in Watte gepackte Frau ihre Füße baumeln ließ. Die gallertartige Masse wurde langsam angehoben als die Schläuche, die unter ihr verborgen lagen, aufgeblasen wurden, sich aus dem Teich und zwischen die Zuschauer schoben und schließlich platzten und weißen Rauch freisetzten. Das verzerrte Bild erweiterte sich somit zusammen mit der Projektionsfläche.

Ein zentraler Punkt im Schaffen Jeffrey Shaws ist die Projektionsfläche (dreidimensional und ohne Begrenzung); immer wieder konfrontiert er sie mit neuen Herausforderungen und stellt ihre spezifischen Eigenschaften in Frage: Leinwände aus Papier wurden zerrissen, Projektionsflächen aus Rauch lösten sich auf, eine Leinwand aus absorbierendem Material saugte sich immer mehr mit schwarzer Tinte voll, in die sie getaucht war.

Nicht mehr das Bild auf dem Filmstreifen steht im Mitelpunkt des Interesses, sondern vielmehr der unbestimmte Status des projizierten Bildes – das im Entstehen begriffene Bild. Die Projektion des Films als solche wird zur Performance.

Die beiden ›Performance-Events‹ *Corpocinema* und *MovieMovie*, die Shaw 1967 in den Niederlanden präsentierte, sind eine Synthese seiner Beschäftigung mit der Idee der Erweiterung

Corpocinema bestand aus einer aufblasbaren durchsichtigen Kuppel, die unter freiem Himmel installiert wurde und auf die Zeichentrickfilme, Dokumentar- und Spielfilme sowie Dias mit abstrakten Bildinhalten projiziert wurden, die jeden Abend einem anderen Thema gewidmet waren.[19] Aufgrund ihrer Transparenz konnte die Kuppel selbst nicht als Projektionsfläche dienen. Sie wurde somit zurückgeworfen auf ihre architektonische Funktion als ›Schutzschirm‹, der jedoch nicht die Installation von anderen Projektionsflächen abschirmte, sondern vielmehr die Entstehung jener Ereignisse beschirmte, die als Projektionsflächen fungierten:

interceptive phenomena, and the metamorphoses of the event-driven screens imparted movement to still images.

The multifarious show also featured intermittent glimpses of the technology and impressive machinery required to produce such celestial artifices – exactly what Robertson, in the 18th century, took great care to disguise when his 'fantascope' projected ghosts onto the smoke.[21]

The piece thus entailed nothing other than the incessant process of materialization of the project image. The 'corpocinematic concept' meant giving body to film, endowing it with volume, the third dimension that it lacked. Shaw's alchemical operation of transmutation employed shapeless substances to render the immaterial material. Since it was all about process, the substrate of representation could never be allowed to jell – only transformation could exist.

MovieMovie took up the principles of *Corpocinema*, but the conical structure onto which the images were projected comprized two surfaces – an outer, transparent one and an inner, opaque one. The partly-inflated nature of the structure was incorporated into the performance, creating a double screen in constant metamorphosis triggered by various actions including the movement of the audience itself onto the surface. This time, Shaw employed a denser collage of imagery and live music that reacted to the kinetic behaviour of the structure. This dynamic flux of causal, if random, interactions between the acoustic environment, the projected images, and the morphology of the structure clearly met the conditions of an 'event'.[22] Gilles Deleuze, commenting on Leibniz, noted that 'an event is produced in chaos, in a chaotic multiplicity, as long as a kind of sieve is employed', a sieve that Deleuze described as 'an elastic membrane, without shape, like an electromagnetic field'.[23] In this case, the sieve is Shaw's phenomenal screen, his field of virtual tensions, the constant osmosis of substances that marry via what might be termed, with a nod to Marcel Duchamp, 'inframince' (infra-thin). 'When tobacco smoke smells also of the / mouth which exhales it, the 2 colours / marry by *infra-thin* (olfactory / in-thin).'[24]

This double, indeed duplicitous, screen that Shaw explored – no longer flat, but a volume – is simultaneously the site and the operator of a process of representational formation and disintegration. It is a zone of contamination yet also of transformation or interference between the actual and the virtual, already prefiguring the principle of interface.

As suggested by Dominique Noguez's fifth comment on expanded cinema, not only does the movie become just one of many elements in a complex web of phenomena, but expansion goes so far as to outrun its historical origin – the film strip itself. Indeed, Shaw has declared that, 'all my works are a discourse, in one way or another, with the cinematic image, and with the possibility to violate the boundary of the cinematic frame – to allow the image to physically burst out towards the viewer, or allow the viewer to virtually

Verbindungen unbeständiger Phänomene und formloser Substanzen in unterschiedlicher Dichte. Das Sichtbarwerden der projizierten Bilder war abhängig von Zonen mit relativer, vorübergehender Opazität, die durch physische Aktionen geschaffen wurden: Farbpuder und farbige Flüssigkeiten wurden auf die Innenhaut der Kuppel gesprüht, Rauch, Feuerlöschschaum und Feuerwerke wurden eingesetzt. Die Kuppel konnte abgelassen werden, während in ihrem Innern Schläuche oder Ballons aufgeblasen wurden, um der Projektionsfläche neue, überraschende Formen zu verleihen. Auf diese Weise kreierte Shaw ein dreidimensionales ›Volumen aus Teilchen [...], auf dem sich die projizierten Bilder materialisieren konnten‹[20]. Die Existenz des filmischen Bildes als solches wurde ebenso angegriffen und radikal in Frage gestellt wie auch die Möglichkeiten des Kinos selbst.

Hier wird die Frage aufgeworfen, was genau das projizierte Bild abbildet. Und wie kann dies festgestellt werden, wenn das, was es abbildet genau das ist, was seiner Existenz gegenüberliegt? Indem Shaw unterschiedliche Materialien miteinander konfrontierte und mit Hilfe verschiedener Prozesse, die dem Kino fremd sind, die Richtung der Lichtstrahlen beeinflußte, gelang es ihm, die Funktion bzw. die Funktionsweise der Projektionsfläche zu enthüllen.

Auf diese Weise demonstrierte Jeffrey Shaw eine Form der Repräsentation jenseits aller Fiktion und schuf ein Interaktionsfeld, ein Theater der konstanten Kollision von Materie und Lichtstrahl, einen Ort des Austausches und der Transformation von Energien: Die Bewegung der Materie wurde in Szene gesetzt. Das Erscheinen/Verschwinden der Bilder entsprach in Umkehrung dem Erscheinen/Verschwinden der im Innenraum der Kuppel vorgenommenen Aktionen. Die Sichtbarkeit des Bildes war abhängig von jenen Aktionen – die Bilder entstanden aus einem zufälligen Zusammenspiel zwischen der Dichte des Rauches und der Beleuchtung des Schauplatzes. Darüberhinaus konstituierten diese wechselseitigen Abhängigkeiten zwischen heterogenen Materialien und mehreren gleichzeitigen Ereignissen eine komplexe zeitliche Vielschichtigkeit. Die Live-Aktionen der Performer im Raum der Kuppel mischten sich mit der auf dem Filmstreifen aufgezeichneten Filmhandlung; die festgelegte Dauer der projizierten Bilder wurde mit der zufallsbestimmten Dauer dazwischentretender Phänomene konfrontiert, und die Metamorphosen der ereignisgebundenen Projektionsflächen versetzten die stehenden Bilder in Bewegung.

Die vielschichtige Show erlaubte auch kurze Einblicke in die Technik und die eindrucksvolle Maschinerie, die hinter jenen ›himmlischen Feuerwerken‹ standen. Eben jene Einblicke versuchte z.B. Robertson mit größter Sorgfalt zu vermeiden, als er im 18. Jahrhundert mit seinem ›Phantascop‹ Gespensterbilder auf Rauch projizierte.[21]

Das Kunstwerk verkörperte somit den fortlaufenden Prozeß der Materialisierung des projizierten Bildes. Das Konzept von *Corpocinema* bestand darin, dem Film einen Körper, ein Volumen, die fehlende dritte Dimension zu geben. Shaw verwendete in seinen alchimistischen Experimenten formlose Substanzen, um dem

enter the image'.[25] He would subsequently interest himself mainly in constituent principles of the cinematic apparatus – the projection of images, light, frame, movement.

Spectator Involvement

It was not the arrival of digital simulation and the resulting possibilities of specifically interactive modes that prompted Jeffrey Shaw to interrogate the relationship between spectator and artwork, nor was this issue grafted onto his œuvre by fashion or technical considerations, since it had clearly been an integral part of his early pieces. His environments, events, and installations, although not employing computer technology, necessarily implied and defined procedures of involvement that went beyond simple levels of contemplation, identification, or interpretation.

Shaw's artistic practice emerged at the moment when the question of spectator involvement was being explicitly raised in all spheres of aesthetic activity; it encountered validation and encouragement, if not its initial impetus, in the anti-establishment movements of the late 1960s. Some of the experiments from that period familiarized the public with new attitudes to art, creating a kind of laboratory of heightened awareness. As early as the 1950s certain kinetic works of art required spectators to move around in order to appreciate the structure of the work, or demanded that certain elements be manipulated, or even reacted to spectator presence. In setting forth some of the 'rules' that governed happenings in 1966, Allan Kaprow argued that there should not be (and normally cannot be) an audience or public that watches a happening – by voluntarily participating in a piece, knowing the overall scenario and their specific role in advance, people become a real and essential part of the work.[26] For Minimal art, meanwhile, which largely helped to define the realm of 'installation', spectators became a critical pole of the 'work in situ' conceived as a system of relationships that 'obliged spectators to perceive themselves as a part of the created situation'.[27] What clearly emerged, then, across a wide range of approaches, was the idea that the audience was responsible for completing the artistic proposition. In addition to familiar ways of soliciting involvement – ranging from rhetorical tropes, to including the spectator in the organization of a painting, to perceiving reading as 'work' done on 'production of the text' (Barthes), to the acknowledging 'gaze at the camera' – what was then called participation or interaction required the spectator to make a deliberate intervention that is an integral part of the overall process. This supposes that the work induces awareness of the possibility of a determining act, that the process of transformation be inscribed in the very conception of the piece.

Shaw's early work involved the audience as protagonist of an event that comprized a multitude of potential interactions between various components. Sometimes spectators were encouraged to perform a specific action; in his first installation, for

Immateriellen Form zu geben. Da es hierbei nur um den Prozeß als solchen ging, durfte die Grundlage der Repräsentation nie in einer Form verfestigt werden, denn einzig die Transformation war von Bestand.

MovieMovie griff die Grundprinzipien von *Corpocinema* auf; die kegelförmige Struktur, auf die die Bilder projiziert wurden, bestand jedoch aus zwei Oberflächen – einer transparenten äußeren und einer undurchsichtigen inneren. Die zur Hälfte aufgeblasene Innenfläche war Teil der Performance und schuf aufgrund der verschiedenen Aktionen – zu denen auch die Bewegung der Zuschauer gehörte – eine doppelte Projektionsfläche, die in ständigem Wandel begriffen war. Hier setzte Shaw eine noch dichtere Collage von Bildern und Live-Musik ein, die auf das kinetische Verhalten der Struktur reagierte. Dieser dynamische Fluß von ursächlichen, wenn auch zufallsbestimmten Interaktionen zwischen akustischem Environment, projizierten Bildern und der Morphologie der Struktur, beinhaltete fraglos sämtliche Bedingungen eines ›Events‹.[22] In Gilles Deleuze' Leibniz-Kommentar heißt es: ›Das Ereignis produziert sich in einem Chaos, in einer chaotischen Mannigfaltigkeit, vorausgesetzt, daß eine Art Sieb dazwischentritt‹, ein Sieb ›wie eine elastische und formlose Membran, wie ein elektromagnetisches Feld.‹[23] Jenes Sieb ist bei Shaw die phänomenale Projektionsfläche, ihr Raum virtueller Spannungen, die fortlaufende Osmose von Substanzen, die sich – um mit Marcel Duchamp zu sprechen – im ›Inframince‹ vereinen: ›Wenn Zigarettenrauch auch nach dem / Mund riecht, der ihn aushaucht, dann vereinen sich die beiden Gerüche / durch *infra-dünn* (Geruch / in-dünn).‹[24]

Die hier von Jeffrey Shaw erforschte doppelte, oder genauer gesagt vervielfachte Projektionsfläche – die nicht mehr flach, sondern ein Volumen ist – ist Ort und Akteur zugleich in einem Prozeß der Repräsentation von Entstehung und Auflösung. Sie ist ein Raum der Kontamination, aber auch der Transformation und der Interferenz von Realität und Virtualität und weist bereits voraus auf das Strukturprinzip des Interfaces.

Wie Dominique Noguez im fünften Kommentar zum ›Expanded Cinema‹ formuliert, wird der Film nicht nur zu einem von vielen Elementen in einem komplexen Netz von Phänomenen, sondern die Erweiterung wird sogar über seinen historischen Ursprung – den Filmstreifen selbst – hinausgetrieben. So erklärt Shaw: ›Alle meine Arbeiten sind auf die eine oder andere Weise ein Diskurs mit dem filmischen Bild und mit den Möglichkeiten, die Begrenzung des Bildrahmens zu sprengen – dem Bild zu ermöglichen, sich physisch zum Zuschauer hin auszudehnen oder dem Zuschauer zu ermöglichen, virtuell in das Bild einzutreten.‹[25] Später wird sich Shaw hauptsächlich mit den Grundkonstituenten des kinematographischen Apparates auseinandersetzen: mit der Projektion von Bildern, Licht, Rahmen und Bewegung.

Die Beteiligung des Zuschauers

Bereits vor Entwicklung der digitalen Simulation und den daraus resultierenden Möglichkeiten spezieller Formen von Interaktivität

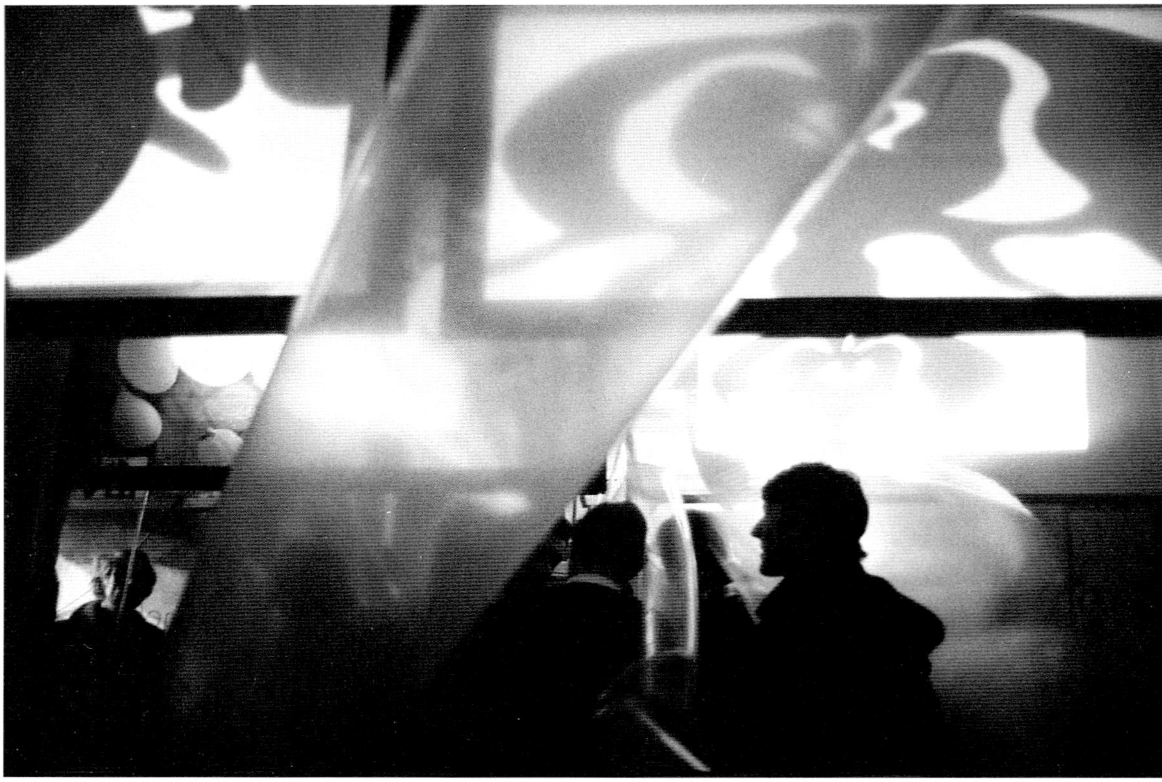

Emergences of Continuous Forms, Better Books, London, UK, 1966. Photo: Pieter Boersma.

hatte Jeffrey Shaw begonnen, sich mit der Beziehung zwischen Betrachter und Kunstwerk zu beschäftigen. Es waren weder modebedingte noch technische Überlegungen, die dazu führten, daß dieses Thema in sein Schaffen einging, vielmehr war es schon integraler Bestandteil seiner frühen Arbeiten. Obwohl er in seinen Environments, Events und Installationen keine Computertechnologie einsetzte, implizierten und definierten sie verschiedene Formen der Beteiligung des Zuschauers, die über das einfache Betrachten, Identifizieren oder Interpretieren hinausgingen.

Shaws künstlerische Arbeit begann zu einem Zeitpunkt, als die Frage nach der Beteiligung des Zuschauers in allen Bereichen der Kunst in den Vordergrund trat. Sie fand Anerkennung und Bestärkung, wenn nicht sogar ihren ursprünglichen Impuls, bei den Anti-Establishment-Bewegungen der späten sechziger Jahre. Einige Experimente jener Zeit machten das Publikum mit neuen Haltungen gegenüber der Kunst vertraut und kreierten eine Art Versuchslaboratorium für ein wachsendes Bewußtsein. Schon in den fünfziger Jahren forderten bestimmte kinetische Kunstwerke den Betrachter zur Bewegung auf, um auf diese Weise ihre Struktur erfassen zu können, oder bestimmte Elemente mußten manipuliert werden oder diese reagierten auf die Präsenz der Zuschauer. Allan Kaprow argumentierte in seinen ›Regeln‹ des Happenings von 1966, daß es kein Publikum geben dürfe, das einem Happening lediglich zuschaut: Erst durch die freiwillige Partizipation, durch das bereits vorab gewonnene Wissen um die Gegebenheiten des allgemeinen Schauplatzes und der eigenen Rolle darin wird das Publikum zu einem wirklichen und wesentlichen Bestandteil der Arbeit.[26] Die Minimal art indessen leistete einen wichtigen Beitrag zur Definition der ›Installation‹; der Zuschauer wurde ein entscheidender Pol der ›Arbeit in situ‹, die als ein System von Beziehungen angelegt war, ›das den Betrachter dazu brachte, sich selbst als Teil der geschaffenen Situation zu begreifen‹.[27] Aus der breiten Vielfalt der Ansätze entwickelte sich die Idee, das Publikum für die Vollendung der künstlerischen Aussage verantwortlich zu machen. Neben den herkömmlichen Mitteln, die zur Beteiligung auffordern – rhetorische Stilmittel, die Einbeziehung des Betrachters in die Komposition eines Gemäldes, das Begreifen der Lektüre als ›Vorgang, der den Text hervorbringt‹ (Barthes), der erwidernde ›Blick in die Kamera‹ – forderte die sogenannte Partizipation oder Interaktion den Zuschauer zum bewußten Eingriff auf, der ein integraler Bestandteil des ganzen Prozesses ist. Dies setzt voraus, daß das Werk beim Zuschauer das Bewußtsein für die Möglichkeit des Eingreifens weckt, daß der Prozeß der Transformation in der Grundkonzeption der Arbeit verankert ist.

Shaws frühe Arbeiten machten den Zuschauer zum Protagonisten eines ›Events‹, das eine Vielzahl möglicher Interaktionen zwischen verschiedenen Komponenten umfaßte. In manchen Arbeiten wurden die Zuschauer zu bestimmten Aktionen aufgefordert; in Shaws erster Installation z.B. sollte das Publikum Ballons, die in einer der Leinwände hingen, aufblasen und so Form und Transparenz dieser vervielfachten Projektionsfläche verändern (*Emergences of Continuous Forms*, 1966). Oder die Besucher konnten sich an

example, they were invited to blow up balloons placed in one of the screens, thereby modifying the shape and transparency of that multiple projection surface (*Emergences of Continuous Forms*, 1966). Sometimes spectators took part in a collective game – not unlike a happening – by providing, for instance, the feet for an imaginary 'inflatable creature', the *Centipede* of 1972, which they paraded through town. In other instances, onlookers and passers-by were provoked into seizing the inflated tubes rising from a canal; by bursting the tubes, spectators released a white smoke and thus simultaneously contributed to the spectacle and to its completion (*Waterquake*, 1970). Other works by Shaw lacked precise instructions or directions – such as certain inflatable objects – yet remained open to the boldness, desire, and imagination of local inhabitants, providing the potential for interaction.

A retrospective look raises one point of particular interest, namely the way in which Shaw immediately generated experimental fields and experiential 'occasions' that involved the human body in playful, poetic actions, and that were, in a way, precursors to the perceptual situation now offered to travellers in virtual worlds. Impressions of immersion, floating, and suspension were all effects engendered at the time by provocative concepts like Shaw's 'soft responsive architecture'. They belong to an initial group of experiments on the notion of environment as organic space.

In *MovieMovie* spectators suddenly took part in the performance by spontaneously jumping into the semi-inflated structure, moving among the projected images, offering their bodies as screen. Being lifted or buried by the soft structures produced an immediate sensorial bliss and euphoria of osmosis and contact with material and sounds (which were thereby modified). Spectators thus contributed to the metamorphosis of the screen-structure. 'Embodying' the work and 'being in touch' with the image were no longer mere metaphors. The violation of the borders and rigidity of the projection screen was accompanied by the breaking of the conventional immobility of movie viewers. The concept of 'expanded cinema' here assumed its full kinesthetic dimension.

Whereas *MovieMovie* was not totally unrelated to the psychedelic ambience of the multi-media events of the day, the inflatable structures subsequently produced by Shaw displayed various interactive virtues via an approach in which humour was more marked: a tube covered with synthetic grass, which could be manipulated (*Grassroll*, 1969); a conically shaped soft structure printed with a brick pattern, onto which people could climb and play (*Brickhill*, 1969); a series of Airgrounds to explore – one in the form of a pyramid (*Airground*, 1968), another partly filled with water so that any movement produces the sound of a pool (*Aqua-Airground*, 1972); and *Three Pavilions* (1971), including one with an auditorium and central stage on the upper level – the audience sat on soft seats sustained by air blown up from the ground floor

einem gemeinschaftlichen Spiel beteiligen – einem Happening nicht unähnlich – indem sie einem imaginären ›aufblasbaren Wesen‹ (*Centipede*, 1972) Beine verliehen und so durch die Stadt marschierten. Ein anderes Mal wurden Zuschauer und Passanten aufgefordert, an aufgeblasenen Schläuchen zu ziehen, die sich aus einem Kanal schoben (*Waterquake*, 1970). Wurden die Schläuche von den Zuschauern zum Platzen gebracht, entstieg ihnen weißer Rauch; somit trug das Publikum gleichzeitig zum Ablauf des Spektakels und dessen Beendigung bei. In anderen Arbeiten Shaws – wie bei bestimmten aufblasbaren Objekten – fehlten jegliche Anleitungen oder Hinweise, sie blieben der Kühnheit, der Lust und der Phantasie ihrer Benutzer überlassen und stellten das Potential zur Interaktion bereit.

Rückblickend zeigt sich ein Aspekt von besonderem Interesse: die Art, in der Shaw von Anfang an experimentelle Schauplätze und erfahrungsbezogene ›Gelegenheiten‹ schuf, die den menschlichen Körper in spielerische, poetische Aktionen verwickelten und in gewisser Weise Vorläufer der perzeptiven Situation sind, die sich dem Reisenden durch virtuelle Welten heute eröffnet. Gefühle wie die des ›Eintauchens‹, des Fließens und des Schwebens waren Effekte, die damals durch provokative Konzepte wie Shaws ›weiche, reagierende Architektur‹ erzeugt wurden. Sie gehören einer ersten Gruppe von Experimenten an, die sich mit der Idee des ›Environments‹ als einem organischen Raum beschäftigen.

In *MovieMovie* wurden die Zuschauer plötzlich Teil der Performance als sie spontan die halb aufgeblasene Struktur betraten, sich zwischen den projizierten Bildern bewegten und ihren Körper als Projektionsfläche anboten. Das Hochgehobenwerden und Versinken in der nachgiebigen Struktur erzeugte ein unmittelbares sensorisches Wohlgefühl und eine Euphorie der Osmose und des Kontaktes mit Materialien und Tönen (die dadurch verändert wurden). Die Zuschauer beeinflußten somit die Metamorphose der Struktur der Projektionsfläche. Die Arbeit zu ›verkörpern‹, die Bilder zu ›berühren‹ – dies waren nicht mehr bloße Metaphern. Die Grenzen und die Starrheit der Projektionsfläche wurden gesprengt und gleichzeitig die herkömmliche Immobilität des Kinobesuchers überwunden. Das Konzept des ›Expanded Cinema‹ wurde hier in seiner ganzen kinästhetischen Bedeutung umgesetzt.

Während sich *MovieMovie* der psychedelischen Atmosphäre der ›Multimedia-Events‹ jener Tage nicht völlig entziehen konnte, entfalteten Shaws später entstandenen aufblasbaren Strukturen ihre vielfältigen interaktiven Fähigkeiten mit Sinn für Humor: ein mit Kunstrasen überzogener Schlauch, der manipuliert werden konnte (*Grassroll*, 1969), ein kegelförmiges, weiches, mit einem Muster aus Backsteinen bedrucktes Objekt, auf dem man herumklettern und spielen konnte (*Brickhill*, 1969), eine Reihe von ›Airgrounds‹ – pyramidenförmig (*Airground*, 1968) oder teilweise mit Wasser gefüllt, so daß jede Bewegung die Geräusche eines Pools assoziierte (*Aqua-Airground*, 1972) und *Three Pavilions* (1971). Einer der Pavillons beherbergte im Obergeschoß einen Zuschauerraum und eine Bühne – die Zuschauer saßen auf nachgiebigen luft-

(where the real show was, rather than on stage). Interaction occurred not only between users and structure (whose shape they modified) but also between participants themselves (obliged to make certain acrobatic gestures, displaying 'intoxicated' behaviour that provided a spectacle for all). The strategy of involvement was straightforward, playful, and collective, and called for unusual sensory-motor exploration, sometimes going so far as to defy the laws of physics. Shaw could even be seen as a pataphysicist, a disciple of the 'science of imaginary solutions' describing 'a universe that can be envisaged and that perhaps should be envisaged in place of the traditional one', as Alfred Jarry suggested.[28] 'Instead of a law for a body falling toward a centre', continued Jarry 'it would be preferable to have a law for a vacuum rising toward the edge.'[29]

Another series of pieces by Shaw from the same period encouraged the public to walk on water, either by entering hermetically sealed, inflated transparent or colored tetrahedrons (*Waterwalk*, 1969), or by using a 250-metre long floating transparent tube that served as bridge (*Waterwalk Tube,* 1970). It was only in 1983 that Allan Kaprow managed to walk on the Sea of Galilee – in a videotape by Nam June Paik.[30]

Without being interactive – although contemporaneous with Shaw's earliest work on virtual reality – the video installation *Heavens Gate* (1986) subordinated the tactile dimension in favour of an exploration of the immersive potential of a visual space. The resulting vertiginous effect was produced by a subtle system of relationships between body, image, and space, based on a closed and totally dark room some six metres high; the ceiling served as projection screen while the floor was covered with a mirror. Viewers who ventured into this space were caught in a vertical vanishing axis. As they hovered between the image and its reflection, the ground gave way under their feet – viewers found themselves above a void even as their eyes were drawn upward. In fact, top and bottom were undifferentiated, locked together in a play of mirrors. It was a Baroque setting par excellence, perfectly integrating image with architecture. Yet here the traditional dome painting was hybridized with an opposing view of the earth as seen from a satellite. Digital effects inextricably wove the two images into a continuous movement of rotation, of ascent, of shattering and exploding, of folding and refolding. This visual profusion, in which electronics held centre stage, contributed to the destabilization and abduction of the body, to the virtual sensation of being absorbed into a space that abolishes 'the boundary between material and immaterial identity'[31].

Employing different techniques, Shaw explored various other principles of interaction, perhaps entailing a simple reaction triggered by the structure itself. For example, the position of air bubbles in the panels of a glass wall of a pool was modified according to the movement of passers-by as detected by infra-red

gefüllten Sitzen, die vom Erdgeschoß aus gestützt wurden (die wirkliche ›Show‹ spielte sich denn auch hier und nicht auf der Bühne ab). Die Interaktion fand nicht nur zwischen den Benutzern und der Struktur (deren Form verändert werden konnte), sondern auch zwischen den Teilnehmern selbst statt (wenn aus unfreiwilligen akrobatischen Verrenkungen und ›torkelnden‹ Bewegungen ein Spektakel für alle wurde). Das Prinzip der Beteiligung war einfach, spielerisch und kollektiv und führte zu ungewohnten sensomotorischen Erfahrungen, die manchmal sogar den physikalischen Gesetzen trotzten. Man könnte Jeffrey Shaw vielleicht als einen ›Pataphysiker‹ bezeichnen, als einen Schüler der ›Wissenschaft der imaginären Lösungen‹, die, wie es Alfred Jarry formuliert, ›ein Universum [beschreibt], das man sehen kann und das man vielleicht statt des Überkommenen sehen sollte‹.[28] Und weiter heißt es bei Jarry: ›Sollte man nicht, statt das Gesetz des freien Falls der Körper auf einen Mittelpunkt hin zu formulieren, vielmehr die These vom Aufsteigen der Leere zur Peripherie hin vorziehen.‹[29]

Eine andere Reihe von Arbeiten Shaws aus dieser Zeit ermunterte das Publikum, auf dem Wasser zu gehen: entweder in hermetisch abgedichteten, luftgefüllten Tetraedern aus durchsichtigem oder farbigem Material (*Waterwalk*, 1969) oder durch eine 250 Meter lange transparente schwimmende schlauchförmige Struktur, die als Brücke diente (*Waterwalk Tube,* 1970). Allan Kaprow schaffte es dagegen erst 1983, auf dem See von Genezareth zu wandeln – in einem Video von Nam June Paik.[30]

Obwohl die Videoinstallation *Heavens Gate* (1986) zeitgleich mit Shaws ersten Virtual Reality-Arbeiten entstand, ist sie nicht interaktiv, sondern ordnet die taktile Dimension der Erforschung der immersiven Möglichkeiten des virtuellen Raums unter. Der hier erzeugte ›schwindelerregende‹ Effekt entsteht aus einem subtilen Beziehungssystem zwischen Körper, Bild und Raum: In einem geschlossenen, völlig abgedunkelten, etwa sechs Meter hohen Raum dient die Decke als Projektionsfläche während der Boden von einem Spiegel bedeckt ist. Besucher, die sich in diesen Raum wagen, sind auf der vertikalen Fluchtachse gefangen und schweben zwischen Bild und Spiegelbild. Der Boden scheint unter den Füßen nachzugeben und der Betrachter wähnt sich, auch wenn er den Blick nach oben richtet, über einem Abgrund. Oben und unten verbinden sich auf undifferenzierte Weise im Spiel der Spiegel. Dies ist ein barocker Schauplatz par excellence, der das Bild in perfekter Weise in die Architektur eingliedert. Doch hier wird das traditionelle Deckengemälde mit seinem Gegenstück vermischt – dem Blick von einem Satelliten herab auf die Erde. Digitale Effekte verweben die beiden Bilder in einer kontinuierlichen Bewegung miteinander – sie drehen sich, steigen auf, zersplittern, explodieren, falten sich zusammen und entfalten sich von neuem. Diese Überfülle der Bilder bewirkt die Schwächung und Entführung des Körpers bis hin zu der virtuellen Empfindung, in einen Raum hineingesogen zu werden, in dem ›die Grenzen zwischen materieller und immaterieller Identität‹[31] aufgehoben sind.

Jeffrey Shaw nutzte die verschiedensten Techniken, um vielfäl-

sensors (*Bubble Wall*, 1979); elsewhere, spectators were invited to collaborate by choosing the texts or words that drive a system (*Propagation of the Luminous Word*, 1988 and *Architext*, 1992); again, the spectator might be confronted by a real-time computer-processed video image of his or her own face (*Video Narcissus*, 1987).

Although these few examples show that the spectator's relationship to the art-work is a constant concern running throughout Shaw's œuvre, it does not necessarily constitute the key issue behind all his projects, and certain forms of participation that might otherwise seem simple or banal only assume their full meaning when related to a specific context or concept behind a given work.

Shaw quickly became interested in another fundamental principle of spectator involvement, namely soliciting the viewer's visual activity and role in actualizing a scene.

Viewpoint on Virtuality

Viewpoint (1975) provides a good example of Jeffrey Shaw's systematic investigation into the nature of virtual images. From that point onward, he began to exploit the specific potential of installations to expose representational processes, all the while spatially deploying the various parameters constituting that representation in order to re-orchestrate them according to new hypotheses or to propose new arrangements. Shaw thus elaborated a veritably critical stagecraft by appropriating and transforming established models (painting, theatre, movies, photography) via multiple hybridization and the introduction of new technical features. What was at stake was no longer the image so much as the whole apparatus which produces and circumscribes that image, namely a complex set of technical, perceptual, discursive, economic, psychological and institutional conditions. This analytical approach, in which a work tests its own conditions of existence, was widely explored by artists in the 1970s, most especially in video installations.[32] Shaw's œuvre testifies to this major artistic shift from interest in representation alone to interest in the generation of that representation and its experiential possibilities.

Well before the use of computers, Shaw developed 'virtual slide projection techniques' that explored the virtualization (rather than materialization) of images. Henceforth images would be disembodied, rather than embodied. Projection then became increasingly pertinent insofar as virtual image is primarily a question of optics.

Viewpoint powerfully inaugurated awareness of the total dependence between image and spectator. An image was no longer given, could not pre-exist its actualization – here, its perception – by a spectator. Seeing became part of what is seen.

The *Viewpoint* installation comprized two basic poles – an optical viewing console that included two programmed slide pro-

tige weitere Prinzipien der Interaktion zu entwickeln, die verbunden sein können mit einer einfachen Reaktion, die von der Struktur selbst ausgelöst wird. So verändert sich beispielsweise die Verteilung der Luftblasen in der gläsernen Wand eines Schwimmbades entsprechend der Bewegung der vorbeigehenden Besucher, die von Infrarotsensoren wahrgenommen wird (*Bubble Wall*, 1979). In anderen Arbeiten können die Besucher Texte oder Worte auswählen, die ein System steuern (*Propagation of the Luminous Word*, 1988 und *Architext*, 1992) oder der Zuschauer wird mit einem in Echtzeit digitalisierten, computerbearbeiteten Videobild seines eigenen Gesichts konfrontiert (*Video Narcissus*, 1987).

Wenn auch diese wenigen Beispiele zeigen, daß die Beziehung zwischen Betrachter und Kunstwerk ein immer wiederkehrendes Motiv ist, das sich durch Shaws gesamtes Œuvre zieht, so ist dies doch nicht unbedingt das zentrale Thema, das hinter all seinen Projekten steht. Denn bestimmte Formen der Partizipation, die in anderen Zusammenhängen simpel oder banal erscheinen mögen, entfalten ihre ganze Bedeutung erst, wenn sie in Beziehung gesetzt werden zu einem bestimmten Kontext oder Konzept, die hinter einer Arbeit stehen.

Schon früh interessierte sich Shaw für ein weiteres grundlegendes Prinzip der Beteiligung des Zuschauers: die Einbeziehung der visuellen Tätigkeit und Rolle des Betrachters bei der Realisierung eines Schauplatzes.

Standpunkte zum Virtuellen

Viewpoint (1975) ist ein gutes Beispiel für Jeffrey Shaws systematische Auseinandersetzung mit dem Wesen der virtuellen Bilder. Von diesem Zeitpunkt an begann er, das spezifische Potential von Installationen zu nutzen, um den Prozeß der Repräsentation darzustellen und gleichzeitig die verschiedenen Parameter, aus denen sich die Repräsentation konstituiert, räumlich umzusetzen, um sie neuen Hypothesen entsprechend umzuarrangieren oder neue Anordnungen vorzuschlagen. Hierbei entwickelte Shaw ein wahrhaft kritisches dramaturgisches Können, wobei er die etablierten Genres (Malerei, Theater, Film, Fotografie) aufnahm und veränderte, indem er sie auf verschiedenste Weise miteinander vermischte und neue technische Mittel einsetzte. Im Mittelpunkt stand nicht mehr so sehr das Bild, sondern der ganze Apparat, der das Bild hervorbringt und beschreibt: eine komplexe Reihe technischer, perzeptiver, diskursiver, ökonomischer, psychologischer und institutioneller Bedingungen. Diese analytische Herangehensweise, bei der ein Werk die Bedingungen seiner eigenen Existenz hinterfragt, war typisch für die Künstler der siebziger Jahre, besonders bei Videoinstallationen.[32] Shaws Œuvre zeugt von dieser wichtigen Wende in der Kunst: vom Interesse an der Darstellung als solcher zum Interesse an der Erzeugung dieser Darstellung und ihren experimentellen Möglichkeiten.

Lange vor Einführung des Computers entwickelte Shaw Techniken zur virtuellen Projektion von Bildern, die die Virtualisierung (im

jectors, and a projection screen covered with a material that reflects light solely in the direction of the light source (and which, moreover, does not require a darkened room).[33] Only the person who stepped up to the console could see the image projected on the screen – other museum visitors perceived only a plain grey surface in front of which they passed without realizing they had become part of the projected scene.

This system shares a certain number of principles with Brunelleschi's prototype perspective method, or *costruzione legittima*: the specular nature of the system and its closure; the fixed, precise place assigned to the viewer (external to the system); and the privileged position of the spectator as the locus around which the representation is organized. As Hubert Damisch describes it, Brunelleschi's system 'attempted to reproduce, on the scale of a proportionally reduced "view", the conditions in which the San Giovanni baptistery could be seen from the framing of the central portal of Florence cathedral by an observer inside the cathedral, at a prescribed distance'.[34] The spectator of *Viewpoint* is also incorporated into a homothetic relationship (i.e. one based on similar placement), because he or she stands at the very spot in the museum where the slides were originally photographed. The construction of optical illusion depends precisely on this perfect coincidence of the photograph frame with the projection frame (like the coincidence between vanishing point and viewpoint in Brunelleschi's system). Whereas the central site intrinsic to Brunelleschi's *costruzione legittima* provides the full effect of depth and perspective, Shaw's system goes beyond that goal in two respects. First of all, the illusion involves not representation, but the image itself; secondly, illusion is not played out in the apparent depth of the scene, but along its edges, on the frontier between the image and the space in which it is set.

The point of view therefore not only organizes the scene, it actualizes it, becoming the very site and condition of visibility. Representation exists only for the person who does the looking and constructing. That is precisely what attracted Marcel Duchamp's lively and somewhat ironic interest in various illusionist techniques like anamorphosis, stereo vision, and anaglyphs, in which images only occur via the intervention of mental activity – only an act of perception endows them with materiality, with 'physicality'.

Anamorphosis, the art of 'projecting forms outside of themselves', requires optical correction from a 'specific point' in order to be legible, to become identifiable.[35] Except at that specific point, the image can not be decoded, will resist 'correct' legibility. *Viewpoint*, however, is not concerned with revealing dissimulation within the image, it is quite simply concerned with making the image appear. Eleven years later Shaw would employ anamorphosis with a mirrored cylinder – an installation titled *Anamorphoses of Memory* (1986) – but there it indeed concerned a text to be deciphered.

Several kinetic works of art in the 1950s, meanwhile, explored

Gegensatz zur Materialisierung) der Bilder erforschten. Bilder wurden fortan entkörpert und nicht mehr verkörpert. Die Projektion gewann zunehmend an Bedeutung, da das virtuelle Bild in erster Linie eine Frage der Optik ist.

Viewpoint enthüllt mit aller Deutlichkeit die totale Abhängigkeit von Bild und Betrachter. Ein Bild ist als solches nicht mehr gegeben, kann vor seiner Verwirklichung – der Wahrnehmung – durch den Betrachter nicht existieren. Sehen wird Teil des Gesehenen.

Die Installation *Viewpoint* bestand aus zwei Polen: einer optischen Sichtkonsole mit zwei synchron arbeitenden Diaprojektoren und einer speziell beschichteten Leinwand, die auftreffendes Licht wieder zur Lichtquelle zurücklenkte (so daß der Raum nicht abgedunkelt werden mußte).[33] Nur die Person, die die Konsole betreten hatte, konnte das auf die Leinwand projizierte Bild sehen; alle anderen Besucher nahmen nur eine leere graue Fläche wahr, an der sie vorbeigingen, ohne zu bemerken, daß sie Teil der projizierten Szene geworden waren.

Dieses System hat viele Gemeinsamkeiten mit Brunelleschis Prinzipien der perspektivischen Konstruktion (*costruzione legittima*): die Geschlossenheit des Systems, der fest definierte Standpunkt des Betrachters (außerhalb des Systems) und dessen besondere Position in einem geometrischen Ort, um den die Darstellung angeordnet ist. So beschreibt Hubert Damisch, auf welche Weise Brunelleschis System versucht, ›im Maßstab einer proportional verkürzten »Sicht« die Bedingungen zu reproduzieren, in denen der Betrachter von einem bestimmten Punkt im Innern der Kathedrale von Florenz aus das Baptisterium von San Giovanni durch das Hauptportal hindurch sieht‹.[34] Auch der Betrachter von *Viewpoint* wurde Teil einer synthetischen Beziehung (z.B. durch eine ähnliche Plazierung), da er sich an exakt demselben Punkt des Museums befand, von dem aus die projizierten Bilder fotografiert worden waren. Die optische Täuschung beruhte gerade auf dieser perfekten Übereinstimmung von Bildrahmen und Projektionsrahmen (vergleichbar mit der Übereinstimmung von Fluchtpunkt und Standpunkt bei Brunelleschi). Während der zentrale Standpunkt das Wesen von Brunelleschis *costruzione legittima* ausmacht und auf das Erreichen einer perspektivischen Tiefenwirkung abzielt, geht Shaws System in zweierlei Hinsicht über dieses Ziel hinaus: Zum einen bezieht sich die Illusion nicht auf die Darstellung, sondern auf das Bild selbst, zum anderen wird diese Täuschung nicht in der scheinbaren Tiefe des Raumes dargestellt, sondern an seinen Rändern, an der Grenze zwischen dem Bild und dem Raum, in den es gestellt wird.

Der Betrachterstandpunkt ist also nicht bloß Bezugspunkt für die Darstellung, sondern er verwirklicht sie, indem er zugleich Ort und Bedingung für deren Sichtbarkeit wird. Die Repräsentation ist nur für jene Person existent, die sie betrachtet und dadurch konstruiert. Es war genau jener Aspekt, der Marcel Duchamps intensives und in gewisser Weise ironisches Interesse an den verschiedenen Illusionstechniken weckte, wie z.B. der Anamorphose, der Stereoskopie und den Anaglyphen, bei denen sich Bilder nur über

approaches to virtual images or movement – surfaces that reflected figures according to the spectator's angle of view, structures perceived solely in peripheral vision or according to certain movements.

Going beyond an investigation of perception as hallucination, beyond the interdependence of image and spectator, *Viewpoint* addressed another illusion, namely that of the unity of representation. The image projected into the environment was that of the environment itself. Of identical scale, it fitted exactly into the space it depicted (the space behind the screen), thereby 'creating a seamless continuity between the virtual and actual spaces'[36]. But this apparent continuity instantly displayed a series of contradictions and divergences – between the surface of the image and the three-dimensional space of the museum, between the immobility of the photographic image and the movement of visitors in the room, and between past actions recorded on slides and events actually taking place. Twelve somewhat humorous, incongruous or self-referential actions were staged and photographed in the museum space prior to the opening of the exhibition (a visitor makes a bed on a museum bench and goes to sleep, the projection screen itself is built). Presented as sequences of still images, they constituted so many autonomous micro-tales animated by the pace of projection, in a deliberately chronophotographic approach. Every new visitor triggered one of the sequences by stepping up to the viewing console; everyone thus possessed his or her own tale concerning tiny differences within sameness.

Finally, *Viewpoint* was presented during the 9th Biennale at the Musée d'Art Moderne of the City of Paris, and therefore represents an example of that other interdependence – between work and site – found throughout Shaw's œuvre, in critical as well as formal terms. Here the museum itself (or, more exactly, its exhibitionist role) was placed on centre stage. The frame-screen apparently placed on view was simply a medium awaiting a work that would remain pure illusion without the active participation of a specific, searching gaze, the very gaze on which today's museological institution depends.

Ten years later, Shaw would produce *Jules Verne* (1985), an installation for an opera in a theatre, based on the same principle but complicating the temporal and spatial dimensions by projecting, onto the inner doors of the theatre, photos of activities taking place outside.

Floating Image

It was probably such reflections on the role of the viewer in bringing the image into existence that spurred Jeffrey Shaw's simultaneous interest in the way images could be generated by computer codes and techniques, as well as stereoscopic vision (which is a pure construct of mental activity). A radicalization of the process of virtualizing images inevitably led to the complete abolition of the

eine geistige Aktivität erschließen; nur der Vorgang der Wahrnehmung verleiht ihnen Materialität, ›Körperlichkeit‹.

Die anamorphotische Abbildung – die ›Projektion von Formen außerhalb ihrer selbst‹ – wird nur durch eine optische Korrektur von einem ›bestimmten Punkt‹ aus lesbar, entzifferbar.[35] Von einem anderen Punkt aus kann das Bild nicht dekodiert werden und entzieht sich jeder ›korrekten‹ Lesart. *Viewpoint* dagegen zielte nicht darauf ab, eine Dissimulation innerhalb des Bildes aufzudecken, sondern es ging schlicht darum, das Bild überhaupt sichtbar zu machen. Elf Jahre später nutzte Shaw die Anamorphose und einen verspiegelten Zylinder für die Installation *Anamorphoses of Memory* (1986), in der der Text aber in der Tat entziffert werden mußte.

In den fünfziger Jahren hatten verschiedene kinetische Kunstwerke eine Annäherung an virtuelle Bilder oder Bewegungen versucht: Oberflächen, die je nach Blickwinkel des Betrachters Figuren reflektierten oder Strukturen, die nur am Rand des Sichtfeldes oder aufgrund bestimmter Bewegungen wahrgenommen werden konnten.

Neben der Erforschung der Wahrnehmung als einer Halluzination und der gegenseitigen Abhängigkeit von Bild und Betrachter beschäftigte sich *Viewpoint* mit einer weiteren Illusion – der Einheit der Repräsentation. Das in den Raum projizierte Bild war das Abbild dieses Raumes. Es hatte denselben Maßstab und paßte exakt in den Raum, den es darstellte (den Raum hinter der Leinwand), so daß ein ›nahtloser Übergang zwischen virtuellem und realem Raum geschaffen wurde‹[36]. Aber diese scheinbare Kontinuität enthüllte sogleich eine Reihe von Widersprüchen und Divergenzen: zwischen der Oberfläche des Bildes und der Dreidimensionalität des Museumsraumes, zwischen der Starrheit des fotografierten Bildes und der Bewegung der Besucher im Raum, zwischen vergangenen Ereignissen, die fotografisch festgehalten worden waren und gerade stattfindenden Ereignissen. Zwölf teilweise witzige, abwegige oder metareflexive Handlungsabläufe wurden vor Beginn der Ausstellung im Raum des Museums inszeniert und fotografiert (z.B. ein Besucher, der sich auf einer Bank sein Bett machte und sich dort schlafen legte oder die Projektionsleinwand wurde aufgebaut). Präsentiert als Sequenzen von Standbildern formten sie sich zu verschiedenen autonomen Kurzgeschichten, die – in Anlehnung an die Chronofotografie – durch die Geschwindigkeit, in der sie projiziert wurden, animiert wurden. Jeder neue Besucher löste, wenn er die Sichtkonsole betrat, eine der Sequenzen aus, so daß jeder Betrachter seine eigene Geschichte über die kleinen Unterschiede in einer scheinbaren Gleichheit erhielt.

Viewpoint wurde während der 9. Biennale im Musée d'Art Moderne in Paris gezeigt und veranschaulicht jene andere Abhängigkeit – zwischen Werk und Schauplatz –, die Shaws Œuvre sowohl in kritischer als auch in formaler Hinsicht durchzieht. In *Viewpoint* rückte das Museum selbst (bzw. seine Rolle als Ausstellungsraum) in den Mittelpunkt. Die gerahmte Leinwand, die hier scheinbar ausgestellt wurde, diente ledglich als Medium für

screen. Thus right from the late 1970s, Shaw used his first computer to begin developing a 'see-through virtual reality system' based on stereoscope principles. His optical system coupled a semi-transparent mirror with a computer screen onto which two wire-frame images of a cube were displayed. By turning and rotating this display system (whose position was detected by the computer), the spectator could observe the basic rotation of the cube, projected into the room and integrated into the other elements of the space. This *Virtual Projection Installation* (1978), a forerunner of Head-Mounted Display and BOOM[37], produced a three-dimensional image that seemed to float in space like a ghost. Yet perhaps it is no longer accurate to speak of an 'image', it might be better to allude to what Robert Smithson, in referring to stereo vision experiments, called a 'non-thing' or 'non-object'.[38] For the original function of 'screen' had now completely evolved toward 'viewing system', to become an interface combining optics, catoptrics and computer science. While a mediating system was still required to makes a scene appear, it was henceforth in the hands of the spectator.

Augmented Memory

For *Inventer La Terre* (1986), an interactive sculpture shown at the Cité des Sciences et de l'Industrie de la Villette in Paris, Shaw developed another system comprising a small video monitor and a periscope installed in a column with an opening in the middle, through which the spectator looked. By rotating the column, the viewer selected various sites to explore within a virtual panorama; floating travelogue images of the selected site then appeared superimposed on the exhibition space. The material involved tales, signs, and symbols taken from ancient times and cultures on various continents, expressing the multiplicity of representations of the world, constituting what Shaw calls a kind of 'museum within the museum'. The virtual integration of the environment via transparency was essentially symbolic. As in *Viewpoint*, the piece referred to the very function of museums. But that function here became one of conservation, of the museum as communal memory of the human culture.

Shaw here produced a form of 'augmented reality'[39] via memory, yanking into the present-day museum path pieces of past information that constitute human history like so many milestones triggering the powerful imaginative faculty.

Impression of Totality

Wittgenstein, in the *Tractatus*, argued that total reality is the world; Shaw's *Inventer La Terre*, meanwhile, crystallized a major notion within his own œuvre, namely virtual totality. It inaugurated the twin principles of the viewing window and panorama. Although the gaze never perceives more than a fraction of the environment at any instant, cerebral activity completes the information, incorporating all senses, knowledge, and memory into the

ein Werk, das reine Illusion bleiben würde ohne die aktive Beteiligung eines spezifischen, suchenden Schauens – jenes Schauen, auf dem die Institution Museum heutzutage beruht.

Zehn Jahre später entwickelte Shaw in einem Theater für eine Oper die Installation *Jules Verne* (1985), die auf denselben Prinzipien aufbaute, aber kompliziertere zeitliche und räumliche Dimensionen besaß, da auf die Innenseiten der Eingangstüren des Theaters Fotos von Ereignissen, die draußen vor dem Theater stattfanden, proijziert wurden.

Schwebende Bilder

Das Nachdenken darüber, welche Rolle der Betrachter bei der Entstehung des Bildes spielt, war sicherlich der Grund für Shaws gleichzeitiges Interesse an der Erzeugung von Bildern mit Hilfe von Computercodes und -techniken und am stereoskopischen Sehen, diesem ausschließlich auf mentaler Aktivität basierenden Konstrukt. Eine Radikalisierung im Prozeß der Virtualisierung von Bildern führte zwangsläufig zur völligen Abschaffung der Leinwand. So benutzte Shaw Ende der siebziger Jahre schon seinen ersten Computer zur Entwicklung eines ›See-Through-Virtual-Reality-Systems‹, das auf stereoskopischen Prinzipien basierte. Sein optisches System koppelte einen halbdurchlässigen Spiegel mit einem Computermonitor, auf dem zwei Drahtgittergrafiken eines Würfels zu sehen waren. Indem der Betrachter dieses Visualisierungssystem drehte und wendete (wobei der Computer die jeweilige Position errechnete), konnte er die gesamte Drehung des Würfels verfolgen, der in den Raum projiziert und zwischen die anderen dort vorhandenen Elemente eingefügt wurde. Diese *Virtual Projection Installation* (1978), ein Vorläufer des ›Head-Mounted-Display‹ und des BOOM[37], produzierte ein dreidimensionales Bild, das im Raum wie ein Geist zu schweben schien. Allerdings ist es wohl nicht länger angebracht, von einem ›Bild‹ zu sprechen, man sollte eher auf die von Robert Smithson im Zusammenhang mit stereoskopischen Experimenten verwendeten Begriffe ›non-thing‹ oder ›non-object‹ zurückgreifen.[38] Die ursprüngliche Funktion des ›Bildschirms‹ hatte sich in Richtung eines ›Sichtsystems‹ verändert, das zu einem Interface werden sollte, welches Optik, Katoptrik und Informatik kombinieren konnte. Damit eine Szene, ein Bild erscheinen kann, bedarf es zwar immer noch eines vermittelnden Systems, aber es befindet sich von nun an in der Hand des Betrachters.

Erweitertes Gedächtnis

Für die interaktive Skulptur *Inventer la Terre* (1986), die in der Cité des Sciences et de l'Industrie de la Villette in Paris gezeigt wird, entwickelte Shaw ein anderes System: es besteht aus einem kleinen Videomonitor und einem Periskop, die in eine Säule eingelassen sind, in deren Mitte sich ein Sichtfenster befindet, durch das der Betrachter schaut. Durch Drehung der Säule kann der Betrachter verschiedene Schauplätze in einem virtuellen Panorama auswählen, um sie zu erkunden; daraufhin wird der reale Ausstellungsraum überlagert von Bildern des ausgewählten Schauplat-

cognitive process.

The viewing window, present as a crucial element in several of Shaw's works, precisely incites the spectator to reconstruct the totality of a scene, a text, or an object. Indeed, it is not a window with fixed frame that allows exploration of depth alone, but rather a dynamic framework whose movement triggers the discovery mode. Rather than creating the illusion of transparence, the viewing window underscores one part of a whole via the continuous displacement of the borders it circumscribes. The impression of a virtual totality is produced by the twin processes of marking a fragment and encouraging omnidirectional movement (which, furthermore, is constantly reversible). It differs from cinematic panorama devices, in the first instance, in the control that the spectator exercises over the window.

The television screen of *Revolution* (1990), which here fully assumed the metaphor of a 'window on the world' and its mediatizing function (now participating in the very occurrence of events), displayed the vast visual memory of revolutions since 1789. The context for this piece was an historic celebration, and visitors were invited to turn the wheel of history. A complete rotation, in one direction, of the window on its axis (the initial sense of the term revolution) enabled the visitor to access a series of images constituting humanity's collective memory. In the other direction, the visitor simply ground grain, this task making him or her a motor of history rather than a spectator. Totality is thus no longer a question of accumulation, but of dialectic.

Shaw renewed this attempt to exhaust visibility and legibility in two kinetic works that combined and contrasted a mobile viewing window with the image it conveyed. The first piece, a 'textual sculpture' titled *Word Play* (1989), entailed the chance encounter of meanings doubly dependent on a random choice of texts and a random combination of the two 'moving windows' on which those texts are displayed (one shifted horizontally, the other vertically). 'Reading' then became a question of crossed lines, of a double text simultaneously fragmented and moving, which had to be constantly constructed by each individual spectator.

The second piece was a video installation, *Disappearance* (1993), which showed the window at work by confronting that window with what it decomposes and reveals. This voyeuristic mechanism was applied here to a little automaton of a ballerina. As Christian Metz has pointed out, 'framing and its displacement [...] have an inner affinity with the mechanism of desire, its postponements, its new impetus'[40]. The voyeuristic process behind this 'constant undressing' was all the more manifest in the choice of a feminine object in *Disappearance* – the little ballerina was continuously scanned from top to bottom by a camera whose image was displayed on a live video monitor that rose and descended in synchronized fashion. This vertical exploration was complicated by the pivoting movement of the forklift truck that supported the whole system, not to mention the inverse pivotal

zes, die durch den Raum zu schweben scheinen. Das verwendete Material besteht aus Erzählungen, Zeichen und Symbolen aus vergangener Zeit und von Kulturen verschiedener Kontinente. Es zeigt die Vielfältigkeit in der Darstellung der Welt und schafft so eine Art ›Museum im Museum‹, wie Shaw es nennt. Die virtuelle Integration der Umgebung durch Transparenz ist ihrem Wesen nach symbolisch. Wie *Viewpoint* bezieht sich auch diese Arbeit auf die ureigensten Funktionen des Museums, in diesem Falle auf die Funktion des Konservierens: das Museum als kommunales Gedächtnis der menschlichen Kultur.

Shaw produziert hier eine Art ›erweiterter Realität‹[39] mit Hilfe des Erinnerungsvermögens, indem er in die Gegenwart des musealen Parcours' Fragmente vergangenen Wissens einfügt, das die Menschheitsgeschichte konstituiert – wie Meilensteine, die die mächtige Kraft der Phantasie auslösen.

Impressionen von Totalität

Wittgenstein vertritt im *Tractatus* den Standpunkt, daß die Gesamtheit der Realität die Welt sei. In *Inventer la Terre* kristallisiert sich ein Hauptgedanke des Gesamtwerks von Jeffrey Shaw heraus: virtuelle Totalität. Hier wird das Doppelprinzip Sichtfenster/Panorama eingeführt. Obwohl der Blick in keinem Moment mehr als einen kleinen Ausschnitt der Umgebung wahrnehmen kann, vervollständigt das Gehirn die Informationen, indem es Wissen, Erinnerung und alle Sinne in den kognitiven Prozeß einbezieht.

Das Sichtfenster, wesentliches Element in verschiedenen Arbeiten Shaws, fordert den Betrachter geradezu heraus, die Gesamtheit eines Schauplatzes, eines Textes oder eines Objekts zu rekonstruieren. Tatsächlich ist es nicht allein das durch einen festgelegten Rahmen begrenzte Fenster, das Erkundungen in die Tiefe des Bildes zuläßt, sondern es ist vor allem die Beweglichkeit des Rahmens, die die Art und Weise der Entdeckungsreise bestimmt. Es geht nicht so sehr um die Schaffung einer Illusion von Transparenz, vielmehr unterstreicht das Sichtfenster durch die ständige Verschiebung der Grenzen des gezeigten Ausschnitts die Bedeutung des Details gegenüber dem Ganzen. Der Eindruck virtueller Totalität wird durch zwei parallele Prozesse hervorgerufen: Markierung eines Auschnitts und Aufforderung zu Bewegung in alle Richtungen (jederzeit umkehrbar). Der Unterschied zu filmischen Panorama-Apparaturen liegt in erster Linie darin, daß der Betrachter das Sichtfenster selbst steuert.

Der Fernsehbildschirm in *Revolution* (1990), der vollkommen der Metapher des ›Fensters zur Welt‹ und seiner Mittlerfunktion (das bedeutet in unserer Zeit die direkte Teilnahme an den Geschehnissen) entspricht, zeigt als gewaltiges visuelles Gedächtnis Erinnerungen an Revolutionen seit 1789. Die Arbeit stand ursprünglich im Kontext einer historischen Gedenkfeier und lädt die Besucher ein, am Rad der Geschichte zu drehen. Mit einer ganzen Umdrehung des Bildschirms um die eigene Achse (die ursprüngliche Bedeutung des Begriffs Revolution) kann der Besucher eine Reihe von Bildern auslösen, die zum kollektiven Gedächtnis der Menschheit gehören. Dreht er in die Gegenrichtung, mahlt er Korn; er ist nicht

motion of the ballerina herself, creating a double spiral movement. The precision of the mechanism, its automaticness, and the heaviness of the machinery as opposed to the ballerina all yielded a simultaneously ridiculous and implacable effect. *Disappearance* is a bachelor machine par excellence – a pointless and startling machine, a 'simulacrum of machine' that can be divided into a sexual subunit and a mechanical subunit designed to carry out a lethal operation – the disappearance of the little automaton.[41] Subjected to a kind of X-ray performed on some vestige or skeleton of a vanished species, the ballerina evokes the memory of 'a first generation robot', while the electronic-cinematic-industrial robot of the installation 'generates her virtual reconstruction to the extent that the machinery of reproduction itself now incarnates her pirouettes'.[42] Given the collapse of a totalizing representation of things, it is the machines themselves that are now called upon to keep up appearances.

A Mobile Gaze within the Scene

Reformulating the question of viewpoint using digitized, interactive imagery necessarily underscored the relativity of observation. The shift from *Viewpoint* (1975) to *Points of View* (1983) entailed more than just the plurality and the mobility of the gaze. The image became an environment in which the spectator can act, transforming it through his or her movements. This interdependence between viewer and image, which *Viewpoint* heralded, henceforth became critical. Once the spectator entered the scene, representation lost its autonomy. The very question of viewpoint has become less pertinent than the positions and roles adopted by the spectator in what has become a theatre of operations.

The sole elements of *Points of View* were a bare stage, sixteen hieroglyphs as 'actors', and sixteen off-screen voices recounting sixteen visions of the world. This initial 'theatre of signs' hosted a gaze that assumed its freedom and the consequences of a nomadic condition. The virtual architecture comprized a half-sphere of sixteen areas of text, organized according to a kind of cosmology in which each text was linked to a conventional position in a space of ideas and practices.[43] When moving through this space, voices overlapped and differing conceptions collided. Point of view was here invoked in its metaphorical sense: a physical viewpoint also corresponds to an opinion, it means 'adopting a position'.

Points of View was the first of Shaw's interactive installations to propose an omnidirectional, real-time pathway through a computer-generated 3-D scene. Despite its simplicity – which to a certain extent represented its strength – it played an inaugural role in the sphere of interactive creativity. At that time, most experiments still employed videodisks, and although digital imagery was undergoing full development, interactive processes still had to be mastered. It was research with flight simulators – the most sophisticated equipment at the time – that inspired Shaw. Yet *Points of*

mehr nur Zuschauer, sondern wird zum Motor der Geschichte. Totalität ist nicht länger eine Frage von Akkumulation, sondern von Dialektik.

In zwei kinetischen Arbeiten, in denen er ein bewegliches Sichtfenster mit dem darin gezeigten Bild verknüpft und kontrastiert, unternimmt Shaw erneut den Versuch, Sichtbarkeit und Lesbarkeit erschöpfend zu behandeln. Die eine Arbeit, eine ›Textskulptur‹ mit dem Titel *Word Play* (1989), behandelt die zufällige Begegnung von Bedeutungen, die in doppelter Weise abhängig sind: von einer zufälligen Auswahl der Texte und von der zufälligen Kombination zweier beweglicher Fenster, in denen diese Texte auftauchen (das eine Fenster bewegt sich in der Horizontalen, das andere in der Vertikalen). ›Lesen‹ wird hier zur Frage sich kreuzender Linien und eines doppelten Textes, der zugleich fragmentiert ist und sich bewegt und der von jedem Zuschauer immer wieder neu zusammengesetzt werden muß.

Das andere Werk ist eine Videoinstallation, *Disappearance* (1993), die die Arbeitsweise des Sichtfensters zeigt, indem es dieses Fenster mit dem konfrontiert, was es zerlegt und wieder zusammensetzt. Der voyeuristische Mechanismus dreht sich hier um eine kleine mechanische Ballerina. Christian Metz hat darauf hingewiesen, daß ›der Bildrahmen und seine Bewegungen eine innere Affinität zum Mechanismus der Lust besitzen, zum Aufschieben oder plötzlichen Aufwallen der Lust‹[40]. Der voyeuristische Prozeß hinter dem ›ununterbrochenen Entkleiden‹ wird in *Disappearance* durch die Wahl eines weiblichen Objekts noch unterstrichen. Die kleine Tänzerin wird beständig von Kopf bis Fuß von einer Kamera gefilmt und diese Aufnahmen werden live auf einem Videomonitor gezeigt, der sich synchron auf- und abbewegt. Diese Erkundungen in vertikaler Richtung werden durch die Drehung des Gabelstaplers, der das ganze System trägt, verkompliziert. Nicht zu vergessen die gegenläufigen Pirouetten der Ballerina selbst, wodurch insgesamt eine doppelte spiralenförmige Bewegung entsteht. Die Präzision des gesamten Mechanismus', sein Automatismus und die Schwerfälligkeit der Maschinerie im Gegensatz zur zierlichen Ballerina wirken lächerlich und unvereinbar zugleich. *Disappearance* ist eine Junggesellenmaschine par excellence, eine nutzlose und gleichzeitig erstaunliche Maschine, ein ›Simulacrum von Maschine‹, das in eine sexuelle und eine mechanische Untereinheit geteilt werden kann und dazu dient, eine tödliche Operation durchzuführen: das Verschwinden des kleinen Roboters.[41] Die Ballerina ist das Opfer einer Art Röntgenuntersuchung, die am Rudiment bzw. am Skelett einer ausgestorbenen Spezies durchgeführt wird, und sie evoziert die Erinnerung an einen ›Roboter der ersten Generation‹, während der elektronisch-filmische Industrieroboter der Installation ihre ›virtuelle Rekonstruktion so weit [treibt], daß nun die Reproduktionsmaschinerie selbst die Pirouetten der Ballerina verkörpert‹.[42] Vor dem Hintergrund des Zusammenbruchs einer totalisierenden Repräsentation der Dinge sind nun die Maschinen an der Reihe, den Schein zu wahren.

View did not limit itself to a definition of the key elements of 'virtual voyages', it above all launched a unique type of voyage across ideas, across accounts made up of everyday comments, poetry, or philosophy. At the time, there was nothing comparable to Shaw's approach in the emerging sphere of virtual technology.

Two major aspects of scopic activity and trajectory were at work in these interactive installations: omnidirectional exploration of the surface of the world (whether flat or hemispheric), and in-depth penetration into the matter and meaning of things. A global grasp and a detailed grasp of things, according to Christine Buci-Glucksman, are 'the two fantasy drives generating a worldliness that stimulates travel, wanderlust, and discovery'[44]. Models for this infinite geometry of the gaze come from horizontal maps and vertical strata, suggesting scanning and tunnelling movements.

On a horizontal level, this translated into a bike ride through the labyrinthine streets of *The Legible City* (1988-91) or, to the contrary, a straightforward path (marked like a runway) in *Going to the Heart of the Center of The Garden of Delights* (1986). On a vertical level, visitors had to lean over a well of images in *The Narrative Landscape* (1985) to select a zone of exploration comprising three levels.

The circular or environmental level was incarnated by installations structured around a central viewpoint, notably defined by a platform, such as *The Virtual Museum* (1991) and *Place – a user's manual* (1995).

Panoramas

Shaw's first panoramic proposition was made in *Diadrama* (1974), devised for a theatrical stage. The theme of that audiovisual performance was the idea of panorama and a collage of events from different epochs. Six projectors working simultaneously flashed over 2,000 slides onto a semi-circular screen twelve metres long by three metres high, producing an impression of visual immersion. The camera that recorded the panorama was rotated along three positions, covering a 270-degree field of vision. Shaw subsequently developed his work on environmental projection through installations which exploited the model of circular panorama more directly – that of *Inventer La Terre* remained virtual, whereas that of *Place – a user's manual* could also be physically experienced by visitors.

The first modern system for placing spectators at the centre of the scene entailed painting a panorama on a cylinder. The viewing platform was raised significantly in order to provide an overview and give the most total illusion possible, all the while generating a feeling of infinity (which Edmund Burke identified as an attribute of the sublime), enhanced by the circularity of the scene.[45]

The panorama of *Place – a user's manual* combined two key elements of those 19th-century panoramas: the circular image and the central observation platform. The image in *Place – a user's manual* was projected onto a cylindrical screen (nine metres in diameter, two metres high) from a small platform that held several

Der Blick als Agens und Akteur

Stellt man die Frage nach dem Betrachterstandpunkt durch die Verwendung interaktiver, digitalisierter Bilder neu, so bedeutet das zugleich, den Akt des Sehens/Beobachtens als relativ zu begreifen. Der Übergang von *Viewpoint* (1975) zu *Points of View* (1983) brachte mehr als nur Pluralität und Mobilität des Blicks mit sich. Das Bild wurde zu einer Umgebung, in der der Zuschauer agieren und die er durch seine Bewegungen verändern konnte. Diese wechselseitige Abhängigkeit zwischen Betrachter und Bild, die sich in *Viewpoint* schon ankündigte, wird nun entscheidend. Sobald der Zuschauer die Szene einmal betreten hat, verliert die Darstellung ihre Autonomie. Die Frage nach dem Standpunkt verliert an Bedeutung gegenüber der Frage nach der Position und der Rolle, die der Zuschauer in diesem ›Theater der Funktionen‹ einnimmt.

Eine leere Bühne, sechzehn Hieroglyphen, die als ›Schauspieler‹ fungieren, sechzehn Stimmen aus dem Off, die sechzehn Weltanschauungen vertreten – das waren die Bestandteile von *Points of View*. Dieses erste ›Theater der Zeichen‹ lancierte einen Blick, der seine Freiheit und die Konsequenzen seines Nomadentums akzeptiert hat. Die virtuelle Architektur der Arbeit bestand aus einer Semisphäre mit sechzehn Textbereichen; sie waren einer Art Kosmologie entsprechend angeordnet, in der jeder Text mit einem traditionellen Standpunkt in einem Raum aus Ideen und Praktiken verknüpft war.[43] Bewegte man sich durch diesen Raum, vermischten sich die Stimmen, und die verschiedenen Konzepte prallten aufeinander. Der Begriff des ›Standpunkts‹ wird hier in seiner metaphorischen Bedeutung veranschaulicht: Der Punkt, an dem man steht impliziert hier gleichzeitig, eine bestimmte Meinung zu vertreten.

Points of View war Shaws erste interaktive Installation, die es erlaubte, einen computergenerierten, dreidimensionalen Schauplatz in allen Richtungen und in Echtzeit zu durchqueren. Trotz des einfachen Aufbaus – der in gewisser Hinsicht auch seine Stärke ist – spielt das Werk eine Vorreiterrolle im Bereich interaktiver Kreativität. Zu dieser Zeit benutzten die meisten experimentellen Arbeiten Bildplatten, und obwohl sich die digitale Bildbearbeitung rasant entwickelte, mußten interaktive Prozesse erst noch gemeistert werden. Jeffrey Shaw ließ sich von der damals fortschrittlichsten Technologie, der Flugsimulation, inspirieren. *Points of View* beschränkte sich aber nicht auf die Bestimmung der Grundelemente einer ›virtuellen Reise‹, sondern stellte vor allem ein einzigartiges Genre vor: die ›Ideenreise‹, die durch Erzählungen führt, in die alltägliche Bemerkungen, Poesie und Philosophie verwoben sind. In diesem damals neuen Bereich der virtuellen Technologie hatte es bis dahin nichts vergleichbares gegeben.

Für die Aktivität und Richtung des Schauens sind in diesen interaktiven Installationen zwei Aspekte von Bedeutung: zum einen die Erkundung der Oberfläche einer Welt (die flach oder kuppelförmig sein kann) in allen Richtungen, zum anderen das Eindringen in die Tiefe, in die Beschaffenheit und Bedeutung der Dinge. Erfassen des Allgemeinen und erfassen des Einzelnen – das sind laut Chri-

spectators, providing a special point of observation. Once in movement – here, it is the platform that rotates, along with the three projectors – visitors are simultaneously at the source of projection and the very site of original camera view. This arrangement, not unlike *Viewpoint*, reconstituted the conditions of recording: the location of the lens in the environment and the movement of the panoramic camera. The virtual panorama and the cylindrical screen being homothetic, when a visitor decides to visit one of the eleven panoramas, he or she is automatically placed at its centre.

Although the platform of *Place – a user's manual* is only raised six inches (so that spectators lose the lofty positions formerly occupied when contemplating painted panoramas), the viewer now determines the rotation of the platform according to the orientation given to a camera. This simple interface, given the normal use of a camera, becomes a metaphor for the act of realization, thus producing a strange illusion of live vision. The spectator thereby assumes the place and role of the creator, largely regaining mastery of the scene. While spectators can visit panoramas at their own pace, they nevertheless only control their discovery by remaining part of the system, by 'embodying' the interface, accepting relative immobility. On the platform, hand controls replace the pedestrian stroll in which other visitors can indulge.

Since the projected image covers only one third of the circular screen, the spectator can generate a total view of the panorama solely through time and a continuous sweep. So even though the scene is totally present on a virtual level, it can only be revealed by partial actualization. It is not automatically there, immediately open to contemplation – it only succumbs to a searching gaze. The spectator's memory and capacity for anticipation are required to complete the environment. The dialectic between global and fragmented view, already present in several of Shaw's pieces, becomes all the more striking in *Place – a user's manual* insofar as total vision is precisely what the panorama promises.

The shifting display band (it is perhaps no longer appropriate to speak of 'window' when the visual field is 120°) that reveals an environment recorded by photography evokes another model contemporary with painted panoramas, namely the 'moving panorama'. That system entailed unrolling views behind a fixed frame in front of seated spectators, an experience often compared to looking out a train window, a key metaphor for cinema. The frame of the image in *Place – a user's manual* is fixed in relation to viewers on the platform but, since they share the same movement, the perceptual contradiction inherent in 'moving panorama' – between the immobility of the view and the motion of the images – is eliminated here.

Shaw's decision to use still photographs may seem surprising, coming as it did a century after Grimoin-Sanson's Cinéorama (patented in 1896), which simultaneously projected – onto a circular screen – moving images from ten motion-picture cameras placed on the gondola of a hot-air balloon rising above Paris ('spectators

stine Buci-Glucksman ›die beiden Antriebskräfte der Phantasie, die Grundlage für die Erkenntnis der Welt durch Reisen, Umherschweifen und Entdecken‹[44]. Landkarte und Querschnitt sind die horizontalen bzw. vertikalen Modelle für diese unendliche Geometrie des Blicks, Abtasten und Durchqueren die angebotenen Formen der Bewegung.

Auf der horizontalen Ebene wird daraus die Fahrradfahrt durch das Straßenlabyrinth von *The Legible City* (1988–91) oder, im Gegensatz dazu, der wie eine Startbahn markierte schnurgerade Weg in *Going to the Heart of the Center of The Garden of Delights* (1986); auf der vertikalen Ebene ist es der ›Bilderbrunnen‹ in *Narrative Landscape* (1985), über den sich der Besucher beugt, um einen Bereich auszuwählen, den er in drei Ebenen erkunden kann.

Schließlich gibt es Installationen, die kreisförmig um einen zentralen Punkt herum angeordnet sind, an dem zumeist eine Plattform plaziert ist, wie z.B. in *The Virtual Museum* (1991) oder *Place – a user's manual* (1995).

Panoramen

Diadrama (1974), das für eine Bühne entwickelt wurde, war Jeffrey Shaws erster Entwurf für ein Panorama. Thema dieser audiovisuellen Performance war die Idee des Panoramas selbst und die Zusammenstellung von Ereignissen aus verschiedenen Epochen. Sechs synchron arbeitende Diaprojektoren projizierten über 2000 Dias auf eine halbkreisförmige Leinwand von zwölf Metern Breite und drei Metern Höhe, wodurch der Eindruck visueller Überflutung entstand. Die Kamera, mit der das Panorama aufgenommen worden war, war in drei verschiedenen Positionen gedreht worden, so daß ein Blickfeld von 270 Grad eingefangen werden konnte. In mehreren nachfolgenden Installationen verwendete Shaw Projektionen von Umgebungen und entwickelte das Modell des kreisförmigen Panoramas auf direkterem Wege weiter – das Panorama in *Inventer la Terre* bleibt virtuell, während es in *Place – a user's manual* von den Besuchern auch körperlich erfahren werden kann.

Das auf einen Zylinder gemalte Panorama stellte zum ersten Mal in der Moderne den Zuschauer ins Zentrum des Geschehens. Die Beobachterplattform war deutlich erhöht, um dem Betrachter einen Überblick zu ermöglichen und eine möglichst vollkommene Illusion zu erzeugen. Zugleich entstand der Eindruck von Unendlichkeit (was Edmund Burke als ein Attribut des Erhabenen bezeichnete), der durch die Kreisförmigkeit des Schauplatzes noch verstärkt wurde.[45]

Das Panorama in *Place – a user's manual* kombiniert zwei wesentliche Elemente der Panoramen des 19. Jahrhunderts: das kreisförmige Bild und die Beobachterplattform im Zentrum. Das Bild wird von einer kleinen Plattform aus auf eine zylindrische Leinwand (mit einem Durchmesser von neun Metern und einer Höhe von zwei Metern) projiziert. Diese Plattform, die von mehreren Zuschauern betreten werden kann, ist ein besonderer Beobachtungspunkt: einmal in Bewegung – in dieser Arbeit rotiert die Plattform, zusammen mit den drei Projektoren – befindet sich der Zuschauer gleichzeitig am Ausgangspunkt der Projektion und an

seeing the ground fall away will have the feeling of rising into the air'.[46]) Yet it is clear that *Place – a user's manual* did not seek to perfect the 'illusion situation' of spectators in a traditional panorama.[47] The control that users exercise over projection, the visible limits of the image, the opening in the cylinder, and the reversibility of the screen (which allows the panorama to be seen from outside) all run counter to the effects sought by the 19th-century models. Nor does Shaw try to reconstruct simple, circular photographic panoramas such as they were produced from 1893 onwards.[48] Here, photography is the condition (in the current state of technology, at least) of another movement, that of movement within virtual space, circulation within a universe of panoramas. Photography is a condition for entry into representation.

To a certain extent, *Place – a user's manual* reflects the original panorama genre by offering 'surrogate voyages' like those that attracted 19th-century spectators. In *Place – a user's manual*, however, the eleven panoramas photographed all over the world – a beach on Bali, a monastery in Germany, gas tanks in Australia, a Roman amphitheatre in France, a cemetery in La Palma – are not tourist sites, but rather deserted sites, or sites of memory (whether personal or communal), devoid of movement. Shaw thus fully exploits photography's propensity for recording a trace of existence (to which computed worlds, by their very nature, cannot testify), as well as for its capacity for capturing nuances, details and atmosphere often cruelly lacking in the digital universe.

By mapping photographs – themselves rich in circular forms – onto computer-generated cylinders, Shaw hybridizes techniques and weds the unique contribution of mechanical imagery with the omnidirectional mobility afforded by digitized space. A certain euphoria, like that described by certain visitors to the earliest panoramas, is provoked by exploring landscapes that effortlessly shift and flow by, reproduced indefinitely in a no-man's-land.

There is no human presence in these spaces. It is as though a visitor were awaited. The only life comes from the architectured phrases that emerge from the background to cross, independently, the screen, and then slowly vanish as they become increasingly transparent. These texts are triggered by the words and noises made by the viewer on the platform, and their physical arrangement is affected by movement detected by the interface as they are being generated. Language thus incarnates the presence and power of viewers over the scene, reinforcing their role as subjects dialoguing with the artist – the speech of the former triggers the speech of the latter. The phrases, which sometimes directly address the visitor, were taken from various literary and non-literary sources, and were selected for the poetic impact of their description or evocation of landscape, for their rhythm, their harmony, their mystery. Invoking elements of nature as well as myth, they interrogate the world, boundaries, and maps, alluding to pathways through a space that appears as a labyrinth. The text is not a mirror of the visual panoramas, it is their imaginary construction.

der Stelle des urspünglichen Kamerastandpunkts. Diese Anordnung rekonstruiert, ähnlich wie *Viewpoint*, die Bedingungen der Aufnahme: die Position des Objektivs innerhalb der Umgebung und die Bewegung der Panoramakamera. Die virtuellen Panoramen und die zylindrische Projektionswand sind untrennbar miteinander verknüpft: entscheidet sich ein Besucher, eines der elf Panoramen zu besuchen, so wird er automatisch ins Zentrum dieses Panoramas versetzt.

Die Plattform in *Place – a user's manual* ist nur fünfzehn Zentimeter hoch; damit verliert der Zuschauer seine luftige Position, die er bei der Betrachtung der gemalten Panoramen innehatte. Stattdessen steuert er nun die Rotation der Plattform, und zwar durch die Ausrichtung einer Kamera. Dieses einfache Interface, das genau wie eine gewöhnliche Kamera funktioniert, wird hier zur Metapher für den Akt der Verwirklichung und schafft so die merkwürdige Illusion von Unmittelbarkeit. Der Zuschauer nimmt den Platz und die Rolle des Schöpfers ein und beherrscht größtenteils den Schauplatz. Auch wenn der Zuschauer die Geschwindigkeit, in der er die Panoramen besucht, bestimmen kann, steuert er seine Entdeckungsreise nur insofern er ein Teil des Systems bleibt, indem er das Interface ›verkörpert‹ und eine gewisse Unbeweglichkeit in Kauf nimmt. Das Flanieren, dem sich andere Besucher hingeben können, muß der ›operierende‹ Zuschauer auf der Plattform auf Bewegungen seiner Hand reduzieren.

Da das projizierte Bild nur ein Drittel der zylindrischen Leinwand bedeckt, kann der Zuschauer eine Gesamtansicht des Panoramas nur in der Zeit und durch kontinuierliche Schwenks erzeugen. Auch wenn der Schauplatz auf einer virtuellen Ebene vollständig präsent ist, kann er nur teilweise enthüllt, verwirklicht werden; er offenbart sich nicht von selbst, bietet sich nicht automatisch zur Betrachtung an – er ergibt sich nur dem suchenden Blick. Es bedarf des Erinnerungsvermögens und der Fähigkeit zur Antizipation des Betrachters, um die Umgebung zu vervollständigen. Die bereits aus anderen Werken Shaws bekannte Dialektik zwischen Gesamt- und Teilansicht ist bei *Place – a user's manual* besonders auffällig, da es gerade die Gesamtansicht ist, die das Panorama verspricht.

Der breite, bewegliche Streifen (man kann kaum noch von einem ›Fenster‹ sprechen, wenn das visuelle Feld 120 Grad umfaßt), der eine fotografierte Umgebung enthüllt, evoziert ein anderes Modell aus der Zeit der gemalten Panoramen: das ›Moving Panorama‹. Das sitzende Publikum sah Bilder, die hinter einem feststehenden Rahmen vorbeizogen; die Erfahrung ähnelte dem Blick aus einem Zugfenster, eine Schlüsselmetapher des Kinos. In *Place – a user's manual* verändert sich zwar das Verhältnis des Bildrahmens zum Betrachter auf der Plattform nicht, da beide aber die gleiche Bewegung ausführen, ist der im ›Moving Panorama‹ auftretende Widerspruch in der Wahrnehmung – zwischen der Unbeweglichkeit des Blicks und der Bewegung der Bilder – aufgehoben.

Shaws Entscheidung für den Einsatz von Fotografien mag überraschen – ein Jahrhundert nach dem Cinéorama Grimoin-Sansons (es wurde 1896 patentiert), bei dem auf eine zylindrische Leinwand

New forms of representation and the original experiences they trigger inevitably stimulate and indeed demand, during every epoch, new concepts of space where they can be fully exploited. This necessity can be detected in the history of theatre architecture, for instance, from Shakespeare's Globe theatre to Omnimax cinemas. Thus the rotundas of 19th-century panoramas were specially built to 'exhibit' a certain type of depiction, thereby controlling the modalities of perception and specific effects.

With *EVE (Extended Virtual Environment,* 1993), Jeffrey Shaw raised the question of a specific architecture for the exploration of virtual universes. As he himself has explained, this project is still at the prototype stage: 'It encompasses the conceptual and technical development of a new form of interactive immersive visualization environment.'[49] These last four terms clearly map the terrain of what might be termed experimental architecture. Thus it is not just a question of adapting an existing system, but of rethinking the way in which architecture determines the conditions of an aesthetic experience in which the image has become an interactive stage, and in which the spectator has become operator as well as performer. Within this environmental scheme, the notion of installation must be extended to architecture, or rather to architecture as an integral part of the installation itself.

Twenty-six years after *Corpocinema*, then, Shaw has once again employed an inflatable dome structure (nine metres high, twelve metres wide).[50] In *EVE*, however, the sphere is opaque, and the visitor enters it. In the middle is a robot equipped with two projectors, whose movement is piloted by a visitor wearing a position-tracking sensor on the head. The image, viewed with stereoscopic spectacles, sweeps across the entire inner surface of the dome onto which it is projected. Thanks to hand-held controls, the visitor can also enter the scene.

The numerous proposals for hemispheric screens or theatres made in the 1950s [51] – Phonorama, Coupolorama, Circarama, Cinetarium, Specarium, Panrama, and so on – all sought, in various ways, to efface the screen and produce the impression of total immersion in the scene.[52] The creation of such illusion was usually accompanied by escalation in sensorial experience and the production of 'thrills'.

That is not Shaw's goal, however, even if he has borrowed certain principles and techniques of total immersion; he weds the functionality of a head-mounted display with the spatiality of an Omnimax theater, thereby hybridizing several models. This project stems, he says, from the encounter of two major trends in the history of the technological development of the media: 'One is photography, cinema, and television which establishes the power of media to reassemble space and time as a contemplative experience [...]; the other is the development from panorama painting to 'Virtual Reality' which establishes the power of media to repro-

simultan bewegte Bilder projiziert wurden, aufgenommen von zehn Filmkameras, die sich in der Gondel eines Heißluftballons befanden, der über Paris aufstieg (›Zuschauer, die den Boden unter sich weichen sehen, haben das Gefühl, sich in die Luft zu heben.‹[46]). Es ist offensichtlich, daß *Place – a user's manual* nicht darauf aus ist, die ›Illusionssituation‹ des Zuschauers im traditionellen Panorama zu perfektionieren.[47] Die Kontrolle des Benutzers über den Projektionsvorgang, die sichtbaren Begrenzungen des Bildes, die Öffnung in der zylindrischen Projektionsfläche, die Beschaffenheit der Leinwand, die es ermöglicht, die Projektionen auch von außen zu betrachten – alle diese Elemente konterkarieren den Effekt, den die Modelle des 19. Jahrhunderts anstrebten. Shaw versucht ebensowenig, die einfachen fotografischen Panoramen, wie sie ab 1893 gebaut wurden, zu rekonstruieren.[48] Die Fotografie ist in seinen Arbeiten vielmehr die Bedingung (zumindest nach dem aktuellen Stand der Technik) für eine andere Bewegung, für die Bewegung im virtuellen Raum, die Zirkulation innerhalb eines Universums von Panoramen. Sie ist die Bedingung für das Eintreten in die Darstellung.

In gewissem Sinne reflektiert *Place – a user's manual* das ursprüngliche Genre des Panoramas, indem es einen ›Reiseersatz‹ anbietet – genau das faszinierte auch den Zuschauer im 19. Jahrhundert. Doch sind die elf Panoramen, die an Schauplätzen auf der ganzen Welt fotografiert wurden (ein Strand auf Bali, ein Kloster in Deutschland, Benzintanks in Australien, ein römisches Amphitheater in Frankreich, ein Friedhof auf La Palma) keine Touristenattraktionen, sondern eher verlassene Orte, Stätten der kollektiven oder persönlichen Erinnerung, bar jeder Bewegung. Jeffrey Shaw nutzt hier die Neigung der Fotografie, eine Spur des Gewesenen zu bewahren (was die digitalen Welten ihrer Natur nach nicht bezeugen können) und ihre Fähigkeit, Nuancen, Details und Atmosphäre einzufangen – etwas, das man im digitalen Universum oft schmerzlich vermißt.

Indem er die Fotografien – die selbst wiederum viele kreisförmige Motive enthalten – auf die Oberfläche computergenerierter Zylinder plaziert, kombiniert Shaw verschiedene Techniken, verbindet die beschränkten Möglichkeiten der mechanischen Abbildung mit der Möglichkeit, sich im digitalen Raum in alle Richtungen zu bewegen. Eine gewisse Euphorie, ähnlich derjenigen, die auch Besucher der ersten Panoramen beschrieben, stellt sich ein bei der Erkundung dieser Landschaften, die sich mühelos bewegen, die vorbeiziehen, die unendlich oft reproduziert werden – in einem Niemandsland.

In diesen Räumen sind keine Menschen anwesend. Es ist, als ob ein Besucher erwartet würde. Das einzige Leben kommt von den achitektonischen Sätzen, die aus dem Hintergrund auftauchen, um, unabhängig, die Leinwand zu durchqueren und, indem sie immer durchsichtiger werden, langsam wieder zu verschwinden. Diese Texte werden von der Stimme, den Geräuschen des Zuschauers auf der Plattform ausgelöst, ihre räumliche Anordnung wird beeinflußt von den Bewegungen des Interfaces im Moment ihrer Generierung. Die Sprache verkörpert hier die Gegenwart des

duce space and time as a surrogate experience.'[53]

As he did in *Place – a user's manual*, Shaw has again produced a specific tension between, on the one hand, the impression of immersion (all the more effective here in that the exploration can be done vertically, and the images appear in 3-D) and, on the other hand, the distance created by the frame of the image and the activity of the robot. Visitors are therefore caught up in three spectacles – the imagery itself, the machine projecting that imagery, and the operator-performer controlling the machine. This staging of the interactive process staves off immersion.

One visitor is hooked up to the optical machine, a condition for wielding the power to actualize images. Interaction with the scene stems from an amazing linkage between human operator and robot, between a gear-toting person and an anthropomorphic machine. The latter is placed very precisely at the focal point of the dome, in the center of representation; the spectator identifies with this point, as well as with the movements of the machine being piloted, which waits on the viewer 'hand and foot'. It is the movement of the head, however, that really directs operations.

A second version of *EVE,* presented outdoors in 1995 (*The Telepresent Onlookers*, MultiMediale 4, ZKM Karlsruhe), functioned like a perfect panoptic machine. The installation was no longer based on synthesized imagery but on the live image of the environment in which the dome was set. The images were recorded by a pair of cameras attached to a second pan-and-tilt-head outside, a kind of kinetic sculpture whose roving head, with its extreme mobility, constituted yet another show. The spectator simultaneously controlled camera-robot and projector-robot, thus determining both the recording and reconstitution of the scene. This privileged role is similar to that of a miracle worker, as described by Paul Virilio: 'Another divine attribute is added to the *omnivision* of the sudden trans-appearance of things, namely remote *omnipresence*, a kind of electromagnetic telekinesis.'[54] A new temporal dimension arises, replacing real time with digital computation, present time with electronic recording (or telepresence). Shaw has 'collapsed' that telepresence here, not without humour, by monitoring the immediate environment. Finally, concepts of voyeurism and surveillance are evoked through the sweep of the viewing window that scans the surrounding space like a theatrical follow-spot.

Although the electronic closed circuit pulls the outside in, the observers remain invisible, as in the original Panopticon, 'that machine designed to dissociate seeing from being seen'[55]. However, unlike most surveillance devices, the operator does not vanish, does entirely delegate observation to a machine that autonomously executes an automatic sweep of the surrounding space. The doubling of vision here concerns a kind of aided vision, and remains eminently subjective since the spectator looks wherever he or she desires, all the while remaining entirely subject to the limits and parameters of the viewing machine.

Betrachters und seine Macht über den Schauplatz; sie verstärkt seine Rolle als Subjekt im Dialog mit dem Künstler – das Sprechen des ersteren löst das des letzteren aus. Die Sätze, die zuweilen direkt an den Zuschauer gerichtet sind, stammen aus unterschiedlichen literarischen und nicht-literarischen Quellen; sie wurden aufgrund der poetischen Kraft ihrer Landschaftbeschreibungen oder -evokationen, wegen ihres Rhythmus, ihrer Harmonie, ihres Geheimnisses ausgewählt. Sie beschwören Elemente aus der Natur und der Mythologie, sie befragen die Welt, die Grenzen, die Landkarten, sie deuten Wege an durch einen Raum, der als Labyrinth erscheint. Der Text ist kein Spiegel der visuellen Panoramen, er ist ihre imaginäre Konstruktion.

Eine Architektur des Virtuellen

Neue Darstellungsformen bedingen ganz spezielle Erfahrungen und stimulieren, ja fordern deshalb zwangsläufig in jeder Epoche neue Raumkonzeptionen, um sich vollständig entfalten zu können. Die gesamte Geschichte der Theaterarchitektur, von Shakespeares Globe-Theater bis zum Omnimax-Kino, zeugt von dieser Notwendigkeit. So waren auch die Panorama-Rotunden des 19. Jahrhunderts speziell dafür konstruiert, einen bestimmten Darstellungstypus ›auszustellen‹ und dadurch die Modalitäten der Wahrnehmung und bestimmte Effekte zu kontrollieren.

Mit *EVE* (*Extended Virtual Environment*, 1993) stellt Jeffrey Shaw die Frage nach einer Architektur speziell für die Erkundung virtueller Universen. Es handelt sich hierbei noch um einen Prototyp, wie Shaw selbst sagt: ›Es umfaßt die konzeptuelle und technische Entwicklung einer neuartigen interaktiven immersiven Visualisierungsumgebung.‹[49] Diese Stichworte markieren sehr genau das Terrain einer Architektur, die als experimentelle bezeichnet werden könnte. Dabei geht es nicht darum, einfach ein bestehendes System zu adaptieren, sondern zu überdenken, auf welche Weise Architektur die Bedingungen ästhetischer Erfahrung bestimmt, wenn das Bild zu einer interaktiven Bühne geworden und der Zuschauer sowohl Operateur als auch Performer ist. Innerhalb dieses Entwurfs von Environment muß der Begriff der Installation zur Architektur hin, oder vielmehr zur Architektur als integralem Bestandteil der Installation selbst, erweitert werden.

Sechsundzwanzig Jahre nach *Corpocinema* verwendet Jeffrey Shaw erneut eine aufblasbare, kuppelförmige Struktur (mit einer Höhe von neun und einem Durchmesser von zwölf Metern).[50] Die Kuppel von *EVE* ist allerdings undurchsichtig, und der Besucher kann sie betreten. Im Zentrum befindet sich ein Roboterarm, auf dem zwei Projektoren installiert sind, deren Bewegung von einem Besucher, der einen Positionsmesser auf dem Kopf trägt, gesteuert wird. Das Bild, das durch stereoskopische Brillen betrachtet wird, kann auf jede beliebige Stelle der inneren Kuppeloberfläche projiziert werden. Mit Hilfe einer Handsteuerung kann sich der Betrachter innerhalb der gezeigten Szenerie bewegen.

Die zahlreichen Entwürfe (vor allem aus den fünfziger Jahren[51]) für kuppelförmige Projektionsflächen oder Vorführräume – wie

Fully cognizant of today's hybrid reality, Jeffrey Shaw has examined the modalities of coexistence of the heterogeneous space-times in which people now act and move. He underscores similarities in order to pinpoint differences, thereby etching the circuits where the virtual interacts with the real.

Paradoxically, those installations by Shaw that integrate virtual spaces are intimately linked to the specific site and architecture for which they were produced, which therefore may determine their structure (both virtual and concrete). They might be termed 'virtual site-specific works'.

Hence each version of *The Legible City* – Manhattan, Amsterdam, Karlsruhe – required that a new database be built, new narratives be concocted for an altered urban geography, different letter-architecture be displayed. Although the concept remained the same, the perception of the work necessarily changed according to the specific context. Determining the site of exhibition was equally fundamental for *Going to the Heart of the Center of The Garden of Delights* where the spacing of the vaulting of a church-like, Gothic-revival building (in fact, a meat-market converted into a municipal museum), determined the very placement of the markers indicating the path from spectator to screen. The ritual advance of a spectator through this architecture coincided with the traversal of a virtual space where the sacred and the profane are inextricably intertwined. Yet despite this correlation between the virtual and the real, these works are autonomous enough to be presented elsewhere. There are other pieces, however – an early example being *Viewpoint* – whose very functioning depends on an immediate confrontation with the place of exhibition.

Shaw's approach to the sphere of 'virtual reality' is startling. He produces digitally processed universes entirely dependent on an existing site, even though the modalities of their generation render them, to the contrary, completely independent of any concrete reference. In works like *Alice's Room* (1989), *The Virtual Museum* (1991) and *The Golden Calf* (1994), the virtual space duplicates a precise physical space, which is furthermore a site within sight of the visitor (e.g. a museum gallery, the very space in which the piece is located and which therefore can be experienced directly).

Although simulation here, paradoxically, assumes the task of reproduction, it does not produce a realistic scene. Rather, it is more accurate to speak of a realism of reference points. A few architectural elements are simulated – doorways, windows – just enough needed to denote a space, identify its resemblance to the one it describes, provide orientation. They are indicators of similitude, not details designed to create illusion. They are enough to produce sufficient analogy to test the differences between two samenesses. Here duplication has an operative value.

A visit to *The Virtual Museum* starts from a simulated gallery space with, at its centre, another platform with large computer

Phonorama, Coupolorama, Circarama, Cinetarium, Specarium, Panrama etc. – suchten nach (jeweils unterschiedlichen) Lösungen, die Leinwand vergessen zu machen und den Eindruck völligen Eintauchens in das projizierte Bild hervorzurufen.[52] Die auf diese Weise entstandene Illusion wurde im allgemeinen begleitet von überwältigenden sinnlichen Erfahrungen und der Erzeugung von ›Nervenkitzeln‹.

Dies ist aber nicht das von Jeffrey Shaw anvisierte Ziel, obwohl er sich einige Prinzipien und Techniken der Immersion zunutze macht; er kombiniert die Funktionalität eines ›Head-Mounted-Displays‹ mit dem Raumeindruck eines Omnimax-Kinos und mischt auf diese Weise verschiedene Modelle. Sein Projekt resultiert, so Shaw, aus dem Zusammentreffen zweier Hauptströmungen der historischen Entwicklung von Technologien medialer Darstellung: ›Auf der einen Seite Fotografie, Film und Fernsehen, die die Macht und die Möglichkeiten der Medien einsetzen, um das Wiederzusammenführen von Raum und Zeit als kontemplative Erfahrung zu erreichen [...]. Auf der anderen Seite entwickelt sich das Panoramabild zur virtuellen Realität, die die Macht und die Möglichkeiten der Medien einsetzt, um die Reproduktion von Raum und Zeit als Erfahrungssurrogat anzubieten.‹[53]

Wie auch in *Place – a user´s manual* erzeugt Jeffrey Shaw eine spezifische Spannung zwischen dem Eindruck der Immersion einerseits (umso effektiver hier, da die Szenerie auch in vertikaler Richtung erkundet werden kann und die Bilder dreidimensional erscheinen) und der Distanz andererseits, die durch den immer präsenten Bildrahmen und die Aktivität des Roboters entsteht. Der Besucher wird so von drei verschiedenen Spektakeln gefangengenommen: von der projizierten Szenerie selbst, der Projektionsmaschinerie und von der Aktion des Operateurs/Performers, der diese Maschinerie kontrolliert. Diese Art der Inszenierung des interaktiven Prozesses behindert die Immersion.

Einer der Besucher ist an den optischen Apparat gekettet – das ist die Bedingung für die Macht, Bilder heraufbeschwören zu können. Die Interaktion mit der Szenerie resultiert aus einer besonderen Verbindung zwischen menschlichem Operateur und Roboter, zwischen verkabeltem Individuum und anthropomorpher Maschine. Letztere befindet sich genau im Brennpunkt der Kuppel, im Zentrum der Darstellung; der Betrachter identifiziert sich mit diesem Punkt ebenso wie mit den Bewegungen der Maschine, die er steuert, die ihm gehorcht – ›auf einen Fingerzeig, ein Augenzwinkern‹. Tatsächlich sind es aber seine Kopfbewegungen, die das Geschehen dirigieren.

Eine zweite Version von *EVE*, die 1995 im Freien gezeigt wurde (*Die telepräsenten Betrachter,* MultiMediale 4, ZKM Karlsruhe), funktioniert wie eine perfekte panoptische Maschine. In dieser Installation werden keine computergenerierten Bilder verwendet, sondern Live-Aufnahmen der Umgebung, in der sich die Kuppel befindet. Die Bilder werden von einem Kamerapaar aufgenommen, das außerhalb der Kuppel auf einem zweiten Schwenk-Neige-Kopf montiert ist. Dieses Ensemble wird – mit dem umherschweifenden Kopf, seiner extremen Beweglichkeit – zu einer Art kinetischen

monitor and chair, where the visitor sits. But in the virtual version, the visitor is not depicted, the chair remains empty, inviting him to take a seat and thereby travel into other rooms. Like *Viewpoint*, this piece keys the virtual into the real. The monitor's field of vision initially replaces a fragment of space in which the spectator is located. The question of matching, however, is addressed differently. The edge of the monitor at any rate frustrates the illusion of continuity between the two spaces. Shaw simulates them by placing a grey horizontal band along the walls, which can be optically aligned to provide a distant reference point for the virtual space, a referential horizon. This artifice, however, does not resolve the complexity of coordination, which is linked above all to the movement that the spectator is induced to make in both three-dimensional spaces (although one can be traversed only via an image). Assimilation then occurs by making the observation points of each space coincide, and by synchronizing the speed and direction of movements. It is the platform that operates this conjunction, the interface which guarantees a match between these heterogeneous spaces.

This exploration of simulacra – of the boundaries and intersections between various orders of reality and heterogeneous spaces – characterizes Shaw's entire œuvre and also invokes the notion of 'inframince' ('infra-thin') developed by Marcel Duchamp in some forty notes made between 1912 and 1968.[56] Duchamp notably defined 'inframince' as the difference between two samenesses, where they are the most indeterminate. Thus in note 35 (recto): 'Infra-mince separation [...]. All "identicals", as / identical as they may be (and / the more identical they are) / move towards this / infra thin separative / difference.'

Even though Duchamp refers to a separation, a gap, in his last note (No. 46), he also conceives of 'inframince' in terms of a 'conductor', the operator of a passage, the site of an exchange between dimensions: 'Inframince. Reflections / of light on diff. surfaces / more or less polished – Matt reflections giving an / effect or reflection – mirror in / depth / could serve / as an optical illustration of the idea / of the infra-thin as / "conductor" from the 2nd to / the 3rd dimension.'

Coalescence of Virtual and Real

In *The Golden Calf*, the virtual indirectly reproduces the real, for it must be adapted to each place of presentation, even though the surrounding environment is not the immediate object of simulation here. While Shaw takes up the model of panorama again, this time he inverses it by drawing the environment in toward the centre, into an object, a small LCD screen set on a plinth like a sculpture.

The exhibition space was first photographed with a fish-eye camera, then the photographs were digitized to create a virtual panorama around a computer-generated golden calf, which reflected that panorama. So here again, since the location of the physical screen was electronically linked to the photographed space,

Skulptur und einem ganz eigenen Schauspiel. Der Zuschauer kontrolliert gleichzeitig den Projektions- und den Kamera-Roboter und bestimmt dadurch sowohl die Aufnahme als auch die Rekonstruktion des Schauplatzes. Diese privilegierte Position ist dieselbe wie die des Thaumaturgen, wie sie Paul Virilio beschreibt: › [...] der *Allsichtbarkeit* der plötzlichen Hin-durch-Sichtbarkeit der Dinge fügt sich ein anderes göttliches Attribut hinzu, die *Allgegenwart* aus der Ferne, eine Art elektromagnetische Telekinese.‹[54] Eine neue zeitliche Dimension entsteht: Die reale Zeit wird ersetzt durch digitale Berechnung, die gegenwärtige Zeit durch die elektronische Videoaufzeichnung, durch Telepräsenz. Eine Telepräsenz, die Jeffrey Shaw hier nicht ohne eine gewisse Ironie ins Leere laufen läßt, da nur die unmittelbare Umgebung kontrolliert wird. Und schließlich werden durch die Bewegungen des Sichtfensters, das die Umgebung wie ein Verfolgerspot absucht, Prinzipien von Voyeurismus und Überwachung inszeniert.

Obwohl der elektronische ›Closed-Circuit‹ das Äußere nach innen holt, bleibt der Beobachter unsichtbar wie im ursprünglichen Panoptikum, dieser ›Maschine zur Scheidung des Paares Sehen/Gesehenwerden‹[55]. Im Unterschied zu den meisten Überwachungsapparaturen verschwindet der Operateur jedoch nicht ganz, er delegiert das Beobachten nicht völlig an eine Maschine, die selbständig und automatisch die Umgebung absucht. Die Doppelung des Blicks bedingt hier eine Art Unterstützung des Sehens, das ausgesprochen subjektiv bleibt: Der Betrachter schaut zwar dorthin, wohin er möchte, bleibt aber abhängig von den Grenzen und Bedingungen der Sehmaschine.

Raumbezogene Virtualität

Im Bewußtsein des hybriden Charakters unserer heutigen Wirklichkeit untersucht Jeffrey Shaw die Bedingungen für die Koexistenz heterogener Raum-Zeit-Dimensionen, in denen Menschen heute handeln und sich bewegen. Er inszeniert Ähnlichkeiten, um die Unterschiede aufzuzeigen und so die Kreisläufe, in denen das Virtuelle und das Reale interagieren, einzufangen.

Paradoxerweise sind gerade diejenigen Installationen Shaws, die virtuelle Räume einbeziehen, eng mit der Spezifik und der Architektur der Orte, für die sie entworfen wurden, verbunden. Davon wird sowohl ihre virtuelle als auch ihre konkrete Struktur beeinflußt. Man könnte von ›virtuellen raumbezogenen Werken‹ sprechen.

So erforderte jede Version von *The Legible City* – Manhattan, Amsterdam, Karlsruhe – eine komplett neue Datenbank, neue Erzählungen für eine veränderte urbane Geographie und eine andere Buchstabenarchitektur. Auch wenn das Konzept gleichbleibt, verändert sich notwendigerweise die Wahrnehmung des Werkes entsprechend des jeweiligen Kontextes. Auch *Going to the Heart of the Center of The Garden of Delights* wird grundlegend durch die Gegebenheiten des Ausstellungsraums bestimmt: die Abstände der neogotischen Gewölbebögen eines kirchenähnlichen Gebäudes (das vor der Umwandlung zum städti-

the viewer could, by manoeuvering the screen, explore the digitized reflection of the site in which he or she was currently located. Reflection of a past time, computed in real time! And, depending on lighting, there might also be direct reflections of the real environment onto the screen, potentially including the image of the spectator. This second, aleatory visual layer provides the only opportunity of being present in a scene that the spectator manipulates and contemplates; he or she is normally invisible, all the while being part of the very environment that is reflected. The installation constitutes an ironic series of staggered illusions, a real vanishing point in the simulated reflection of the spectator's image on a virtual golden calf.

The Golden Calf thus weaves a set of subtle paradoxes into a web of virtualization and actualization, similar to the crystal image described by Gilles Deleuze as a 'bifacial image, real and virtual all at once'[57]. Two faces that cannot be collapsed into one but remain in constant touch.

Inventing the Interface

Interactive systems demand a rethinking and reformulation of the question of aesthetic experience. Indeed, the confrontation between two different levels of reality entails a composite experience, an inevitable twinning of contradictory perceptions for a spectator who is simultaneously active in both. The observation and contemplation of a scene compete with the act of bringing it into being and especially with conducting operations there – the bliss of losing oneself in the work must be constantly negotiated against exercising control over it.

The interface, as the special executor of transactions between the virtual and real, is necessarily at the heart of artistic research involving interactivity. It is absolutely indissociable from the artistic apparatus, and is a constitutive and conceptual part of every installation; it is via the interface that visitors are able to grasp virtual space. However, the interface cannot be identified solely with a technical apparatus, however complex that may be, since the interface also includes the virtual architecture defining the exploratory modalities of a work – the manipulations that it implies are not only of a functional nature, but also *make* sense. In addition to its own visual and plastic qualities, the interface is above all part of a web of metaphors. Much of the artistic activity now employing advanced technology focuses on this complex elaboration.

Shaw, meanwhile, has been inventing interfaces ever since his earliest computer pieces, exploiting highly diverse systems from traditional optical devices (like the periscope) to sophisticated industrial technology (like flight simulators); he has hybridized a whole range of audiovisual techniques with cinematic equipment, assembling a whole arsenal of computer and robot materials in order to produce the immaterial.

schen Museum einen Fleischmarkt beherbergte) bestimmen die Positionierung der Wegmarkierungen vom Eingang zur Leinwand. Das rituelle Schreiten eines Betrachters durch diese Architektur hindurch zur Leinwand fällt mit der Durchquerung eines virtuellen Raumes zusammen, in dem Sakrales und Profanes unlösbar miteinander verknüpft sind. Trotz dieser engen Wechselbeziehung von Virtuellem und Realem sind die genannten Werke doch autonom genug, um auch an anderen Orten gezeigt zu werden. Andere Arbeiten allerdings – wie, als frühes Beispiel, *Viewpoint* – funktionieren nur in der unmittelbaren Konfrontation mit dem Ausstellungsraum.

Shaw hat eine bemerkenswerte Strategie entwickelt, sich dem Bereich der ›virtuellen Realität‹ anzunähern. Er produziert digitale Universen, die gänzlich von einem bestehenden Raum abhängig sind, obwohl sie aufgrund der Modalitäten ihrer Generierung gerade unabhängig von jeder konkreten Referenzialität berechnet werden. In Arbeiten wie *Alice's Room* (1989), *The Virtual Museum* (1991) und *The Golden Calf* (1994) dupliziert der virtuelle Raum einen bestimmten realen Raum, der sich darüberhinaus im Blickfeld des Besuchers befindet (etwa der Ausstellungsraum, in dem das Werk präsentiert wird und somit direkt erfahren werden kann).

Obwohl Simulation hier – paradoxerweise – die Aufgabe der Reproduktion übernimmt, produziert sie doch keine realistische Szenerie. Man sollte eher von einem Realismus der Referenzpunkte sprechen. Einige wenige architektonische Elemente, Fenster oder Türen etwa, werden reproduziert; gerade ausreichend, um einen Raum zu bezeichnen, um die Ähnlichkeit mit dem Raum, der beschrieben wird, aufzuzeigen, eine Orientierung zu bieten. Diese Elemente sind Hinweise auf eine Ähnlichkeit, und nicht Details, die dazu dienen, eine Illusion zu erzeugen. Sie ermöglichen die Produktion einer hinreichenden Analogie, mit deren Hilfe sich Unterschiede zwischen zwei Gleichen überprüfen lassen. Verdopplung hat hier operativen Wert.

Ein Besuch des *Virtual Museum* beginnt im simulierten Ausstellungsraum, in dessen Mitte sich dieselbe Plattform mit demselben großen Monitor und dem Stuhl davor befindet, auf dem der Besucher sich gerade niedergelassen hat. Aber in diesem virtuellen Raum wird der Besucher nicht dargestellt, sein Stuhl bleibt leer und lädt ihn ein, Platz zu nehmen und die anderen Räume zu erkunden. Wie in *Viewpoint* wird hier das Virtuelle in das Reale eingefügt, eingearbeitet. Das Bildfeld des Monitors ersetzt zu Anfang ein Fragment des Raums, in dem der Betrachter sich befindet. Das Problem der Verbindung wird jedoch anders gelöst: Die Begrenzung des Monitors steht der Illusion einer Kontinuität zwischen den beiden Räumen in jedem Fall entgegen. Shaw simuliert sie, indem er einen grauen Streifen horizontal die Wand entlangzieht, der optisch so ausgerichtet werden kann, daß er einen fernen Referenzpunkt für den virtuellen Raum schafft, einen referentiellen Horizont. Allerdings vereinfacht dieser Kunstgriff nicht die komplexe Koordination, die nötig ist, da sich der Zuschauer in beiden dreidimensionalen Räumen zugleich bewegt (auch wenn der eine nur im Bild durchquert werden kann). Es kommt zu einer

Shaw's interactive installations are essentially visits or voyages, with the artist providing the 'means of transportation'. There is nothing necessarily futuristic about such transportation, which is usually a familiar object like a bicycle or armchair. When compared to the vehicles and equipment proposed by the entertainment industry for entering cyberspace, Shaw's interfaces assume an ironic, critical role.

In *The Legible City*, for instance, a bicycle-interface requires the visitor to make a physical effort in order to move through a resistance-free universe, or to slow down in order to read its streets ('slowing down' in the virtual realm is as provocative as making architecture 'soft and responsive'). It seems as though the more immaterial an image becomes, the more it must be earned. The effects of this approach could be inscribed in the pataphysical tradition of the velocipede, from the Quintuplette in Jarry's *Sûrmale* to Tinguely's *Cyclograveur*.

In contrast, the armchair in *The Virtual Museum* encourages (almost) total inactivity – the desire to see can be expressed by slightly leaning the body in one direction or another. It is a sensor-seat for motionless voyagers, producing 'over-equipped able-bodied people' in almost perfect symmetry to 'equipped disabled people', as Paul Virilio suggested.[58] This armchair conflates the movie-goer's seat with the tele-viewer's and even the businessman's. Art is remote-controlled, and the virtual museum can be consumed like everything else – in comfort, from a distance.

The coupling of visitor and machine is sometimes spectacular, as in *EVE*, and sometimes parodistic, as in the screen manipulations that induce the viewer to bow and kneel in idolatrous fashion in order to perceive the reflections on *The Golden Calf*. But it is above all the actualization of each piece by every operator that turns it into a performance. A given performance expresses the visitor's curiosity and skill, and is always just one example among many of an infinite number of potential explorations.

Departure Platform

When not actually absorbed into it, the plinth or base of modern sculpture largely contributes to its autonomy vis-à-vis site or building. It is the platform that performs this function in kinetic work, simultaneously providing a motorized core and a base endowing it with independence. Moholy-Nagy's *Light-Space Modulator* (1930) was set on a rotating circular platter, as was Nicolas Schöffer's early cybernetic sculpture *CYSP 1* (1956) and many others.

Shaw has employed a circular platform in many pieces; sometimes it pivots completely *(The Virtual Museum, Place – a user's manual)*, but at other times remains fixed while incorporating a central element which rotates on its own axis *(Inventer La Terre, Revolution, Alice's Room)* and which may also function as a showcase for a precious object within the installation *(Disappearance)*.

A high-tech model for these platforms is provided by the flight-simulator,[59] whereas a nostalgic model is the carousel. As the

Angleichung, wenn die Beobachtungspunkte beider Räume übereinstimmen und wenn Geschwindigkeit und Richtung der Bewegungen synchronisiert werden. Diese Verbindung wird durch die Plattform hergestellt; sie fungiert als Interface, das das Zusammenpassen dieser heterogenen Räume garantiert.

Die Erkundung der Simulacra, der Grenzen und Schnittpunkte zwischen unterschiedlichen Ordnungen von Realität und heterogenen Räumen, charakterisiert das gesamte Werk Jeffrey Shaws. Darüberhinaus evoziert dies den Begriff des ›Inframince‹ (›Infradünn‹), den Marchel Duchamp in rund vierzig Notizen zwischen 1912 und 1968 entwickelte.[56] Duchamp definierte das ›Inframince‹ vor allem als Differenz zwischen zwei Gleichen, dort, wo sie am ununterscheidbarsten sind. So schreibt er in der Notiz 35 (Vorderseite): ›Trennung Infra-mince [...]. Alle »Identischen«, so / identisch sie sein mögen (und / je identischer sie sind) / nähern sich diesem / infradünnen Unterschied.‹

Auch wenn Duchamp von einer Trennung, einer Lücke spricht, entwirft er in seiner letzten Notiz (Nr. 46) das ›Inframince‹ auch als ›Führer‹, als Operateur eines Übergangs, als Ort eines Austausches zwischen Dimensionen: ›Inframince. Reflexe / des Lichts auf versch. Oberflächen / mehr oder minder glänzend – Matte Reflexe, die einen / Effekt oder eine Reflektion hervorrufen – ein Tiefen- / Spiegel – könnte dienen / als eine optische Illustration der Idee / des Infra-dünnen als / »Führer« von der 2. zur / 3. Dimension.‹

Verbindung von Virtualität und Realität

In *The Golden Calf* wird das Reale auf indirekte Weise vom Virtuellen reproduziert, da die Arbeit an jeden Ausstellungsort angepaßt werden muß – auch wenn hier die Umgebung nicht das unmittelbare Objekt der Simulation ist. Wieder greift Shaw das Modell des Panoramas auf, kehrt es aber um: die Umgebung wird zum Zentrum hin zusammengefaßt, in einem Objekt, einem kleinen LCD-Bildschirm, der wie eine Skulptur auf einem Sockel steht.

Zunächst wurde der Ausstellungsraum mit einem Fischaugenobjektiv fotografiert; anschließend wurden die Aufnahmen digitalisiert, um ein virtuelles Panorama um ein computergeneriertes goldenes Kalb herum zu schaffen, dessen Oberfläche dieses Panorama spiegelt. Durch Bewegen des Monitors, dessen tatsächliche Position elektronisch mit dem fotografierten Raum verbunden ist, kann hier der Betrachter wiederum die digitale Spiegelung des Raums, in dem er sich gerade befindet, erforschen. Spiegelung einer vergangenen Zeit, berechnet in Echtzeit! Und, abhängig von den Lichtverhältnissen, kann die Bildschirmoberfläche die reale Umgebung auch direkt spiegeln, möglicherweise zusammen mit dem Bild des Betrachters. Diese zweite, zufallsabhängige visuelle Ebene stellt für den Zuschauer die einzige Möglichkeit dar, an einem Schauplatz anwesend zu sein, den er manipuliert und betrachtet; obwohl er Teil eben jener Umgebung ist, die gespiegelt wird, bleibt er normalerweise unsichtbar. Die Installation besteht aus einer ironischen Kaskade von Illusionen: ein wirklicher Fluchtpunkt innerhalb der simulierten Spiegelung vom Bild des Betrach-

casting-off point for a more or less extraordinary elsewhere, the platform is a site of rupture, a departure zone for an imaginary voyage.

However, unlike most virtual systems that create immersion effects and do their utmost to detach spectators from the surrounding reality, Shaw's pivoting platforms are a key element of a subtle mechanism that functions in a paradoxical way. They do, of course, isolate the viewer from the surrounding space, but only in order to give that spectator a new posture within it, not to remove him or her to a different universe (which dimming the lights does in the movies). A platform thus lifts the spectator off the ground, which is an initial condition for the experience, but the speed of movement remains that of an observation deck.

In fact, the primary role of this cinematic apparatus (usually combined with a viewing window) is to get two heterogeneous spaces in phase – the space the window reveals and the space the spectator physically occupies. Such is the twin operation of the twin sites of Shaw's pieces.

Architextures

The importance of texts in Jeffrey Shaw's work is striking – texts displayed on electronic billboards, architectured words, tales woven through virtual worlds. For although language abounds in hypermedia (usually in the form of commentary, captions, or literary quotations), it is generally absent from the universe of digital synthesis. Shaw did not add language by default, in order to overcome certain technical inadequacies or to effect a conceptual 'reduction' of his work, but rather to get back into touch with the 'symbolic thinking' that characterizes human development.[60] Virtual spaces are worlds devoid of territorial lines and referential space – they are mental sites where anything can happen. Shaw introduces ideas, relationships, imaginings, and operations for which language functions as a crucial point of departure. In this respect, his oeuvre can certainly be described as conceptual.

Writing is thus an essential, if not the only essential, visual component of several interactive pieces, from the sixteen hieroglyphs in *Points of View* to the 'telepictoglyphs' of *Televirtual Chit Chat* (1993). It was through Shaw's exploration of computer logic, processes and language that texts began to impose themselves. The installation *Propagation of the Luminous Word* (1988) was precisely a visualization of binary coding. The digital transformation of words selected at random from among all the key words entered in an electronic catalogue by library users was displayed in a luminous labyrinth of 0s and 1s hanging from the ceiling of the building. The translation process at the base of all computer operations was thereby spatialized. Below this labyrinth, a plinth supported a mirrored sphere that reflected the surroundings and displayed the selected word, which visitors could modify. Visitors were thus presented with two states of the word for comparison, and could

ters auf einem virtuellen goldenen Kalb!

The Golden Calf verknüpft auf diese Weise eine Reihe subtiler Paradoxien zu einem Netz von Virtualisierungen und Aktualisierungen, ähnlich jenem Kristallbild, das Gilles Deleuze als ein ›zweiseitiges Bild: ein aktuelles *und* ein virtuelles‹[57] beschreibt. Zwei Seiten, die nicht zu einer zusammenfallen können, aber doch in ständiger Verbindung stehen.

Das Interface erfinden

Interaktive Systeme erfordern ein Nachdenken über die Frage der ästhetischen Erfahrung in neuen Begriffen. Denn tatsächlich bewirkt die Konfrontation mit zwei verschiedenen Realitätsebenen eine vielschichtige Erfahrung, eine unvermeidliche Vermischung widersprüchlicher Wahrnehmungen für einen Zuschauer, der gleichzeitig auf beiden Ebenen aktiv ist. Das Beobachten und Betrachten einer Szene konkurriert mit dem Akt, sie überhaupt erst hervorzubringen und zu steuern – der Reiz, sich im Werk zu verlieren, steht in ständigem Widerspruch zu der Aufgabe, den Ablauf zu steuern.

Das Interface, dieser privilegierte Mittler zwischen Virtualität und Realität, steht notwendigerweise im Zentrum einer künstlerischen Erforschung von Interaktivität. Es ist von der künstlerischen Apparatur keinesfalls zu trennen und ist konstitutiver und konzeptueller Teil jeder Installation; über das Interface kann der Besucher auf den virtuellen Raum zugreifen. Das Interface kann aber nicht einfach nur als Teil der technischen Apparatur gesehen werden, sei diese auch noch so kompliziert. Es enthält auch die virtuelle Architektur, die die Bedingungen für die Erkundung eines Werkes vorgibt; die sich daraus ergebenden Manipulationen sind nicht nur funktionaler Natur, sondern *machen* auch Sinn. Über seine visuellen und skulpturalen Qualitäten hinaus ist das Interface vor allem Teil eines Netzes von Metaphern. Viele der Künstler, die moderne Technologien einsetzen, konzentrieren sich in ihren Arbeiten auf diese komplexen Zusammenhänge.

Schon in seinen frühesten computergestützten Arbeiten erfand Jeffrey Shaw Interfaces, wobei er die verschiedensten Systeme nutzte: von traditionellen optischen Geräten (wie das Periskop) bis hin zu hochentwickelter industrieller Technologie (wie den Flugsimulator). Er kreuzt die gesamte Palette audiovisueller Technologien mit dem Equipment der Filmkunst und hat daraus ein ganzes Arsenal von Computer- und Robotertechniken zur Herstellung des Immateriellen zusammengetragen.

Shaws interaktive Installationen sind im wesentlichen Besuche oder Reisen, wobei der Künstler dem Besucher die ›Fortbewegungsmittel‹ zur Verfügung stellt. Diese Fortbewegungsmittel haben nichts Futuristisches, sondern sind vertraute Gegenstände wie ein Fahrrad oder ein Sessel. Vergleicht man sie mit den Vehikeln und der Ausrüstung, die die Unterhaltungsindustrie für die Reise durch den Cyberspace anbietet, übernehmen Shaws Interfaces eine ironische, kritische Rolle.

In *The Legible City* z.B. verlangt das Fahrrad dem Besucher kör-

observe the process of conversion.

Shaw also exploited LED[61] alphanumeric display techniques, as seen in the huge screen of *Architext* (1992), where a panel set up in front of a theatre displayed texts excerpted from shows being presented. This piece explored new relationships, notably those between the perception and reading of a text, in which various parameters like proximity are brought into play: from a distance, the text looks like a more or less abstract figure whereas from close up the gaps dominate, gaps that perhaps suggest other meanings or reconstructions of the text, just as elsewhere Shaw undertook to reconstruct the image.

Here the text – pure, fluid light – is inscribed in the architecture that it animates. Elsewhere it becomes architecture itself, constituting the scene. Back in the 1950s, the Concrete Poetry movement, inspired by Mallarmé and Joyce as well as by avant-garde typographical experiments, rediscovered the space and mobility of a text, got it off the page and presented it as concrete material independent of its semantic value. Shaw has similarly explored the physicality of a text, giving the same volume to letters that he gave to images, endowing them with the plastic and dynamic qualities normally accorded figures, sometimes even endowing them with a life of their own – the phrases in *Place – a user's manual* swirl across the panorama until they fade into oblivion. The letter has become a concrete graphic sign with which Shaw creates the 'poetry in space' sought by Antonin Artaud.

The most remarkable example of Shaw's use of text is certainly the virtual city in *The Legible City*, whose urban profile is formed exclusively by three-dimensional computer-generated letters that replace urban buildings. They sometimes evoke the city's architectural forms and dominant colours, but above all recount its history and stories, since every alignment of house-words constitutes so many lines of narrative to skim. Shaw uses letters in a figural way – their presence is never exclusively formal.

The four galleries of *The Virtual Museum* comprise a kind of inventory-manifesto of the intertextuality of language and the arts in the 20th century: a circular aphorism[62] fills the empty frames of the painting gallery, in a nod to Conceptual art; in the sculpture gallery, five arrangements of solid letters – like Constructivist or Dadaist compositions – form the words of the five senses; two lines of a Japanese haiku run through the cinema gallery in opposite directions, the Kanji letters serving as screen to Muybridge photos whose movement is reconstituted by the shifting text; finally, the fourth gallery, devoted to high-tech arts, is illuminated by the random circulation of three characters – A, 2, Z – that function as primary tri-colour light sources (getting from A to Z requires the 2 of binariness). Thus the computer-generated scene is totally and tautologically reduced to the basic codes of its constitution. Shaw's other exploration of the theme of museums take on a new critical dimension in this virtual museum in which multiple techniques, approaches, and modes of representation inextricably

perliche Anstrengung ab, um sich durch ein Universum ohne Widerstände bewegen zu können; um die Straßen zu lesen, muß er langsamer werden. ›Verlangsamung‹ im Bereich des Virtuellen ist so provokativ wie die Entwicklung einer ›weichen, reagierenden‹ Architektur. Je immaterieller ein Bild wird, desto mehr muß man es sich verdienen, so scheint es. Man könnte die Wirkungen dieser Vorgehensweise der pataphysikalischen Tradition des Velozipedes zuordnen: von der Quintuplette aus Jarrys *Surmâle* bis zum *Cyclograveur* von Tinguely.

Der Sessel in *The Virtual Museum* dagegen lädt ein zu (beinahe) vollständiger Passivität – um dem Wunsch, etwas zu sehen, Ausdruck zu verleihen, genügt es, den Oberkörper leicht zur einen oder anderen Seite zu neigen: Es handelt sich um einen mit Sensoren ausgestatteten Sessel für den bewegungslos Reisenden, für den ›überrüsteten Nicht-Behinderten‹ von heute, dem fast perfekten Gegenstück zum ›mit entsprechenden Hilfsmitteln ausgerüsteten Behinderten‹, wie Paul Virilio es formuliert.[58] Der Sessel ist Kinosessel, Fernsehsessel und Chefsessel zugleich. Die Kunst wird ferngesteuert, und das virtuelle Museum kann genau wie alles andere konsumiert werden – mit allem Komfort und mit gehörigem Abstand.

Die Verbindung zwischen Besucher und Maschine kann bisweilen spektakulär sein, wie in *EVE*, oder parodistisch wie in *The Golden Calf*, wo der Betrachter niederknien und sich in heidnischer Anbetung verrenken muß, um die Spiegelungen auf dem goldenen Kalb erkennen zu können. Was es aber zu einer Performance werden läßt ist vor allem die Verwirklichung jeder Arbeit durch jeden einzelnen Betrachter/Benutzer. Jede Performance ist Ausdruck der Neugier und der Fähigkeiten des Besuchers und dabei doch immer nur eines von vielen Beispielen aus einer unbegrenzten Anzahl möglicher Entdeckungsreisen.

›Abflugsplattform‹

Falls er nicht vollständig integriert ist, verhilft der Sockel der modernen Skulptur zu mehr Autonomie gegenüber ihrer Umgebung. Bei einem kinetischen Werk übernimmt die Plattform diese Funktion; sie ist sein motorisiertes Zentrum und zugleich die Basis seiner Unabhängigkeit. Moholy-Nagys *Licht-Raum Modulator* (1930) stand ebenso auf einem Drehteller wie Nicolas Schöffers frühe kybernetische Skulptur *CYSP 1* (1956) und viele andere.

Jeffrey Shaw verwendet die kreisförmige Plattform in vielen Arbeiten; manchmal dreht sie sich als ganze *(The Virtual Museum, Place – a user's manual)*, manchmal ist sie fixiert und enthält ein zentrales Element, das sich um die eigene Achse dreht *(Inventer La Terre, Revolution, Alice's Room)* – oder sie kann auch als Schaufenster für ein kostbares Objekt innerhalb der Installation dienen *(Disappearance)*.

Das High-Tech-Modell für diese Plattformen ist der Flugsimulator[59], das nostalgische Vorbild das Karussell. Als Ausgangspunkt zu einem mehr oder weniger ungewöhnlichen Anderswo ist die Plattform ein Ort des Aufbruchs, sie ist der Startpunkt zu einer imaginären Reise.

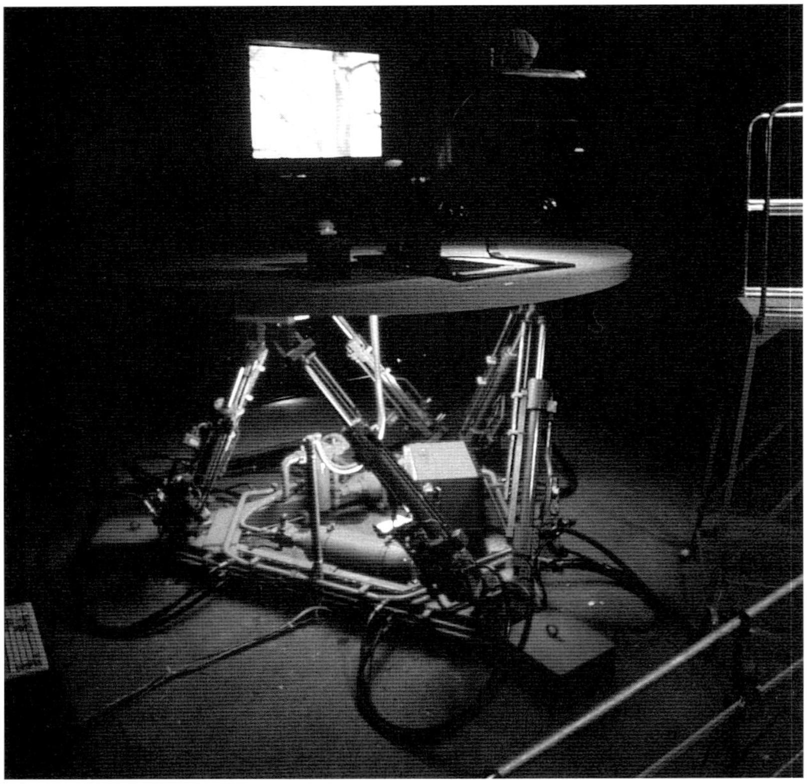

The Forest (Sebastian Egner, Jeffrey Shaw, Tamás Waliczky), MultiMediale 3, ZKM Karlsruhe, Karlsruhe, Germany, 1993. Photo: Jeffrey Shaw.

Im Gegensatz zu den meisten virtuellen Systemen, die Immersionseffekte schaffen und außerordentlich bemüht sind, die Zuschauer aus der sie umgebenden Realität zu lösen, sind Shaws rotierende Plattformen das Schlüsselelement eines subtilen Mechanismus', der auf paradoxe Weise funktioniert. Natürlich isolieren sie den Zuschauer von seiner Umgebung, aber mit dem Ziel, ihm eine neue Position innerhalb dieser Umgebung zu verschaffen und nicht, um ihn in ein anderes Universum zu versetzen (wie es etwa das Verlöschen des Lichts im Kino bewirkt). Die Plattform hebt zwar den Betrachter vom Boden, das ist eine Grundbedingung für die Erfahrung, aber die Geschwindigkeit ihrer Bewegung entspricht der einer Aussichtsplattform.

Die wichtigste Aufgabe dieser filmischen Apparatur (die meist mit einem Sichtfenster gekoppelt wird) ist es, zwei heterogene Räume zu koordinieren – den Raum, den das Sichtfenster enthüllt und den Raum, den der Zuschauer körperlich besetzt. Hierin liegt die doppelte Wirkungsweise der doppelten Räume in Shaws Werken.

Architexturen

Text spielt in Jeffrey Shaws Werk eine erstaunlich große Rolle: Texte auf elektronischen Anzeigetafeln, ›architektonische‹ Worte, mit virtuellen Welten verwobene Erzählungen. Wenn in den Hypermedien Sprache auch im Überfluß vorhanden ist (für gewöhnlich in Form von Kommentaren, Bildunterschriften oder literarischen Zitaten), fehlt sie im allgemeinen im computergenerierten Universum völlig. Shaw verwendet Sprache nicht, um einen Mangel auszugleichen, gewisse technischen Unzulänglichkeiten zu überwinden oder eine konzeptuelle ›Reduktion‹ des Werkes zu bewirken, sondern um an das ›symbolische Denken‹ anzuknüpfen, das die menschliche Entwicklung charakterisiert.[60] Virtuelle Räume sind Welten ohne Grenzlinien und Bezugspunkte; sie sind mentale Orte, in denen alles möglich ist. Shaw inszeniert hier Ideen, Beziehungen, Vorstellungen und Operationen, für die Sprache als entscheidender Ausgangspunkt fungiert. In dieser Hinsicht kann sein Werk durchaus als konzeptuell bezeichnet werden.

Schrift ist also eine – wenn nicht *die* – wesentliche visuelle Komponente mehrerer interaktiver Arbeiten, angefangen bei den sechzehn Hieroglyphen in *Points of View* bis zu den ›Telepiktoglyphen‹ in *Televirtual Chit Chat* (1993). Shaws Beschäftigung mit Computerlogik, Funktionsweise und Sprache führte dazu, daß Texte sich von selbst ergaben. Die Installation *Propagation of the Luminous Word* (1988) ist exakt eine Visualisierung des Binärcodes. Digital transformierte Worte, per Zufallsgenerator ausgewählt aus all den Schlagwörtern, die von Bibliotheksbenutzern in einen elektronischen Katalog eingegeben worden sind, werden über ein leuchtendes Labyrinth aus Nullen und Einsen, das von der Decke des Gebäudes hängt, wiedergegeben. Der Übersetzungsprozeß als Grundlage aller Operationen des Computers wird so räumlich erfahrbar. Unterhalb des Labyrinths befindet sich ein Sockel mit einer verspiegelten Kugel, die die Umgebung reflektiert

overlap. Shaw's highly ironic resumé castigates the categorizations and classifications imposed by art history, and it invokes above all the structuring function of language through the ubiquitousness of text and characters, at the levels of both representation and perception.

Narrative Structures and Virtual Architectures
Shaw has carved a new fictional space from virtual reality, where multiple textual forms intersect – not only aphorisms and quotations, but also stories (in collaboration with writer Dirk Groeneveld) that function as so many points of view, accounts, tales, or impressions of a place.

The texts may be spoken off-screen *(Points of View, The Narrative Landscape)*, inscribed in the scene, or even constitute the scene *(The Legible City, Place – a user's manual)*. Words are aligned to make sense, yet always in a multifarious sense, with meanings largely produced by the spectator from a virtually discontinuous linearity subject to chops and changes. Beyond the text itself, it is the very conception of potential pathways – the manner in which the text/image 'happens' – that inscribes the narration and drives the fiction into the present. What Barthes called 'the scriptible text' is nothing other than 'ourselves in the act of writing'.[63] The viewer's freedom is guaranteed by shifting figures that spark certain associations or methods of transiting from one idea or situation to another. Shaw invents the logic behind the discovery of a city or panorama, the play of parallels and connections that enables a reader to develop his own branching rhizomes. Every pathway is thus absolutely unique, depending on the given entry point and method of 'pacing up and down' the work.

The narrative construction behind such wanderings is extremely rigorous, totally linked to Shaw's staging of the whole piece. As Roland Barthes pointed out, 'the most subjective reading imaginable is never more than a game played according to certain rules'. That game is also a task involving the body, since 'reading means putting the body to work'.[64] Shaw literally formulates this idea through the effort demanded of visitors to *The Legible City* and viewers of *Revolution*.

Structure – that is to say the very conception of these pathways – is expressed through diagrams that function as so many metaphors: hemisphere, grid, stratum, cross, wheel, etc. It is usually built around a limited choice of images (three in *Going to the Heart of the Center of The Garden of Delights*), scenes (six sites for *Inventer La Terre*, four spaces in *Alice's Room*, eleven panoramas in *Place – a user's manual*), or stories (eight tales for the first version of *The Legible City*). This limitation allows – or almost allows, in the context of an installation – for the exhaustion of all possibilities, directing re-directed attention back to what constitutes the scene, thereby rejecting headlong flight into infinite navigation of the virtual (as hyped by the hypermedia).

Thus every piece by Shaw has its own explorational topology.

und das gerade ausgewählte Wort zeigt, das von den Besuchern auch verändert werden kann. Den Besuchern wird auf diese Weise ein Wort in zwei verschiedenen Zuständen, die verglichen werden können, präsentiert. Außerdem können sie den Prozeß des Übergangs vom einen in den anderen Zustand beobachten.

Daneben benutzte Shaw auch die Technik der alphanumerischen LED-Anzeige[61] – z.B. für den riesigen ›Bildschirm‹ in *Architext* (1992), wo an der Außenwand eines Theaters auf einer Tafel Textausschnitte von Aufführungen, die im Theater stattfinden, gezeigt werden. Die Arbeit erforscht verschiedene Beziehungen, vor allem diejenigen zwischen Wahrnehmung und Lektüre eines Textes, wobei verschiedene Parameter ins Spiel kommen: Aus der Ferne sieht der Text aus wie eine mehr oder weniger abstrakte Figur; aus der Nähe dominieren die Zwischenräume, Lücken, die vielleicht andere Bedeutungen, andere Rekonstruktionen des Textes suggerieren – ganz so, wie Jeffrey Shaw es sonst übernimmt, das Bild zu rekonstruieren.

Der Text – reines, flüssiges Licht – ist hier in eine Architektur eingeschrieben und beseelt sie. Andernorts wird der Text selbst zu Architektur, er bildet die Kulisse. In den fünfziger Jahren entdeckt die Bewegung der konkreten Poesie, inspiriert ebenso von Mallarmé und Joyce wie von den typographischen Experimenten der Avantgarde, die Räumlichkeit und Beweglichkeit des Textes wieder, löst ihn von der Buchseite und verwendet ihn als konkretes Material jenseits seiner semantischen Wertigkeit. In gleicher Weise erkundet Shaw die Körperlichkeit eines Textes, gibt den Buchstaben dasselbe Volumen wie zuvor den Bildern, stattet sie mit plastischen und dynamischen Eigenschaften von Figuren aus, schenkt ihnen sogar manchmal ein Eigenleben – die Sätze in *Place – a user's manual* durchqueren die Panoramen, bis sie völlig verblaßt sind. Der Buchstabe ist zu einem konkreten grafischen Zeichen geworden, mit dem Jeffrey Shaw die von Antonin Artaud geforderte ›Poesie im Raum‹ kreiert.

Bemerkenswertestes Beispiel für Shaws Verwendung von Text ist sicherlich die virtuelle Stadt in *The Legible City*, deren urbanes Profil ausschließlich aus computergenerierten dreidimensionalen Buchstaben besteht, die die städtischen Gebäude ersetzen. Manchmal evozieren sie die architektonischen Formen der Stadt oder die in ihr dominierenden Farben, aber vor allem erzählen sie ihre Geschichte und ihre Geschichten, denn jede Reihe dieser Haus-Wörter bildet die Zeile einer Erzählung, die es zu lesen gilt. Shaw benutzt Buchstaben figurativ – sie sind niemals aus bloß formalen Gründen anwesend.

Die vier Ausstellungsräume in *The Virtual Museum* bieten eine Art Inventar-Manifest der Intertextualität von Sprache und Kunst im zwanzigsten Jahrhundert: ein kreisender Aphorismus[62] füllt die leeren Rahmen der Gemäldegalerie – ein Augenzwinkern in Richtung Konzeptkunst; in der Skulpturengalerie bilden fünf Arrangements aus dreidimensionalen Buchstaben – wie konstruktivistische oder dadaistische Kompositionen – die Bezeichnungen der fünf Sinne; in der Filmgalerie durchqueren zwei Zeilen eines japanischen Haiku gegenläufig den Raum, wobei die Kanji-Buchstaben

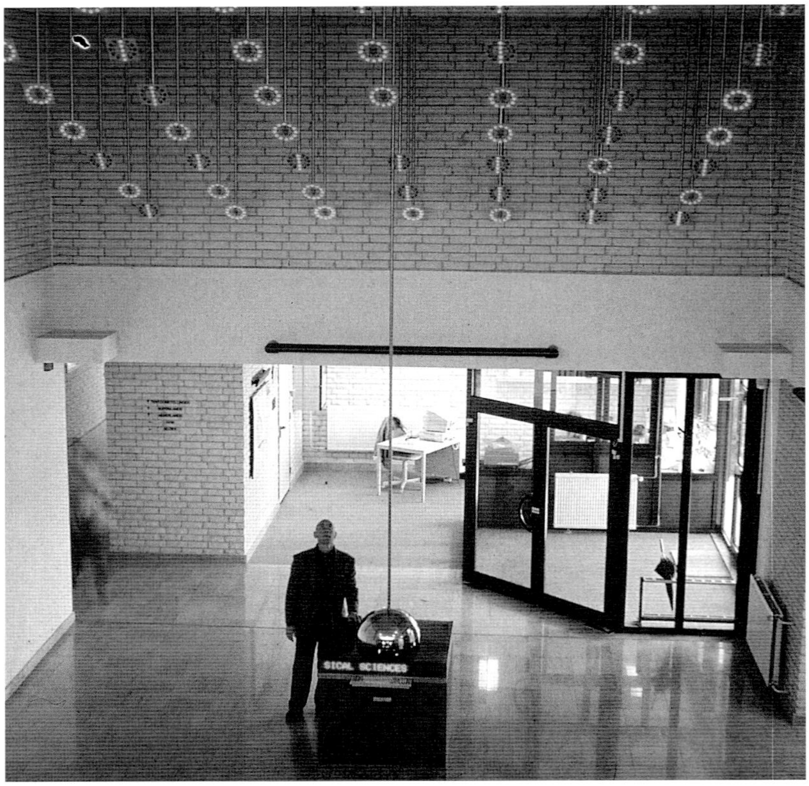

Propagation of the Luminous Word, LBC Landelijk Bibliotheekcentrale, Almere, Netherlands, 1988. Photo: Pieter Boersma.

als Projektionsfläche für Muybridge-Fotos dienen, die durch die Bewegung der Buchstaben in Bewegung geraten; die vierte Galerie schließlich, der High-Tech-Kunst gewidmet, wird beleuchtet von drei Zeichen – A, 2, Z – in den Primärfarben, die zufallsgesteuert durch den Raum schweben und als Lichtquellen fungieren (um von A nach Z zu gelangen, bedarf es der Zweierlogik des binären Systems[63]). Auf diese Weise wird der computergenerierte Schauplatz total und tautologisch auf den grundlegenden Code seines Aufbaus reduziert. Andere Forschungen Shaws zum Thema Museum erhalten eine neue, kritische Dimension durch dieses virtuelle Museum, in dem sich mehrere Techniken, Konzepte und Formen der Darstellung unüberschaubar überlagern. Shaws ziemlich ironisches Resumée verurteilt die von der Kunstgeschichte aufgezwungenen starren Kategorisierungen und Klassifizierungen und erinnert durch die Allgegenwart von Texten und Zeichen vor allem an die strukturierende Funktion der Sprache für Darstellung und Wahrnehmung.

Narrative Strukturen und virtuelle Architekturen

Jeffrey Shaw hat der virtuellen Realität einen neuen fiktionalen Raum abgetrotzt, in dem sich mehrere textuelle Formen kreuzen: nicht nur Aphorismen und Zitate, sondern auch Erzählungen (in Zusammenarbeit mit dem Schriftsteller Dirk Groeneveld), die unterschiedliche Standpunkte, Zeugnisse, Geschichten oder Impressionen eines Ortes darstellen.

Die Texte können aus dem Off gesprochen werden *(Points of View, The Narrative Landscape)*, in die Szene eingeschrieben sein oder sie sogar konstituieren *(Legible City, Place – a user's manual)*. Die Worte sind so aneinandergereiht, daß sie einen Sinn ergeben, einen vieldeutigen Sinn, der größtenteils vom Leser aus einer virtuellen, diskontinuierlichen Linearität, die sich ständig verändert, hergestellt wird. Jenseits des Textes selbst ist es die Anlage potentieller Wege – die Art und Weise, wie Text und Bild ›sich ereignen‹ –, durch die die Erzählung sich einschreibt und die Fiktion in die Gegenwart geholt wird. Was Roland Barthes als ›schreibbaren Text‹ bezeichnet hat, ist nichts anderes als ›wir im Akt des Schreibens‹.[64] Dabei wird die Freiheit des Zuschauers garantiert durch zirkulierende Figuren, die bestimmte Assoziationen wecken und durch Übergangsmodi von einer Idee bzw. Situation zur nächsten. Shaw erfindet die Logik, die sich hinter der Entdeckung einer Stadt oder eines Panoramas verbirgt, das Spiel mit den Parallelen und Verbindungen, das es einem Leser ermöglicht, sein eigenes verzweigtes Rhizom zu entwickeln. So ist jeder Weg absolut einmalig, abhängig vom gewählten Ausgangspunkt und der Methode, sich innerhalb des Werkes fortzubewegen, es zu durchschreiten.

Die narrative Konstruktion hinter diesen Wanderungen ist sehr streng und vollkommen mit der Inszenierung der gesamten Arbeit verbunden. Wie Roland Barthes ausführt, ›ist die subjektivste vorstellbare Lektüre nie mehr als ein Spiel, das nach gewissen Regeln gespielt wird‹. Dieses Spiel ist auch Arbeit, die den Körper miteinbezieht, denn ›lesen heißt unseren Körper arbeiten lassen‹.[65] Shaw setzt diesen Gedanken buchstabengetreu um, indem er den

The surface of *The Narrative Landscape* is divided into nine zones, each offering access to three layers of images via a series of zooms. Each level of imagery corresponds to a different scale and relationship of humankind to the world. This three-tiered trajectory once again implies a virtual totality to be discovered, not unlike Henri Michaux's mescaline visions of crossing a mandala where 'the subject had, or rather "felt", a total knowledge of the world'. Circles repeated within squares 'unendingly, with one or several attributes of primary or secondary signification at each level, to be read and deciphered without ever losing sight of the ultimate truth, into which one dived deeper, ever deeper'.[65]

Progression through *Going to the Heart of the Center of The Garden of Delights* explicitly weds the sacred to the profane, the erotic to the violent, and the cinematic to the painterly, according to a cross-like structure repeated at every level of the work, providing great coherence not only within the symbolism and composition of the imagery and within the grid of pixels being displayed, but also within the very interface – infra-red sensors that detect the progress of the visitor trigger the image sequence. This progress takes viewers back to the painterly origins of cinema, as keyed by the first image: a collage by Shaw in which Yves Klein's blue-painted Arman (*Portrait Relief Arman*) holds a fainted Jane, victim of King Kong (a profane evocation of Christ in the arms of Mary). The second image is taken from Nagisa Oshima's *In the Realm of the Senses* where the sexually-ravaged woman on the ground has arms flung wide, as though nailed to a cross – from behind this image slowly emerges a fragment of Hieronymus Bosch's *The Garden of Delights*. Entering a digitized image means entering the geometry of pixels, where a closer look means greater abstraction. In order for painting to emerge from the raster of a film image, the latter has to sacrifice definition, and therefore its legibility. It must become a frame in order to find its roots in an art of representation. The story ultimately recounts this transition from one visibility to another, the metamorphosis of one ritual into another, the weaving of circuits between various strata of an intellectual, ideological, and aesthetic nature.

Symbolic Spaces

Shaw's works represent so many enigmas to be deciphered. With their multiple readings and constellation of references, they constitute a kind of hermeneutics. While his virtual architectures can be traversed without difficulty, they do offer another kind of resistance. They are coded worlds, initiatory sanctums, esoteric sites. A given piece is not open to instant understanding, potential interpretations can never be exhausted. Instead of simply borrowing everyday hierarchic procedures, arrangements, and models, Shaw's symbolic structures provide both meaning and mystery to pathways through the unsignposted space of virtuality. The mythic

Besuchern von *The Legible City* oder *Revolution* körperliche Anstrengungen abverlangt.

Die Struktur – also die Anlage der möglichen Pfade, über die das Werk durchquert wird – wird über grafische Darstellungen ausgedrückt, die zugleich Metaphern sind: Halbkugel, Gitter, Schicht, Kreuz, Rad etc. Sie ist meist um eine begrenzte Auswahl von Bildern (drei in *Going to the Heart of the Center of The Garden of Delights*), Szenen (sechs Schauplätze in *Inventer la Terre*, vier Räume in *Alice's Room*, elf Panoramen in *Place – a user's manual*) oder Erzählungen (acht Geschichten für die erste Version von *The Legible City*) gebaut. Diese Begrenzung erlaubt es, alle – im Kontext der Installation jedenfalls fast alle – Möglichkeiten auszuschöpfen und so die Aufmerksamkeit (zurück) zu lenken auf das, was die Szenerie ausmacht. Auf diese Weise wird dem Betrachter das überstürzte Abtauchen in die grenzenlose Navigation durch das Virtuelle (die große Verführung der Hypermedien) verweigert.

Jedes Werk Jeffrey Shaws hat somit eine eigene Topologie seiner Erschließung. Die Oberfläche von *The Narrative Landscape* ist in neun Bereiche unterteilt, von denen jeder (über eine Abfolge von Zooms) den Zugang zu jeweils drei Bildebenen ermöglicht. Jeder der drei Bildebenen entspricht eine andere Stufe und ein andersartiges Verhältnis des Menschen zur Welt. Dieser dreistufige Parcours impliziert einmal mehr eine virtuelle Totalität, die es zu entdecken gilt – vergleichbar vielleicht den Visionen Henri Michaux' unter dem Einfluß von Meskalin, z.B. von der Durchquerung eines Mandala, wobei ›das Subjekt ein allumfassendes Verständnis der Welt hatte, vielmehr »fühlte«.‹ Kreise wiederholten sich in Quadraten, ›unendlich oft, mit einem oder mehreren Bedeutungsattributen erster oder zweiter Ordnung, man konnte sie lesen und entziffern ohne jemals die ultimative Wahrheit aus den Augen zu verlieren, in die man tief eindrang, immer tiefer‹.[66]

Das Voranschreiten in *Going to the Heart of the Center of The Garden of Delights* verknüpft, wie der Titel schon andeutet, Sakrales und Profanes, Erotisches und Gewalttätiges, Filmisches und Malerisches, und zwar mithilfe einer Kreuzstruktur, die sich auf allen Ebenen des Werkes wiederholt. Diese Kreuzstruktur konstituiert einen Zusammenhang nicht nur zwischen Symbolgehalt, Bildkomposition und Pixelraster, sondern auch mit dem Interface selbst: auf seinem Weg zur Leinwand kreuzt der Betrachter Infrarotsensoren und löst so die Bildsequenz aus. Das Voranschreiten des Betrachters im Raum läßt ihn auf der Bildebene zurückgehen zu den Wurzeln des Films in der Malerei; das erste gezeigte Bild spielt hier die Schlüsselrolle: eine Collage von Shaw, in der Yves Kleins blauer Arman (*Portrait Relief Arman*) die ohnmächtige Jane, King Kongs Opfer, in den Armen hält – eine profane, inverse Pietà. Das zweite Bild stammt aus dem Film *Im Reich der Sinne* von Nagisa Oshima und zeigt eine am Boden liegende vergewaltigte Frau, die die Arme wie gekreuzigt ausbreitet; hinter diesem Bild taucht langsam ein Ausschnitt aus Hieronymus Boschs *Der Garten der Lüste* auf. In ein digitales Bild hineinzugehen bedeutet, sich auf die Geometrie der Pixel einzulassen: sich nähern, genauer hinzuschauen

order is marked by its own necessity.

Shaw draws his symbols from various, usually archaic, sources such as the Jewish Cabbala, alchemy, astrology, and pagan and Christian mythology, whether from Egypt or the Far East. He was inspired by the hermetic-cabbalistic tradition, for example, in employing connections posited by the Sephirotic Tree to organize the eleven panoramas of *Place – a user's manual*. Trails lead from one panorama to another according to correspondences that the uninitiated cannot grasp. But the complex symbolism of the Sephiroths, the realm of Ideas, and the attributes of God and 'divine measures' all constitute a totality governing the set of panoramas, making a single world of them. The establishment of this logic is detectable in Shaw's use of the cabbalistic diagram; the presence of such references, however mysterious they may be, stimulates exploration. The space of computerized data is thus organized according to the most ancient representations of the universe. This symbolic space also evokes Renaissance theatres of memory like the one devised by Giulio Camillo as 'a vision of the world and of the nature of things seen from a height, from the stars themselves and even from the supercelestial founts of wisdom beyond them'.[66] A system of 'memory sites' is thus linked to mnemonic images that have the magic power to trigger associations.

The structural logic of Shaw's interactive works therefore reinvents a kind of mental theatre, a theatre 'used in that higher sense' which Artaud, when posing the question of 'the intellectual efficiency of art', hoped would 'objectively express secret truths'.[67]

Translated from the French by Deke Dusinberre.

1 Gérard Genette: *L'oeuvre de l'art*, Éditions du Seuil, Paris, 1994, p. 73.
2 Margarethe Jochimsen: 'Le temps dans l'art d'aujourd'hui: Entre la borne et l'infini.' – *L'art et le temps*, Ed. Michel Baudson, Société des Expositions du Palais des Beaux-Arts, Brussels, 1984, p. 229. John Latham taught film at Saint Martin's School of Art, London, where Shaw studied in 1966.
3 Ilya Prigogine and Serge Pahaut: 'Redécouvrir le temps.' – *L'art et le temps*, ibid, p. 27.
4 Robert Smithson: 'Entropy and the New Monuments.' – *Artforum*, June 1966.
5 Lucy Lippard and John Chandler: 'The Dematerialization of Art.' – *Art International*, Vol. XII, No. 2, February 1968.
6 Rosalind Krauss: 'Sculpture in the Expanded Field.' – *October*, No. 8, Spring 1979.
7 Jeffrey Shaw: 'Concepts for an Operational Art.' – *Art and Artists*, No. 10, January 1969, p. 47. See also p. 148 of this book.
8 Marcos Novak is now developing the notion of 'liquid architecture' in cyberspace. See his article 'Transmitting Architecture.' – *Art & Design*, Vol. 65, No. 11/12, 1995.
9 See work description Architext, p. 97.
10 Kinetic art was the object of several exhibitions when Shaw arrived in Europe. Lázló Moholy-Nagy's Lichtmaschine (1922–1930), for instance, was shown at the Stedelijk van Abbemuseum in Eindhoven, Netherlands, in 1966. (See catalogue Moholy-Nagy, Ed. Stedelijk van Abbemuseum, Eindhoven, 1967. Editor's note)
11 Walter Benjamin: 'The Work of Art in the Age of Mechanical Reproduction.' – *Illuminations*, New York, 1969. Reprinted in: *Videoculture*, Visual Studies Work-

bewirkt eine zunehmende Abstraktion. Das Raster, die Auflösung des Filmbildes muß gröber, also weniger lesbar werden, um das Gemälde zu enthüllen. Es muß zu einem Rahmen werden, um seinen Ursprung in einer Kunst der Repräsentation zu finden. Die Geschichte erzählt letztlich diesen Übergang von einem Sichtbaren zum anderen, die Metamorphose eines Rituals in ein anderes, die Verknüpfung verschiedener geistiger, ideologischer und ästhetischer Schichten.

Symbolische Räume

Jeffrey Shaws Werke sind ausnahmslos Rätsel, die es zu lösen gilt. Sie bieten verschiedene Lesarten an und unterschiedliche Konstellationen von Bezügen; sie konstituieren eine Art Hermeneutik. Ihre virtuellen Architekturen können ohne Schwierigkeiten durchquert werden, sie leisten eine andere Art des Widerstands. Es sind kodierte Welten, heilige Orte der Initiation, esoterische Stätten, die man weder sofort verstehen noch erschöpfend interpretieren kann. Shaw übernimmt nicht einfach alltägliche hierarchische Verfahren, Anordnungen und Modelle, sondern entwickelt symbolische Strukturen, die die Pfade durch den virtuellen Raum, in dem es keine Markierungen, keine ›Straßenschilder‹ gibt, mit Bedeutungen sowie mit Geheimnissen füllen. Die mythische Ordnung gehorcht ihren eigenen Gesetzen.

Die Symbole stammen aus verschiedenen, meist archaischen Quellen – von Ägypten bis zum Fernen Osten – wie der jüdischen Kabbala, der Alchimie, der Astrologie und der heidnischen oder christlichen Mythologie. So ist etwa die Anordnung der elf Panoramen in *Place – a user's manual* von der hermetischen kabbalistischen Tradition inspiriert und verwendet durch den Sephiroth-Baum definierte Zusammenhänge. Die Pfade, mit denen die Panoramen verknüpft sind, folgen Gesetzmäßigkeiten, die ein Uneingeweihter nicht nachvollziehen kann. Aber der komplexe Symbolismus des Sephiroth, das Reich der Ideen, die Attribute Gottes und die ›göttlichen Maße‹ machen aus dem Ensemble der Panoramen *eine* Totalität, eine abgeschlossene Welt. Die Etablierung einer solchen Logik wird spürbar in der Art und Weise, wie Shaw das kabbalistische Diagramm einsetzt; die Anwesenheit solcher Bezüge, wie mysteriös sie auch immer sein mögen, fordert dazu auf, auf Entdeckungsreise zu gehen. Der computergenerierte Datenraum ist hier entsprechend der ältesten Darstellungen des Universums organisiert. Dieser symbolische Raum evoziert darüberhinaus das Theater der Erinnerung der Renaissance, wie es etwa Giulio Camillo entwarf: ›Das Theater ist also die Ansicht der Welt und der Natur der Dinge, wie sie sich aus der Höhe, von den Sternen und sogar von den überhimmlischen Quellen der Weisheit und noch jenseits davon bietet.‹[67] Ein System aus ›Stätten der Erinnerung‹ wird so verbunden mit den ›Bildern der Erinnerung‹, die die magische Kraft besitzen, Assoziationen auszulösen.

Die strukturelle Logik der interaktiven Werke von Jeffrey Shaw erfindet eine Art mentales Theater neu, ein Theater, das ›im höheren Sinne genutzt wird‹ und von dem sich Antonin Artaud, als er die

shops Press, New York, 1987, pp. 27-52.

12 Originally employed by Stan VanDerBeek, the term was taken up by Jonas Mekas in 1965 and became the title of a book by Gene Youngblood: *Expanded Cinema*, Studio Vista, London, 1970.

13 Gene Youngblood: *Expanded Cinema*, ibid, p. 346.

14 Dominique Noguez: 'Le Cinéma prend le large.' – *Eloge du cinéma expérimental*, Éd. MNAM, Centre Georges Pompidou, Paris, 1979, p. 153.

15 Abel Gance (1889-1981) developed for his silent film *Napoléon* (1923–27) a special wide-screen process ('Polyvision') using three screens and projectors simulaneously. (Editor's note)

16 See also *telehor*, special edition on László Moholy-Nagy, 1936, p. 123: 'For instance, one could – as I suggested already for silent film – bring all the walls in the picture house under a crossfire of films: "Polycinema".' (Editor's note).

17 In the 1920s, Moholy-Nagy envisaged a totalizing theater as 'a great dynamic-rhythmic process, which can compress the greatest clashing masses or accumulations of media – as qualitative and quantitative tensions – into elemental form', thereby encouraging the use of all sorts of complex apparatus 'such as film, automobile, lift, aeroplane, and other machinery, as well as optical instruments, reflecting equipment, and so on'. – László Moholy-Nagy: 'Theatre, Circus, Variety.' – *Die Bühne im Bauhaus*, Oskar Schlemmer, László Moholy-Nagy, Farkas Molnár, Bauhausbücher 4, Munich, 1925. Reprinted with an epilogue by Walter Gropius, Mainz and Berlin, 1965, p. 52 and p. 54.

18 See Deke Dusinberre: 'On Expanding Cinema.' – *Studio International*, November/December 1975.

19 The first performances in Rotterdam employed a single projector some 30 meters from the dome. In the Amsterdam version, two 16mm projectors and one slide projector were positioned at three points around the dome. See Theo Botschuijver, Sean Wellesley–Miller, Jeffrey Shaw: 'Structure gonflables et participation.' – *RHOBO*, No. 3, Spring 1968.

20 See work description *Corpocinema*, p. 69.

21 The Belgian Etienne Gaspard Robert (1763–1837), who called himself Robertson, developed in 1799 or thereabouts the 'fantascope' – a magic lantern mounted on wheels – which he developed for 'ghost performances' not unlike the horror film genre created some 125 years later. Since his projection device was on wheels, he could rapidly shift his (always concealed) position on the stage in order to project 'spectres' onto wraiths of smoke or tulle curtains. (Editor's note)

22 See also work description *MovieMovie*, p. 70–73.

23 Gilles Deleuze: *Le pli: Leibniz et le Baroque*, Éditions du Minuit, Paris, 1988, pp. 103-104.

24 Marcel Duchamp: 'Note 11', – *Notes Inframince/Infrathin 1–46*, Centre Georges Pompidou, Paris, 1980.

25 Jeffrey Shaw in discussion with Ueno Toshiya: 'We are Materialists, We Employ Science and Technology to Concretize the Virtual.' – *Media Passage*, Ed. InterCommunication Center, Tokyo, 1993, p. 53.

26 Allan Kaprow: *L'Art et la vie confondus*, Centre Georges Pompidou, Paris, 1996, p. 93.

27 Thierry de Duve: 'Performance ici et maintenant.' – *Alternatives théâtrales*, No 6, 1981, p. 33.

28 Alfred Jarry: *Gestes et opinions du docteur Faustroll*, Éd. Gallimard, Paris, 1980, p. 31. The text dates from 1897–99.

29 Ibid., p. 32.

30 Nam June Paik and Shigeko Kubota: *Allan 'n' Allan's Complaint*, 1983, 28 mins., colour.

31 Jeffrey Shaw: 'Jeffrey Shaw on Jeffrey Shaw.' – *Media Passage*, op. cit., p. 25.

32 See Anne-Marie Duguet: 'Dispositifs.' – *Communications*, No. 48, Éditions du Seuil, Video Issue, Paris, 1988.

33 The same material is on road signs that reflect information solely in the direc-

Frage nach der ›verstandesmäßigen Wirksamkeit der Kunst‹ stellte, erhoffte, daß es ›auf objektive Weise verborgene Wahrheiten zum Ausdruck bringen‹ werde.[68]

Aus dem Französischen von Agnes Choma, Manuela Abel und Astrid Sommer.

1 Gérad Genette: *L'oeuvre de l'art*, Paris, 1994, S. 73.

2 Magarethe Jochimsen: ›Zeit zwischen Entgrenzung und Begrenzung der Bildenden Kunst heute.‹ – *Zeit, die vierte Dimension in der Kunst*, Hg. Michael Baudson, Weinheim, 1985, S. 230. John Latham lehrte Film an der St. Martin's School of Art in London, wo Shaw 1966 studierte.

3 Ilya Prigogine und Serge Pahaut: ›Die Zeit wiederentdecken.‹ – *Zeit, die vierte Dimension in der Kunst*, a.a.O., S. 27.

4 Robert Smithson: ›Entropy and the New Monuments.‹ – *Artforum*, Juni 1966.

5 Lucy Lippard und John Chandler: ›The Dematerialization of Art.‹ – *Art International*, Bd. XII, Nr. 2, Februar 1968.

6 Rosalind Krauss: ›Sculpture in the Expanded Field.‹ – *October*, Nr. 8, Frühjahr 1979.

7 Jeffrey Shaw: ›Concepts for an Operational Art.‹ – *Art and Artists*, Nr. 10, Januar 1969, S. 47. Siehe auch S. 148 dieses Buches.

8 Marcos Novak entwickelt heute die Idee der ›liquid architecture‹ im Cyberspace. Vgl. seinen Aufsatz ›Transmitting architecture.‹ – *Art & Design*, Bd. 65, Nr. 11/12, 1995.

9 Vgl. Werkbeschreibung Architext, S. 97.

10 Als Shaw nach Europa kam, wurden mehrere Ausstellungen kinetischer Kunst gezeigt. László Moholy-Nagys *Lichtmaschine* (1922–1930) bespielsweise war 1966 im Stedelijk van Abbemuseum in Eindhoven, Niederlande zu sehen. (Siehe auch Katalog zur Ausstellung: *Moholy-Nagy*, Hg. Stedelijk van Abbemuseum, Eindhoven, 1967. Anm. d. Red.).

11 Walter Benjamin: *Das Kunstwerk im Zeitalter seiner technischen Reproduzierbarkeit*, Frankfurt a. M., 1963, S. 45.

12 Der Begriff wurde geprägt von Stan VanDerBeek, 1965 griff ihn Jonas Mekas auf und 1970 schrieb Gene Youngblood ein Buch mit dem Titel: *Expanded Cinema*, London, 1970.

13 Gene Youngblood: *Expanded Cinema*, a.a.O., S. 346.

14 Dominique Noguez: ›Le cinéma prend le large.‹ – *Eloge du cinéma expérimental*, Éd. MNAM, Centre Georges Pompidou, Paris, 1979, S. 153.

15 Für seinen Stummfilm *Napoléon* (1923–27) entwickelte Abel Gance (1889–1981) ein spezielles Breitwandverfahren mit drei gleichzeitigen Projektionen. (Anm. d. Red.)

16 Vgl. *telehor*, Sonderheft über László Moholy-Nagy, 1936, S. 123: ›Man könnte z.B. – wie von mir schon früher für den stummen Film vorgeschlagen – alle Wände des Filmtheaters unter einem Kreuzfeuer von Filmen halten: »Simultankino«.‹ (Anm. d. Red.)

17 In den zwanziger Jahren hatte László Moholy-Nagy sein ›Theater der Totalität‹ entworfen als einen ›dynamisch-rhythmischen Gestaltungsvorgang, welcher die größten miteinander zusammenprallenden Massen (Häufung) von Mitteln – Spannungen von Qualität und Quantität – in elementarer Form zusammenfaßt‹. Dadurch lancierte er die ›Verwendung von komplizierten Apparaten, wie Film, Auto, Lift, Flugzeug und anderen Maschinen, auch optischen Instrumenten, Spiegelvorrichtungen usw.‹ – László Moholy-Nagy: ›Theater, Zirkus, Varieté.‹ – *Die Bühne im Bauhaus*, Oskar Schlemmer, László Moholy-Nagy, Farkas Molnár, Bauhausbücher 4, München 1925. Zitiert nach dem Faksimile-Nachdruck mit einem Nachwort von Walter Gropius, Mainz und Berlin, 1965, S. 52 und S. 54.

18 Vgl. Deke Dusinberre: ›On Expanding Cinema.‹ – *Studio International*, November/Dezember 1975.

19 Für die ersten Performances in Rotterdam wurde ein einzelner Projektor in ca. 30 m Entfernung von der Kuppel plaziert. In der Amsterdamer Version wurden zwei 16 mm Filmprojektoren und ein Diaprojektor an drei verschiedenen Punkten um die Kuppel herum positioniert. Vgl. Theo Botschujiver, Sean Wel-

tion of the headlights shining on it.

34 Hubert Damisch: *L'origine de la perspective,* Flammarion, Paris, 1993, p. 388.

35 Jurgis Baltrusaitis: *Anamorphoses ou magie artificielle des effets merveilleux,* Chadwyck-Healey, Cambridge, 1977, p. 4

36 See work description *Viewpoint,* p. 86.

37 BOOM: Binocular Omni-Orientation Monitor. 'This is referred to as a "head-coupled" display. The BOOM is a counterbalanced CRT-based stereoscopic viewing device which enables interactive, real-time viewpoint control in a 3-D environment generated by computer or camera.' Scott Fisher – *Revue Virtuelle,* No. 4, Centre Georges Pompidou, Paris, 1992.

38 Smithson: 'Pointless Vanishing Points.' – *The Writings of Robert Smithson,* Ed. Nancy Holt, NYU Press, New York, 1979, pp. 208–209.

39 Augmented reality' refers to the use of translucent glasses onto which information can be displayed, and therefore superimposed on direct vision of the environment.

40 Christian Metz: *The imaginary signifier,* Macmillian, London, 1990, p. 77.

41 On this subject, see the exhibition catalogue *Junggesellenmaschinen/Les Machines Célabataires,* Ed. Marc LeBot, Alfieri, Venice, 1976.

42 See work description *Disappearance,* p. 136–137.

43 In the first version, for example, moving to the right triggered a text by Marinetti, to the left a text by the Russian anarchist Nechaynev, straight ahead a live radio broadcast, rearward (psychologically) a text by R. D. Laing, and vertically toward a more spiritual level, to the top of the dome.

44 Christine Buci-Glucksman: *L'œil cartographique de l'art,* Éd. Galilée, Paris, 1996, p. 51.

45 See Bernard Comment: *Le XIXème siècle des panoramas,* Éd. Adam Biro, Paris, 1993.

46 Ibid, p. 46.

47 See Michel Frizot: 'Revoir le panorama ou les yeux ont aussi des pieds.' – *Cinémathèque,* No. 6, Autumn 1994, and Philippe Dubois: 'La question du panorama, entre photographie et cinéma.' – *Cinémathèque,* No. 4, Autumn 1993.

48 Notably Charles A. Close's Electric Cyclorama (1893), Thomas W. Barber's Electrorama (1898), and the Lumière brothers' Photorama (1899).

49 See work description *EVE,* p. 138.

50 The advantage of inflatable technology here is that it favours a spherical, transportable, and temporary architecture suited to constantly evolving installations.

51 This phenomenon partly resulted from economic crisis in the film industry, prompting it to seek new systems and outlets.

52 On this issue, see *L'influence du matériel technique sur la création artistique audiovisuelle,* research report, CRECA Research Center, Université de Paris I, 1985–1987.

53 Jeffrey Shaw: 'EVE – Extended Virtual Environment.' – *MultiMediale 3,* Ed. ZKM Karlsruhe, Heinrich Klotz, Karlsruhe, 1993, pp. 60–61.

54 Paul Virilio: *L'inertie polaire,* Éd. Christian Bourgois, Paris, 1990, p. 129.

55 Michel Foucault: *Surveiller et Punir,* Gallimard, Paris, 1975, p. 235. For security reasons, however, the MultiMediale 4 version of EVE incorporated one infrared camera within the dome, externally transmitting images of the observers inside.

56 Marcel Duchamp: *Notes Inframince/Infrathin 1–46,* ibid.

57 Gilles Deleuze: *L'image-Temps,* Éditions de Minuit, Paris, 1985, p. 93.

58 Paul Virilio: *La vitesse de libération,* Éd. Galilée, Paris, 1995, p. 23.

59 Jeffrey Shaw in fact adapted a flight simulator when presenting Tamas Waliczky's *The Forest* at Multimediale 3 (ZKM Karlsruhe, 1993).

60 See André Leroi-Gourhan: *Gesture and Speech,* MIT Press, Cambridge, 1993, especially chapter six.

61 Light Emitting Diode

62 'Something that seems like nothing can take the place of the something' or

lesley-Miller, Jeffrey Shaw: ›Structure gonflables et participation.‹ – *RHOBO,* Nr. 3, Frühjahr 1968.

20 Vgl. Werkbeschreibung *Corpocinema,* S. 69.

21 Der Belgier Etienne Gaspard Robert (1763–1837), der sich Robertson nannte, entwickelte um 1799 sein ›Phantascop‹ als eine auf einem Rädergestell montierte Laterna magica mit der er ›Geistervorstellungen‹ gab, die dem 125 Jahre später erfundenen Gruselfilm nicht unähnlich waren. Da er seinen Projektionsapparat mit Rädern ausgestattet hatte, konnte er seinen stets verdeckten Standpunkt auf der Bühne in rascher Folge wechseln, um seine ›Gespenster‹ auf Rauchschwaden oder Tüllvorhängen erscheinen zu lassen. (Anm. d. Red.)

22 Vgl. Werkbeschreibung *MovieMovie,* S. 70–73.

23 Gilles Deleuze: *Die Falte: Leibniz und der Barock.* Frankfurt a. M., 1995, S. 126f.

24 Marcel Duchamp: ›Note 11.‹ – *Notes Inframince/Infrathin 1–46,* Centre Georges Pompidou, Paris, 1980.

25 Jeffrey Shaw im Gespräch mit Ueno Toshiya: ›We are Materialists, We Employ Science and Technology to Concretize the Virtual.‹ – *Media Passage,* Hg. Inter-Communication Center, Tokyo, 1993, S. 53.

26 Allan Kaprow: *L'Art et la vie confondus,* Centre Georges Pompidou, Paris, 1996, S. 93.

27 Thierry de Duve: ›Performance ici et maintenant.‹ – *Alternatives théâtrales,* Nr. 6, 1981, S. 33.

28 Alfred Jarry: *Heldentaten und Ansichten des Doktor Faustroll, Pataphysiker,* Frankfurt a. M., 1987, S. 35f. Der Text entstand in den Jahren 1897–99.

29 Ebd., S. 35.

30 Nam June Paik und Shigeko Kubota: *Allan 'n' Allan's Complaint,* 1983, 28 Min., Farbe.

31 Jeffrey Shaw: ›Jeffrey Shaw on Jeffrey Shaw.‹ – *Media Passage,* a.a.O., S. 25.

32 Vgl. Anne-Marie Duguet: ›Dispositifs.‹ – *Communications,* No. 48, Videoausgabe, Paris, 1988.

33 Dasselbe Material wird auch für Straßenschilder verwendet, die Informationen nur in Richtung des auftreffenden Lichtstrahls reflektieren.

34 Hubert Damisch: *L'origine de la perspective,* Paris, 1993, S. 388.

35 Jurgis Baltrusaitis: *Anarmorphose ou magie artificielle des effets merveilleux,* Paris, 1969, S. 5.

36 Vgl. Werkbeschreibung *Viewpoint,* S. 86.

37 BOOM: Binocular Omni-Orientation Monitor. ›Man spricht von einem sogenannten »Head-Coupled-Display«. BOOM ist ein ausgeglichenes, auf CRT (Cathode-ray tube/Kathodenstrahlröhre) basierendes stereoskopisches Sichtgerät, das eine interaktive Steuerung des Standpunktes in Echtzeit innerhalb einer dreidimensionalen computer- oder kameragenerierten Umgebung ermöglicht.‹ Scott Fisher – *Revue Virtuelle,* Nr. 4, Centre Georges Pompidou, Paris, 1992.

38 Robert Smithson: ›Pointless Vanishing Points.‹ – *The Writings of Robert Smithson,* Hg. Nancy Holt, New York, 1979, S. 208 f.

39 ›Erweiterte Realität‹ bezieht sich hier auf die Benutzung lichtdurchlässiger Brillen, auf denen Informationen gezeigt werden können, die so die direkte Wahrnehmung der Umgebung überlagern.

40 Christian Metz: *Le Signifiant Imaginaire,* UGE 10/18, Paris, 1977, S. 105.

41 Zu diesem Thema vgl. den Ausstellungskatalog *Junggesellenmaschinen/Les Machines Célabataires,* Hg. Marc LeBot, Venedig, 1976.

42 Vgl. Werkbeschreibung *Disappearance,* S. 136 f.

43 In der ersten Version beispielsweise rief eine Bewegung nach rechts einen Text von Marinetti auf, nach links den Text des russischen Anarchisten Nechaynev, nach vorne eine Live-Radiosendung, nach hinten (psychologisch verstanden) einen Text von R. D. Laing. Bewegte man sich in der Vertikalen in Richtung Kuppelspitze, erreichte man eine spirituellere Ebene von Texten.

44 Christine Buci-Glucksman: *L'oeil cartographique de l'art,* Paris, 1996, S. 51.

45 Vgl. Bernard Comment: *Le XIXème siècle des panoramas,* Paris, 1993.

46 Ebd., S. 46.

47 Vgl. Michel Frizot: ›Revoir le panorama ou les yeux ont aussi des pieds.‹ – *Cinémathèque,* Nr. 6, Herbst 1994 und Philippe Dubois: ›La question du panorama, entre photographie et cinéma.‹ – *Cinémathèque,* Nr. 4, Herbst 1993.

48 Beispielsweise Charles A. Closes elektrisches Cyclorama (1893), Thomas W.

'Nothing can take the place of something that seems like nothing.'

63 Roland Barthes: *S/Z*, Éditions du Seuil, Paris, 1970, p. 11.

64 Roland Barthes: *Le Bruissement de la langue*, Essais critiques IV, Éditions du Seuil, Paris, 1984, p. 35.

65 Henri Michaux: *Emergences-Résurgences*, Albert Skira, Geneva, 1972, pp. 102–103.

66 Frances A. Yates: *The Art of Memory*, The University of Chicago Press, Chicago, 1966, p. 144.

67 Antonin Artaud: *Le théâtre et son double*, Éd. Gallimard, Paris, 1964, p. 105.

Barbers Electrorama (1898) oder das Photorama der Gebrüder Lumière (1899).

49 Vgl. Werkbeschreibung *EVE*, S. 138.

50 Der Vorteil der Tragluft-Technologie ist in diesem Falle, daß sich mit ihr kuppelförmige, transportable und temporäre Architekturen leicht realisieren lassen – ideal für Installationen, die ständig weiterentwickelt werden.

51 Zum Teil ist dieses Phänomen die Folge einer wirtschaftlichen Krise der Filmindustrie, die nun versuchte, neue Systeme und Absatzmöglichkeiten zu finden.

52 Vgl. *L'influence du matériel technique sur la création artistique audiovisuelle*, Forschungsbericht, CRECA Centre de Recherche, Université de Paris I, 1985–87.

53 Jeffrey Shaw: ›EVE – Extended Virtual Environment.‹ – *MultiMediale 3*, Hg. ZKM Karlsruhe, Heinrich Klotz, Karlsruhe, 1993, S. 60f.

54 Paul Virilio: *Rasender Stillstand*, München, Wien, 1992, S. 118.

55 Michel Foucault: *Überwachen und Strafen. Die Geburt des Gefängnisses*, Frankfurt a. M., 1994, S. 259. Aus Sicherheitsgründen war jedoch in der auf der MultiMediale 4 gezeigten Version eine Infrarotkamera im Innern der Kuppel angebracht, die Aufnahmen von den Besuchern im Innern nach draußen übertrug.

56 Marcel Duchamp: *Notes Inframince/Infrathin 1–46*, a.a.O.

57 Gilles Deleuze: *Das Zeit-Bild. Kino 2*, Frankfurt a. M., 1995, S. 95.

58 Paul Virilio: *Fluchtgeschwindigkeit*, München, Wien, 1996, S. 36.

59 Für die Präsentation von Tamás Waliczkys *The Forest* verwendete Jeffrey Shaw tatsächlich eine modifizierte Flugsimulationsplattform (MultiMediale 3, ZKM Karlsruhe, 1993).

60 Vgl. André Leroi-Gourhan: *Hand und Wort. Die Evolution von Technik, Sprache und Kunst*, Frankfurt a. M., 1984; insbes. Kap. VI., ›Sprachliche Symbole‹, S. 237–270.

61 Light Emitting Diode

62 ›Something that seems like nothing can take the place of something‹ (›Etwas, das nichts zu sein scheint, kann an die Stelle von etwas treten‹) oder ›Nothing can take the place of something that seems like nothing‹. (›Nichts kann an die Stelle von etwas treten, das nichts zu sein scheint.‹).

63 Unübersetzbares Wortspiel: die Worte für bis (to) und zwei (two) sind im Englischen homophon. (Anm.d.Übers.)

64 Roland Barthes: *S/Z*, Frankfurt a. M., 1976, S. 8.

65 Roland Barthes: *Le bruissement de la langue*, Essais critiques IV, Paris, 1984, S. 35.

66 Henri Michaux: *Emergences – Résurgences*, Genève, 1972, S. 102f.

67 Frances A. Yates: *Gedächtnis und Erinnern. Mnemonik von Aristoteles bis Shakespeare*, Weinheim, 1990, S. 133.

68 Antonin Artaud: *Das Theater und sein Double*, Frankfurt a. M., 1969, S. 74f.

Objects, Events and Installations

With Descriptions by Jeffrey Shaw

Objekte, Events und Installationen

Mit Werkbeschreibungen von Jeffrey Shaw

Aus dem Englischen von Manuela Abel und Astrid Sommer

Continuous Sound and Image Moments 1966

Continuous Sound and Image Moments is a hand-drawn black-and-white animated film loop . Conceived as a cinematic expansion of pictorial means, the process of making thousands of drawings (rather than any individual picture) is the subject of the aesthetic experience. Each image is shown for only a few frames, constituting momentary retinal impressions that assimilate in time into an insubstantial yet coherent multiformity. The film was later used in many events/performances and situations/installations such as *Emergences of Continuous Forms* (1966), *This is No Thing – This is a Situation of Opportunity* (1967), *Glove Screen* (1967), *Corpocinema* (1967) and *MovieMovie* (1967).

.SYNCPSIS OF FIIM PROJECT .... T.VAN.TIJEN. J.SHAW. W.BREUKER.

Towards a new dynamic of Sound and Image as a Space/Time experience.

I.The film presents itself as a FLUX of sound and image moments during which the observer experiences a growing perception of the underlying forms.

The term "moments" refers to the character of the sound and image time intervals which are relatively short. The film explores the boundaries of audio/visual perception and comprehension in time. This involves the expressive exploitation of the very short time intervals possible on film down to one frame or 0.04sec for an image moment. Seen on such a time scale, the images are percieved subliminally and only in the experiece of the film as a continuous repetition will the identity and sequence of the images become more or less fully realized.

Thus the inner forms of the film will grow within the observer as a time experience — the appearance, perception of order from fleeting sound and image moments (i.e. from an audio/visual flux).

The simultaneous showing of the film, in a loop, on four screens will accelerate and intensify this process of perception by exercising more forcefully the observer's capacities of comprehension, i.e. memory, association, feeling, etc.

2.Moments and continuous repetition are the means of effecting an expression of he multiplicity of sound and image ideas, and the essential continuity of the process of creation.

The film was concieved from the need to explore a graphic idea throughout the infinite possibilities of its forms. To approximate its unending capacity for developement, extention, growth, disintergration,contra-statement, dialogue, etc And to expand this capacity even further through a co-exploration by two makers.

It is a response to the inadequacy of the drawing as such which contains in its unity of oneness, an implicit relationship to absolute ideas and a determined universe. The continuous series, by its a-Platonic multiplicity and documentation of change and the relativity of one among many, becomes a far more significant vehicle of expression than the single work as such.

The film as a continuous series of sound and image moments, is an expression of BECOMING, an approximation of the human condition of eternal change, infinite shades of forms and fleeting identities. It seeks to excite the perceptive process for indeterminate form within the total flux.

3.The spatial multiplicity of this film goes beyond the known dynamic of I.film/audience 2.artwork/observer 3.music/audience. The free movement of the audience through the fourfold spatial complex of sound and image emphasises again the essential continuity of this film experience. The four sound and image sources will function simultaneously but will not be synchronized. The resultant indèterminate image/image, sound/sound associations will effect the spatial expression of flux and multiplicity already contained in the film as a time experience. In that the observer will himself propose the beginning of the five minute continuous repetition when entering the space of the showing, the resultant subjectivity of form in this film will echo the subjectivity of all orderings of experience.

Form will be dependant on the participation of the observer, beginning with his act of entering and then through the working of his capacities of perception and comprehension.

4.Each image contains an implicit idea of its continuity beyond the given frame. The showing of these images on four screens will emphasise this by appearing as four areas of limited materialization of an implicit unlimited spatial continuity of the image forms. Activities outside the film project itself such as street drawing, tatooing, distribution of stickers etc.will affirm again the character and capacity of these forms as a world spatial continuity. The forms themselves become generative organisms.

5.This film partakes of a general program for DISILLUSION. Disillusion as applied to film involves the disolution of its conventional theatric experience as a phantasy window. The spatial and visual character of this film will act to confront the observer with art-presence and personal-presence as equal immediacys,

Continuous Sound and Image Moments

Kontinuierliche Ton- und Bildmomente 1966

Continuous Sound and Image Moments ist eine Endlosfilmschleife animierter Handzeichnungen in schwarzweiß. Konzipiert als filmische Erweiterung bildlicher Mittel, stellt der Prozeß des Zeichnens von tausenden von Bildern (mehr als jedes individuelle Bild) das Subjekt ästhetischer Erfahrung dar. Im Film ist jedes Bild nur für einen kurzen Moment zu sehen – flüchtig wahrgenommene Impressionen verbinden sich in der Zeit zu einer zwar immateriellen, aber dennoch kohärenten Vielgestaltigkeit. Der Film wurde später in vielen Events/Performances und Situationen/Installationen eingesetzt; so z.B. in *Emergences of Continuous Forms* (›Das Entstehen kontinuierlicher Formen‹, 1966), *This is No Thing – This is a Situation of Opportunity* (›Dies ist kein Ding – Dies ist eine mögliche Situation‹, 1967), *Glove Screen* (›Leinwand aus Handschuhen‹, 1967), *Corpocinema* (›Körperkino‹, 1967) und *MovieMovie* (1967).

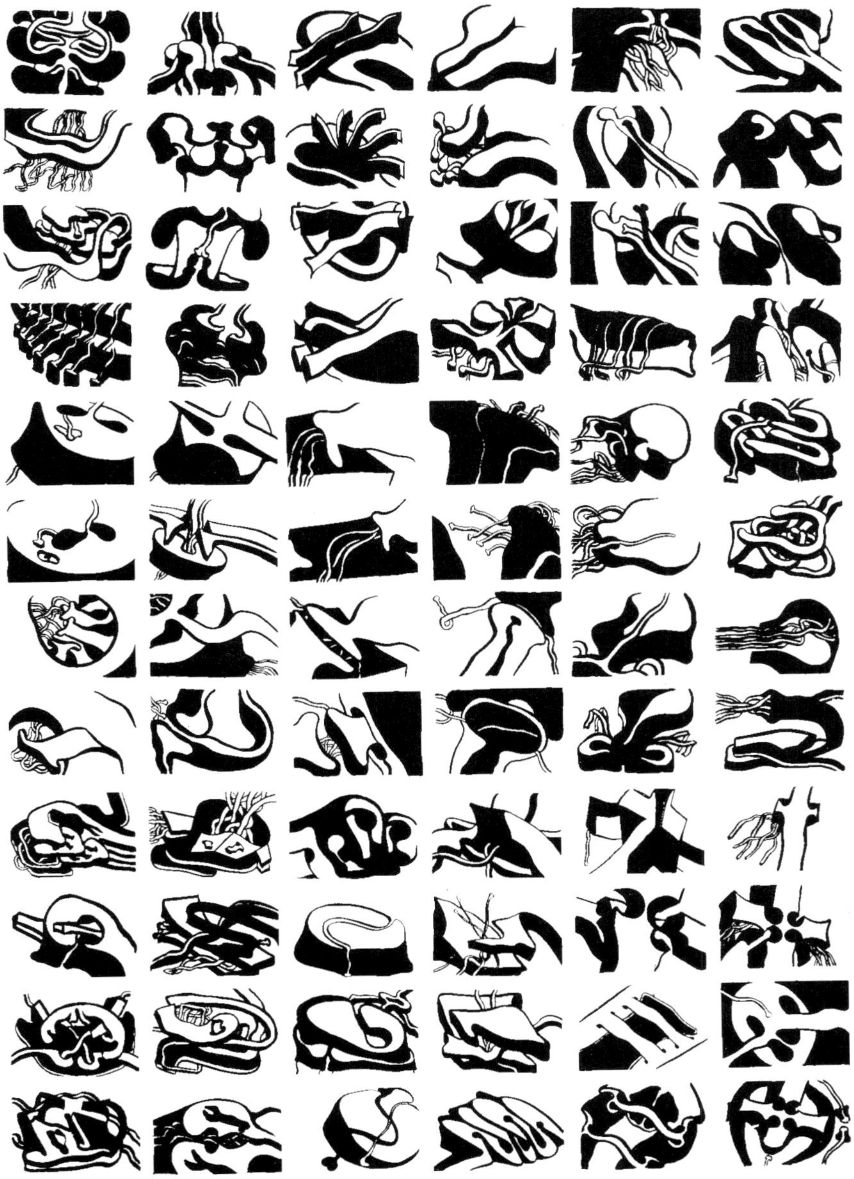

Emergences of Continuous Forms 1966

Emergences of Continuous Forms (Better Books, London, UK, 1966) was one of a series of performances and installations in this period which explored various methods of extending the cinematic image into the space of the viewers and of provoking the viewer's physical interactivity in the cinematic experience. Multiple semi-transparent projection screens were hung in two rows over the length of the gallery producing a spatial materialization of the film images. One of these screens had a transparent compartment filled with white balloons. Tubes coming out of the screen allowed the public to inflate these balloons and so control the shape of the projection surface. Smoke was also used to create another three-dimensional medium for the projected image as it passed from one screen surface to another.

This installation extended out into the streets of London with a procession of costumed performers and musicians.

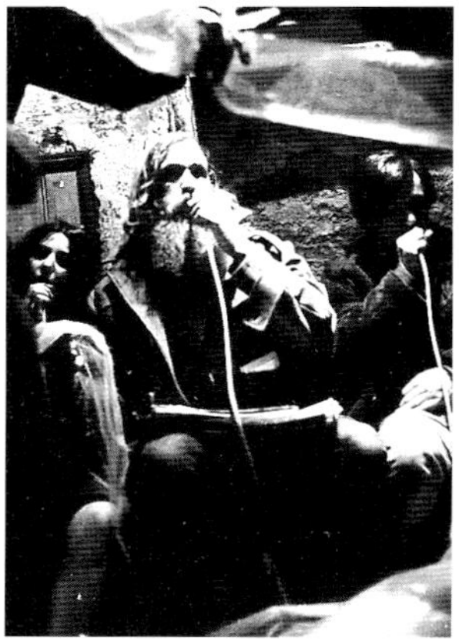

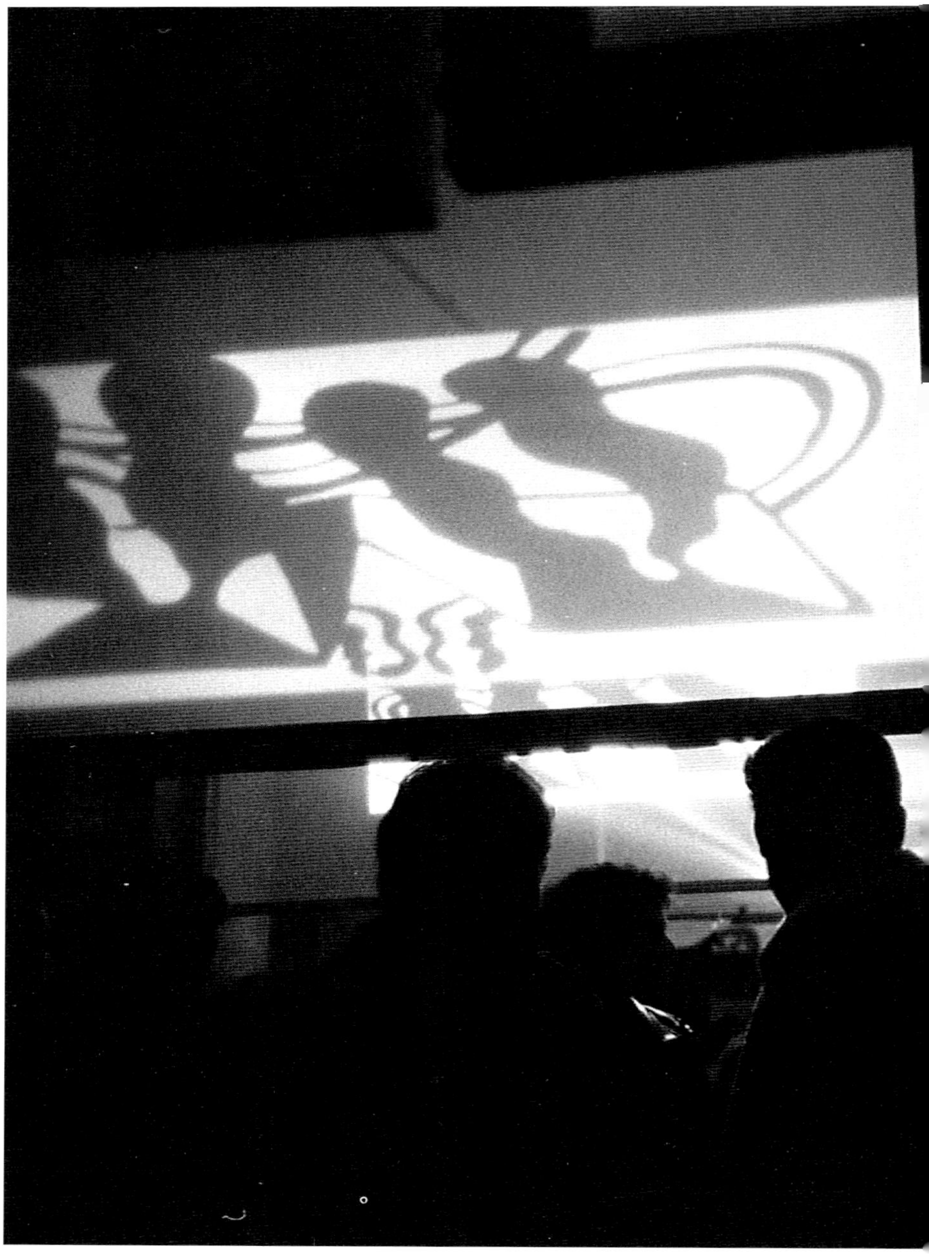

Emergences of Continuous Forms

Das Entstehen kontinuierlicher Formen 1966

Emergences of Continuous Forms (Better Books, London, UK, 1966) gehörte zu einer Reihe von Performances und Installationen jener Zeit, in denen verschiedene Methoden entwickelt wurden, um das filmische Bild in den Zuschauerraum hinein zu erweitern und die physische Interaktion des Betrachters während des Filmerlebnisses zu provozieren. Mehrere semitransparente Projektionsleinwände hingen in zwei Reihen über die ganze Länge der Galerie, so daß es zu einer ›räumlichen Materialisation‹ der Filmbilder kam. Eine Leinwand hatte ein transparentes Innenfach, in dem weiße Ballons hingen. Mit Schläuchen, die aus der Leinwand kamen, konnte das Publikum die Ballons aufblasen und so die Form der Projektionsfläche bestimmen. Außerdem wurde Rauch eingesetzt, um dem projizierten Bild, das von einer Leinwand zur nächsten wanderte, ein weiteres dreidimensionales Medium zu bieten.

Diese Installation dehnte sich mit einem Umzug kostümierter Performer und Musiker in die Straßen Londons aus.

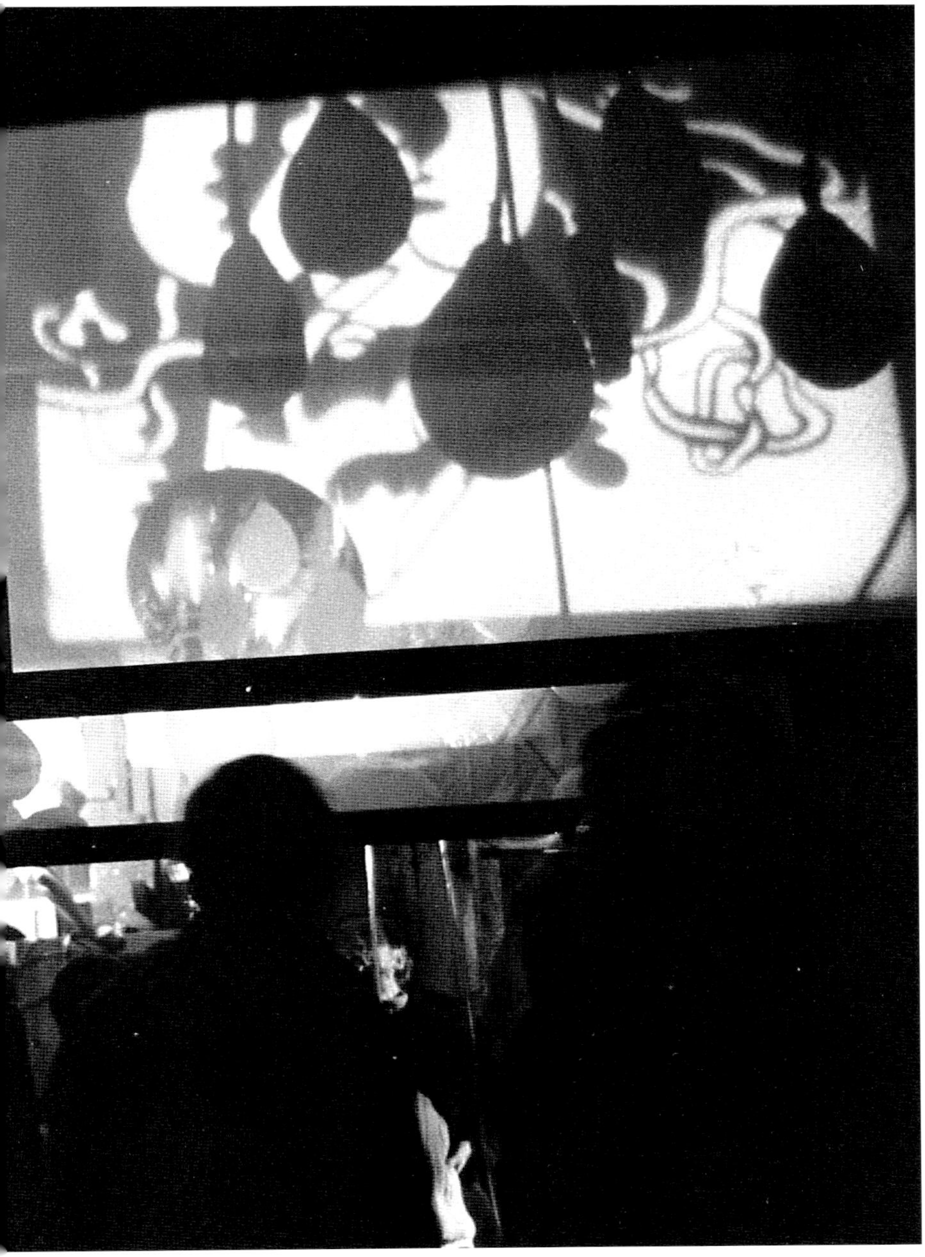

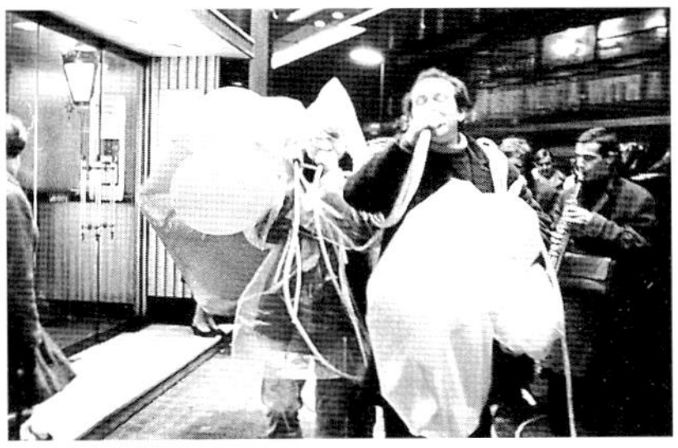

Disillusionary Events and Situations
1966–69

Many 'disillusionary' events were performed in clubs and venues in London (Better Books, Middle Earth, UFO, Roundhouse, Alexandra Palace), Paris and The Hague, often in conjunction with musical performances by groups such as Soft Machine. These happenings were expanded cinema events that incorporated live performance, various material actions, pyrotechnics, inflatable structures and often direct audience participation.

In *Disillusion of a Fish Pond* (26 Kingly Street Gallery, London, UK, 1967) a naked woman swathed in bandages of cotton-wool was sitting at the edge of a large indoor fish-pond. Her feet were embedded in thick yellow gelatine which filled the pond. The film *Continuous Sound and Image Moments* (1966) was projected down onto the surface of the jelly. Polythene tubing laid on under the jelly was slowly inflated with air and smoke, causing the jelly to lift

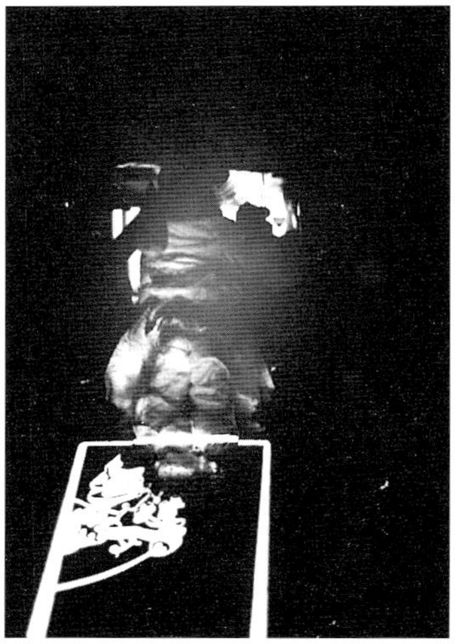

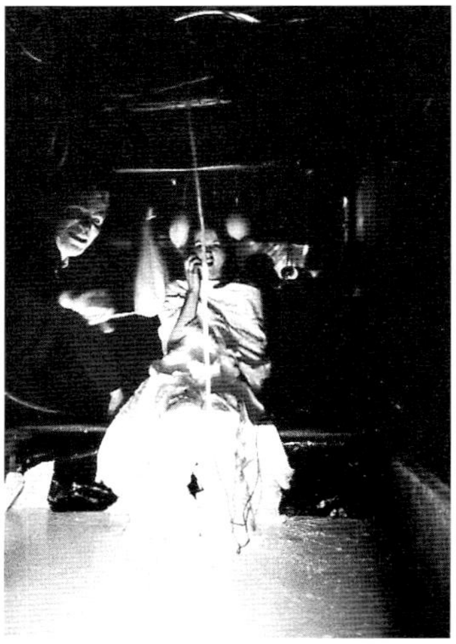

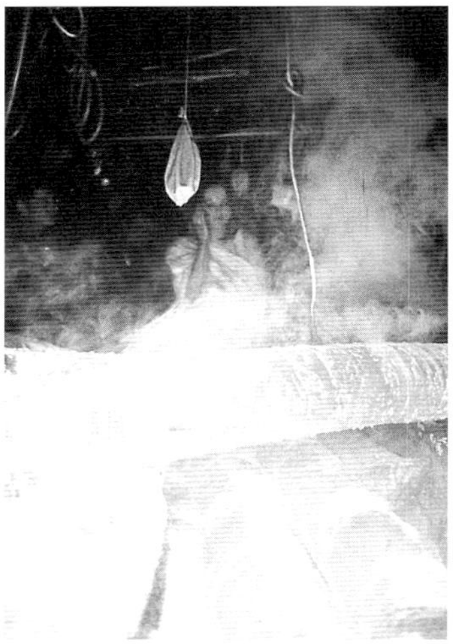

Desillusionierende Events und Situationen 1966–69

Viele ›desillusionierende‹ Events wurden in Clubs und an anderen Orten in London (Better Books, Middle Earth, UFO, Roundhouse, Alexandra Palace), Paris und Den Haag präsentiert, oftmals in Verbindung mit Konzerten von Musikgruppen wie beispielsweise Soft Machine. Diese Happenings waren ›Expanded-Cinema-Events‹, die Live-Performances, Aktionen mit verschiedenen Materialien, Feuerwerke, aufblasbare Strukturen und zumeist die direkte Partizipation des Publikums integrierten.

In *Disillusion of a Fish Pond* (›Desillusionierung eines Fischteiches‹, 26 Kingly Street Gallery, London, UK, 1967) saß eine nackte Frau, deren Körper in Watte gepackt war, am Rand eines großen Fischteiches, der sich in den Räumen der Galerie befand. Ihre Füße waren in dickflüssige gelbe Gelatine getaucht, die den Teich füllte. Der Film *Continuous Sound and Image Moments* (1966) wurde auf die Oberfläche dieser gallertartigen Masse projiziert. Auf dem Grund des Teiches liegende Plastikschläuche wurden langsam mit Luft und Rauch aufgeblasen, so daß die

and crack open. A masked figure burst white balloons that splashed bright yellow liquid over the seated woman. The tubing continued to inflate up out of the pond, pushing itself into the audience, who then dragged the jelly-covered plastic all around the room. When punctured by rough handling, the tubing released jets of white smoke that in turn created another medium for the on-going film projection.

Other 'disillusionary' works exploited materials like fireworks, gases, smoke, air, confetti etc. to create immaterial sculptural situations. At the Sigma 5 festival a room was densely filled with confetti continuously circulated by large blowers (*Wind and Rain*, Bordeaux, France, 1969). In *Smokescreen* (Swansea Art Festival, Wales, 1969) a row of smoke canisters along the front side of Swansea University created a thick smoke-screen behind which the building completely disappeared.

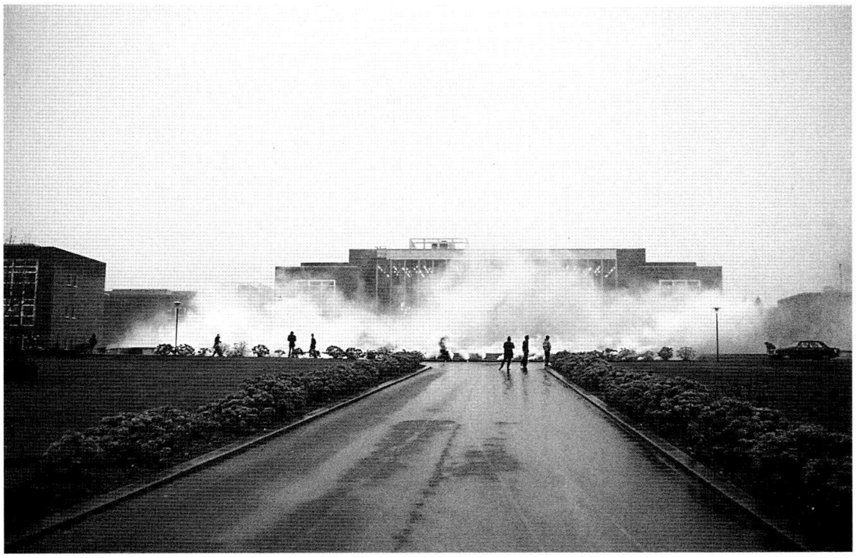

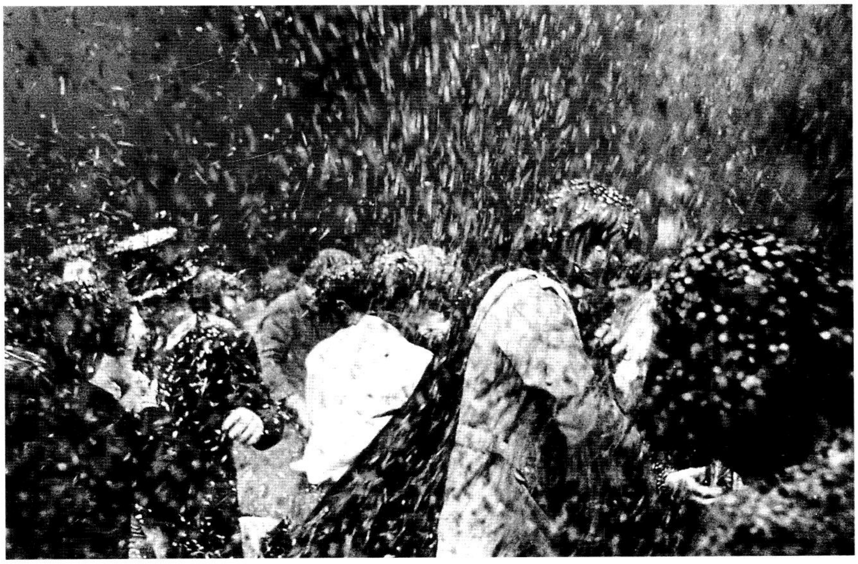

gallertartige Masse allmählich angehoben wurde und aufbrach. Eine maskierte Gestalt brachte weiße Ballons zum Platzen, aus denen sich eine helle gelbe Flüssigkeit über die sitzende Frau ergoß. Währenddessen wurden die Schläuche weiter aufgeblasen, schoben sich aus dem Teich und zwischen die Zuschauer, die das mit Gallert überzogene Plastik durch den ganzen Raum zogen. Wurden die Schläuche zu grob angefaßt, platzten sie und setzten weiße Rauchschwaden frei, die wiederum ein neues Medium für die fortlaufende Filmprojektion bildeten.

Andere ›desillusionierende‹ Arbeiten nutzten Materialien wie Feuerwerkskörper, Gas, Rauch, Luft, Konfetti etc., um immaterielle skulpturale Bedingungen zu schaffen. Während des Festivals Sigma 5 wurde ein Raum mit Konfetti gefüllt, das mit Hilfe von zwei großen Ventilatoren ständig im Raum zirkulierte (*Wind and Rain* (›Wind und Regen‹), Bordeaux, Frankreich, 1969). In *Smokescreen* (›Rauchwand‹, Swansea Art Festival, Wales, 1969) wurden entlang der Vorderseite der Swansea Universität mit Rauch gefüllte Kanister aufgestellt, so daß eine dichte Rauchwand entstand, hinter der das Gebäude verschwand.

Corpocinema 1967

Corpocinema was an expanded cinema environment presented in a series of open-air performances in Rotterdam and Amsterdam in 1967. The basic structure was a large air-inflated transparent PVC dome onto which film and slides were projected from outside.

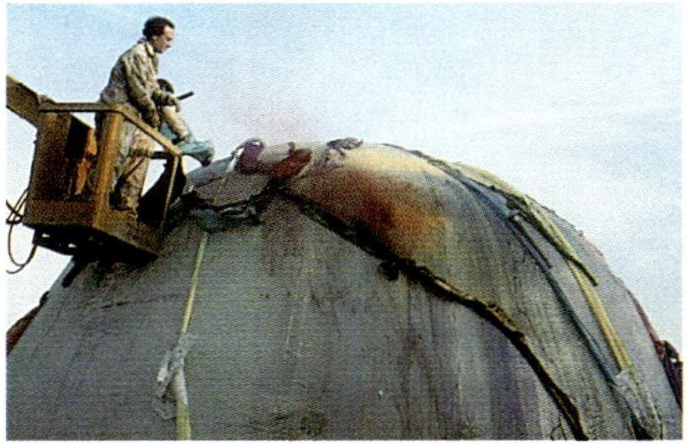

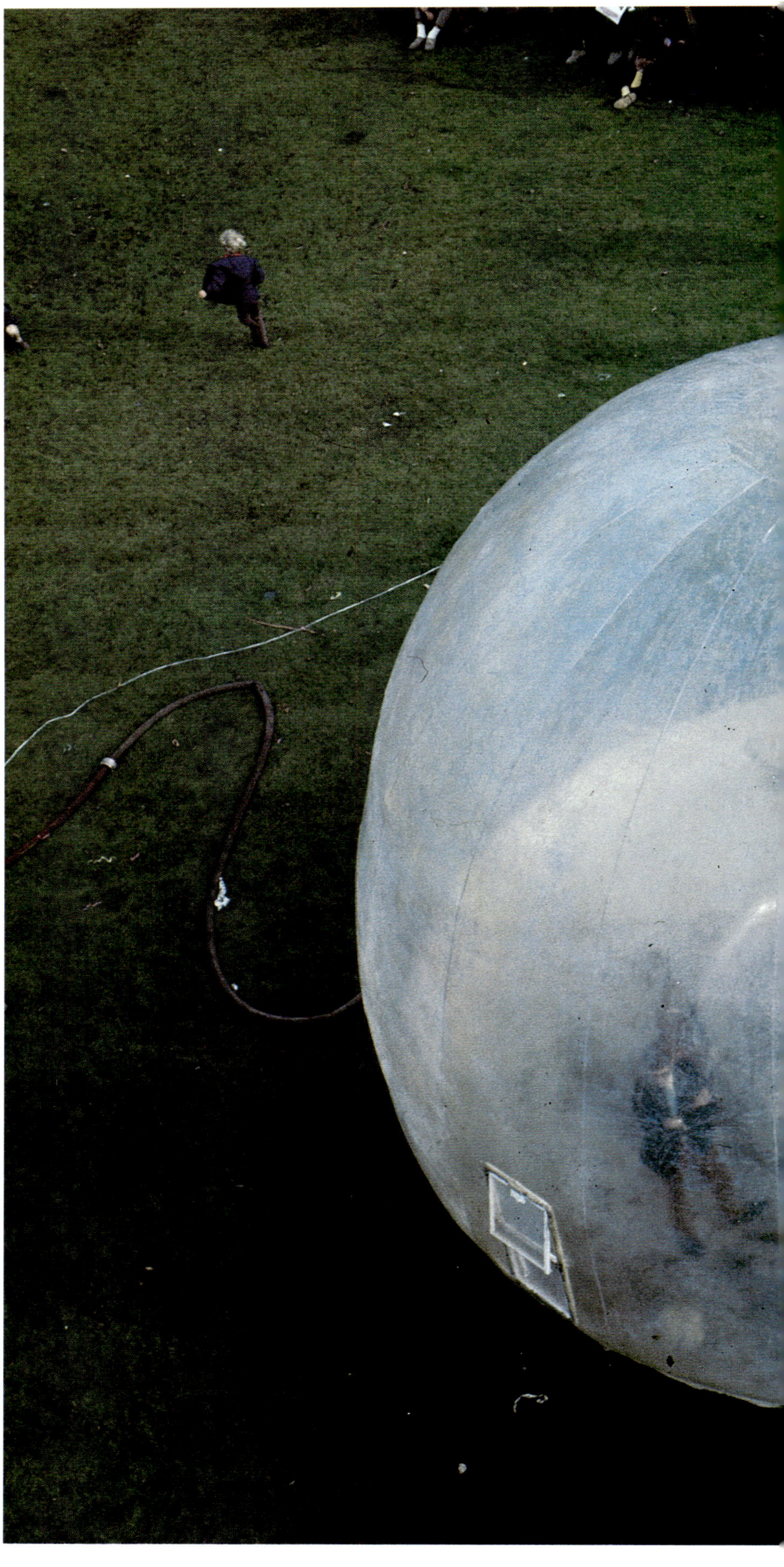

Corpocinema Körperkino 1967

Corpocinema war ein ›Expanded-Cinema-Environment‹, das 1967 in einer Reihe von Open-Air-Veranstaltungen in Rotterdam und Amsterdam präsentiert wurde. Die Grundstruktur bestand aus einer großen, luftgetragenen, transparenten PVC-Kuppel, auf die von außen Filme und Dias projiziert wurden. Im Rah-

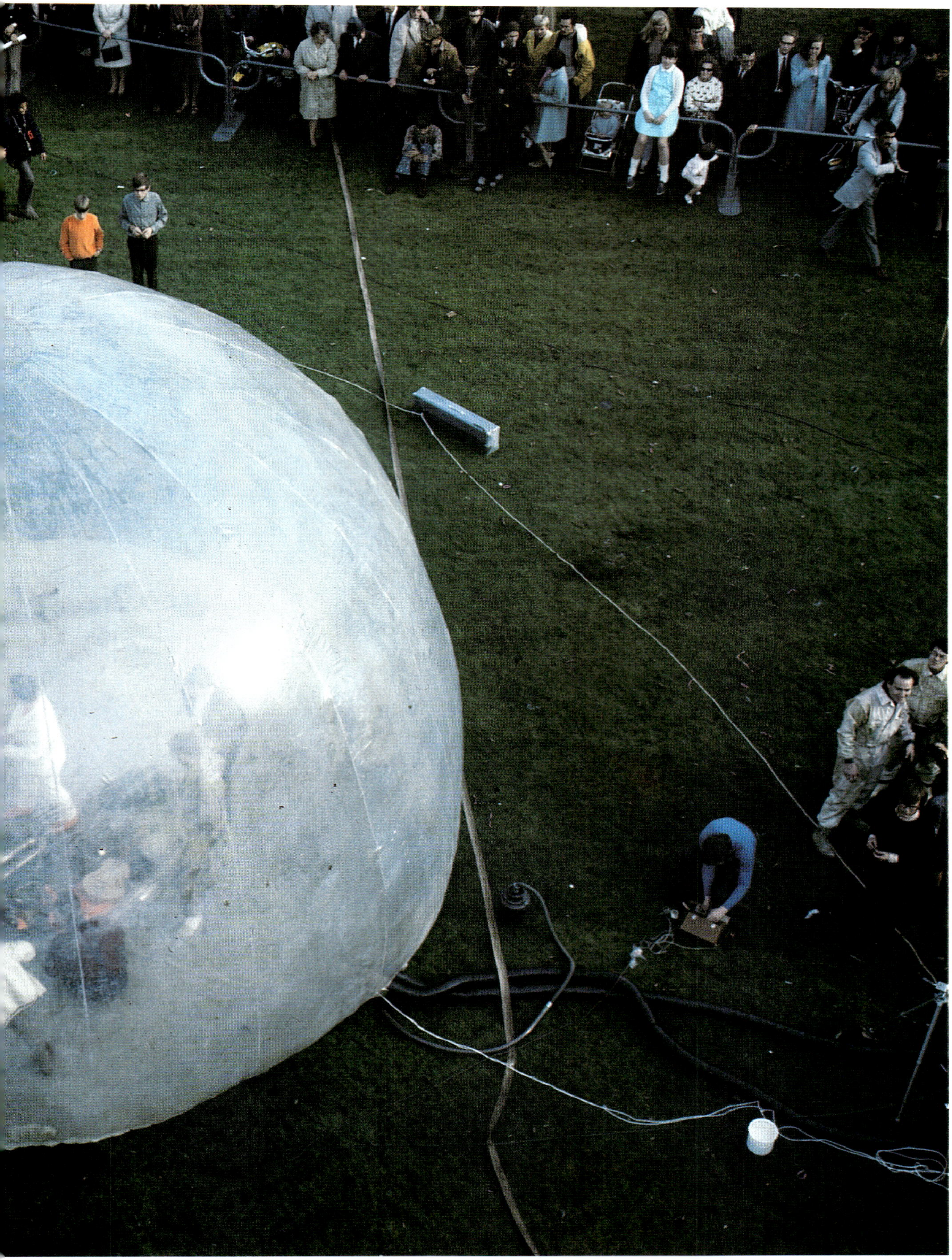

These projections were made visible by physical events and performed actions that created temporary conditions materializing the projected imagery within and on the surface of the dome.
Corpocinema dematerialized the opaque flat projection surface of traditional cinema by creating instead a transparent three-dimensional volume within which the cinematic image could be reconstituted in an equivocal and immediate way. The specific physical and temporal qualities of the various actions and events performed to materialize the projected images also caused dramatic transformations and reconstructions of those images. For example, white polythene tubing was inflated until it filled the interior of the dome, thus creating a complex, growing surface on which the image appeared, and then the dome was deflated over this tubing. Fire-extinguishing foam was sprayed over the entire inner surface of the dome, building up an opaque white projection surface. As the foam dripped off the dome, the projected image disintegrated. Various other sub-

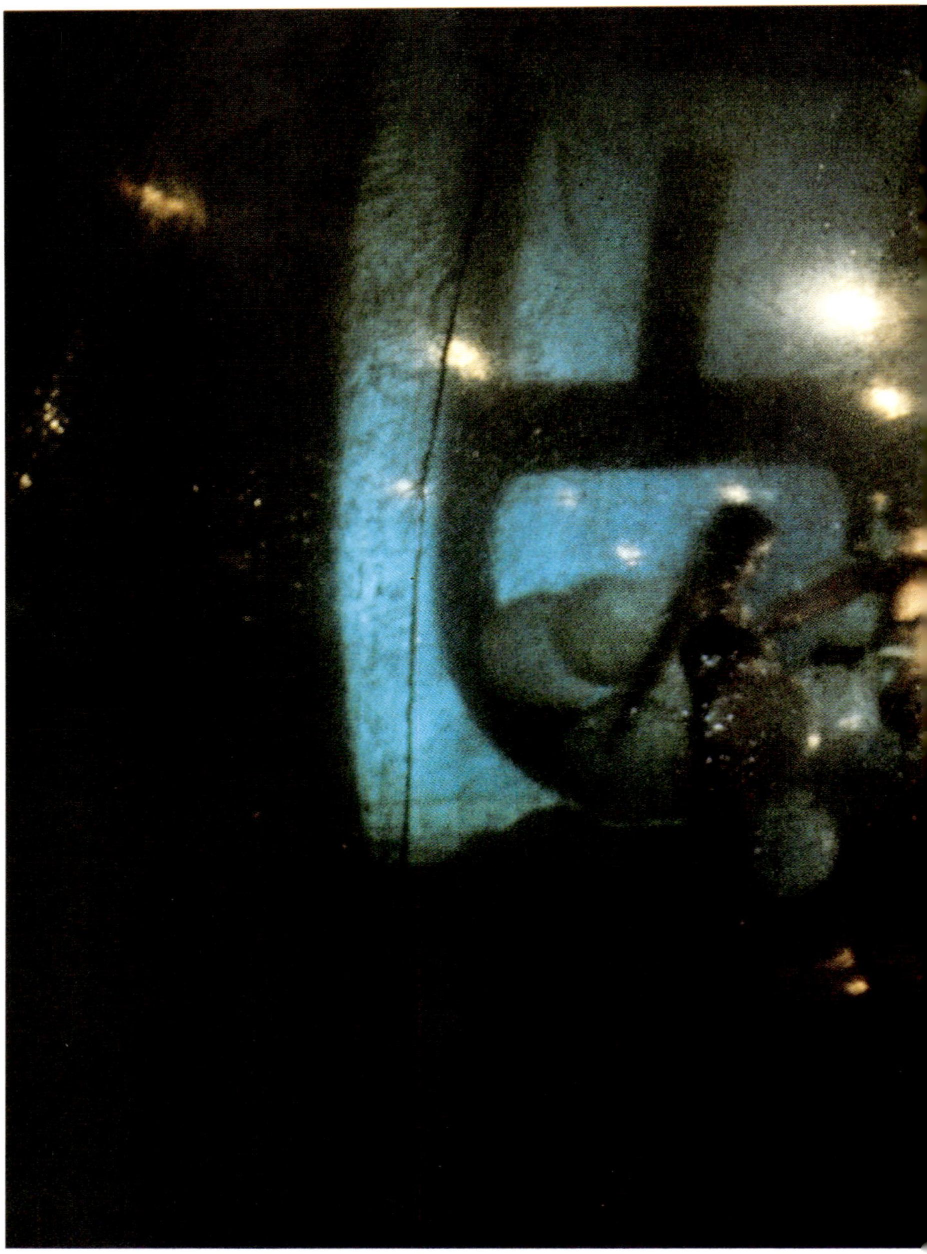

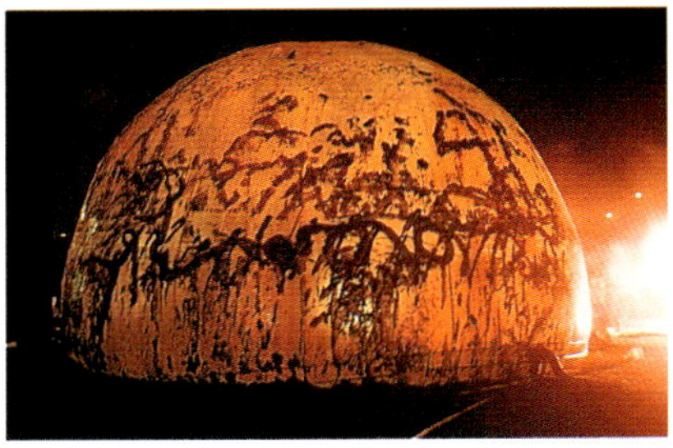

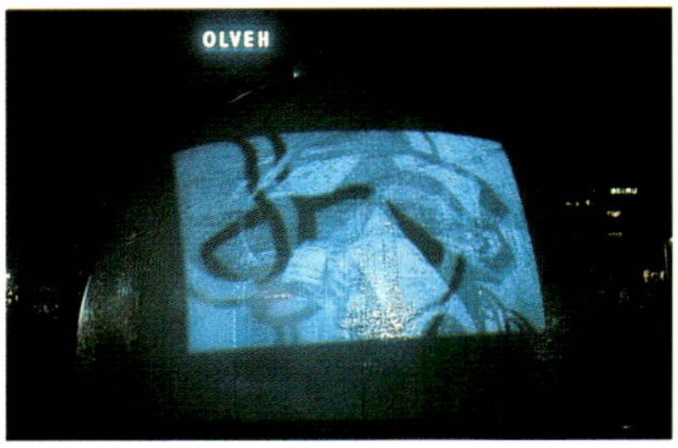

men von Events und Performance-Aktionen wurden vorübergehend Bedingungen geschaffen, die das projizierte Bild in und auf der Kuppel sichtbar werden ließen.

Corpocinema dematerialisierte die undurchsichtige, flache Projektionsfläche des traditionellen Kinos, indem es stattdessen einen transparenten dreidimensionalen Raum schuf, in dem sich das filmische Bild in unbestimmter und unmittelbarer Weise neu konstituieren konnte. Die speziellen physischen und zeitlichen Eigenschaften der verschiedenen Aktionen und Events, die vorgenommen wurden, um die projizierten Bilder sichtbar zu machen, verursachten auch dramatische Veränderungen und Rekonstruktionen dieser Bilder. Beispielsweise wurden weiße Plastikschläuche aufgeblasen, bis sie das Innere der Kuppel völlig ausfüllten und so eine komplexe, wachsende Oberfläche für das projizierte Bild bildeten – dann wurde die Kuppel über den Schläuchen abgelassen. Mit Feuerlöschern wurde Schaum auf die gesamte Innenhaut der Kuppel gesprüht, wodurch eine undurchsichtige weiße Projektionsfläche entstand – sobald der Schaum von der Kuppel abtropfte, löste sich auch das projizierte Bild auf. Eine Vielzahl ande-

stances such as smoke, steam, water spray and confetti were used to fill the interior space of the dome and so constitute a volume of particles on which the projected images were attenuated. Fireworks let off inside the dome created lighting, colour and smoke effects that transformed the projected images. A crane was used to allow performers to spray coloured powders and throw liquid paints and crepe paper over the dome surface, creating an impastoed screen surface. Live performers and musicians were also coactive in the space and discourse of the filmic projections.

Some of the films used in the *Corpocinema* were: *Continuous Sound and Image Moments, Vrig en Onverveerd* (a documentary about the wartime occupation of Holland), *Wasmiddelen Van Nu* (a documentary history of washing powder), *In De Schaduw Van De Mens* (a film about rats), *Duel In Fiet Luchtruim* (a documentary about aircraft dogfights), *De Morgenster* (a film about tramps scavenging through the streets of Amsterdam).

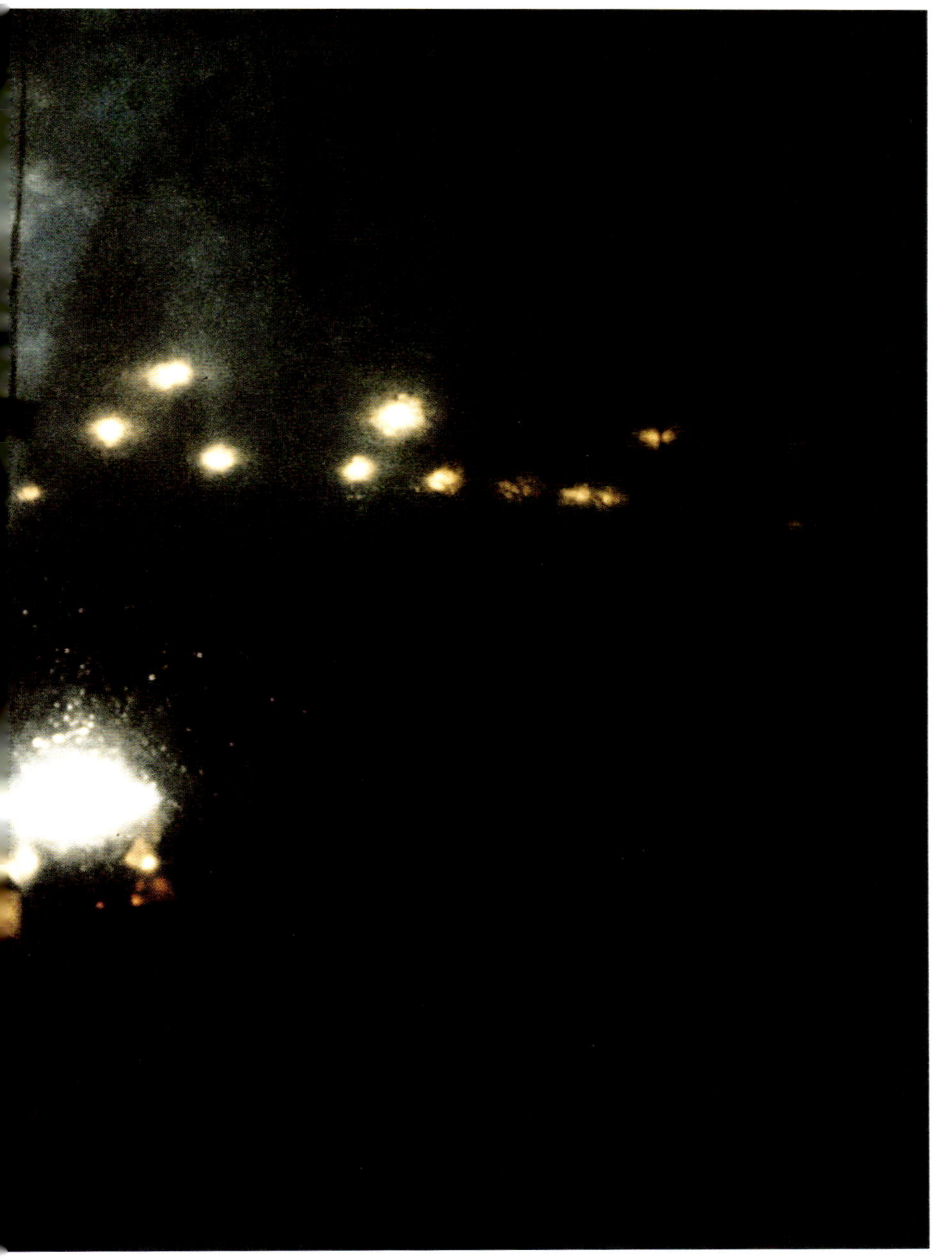

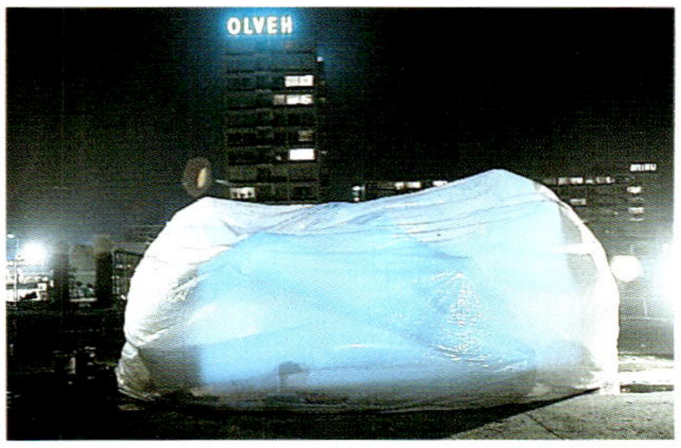

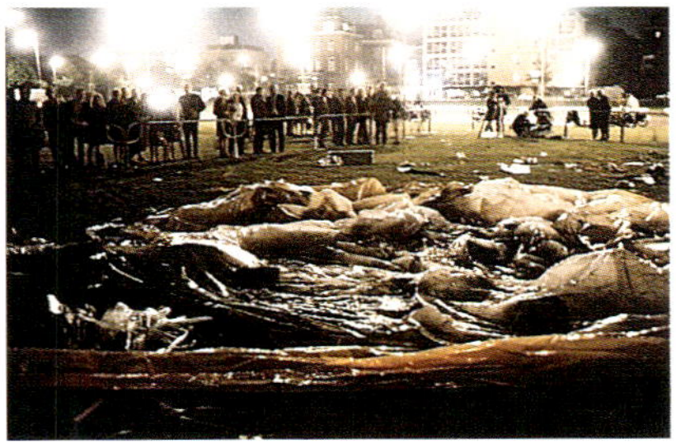

rer Substanzen wie Rauch, Dampf, Wasserspray und Konfetti wurden eingesetzt, um den Innenraum der Kuppel zu füllen und so ein Volumen aus Teilchen zu erzeugen, auf dem sich die projizierten Bilder materialisieren konnten. Feuerwerke im Innern der Kuppel schufen Licht-, Farb- und Raucheffekte, die die projizierten Bilder transformierten. Mit Hilfe eines Krans konnten die Performer Farbpuder über die Außenhaut der Kuppel stäuben und flüssige Farbe und Krepppapier darüber werfen, so daß eine pastellierte Projektionsfläche entstand. Live-Performer und -Musiker ko-agierten ebenfalls im Raum und im Diskurs der Filmprojektionen.

Zu den Filmen, die in *Corpocinema* gezeigt wurden, gehörten: *Continuous Sound and Image Moments, Vrig en Onverveerd* (ein Dokumentarfilm über die Besetzung der Niederlande während des Krieges), *Wasmiddelen Van Nu* (eine Dokumentation über die Geschichte des Waschpulvers), *In De Schaduw Van De Mens* (ein Film über Ratten), *Duel In Fiet Luchtruim* (eine Dokumentation über Luftkämpfe), *De Morgenster* (ein Film über Obdachlose, die in den Straßen von Amsterdam nach Nahrung suchen).

MovieMovie 1967

This expanded cinema performance was specially created for the Experimental Film Festival in Knokke-le-Zoute (Belgium, 1967). It took place in the foyer of the festival building, with the audience sitting on the stairs and balcony. Three performers (Jeffrey Shaw, Theo Botschuijver, and Sean Wellesley-Miller) dressed in white overalls first brought in the inflatable structure and unrolled it on the floor. Then it was gradually inflated while film, slides and liquid-light show effects were projected onto its surface. The architectural form of this inflatable structure was a

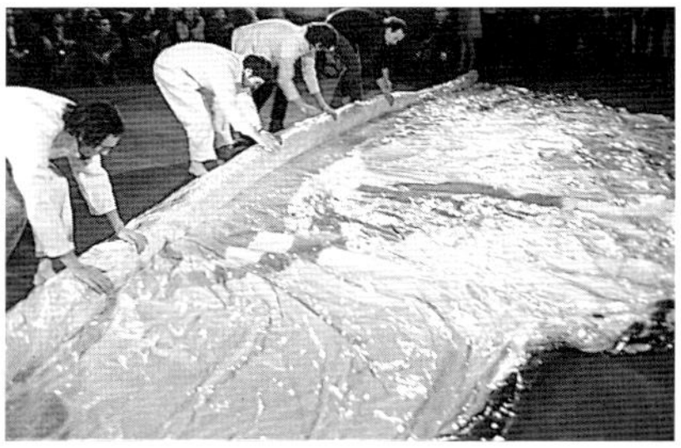

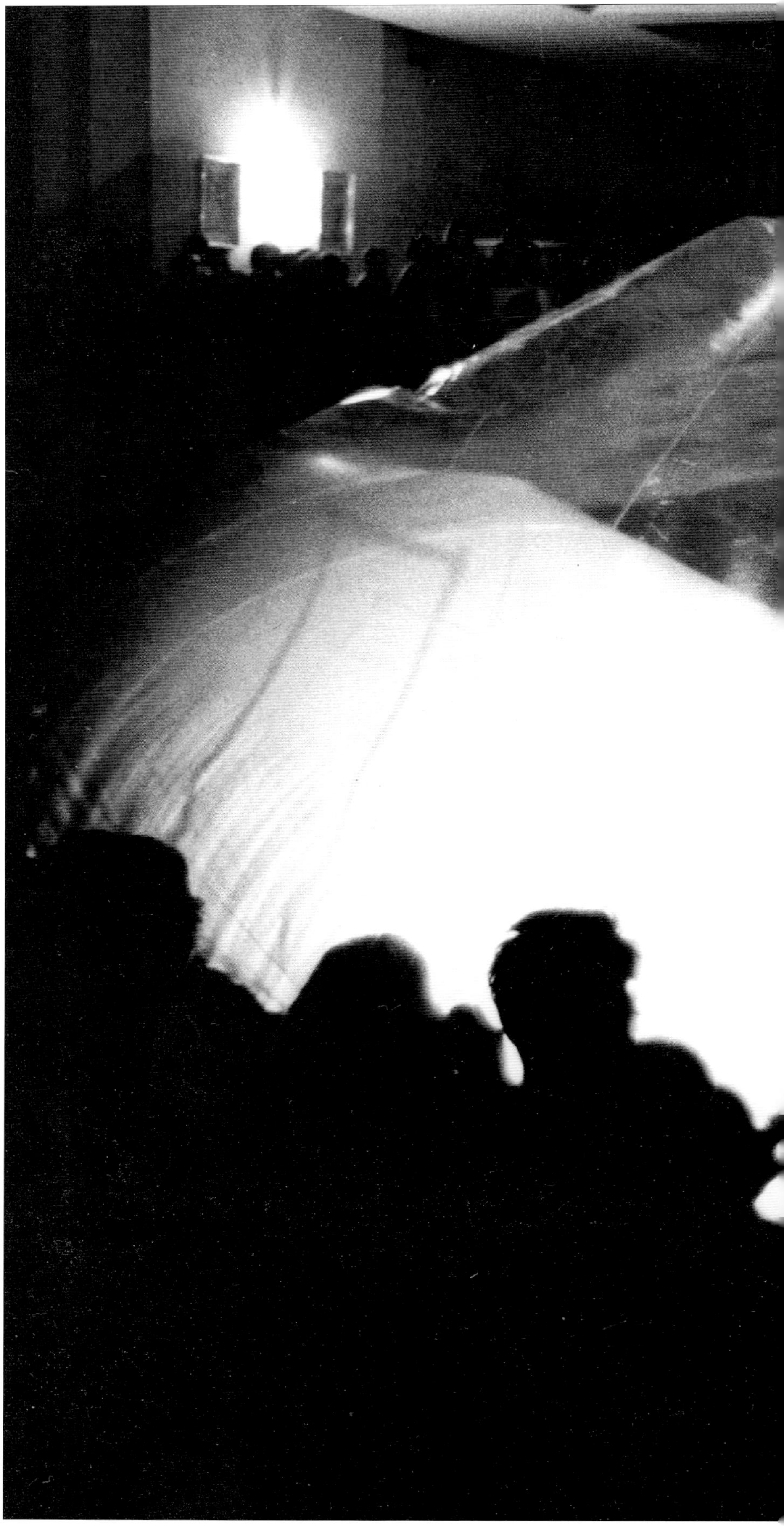

MovieMovie 1967

Diese ›Expanded-Cinema-Performance‹ wurde für das Experimentalfilmfestival in Knokke-le-Zoute (Belgien, 1967) entwickelt und fand im Foyer des Festivalgebäudes statt, wo das Publikum auf den Treppen und dem Balkon saß. Drei Performer in weißen Overalls – Jeffrey Shaw, Theo Botschuijver und Sean Wellesley-Miller – brachten zunächst die aufblasbare Struktur herein und rollten sie auf dem Boden aus. Danach wurde sie langsam aufgeblasen und gleichzeitig wurden Filme, Dias und ineinanderfließende Bild- und Lichteffekte auf ihre Oberfläche projiziert. Die aufge-

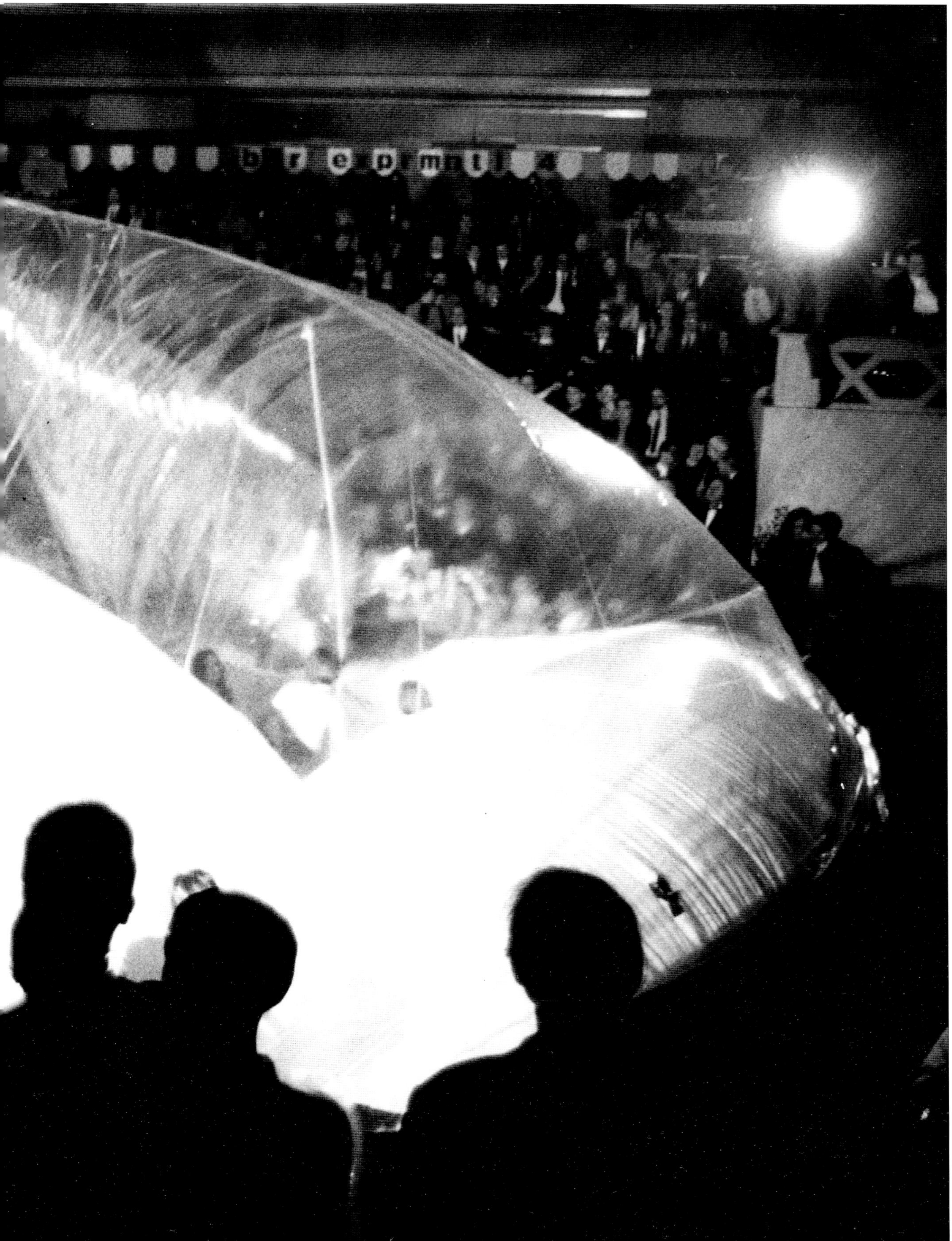

cone with an outer transparent membrane and an inner white surface. The projected imagery first impinged lightly on the tightly inflated outer envelope and then appeared on the semi-inflated inner surface. In the intermediate space between the transparent and white membranes various material actions were performed to materialize the projected images. This included the inflation of white balloons and tubes, and the injection of smoke.

The intention of this work was to transform the conventional flat cinema projection screen into a three-dimensional kinetic and architetonic space of visualization. The multiple projection surfaces allowed the images to materialize in many layers, and the bodies of the performers and then of the audience (many of whom spontaneously jumped in naked) became part of the cinematic spectacle. In this way the immersive space of cinematic fiction included the literal and interactive immersion of the viewers who, modulating the changing shapes of the pneumatic architecture, brought about shifting

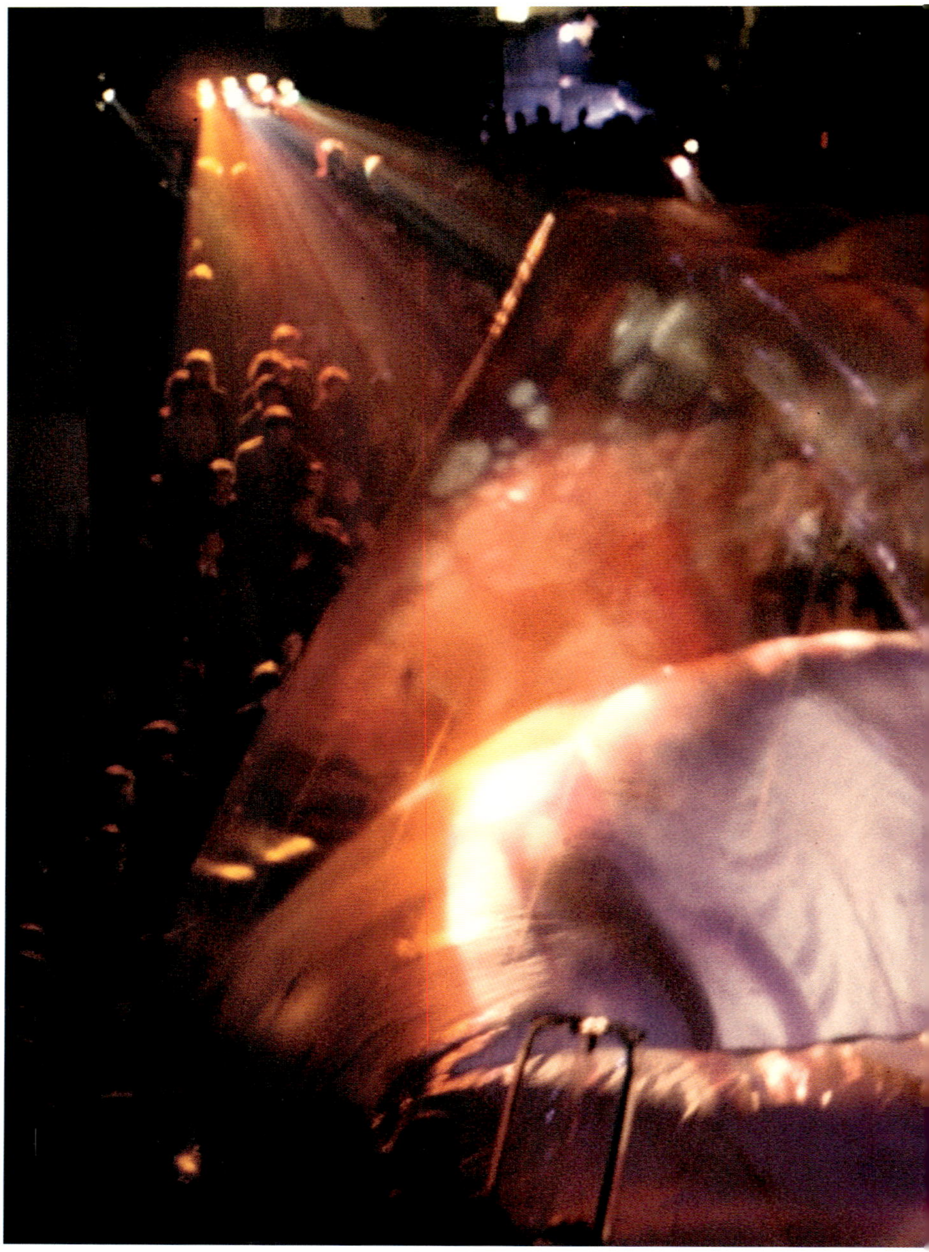

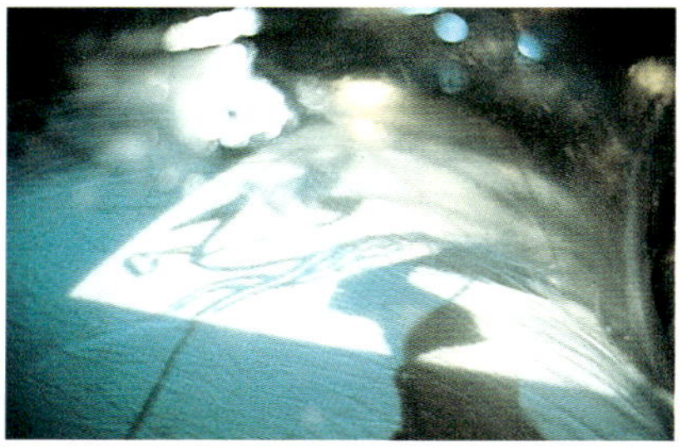

blasene Struktur hatte eine konische Form und besaß eine transparente Außenhaut und eine weiße Innenfläche. Die projizierten Bilder trafen zunächst leicht auf die straffgespannte äußere Hülle und erschienen dann auf der halb aufgeblasenen inneren Oberfläche. Im Raum zwischen der transparenten Außenmembran und der weißen Innenfläche fanden Aktionen mit verschiedenen Materialien statt, um die projizierten Bilder zu materialisieren – weiße Ballons und Schläuche wurden aufgeblasen und Rauch erzeugt.

Es war die Intention dieser Arbeit, die konventionelle flache Kinoleinwand in einen dreidimensionalen, kinetischen und architektonischen Visualisierungsraum zu verwandeln. Die vielfältigen Projektionsflächen ermöglichten eine vielschichtige Materialisierung der Bilder, während die Körper der Performer und auch des Publikums (viele Zuschauer entledigten sich spontan ihrer Kleidung) Teil des filmischen Spektakels wurden. Auf diese Weise konnten die Zuschauer in den immersiven Raum der filmischen Fiktion tatsächlich und interaktiv ›eintauchen‹ und die wechselnden Formen der pneumatischen Architektur gestalten, was wiederum immer neue Deformationen der projizierten Bilder hervorrief.

deformations in the projected imagery. A sensual conjugation of actuality and fiction was achieved through a mediated dematerialization of their respective boundaries.

MovieMovie was also a complex and innovative acoustic eventstructure. The Musica Elettronica Viva was closely involved in its scenography, creating an intense and loud density of electronic sounds that were interactively modulated by the musicians via a spatially distributed sound amplification system placed both outside and inside the inflatable structure. From within, the performers and members of the public could manipulate the shape of the inflatable structure, dragging its skin in one direction and another, and in so doing change the shape of the acoustic spaces. In this way the soft interactive lightweight architecture allowed the public to dynamically modulate the live performance of the music and so add another level of immersive conjugation of the body, architecture and mediated manifestation to the cinematic discourse.

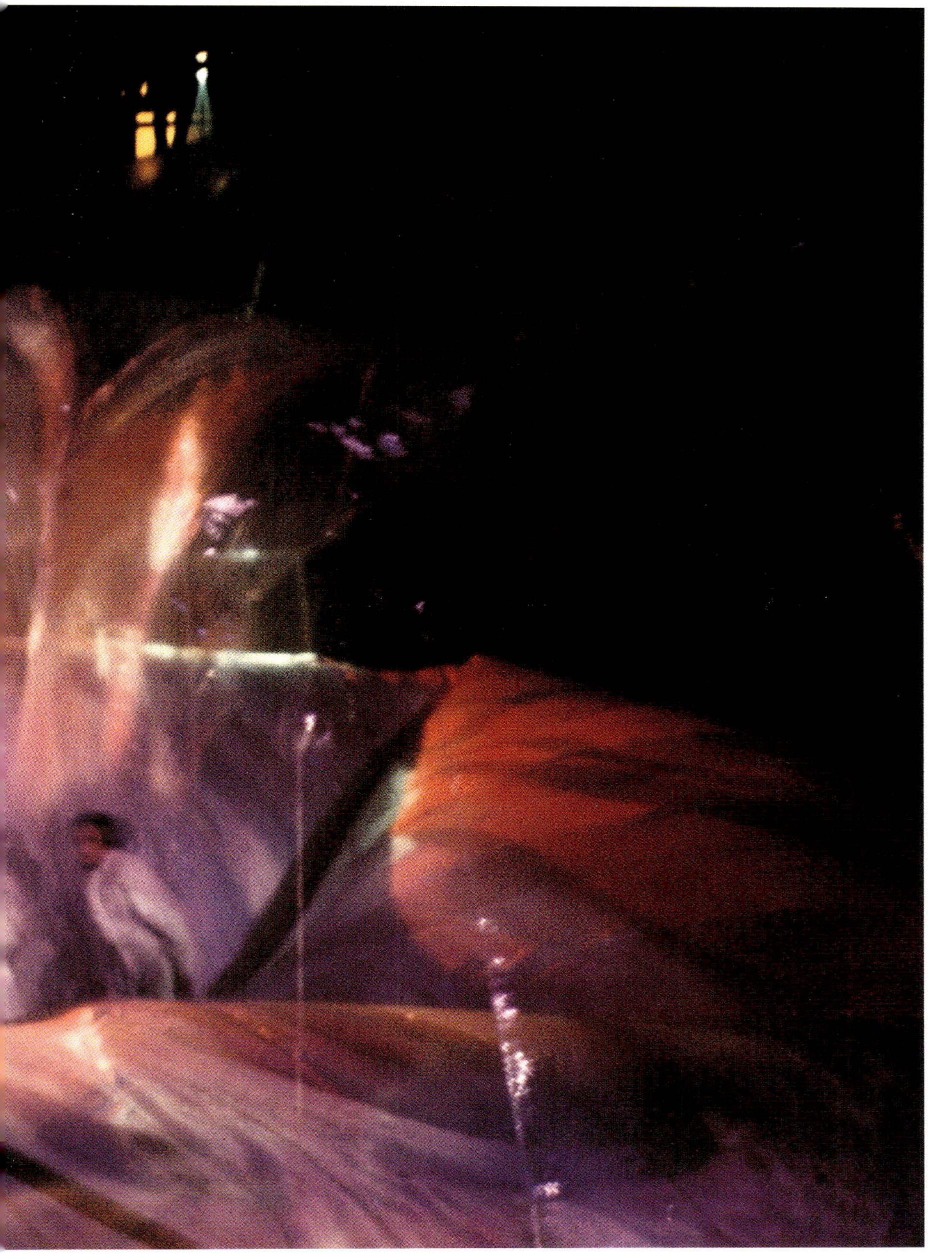

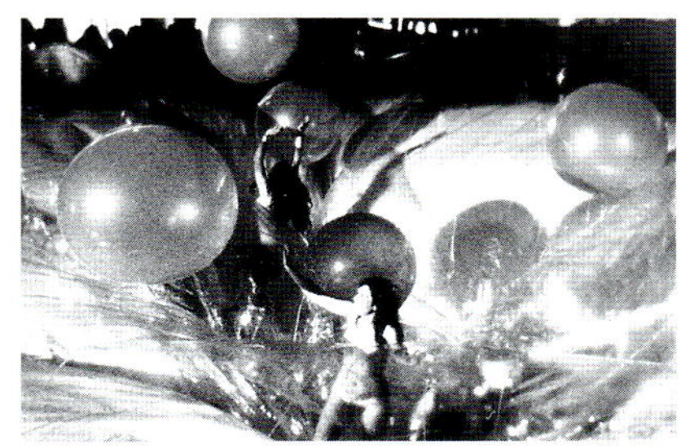

Durch die mittelbare Auflösung der gegenseitigen Grenzen von Realität und Fiktion wurde eine sinnliche Verbindung zwischen ihnen hergestellt.

MovieMovie war gleichzeitig auch eine komplexe und innovative Klangperformance. Die Gruppe Musica Elettronica Viva war eng in das Geschehen eingebunden und kreierte eine laute, intensive Dichte elektronischer Klänge, die von den Musikern über eine sowohl innerhalb als auch außerhalb des pneumatischen Raumes plazierte Verstärkeranlage gesteuert wurde. Im Innenraum konnten die Performer oder das Publikum die Form der aufgeblasenen Struktur verändern, indem sie die Plastikmembran in die eine oder andere Richtung zogen, wodurch sie gleichzeitig auch die Form der akustischen Räume beeinflußten. Die weiche, interaktive und leichte Architektur ermöglichte dem Publikum somit einen dynamischen Eingriff in die Musikperformance, so daß dem filmischen Diskurs eine weitere Ebene der immersiven Verbindung von Körper, Architektur und vermittelndem Ausdruck hinzugefügt wurde.

Inflatable tubes 1968–70

Air-inflated polythene tubing provided a versatile and inexpensive medium for many situations and event-structures. They drew the enthusiastic participation of a public who would manipulate these tubes into complex structures.

In *Waterquake* (Assen, Netherlands, 1970) long lengths of tubing were dropped into a canal and then slowly inflated with air and smoke. The tubing emerged from the water, filling the canal and then spilling over into the surrounding streets. The spectators pulled and knotted these tubes into various forms – when they broke holes in the plastic skin the smoke inside was released.

In the *Alpevent* (Kornhauskeller, Bern, Switzerland, 1968) white polythene tubing was slowly inflated inside a somewhat confined space. The people there dragged and wove the tubing around their bodies, but expanding plastic gradually pushed many of them out of the room.

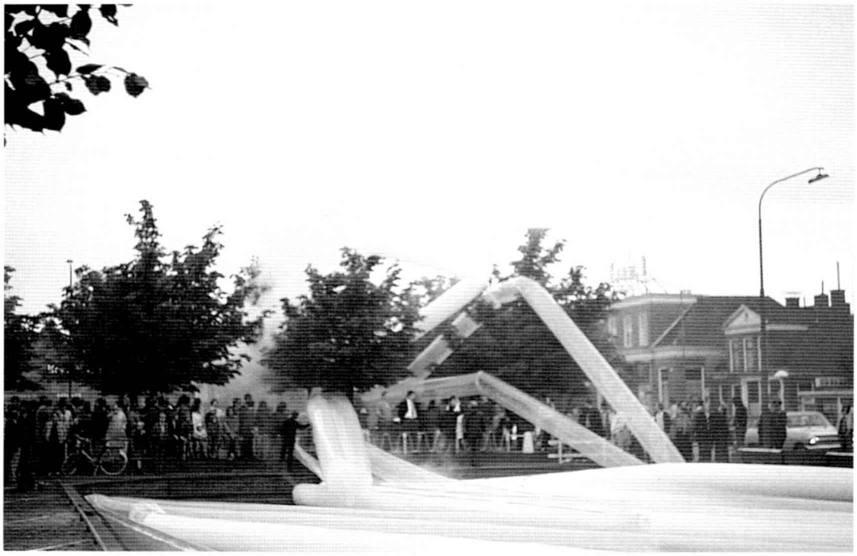

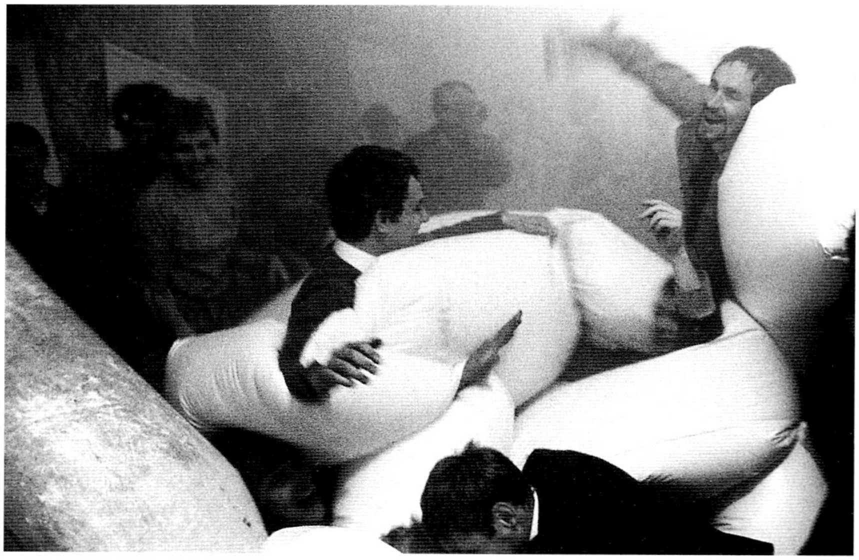

Aufblasbare Schläuche 1968–70

Aufblasbare Schläuche aus Polyäthylen waren ein vielseitiges und preiswertes Medium für zahlreiche Situationen und Ereignisstrukturen (›Eventstructures‹). Sie fanden die begeisterte Partizipation eines Publikums, das aus diesen Schläuchen komplexe Strukturen formen konnte.

In *Waterquake* (›Wasserbeben‹, Assen, Niederlande, 1970) wurden lange Bahnen von Schläuchen in einen Kanal gelassen und dann langsam mit Luft und Rauch aufgeblasen. Die Schläuche tauchten aus dem Wasser auf, füllten den Kanal und breiteten sich dann weiter aus in die umliegenden Straßen. Die Zuschauer zogen und formten die Schläuche; sobald Löcher in der Plastikhaut der Schläuche entstanden, wurde der Rauch freigesetzt.

In *Alpevent* (›Event in den Alpen‹, Kornhauskeller, Bern, Schweiz, 1968) wurden in einem ziemlich beengten Raum weiße Plastikschläuche langsam aufgeblasen. Die Zuschauer zerrten an den Schläuchen und wickelten sie sich um den Körper, doch das sich immer weiter ausbreitende Plastik schob viele von ihnen aus dem Raum.

Airgrounds

The Airgrounds were a new genre of air structures comprising soft, responsive architectures the public could interact with. At the Brighton Festival a pyramid-shaped inflatable with a transparent outer skin and yellow inner skin was set up by the seaside. The visitors could enter and play on its soft inner surface (*Airground*, Brighton, UK, 1968).

At the Floriade festival in Amsterdam (*Aqua-Airground*, 1972) a large air-inflated cushion was also partially filled with water. Another type of Airground resembled a large mattress, its upper and lower surfaces held together by interior ties (*Airground Mattress*, 1970). Airgrounds lost their artistic functionality when they became commercialized as purely recreative devices.

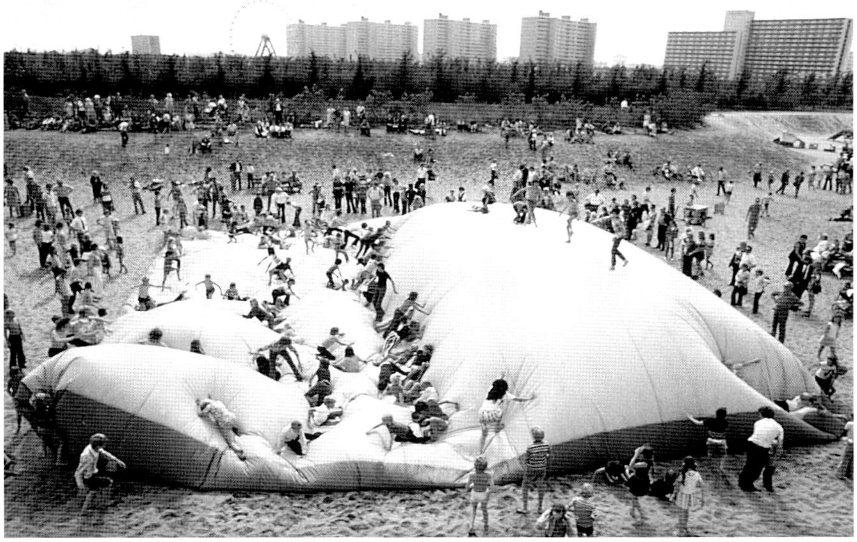

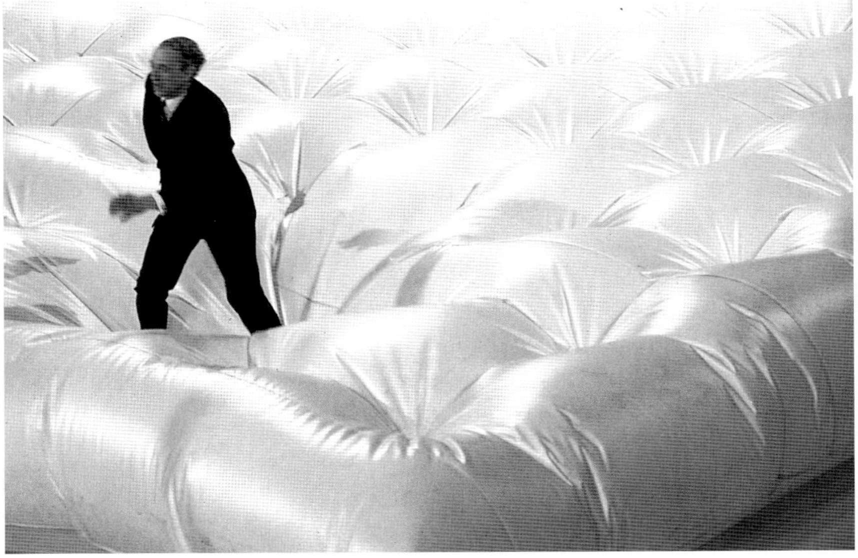

Airgrounds Luftgefüllte Flächen

›Airgrounds‹ bildeten eine neue Gattung aufblasbarer Strukturen, die eine weiche, reagierende Architektur besaßen, mit der das Publikum interagieren konnte. Beim Brighton Festival wurde am Meer eine pyramidenförmige luftgefüllte Struktur aufgebaut, die eine transparente Außenhaut und eine gelbe Innenhaut hatte (*Airground*, Brighton, UK, 1968). Die Besucher konnten hineingehen und sich spielerisch auf der weichen inneren Oberfläche bewegen.

Beim Floriade Festival in Amsterdam wurde ein großes aufblasbares Kissen mit Luft und Wasser gefüllt (*Aqua-Airground* (›Wasser-Luftfläche‹), Niederlande, 1972). Eine andere Form luftgefüllter Flächen ähnelte einer großen Matratze, deren Ober- und Unterseite durch innen befestigte Seile zusammengehalten wurden (*Airground Mattress* (›Luftflächenmatratze‹), 1970). ›Airgrounds‹ verloren ihre künstlerische Relevanz, als sie kommerzialisiert und zu reinen Unterhaltungsobjekten wurden.

Walterwalk Tube 1970

An inflatable tube made from transparent plastic, 250 metres long and three metres in diameter, was placed over the Maschsee lake (Straßenkunstfestival, Hanover, Germany, 1970) connecting its opposite banks. This air-filled floating bridge had airlock revolving doors at each end, and its pliable floor was in direct contact with the water surface. Visitors were able to enter this almost immaterial structure and cross from one side of the lake to the other as if walking on water.

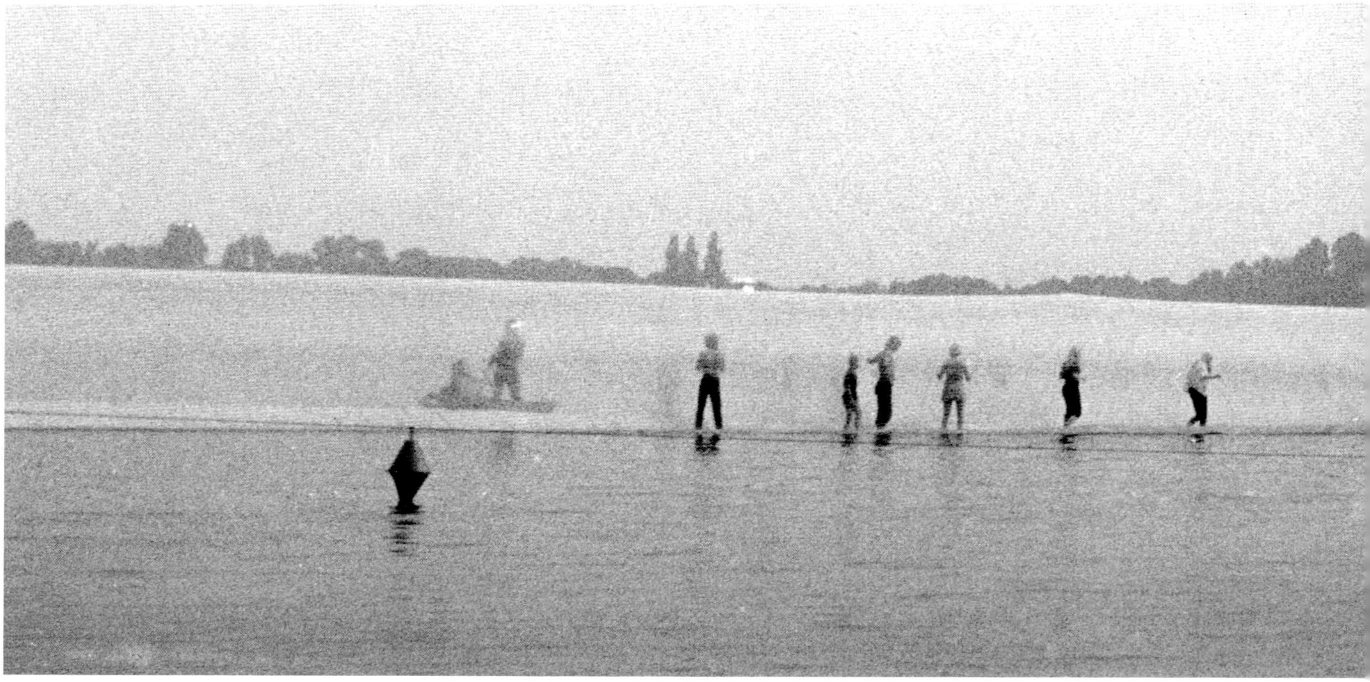

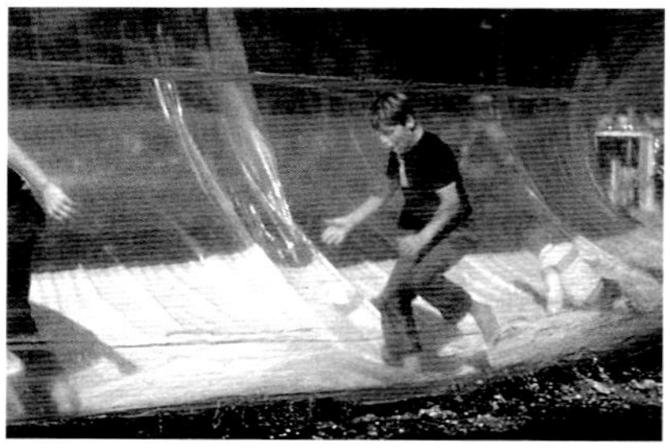

Waterwalk Tube

Tunnel über das Wasser 1970

Ein aufblasbarer Schlauch aus transparentem Plastik mit einer Länge von 250 Metern und einem Durchmesser von drei Metern wurde über den Maschsee in Hannover gelegt, so daß er beide Seeufer miteinander verband (Straßenkunstfestival, Hannover, Deutschland, 1970). Diese luftgefüllte schwimmende Brücke besaß an jedem Ende eine Drehtür; ihr weicher Boden lag direkt auf der Wasseroberfläche. Die Besucher konnten diese nahezu immaterielle Struktur betreten und den See überqueren – so als gingen sie auf dem Wasser.

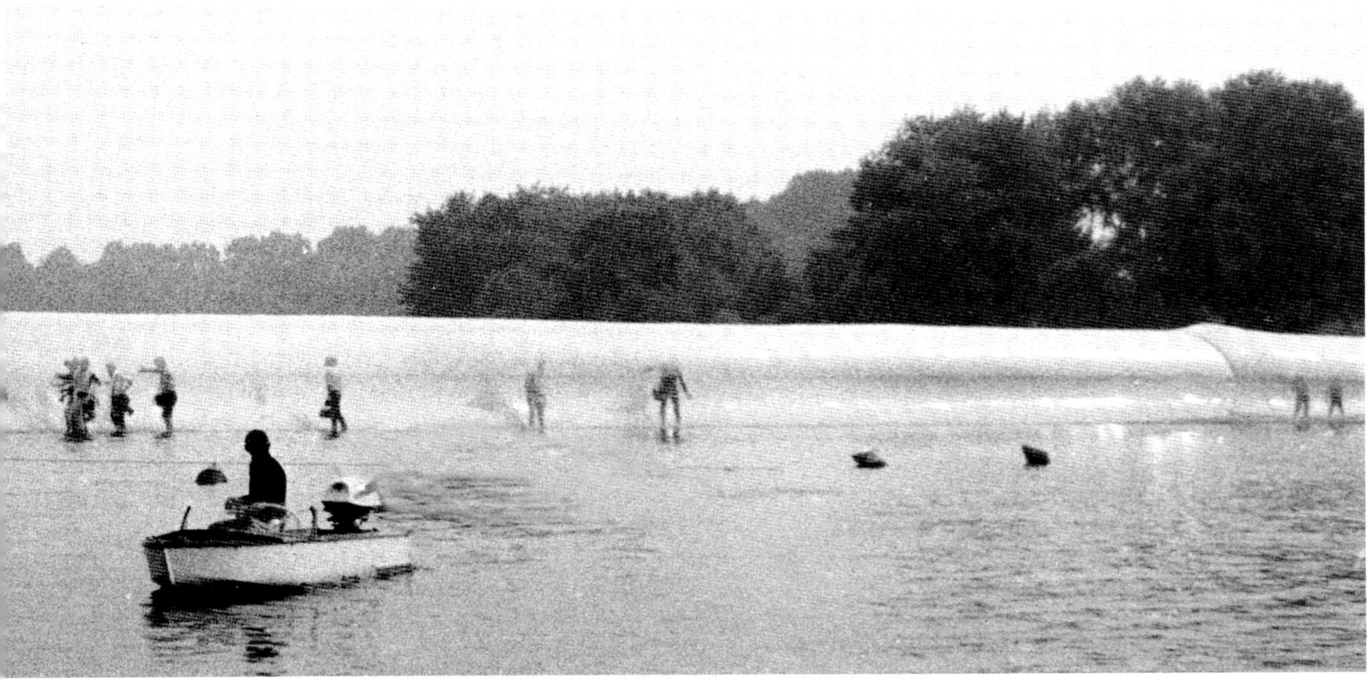

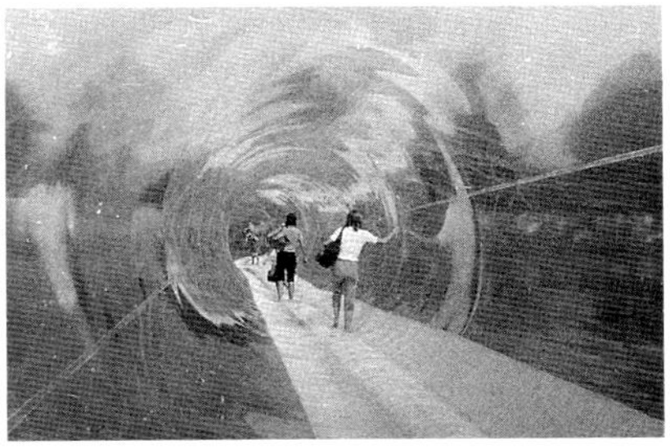

Waterwalk 1969

The *Waterwalk* was a three-metre-high tetrahedron shaped balloon made from transparent (and sometimes coloured) plastic. A watertight zip allowed people to enter and be sealed inside. When this lightweight structure was inflated with air, one or more persons could 'walk on water' by stepping and rotating it like a wheel over the water surface. The large volume of air in the balloon allowed the occupants some time for their journeys – and whenever they wished they could simply unzip themselves out.

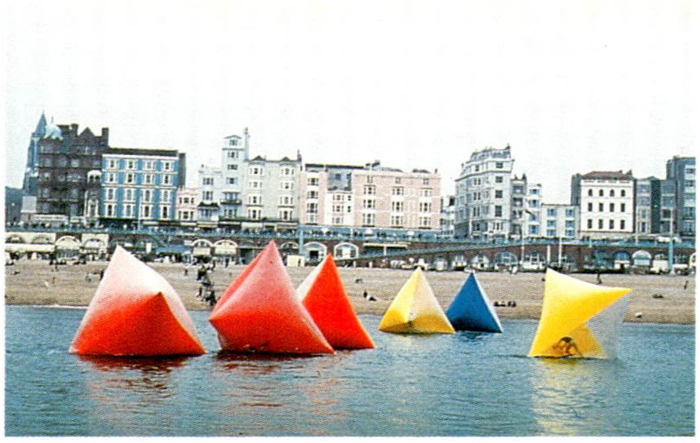

Waterwalk Auf dem Wasser gehen 1969

Waterwalk war ein drei Meter hoher tetraederförmiger Ballon aus transparentem (oder farbigem) Plastik. Durch einen wasserdichten Reißverschluß, der von innen wieder zugezogen werden konnte, konnte man den Ballon betreten. Sobald diese leichte Struktur mit Luft aufgeblasen wurde, konnten eine oder mehrere Personen ›auf dem Wasser gehen‹, indem sie sich schrittweise vorwärtsbewegten und dabei den Ballon wie ein Rad über die Wasserfläche drehten. Aufgrund des großen Luftvolumens im Ballon konnten sich seine ›Insassen‹ über einen längeren Zeitraum in ihm aufhalten, doch zu jeder Zeit war es möglich, den Reißverschluß zu öffnen und den Ballon zu verlassen.

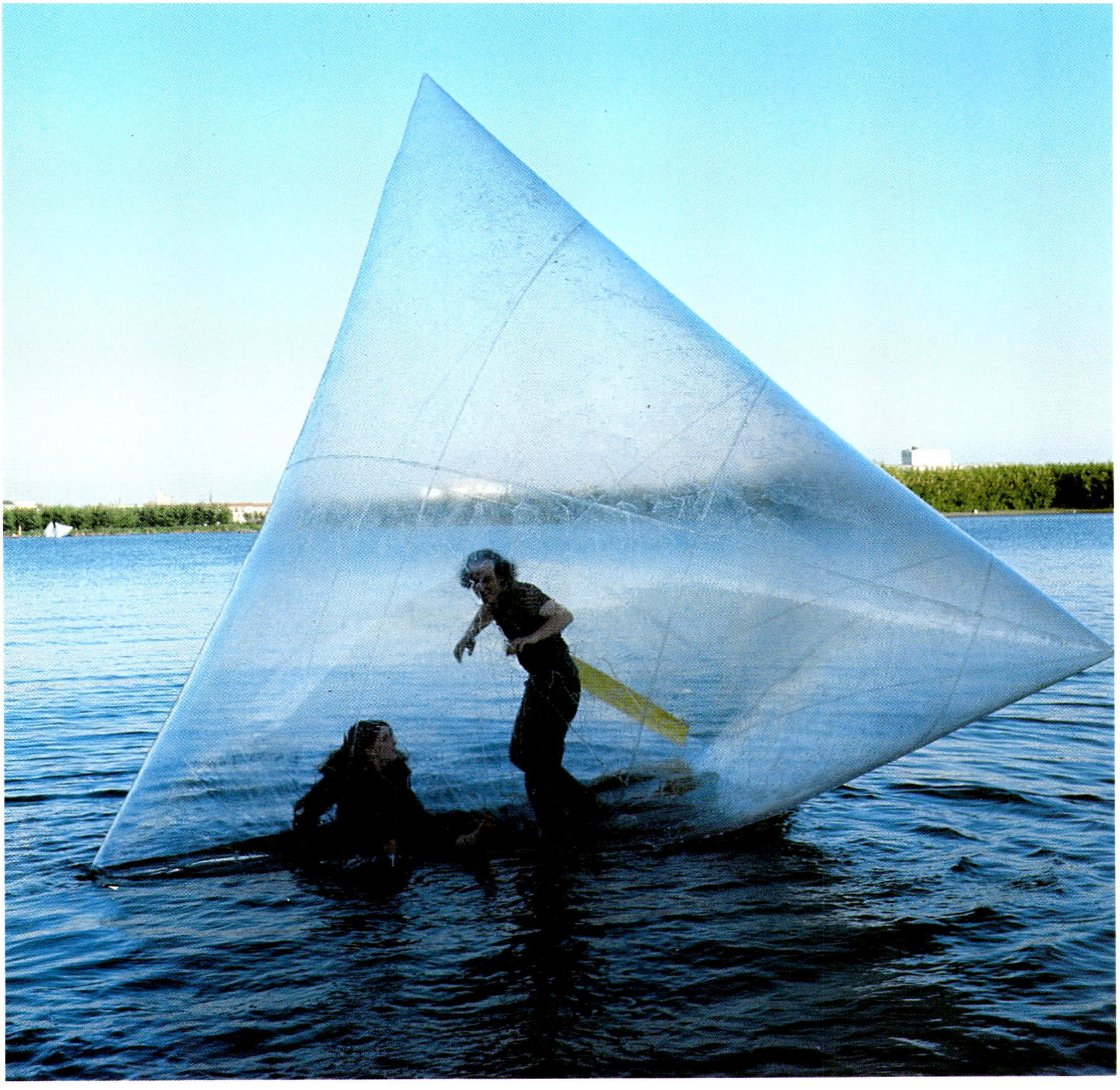

Cloud (of daytime sky at night)

970

A large cloud-shaped and air-inflated structure was suspended from the roof of the Stedelijk Museum (Amsterdam, Netherlands, 1970). During the night an image of a daytime sky and clouds was projected onto it, accompanied by clouds of artificial smoke and the amplified sounds of wind and thunder. This work was one of a series of 'Artificial Landscapes' projects which involved visual and/or temporal displacements of natural situations.

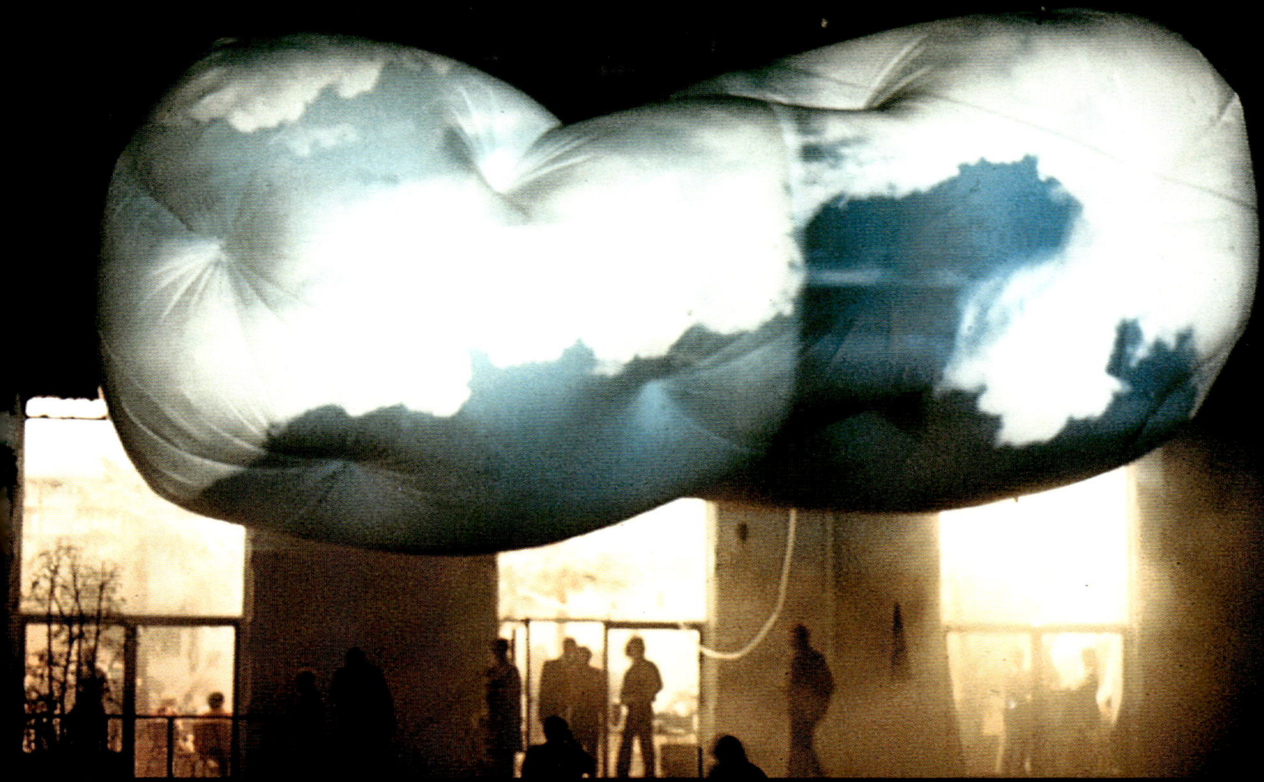

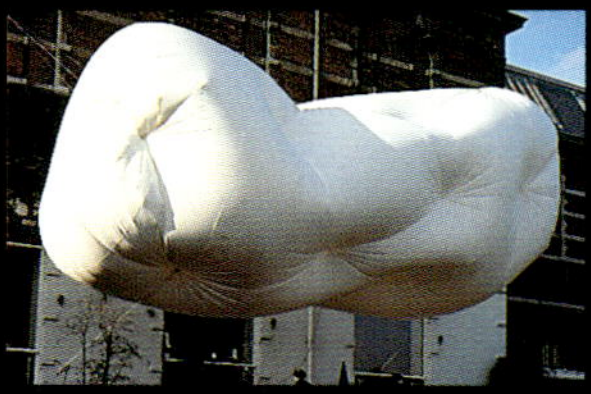

Cloud (of daytime sky at night)

Wolke (am Tageshimmel bei Nacht) 1970

Eine große wolkenförmige, luftgefüllte Struktur wurde vom Dach des Stedelijk Museums (Amsterdam, Niederlande, 1970) gehängt. Bei Nacht wurde das Bild eines wolkenbedeckten Tageshimmels darauf projiziert, begleitet von künstlich erzeugten Rauchwolken und den verstärkten Geräuschen von Wind und Donner. Die Arbeit gehörte zu einer Reihe von Projekten zum Thema ›künstliche Landschaften‹, die sich mit der visuellen und/oder zeitlichen Darstellung von Naturerscheinungen beschäftigten.

Three Pavilions 1971

Three inflatable pavilions, each having a specific function, were specially commissioned for Sonsbeek buiten de perken (Arnheim, Netherlands, 1971). Besides the *Information Pavilion* and the *Video Pavilion* there was a two-level air-supported *Auditorium Pavilion*. The foyer on the ground level had a circular transparent wall and its ceiling, which constituted the floor for the second level, was ballasted by many sandbags. A spiral staircase took the visitors upstairs to the second level where they could sit on the soft air-supported floor around a small stage. The functionality of this structure was often put in question by the audience's preference for simply jumping around on the inflatable floor. The yellow-domed roof could also be removed to create an 'open-air' theatre.

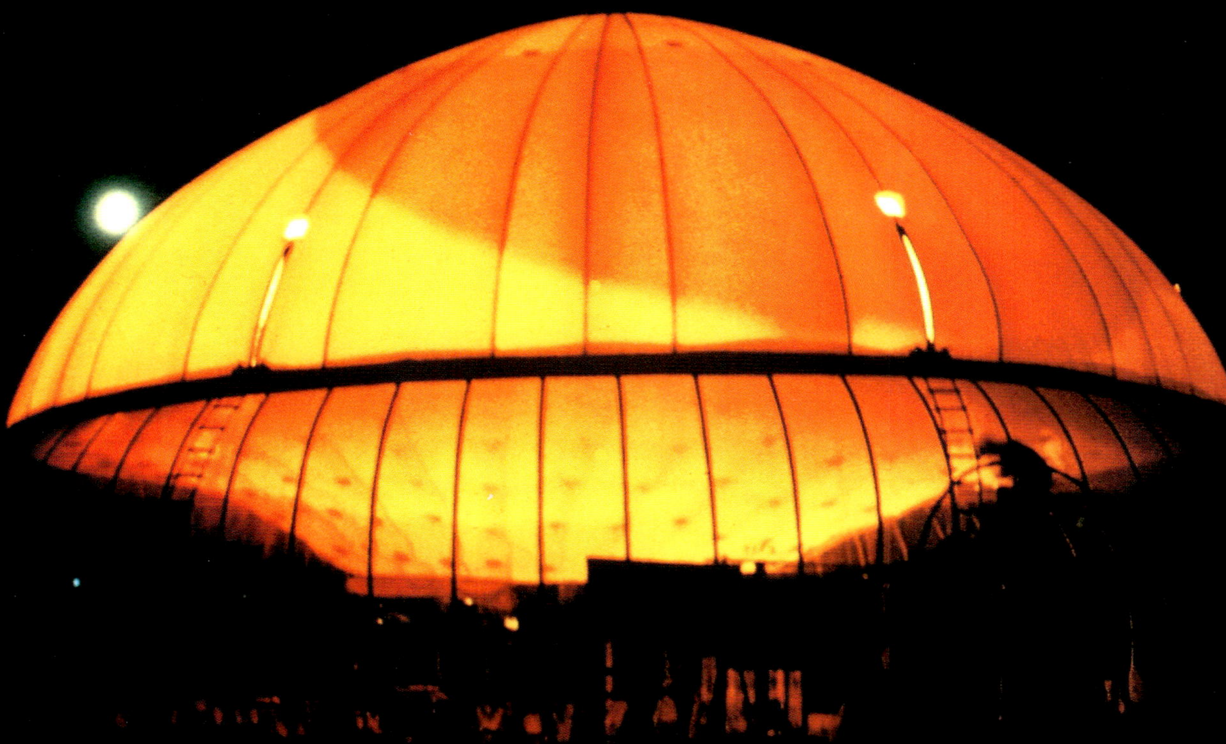

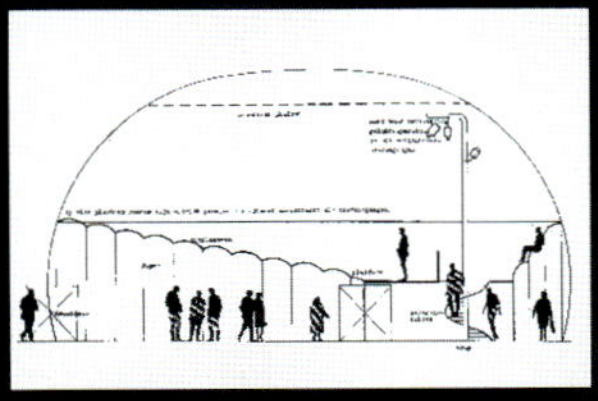

Three Pavilions Drei Pavillons 1971

Drei aufblasbare Pavillons, jeder mit einer bestimmten Funktion, wurden für Sonsbeek buiten de perken (Arnheim, Niederlande, 1971) entwickelt. Neben dem *Informations-* und dem *Videopavillon* gab es einen zweigeschossigen luftgetragenen *Auditoriumspavillon*. Das Foyer im Erdgeschoß war ein runder Raum mit transparenter Wand, während die Decke, die gleichzeitig den Boden für das Obergeschoß bildete, mit Sandsäcken beschwert war. Eine Wendeltreppe führte die Besucher in den oberen Bereich, wo sie auf dem weichen, luftgetragenen Boden um eine kleine Bühne herum Platz nehmen konnten. Die Funktionalität dieser Struktur wurde mehrmals in Frage gestellt, da das Publikum mit Vorliebe auf dem luftgefüllten Boden herumhüpfte. Das gelbe, kuppelförmige Dach konnte abgenommen werden, um ein ›Freiluft‹-Theater zu kreieren.

Diadrama 1974

The *Diadrama* was an audio-visual performance with over 2000 slides being projected onto a large wide screen by three pairs of synchronized slide projectors. The main themes explored in this work were panoramic methods of representation, the collage of visual and temporal events, and the articulation of various simulated and expanded cinema situations. Most of the photography for this work was made by rotating a camera in three positions to capture a 270-degree field of view in order to create an immersive panoramic image.

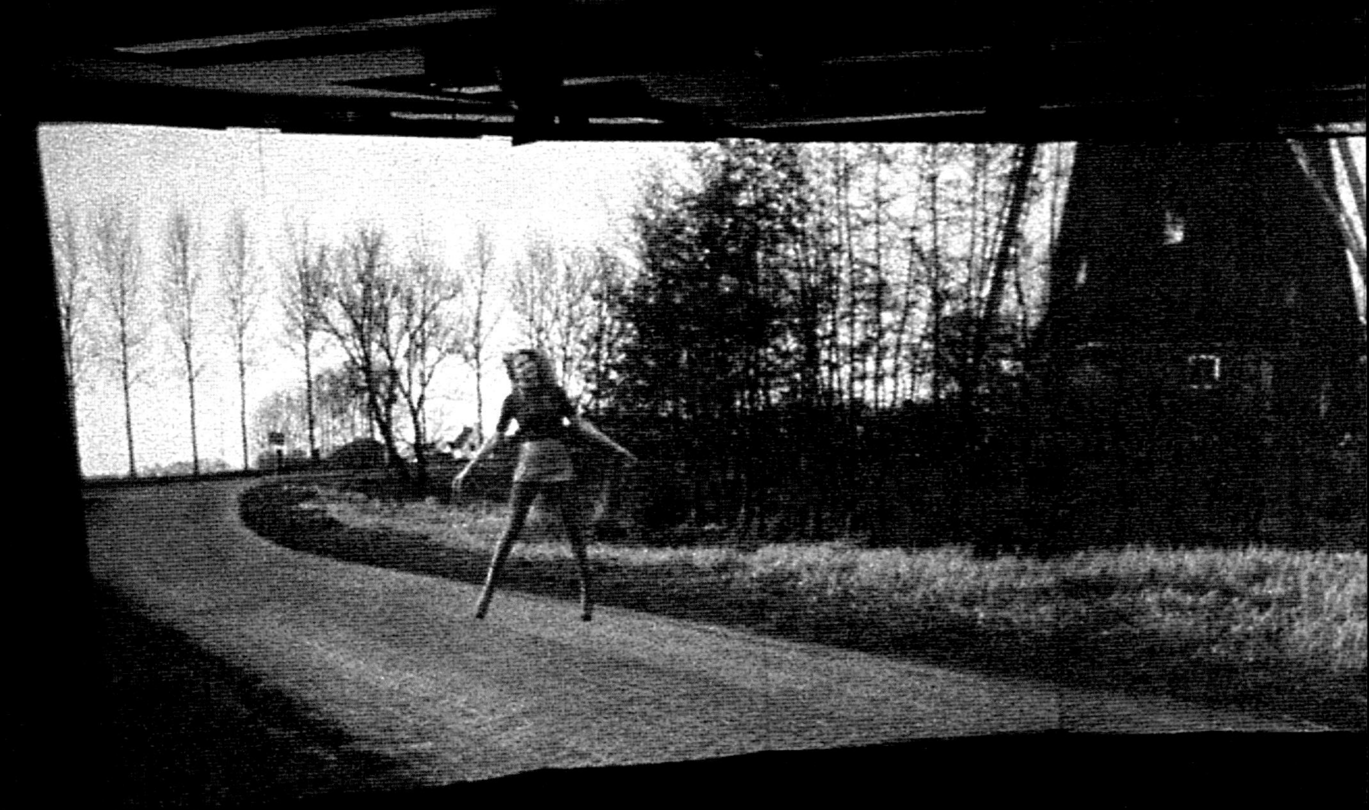

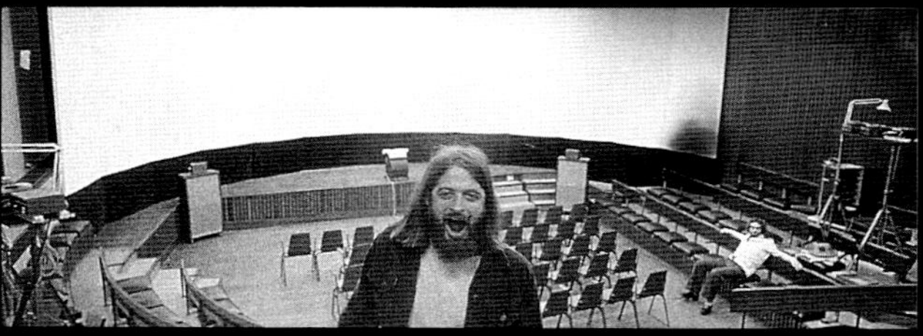

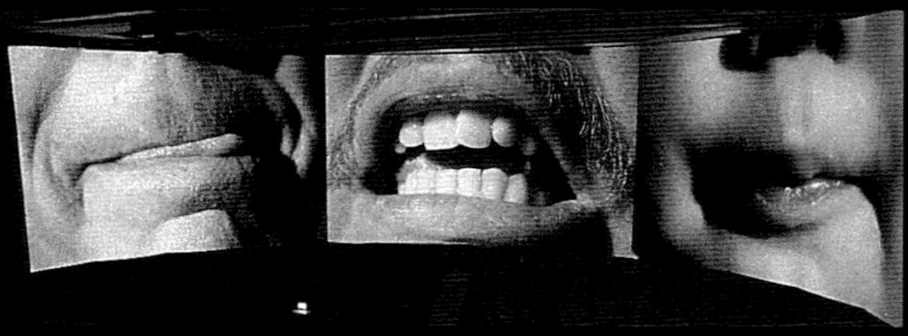

Diadrama 1974

Diadrama war eine audio-visuelle Performance mit mehr als 2 000 Dias, die mit drei Paaren von synchronisierten Diaprojektoren auf eine große Leinwand projiziert wurden. Die Hauptthemen dieser Arbeit waren Panoramamethoden der Darstellung, die Collage von visuellen und zeitlichen Ereignissen und die Verbindung verschiedener simulierter und erweiterter Kinosituationen. Ein Großteil der in dieser Arbeit verwendeten Fotografien war entstanden, indem eine Kamera in drei Positionen gedreht und so ein 270-Grad-Panorama eingefangen wurde, das ein ›immersives‹ Panoramabild kreierte.

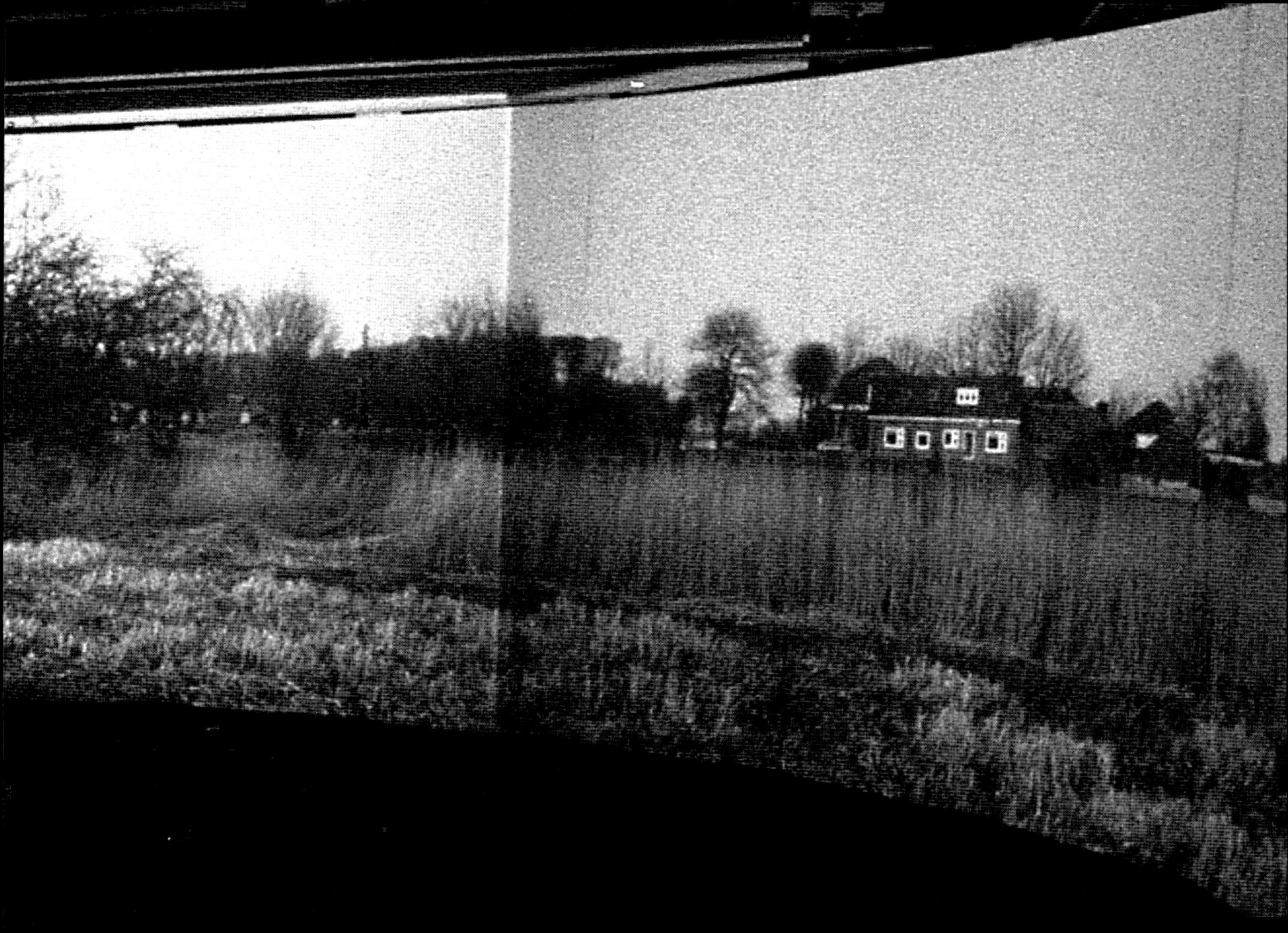

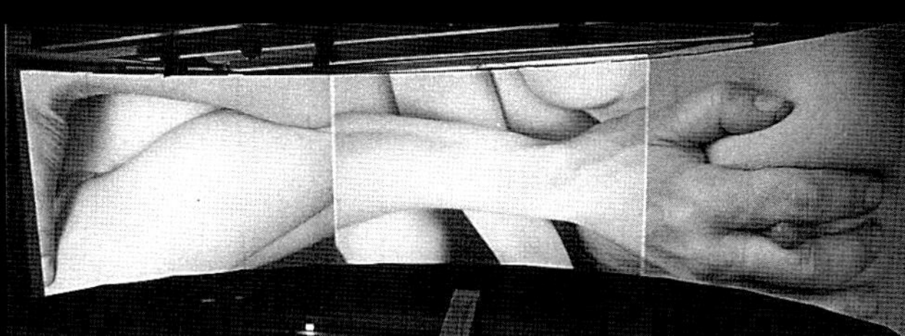

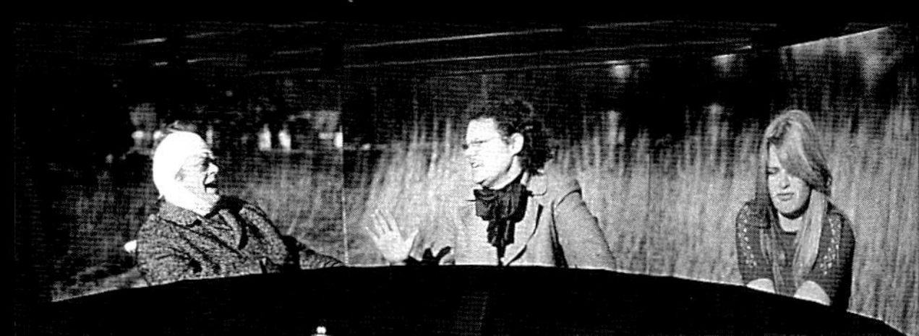

/iewpoint 1975

'his work created a collage of fictional events vithin a museum space (Musée d'Art Moderne de a Ville de Paris, 9th Biennale de Paris, France, 975) by making projected images of the events ppear contiguous with the real space and actual ituations. The work was constituted by two structural elements: an optical viewing console and a arge retro-reflective projection screen. The viewng console was a wood contruction which housed pair of automated slide projectors. A semi-transarent mirror in this console constituted both a vindow which the viewers could look through, and reflective surface which directed the projected mages onto the screen. The screen itself had a pecial surface coating which directed all the light rojected onto it back to the projection source. As consequence the projected image could only be een through the viewing console – from any other osition in the room the screen was a plain grey urface. The inherent brightness of this projection

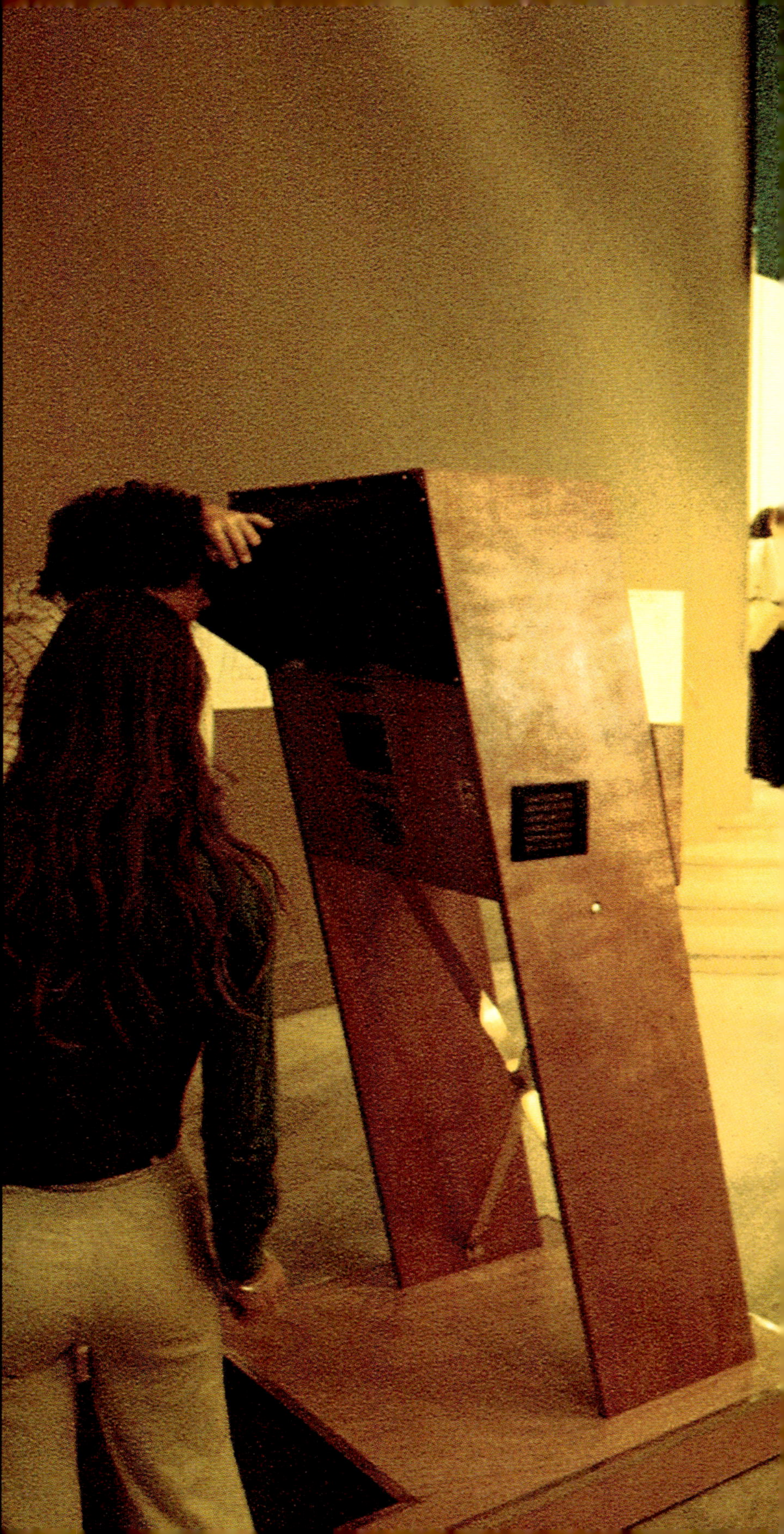

/iewpoint Standpunkt 1975

n dieser Arbeit wurde im Raum eines Museums Musée d'Art Moderne de la Ville de Paris, 9. Bienıale de Paris, Frankreich, 1975) eine Collage fikiver Ereignisse kreiert, indem Bilder solcher Ereignisse projiziert wurden, die mit dem realen Raum und den tatsächlich darin stattfindenden Situationen zusammenzufallen schienen. Zwei Strukturelemente konstituierten diese Arbeit: eine ptische Sichtkonsole und eine große rückreflekierende Projektionsleinwand. Die Sichtkonsole estand aus einer Holzkonstruktion, in die zwei utomatisch gesteuerte Diaprojektoren eingebaut varen. Ein semitransparenter Spiegel, der in die Konsole eingelassen war, diente zum einen als enster, durch das der Betrachter schauen konnte ınd zum anderen als reflektierende Oberfläche, lie die projizierten Bilder auf die Leinwand lenkte. Die Leinwand selbst besaß eine spezielle Oberlächenstruktur, die das auf sie projizierte Licht vieder zum Projektionssystem zurücklenkte. Das rojizierte Bild konnte somit nur durch die Konsole esehen werden – von jedem anderen Standpunkt les Raumes aus erschien die Leinwand nur als ere graue Fläche. Das Projektionssystem funk-

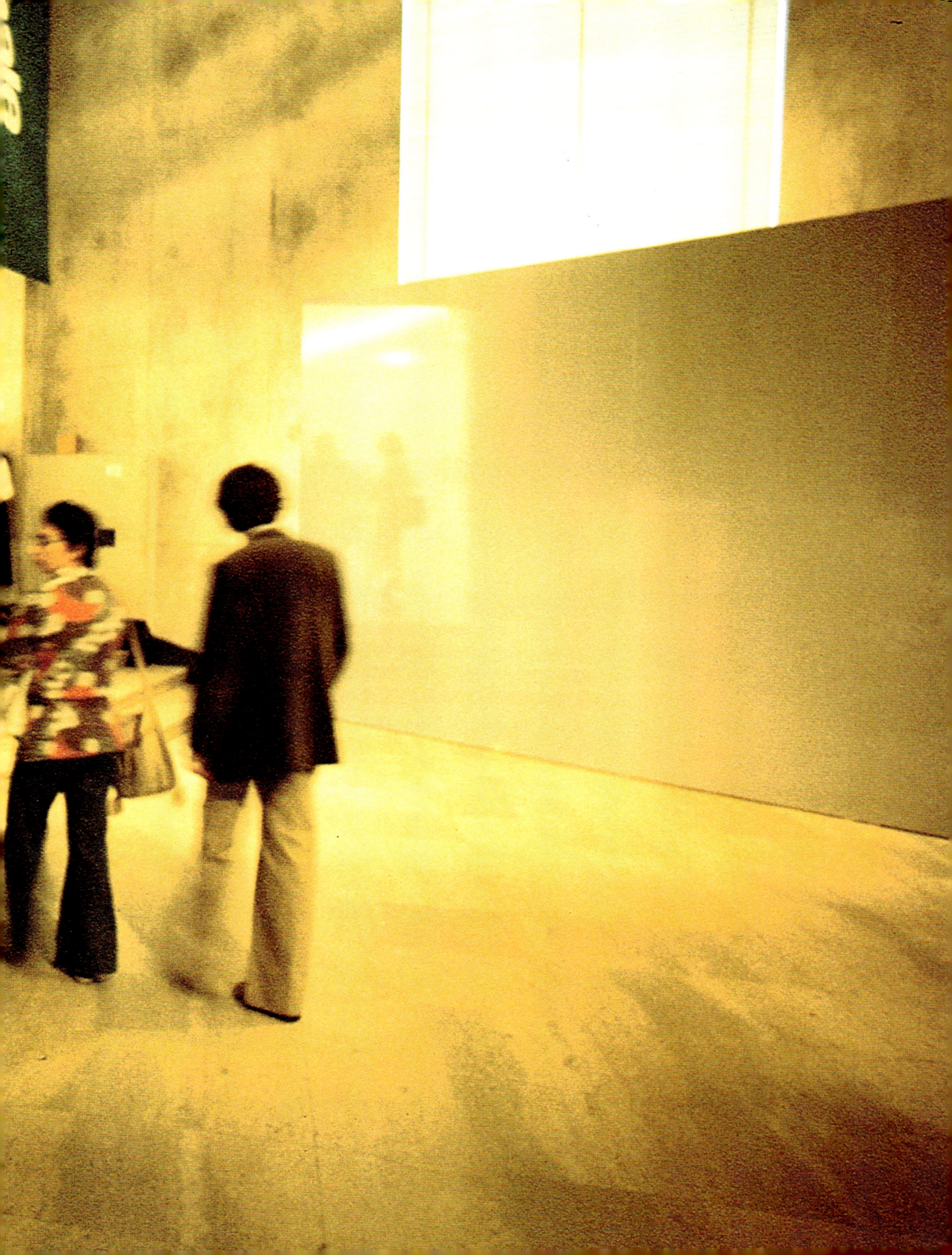

system enabled it to function in the bright ambient lighting in the museum, so that a coherent collage of the projected images with the surroundings was achieved. Furthermore, these images showed exactly that part of the museum room hidden by the screen, creating a seamless continuity between the virtual and actual spaces. Visitors walking by the screen were unaware they had entered and become part of the visual space of the projected image.

Twelve different events had been staged and photographed in the same museum area prior to the exhibition. These projected events were programmed in slides sequences which constituted a synoptic animation of these events. While the optical configuration of this work created a strong illusory conjunction between the real and projected spaces, the use of a slide projection (instead of film or video) enunciated a clear difference between the actual and projected events. The physical reconstitution of past

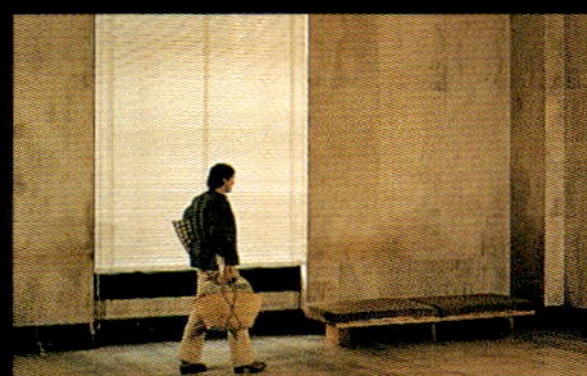

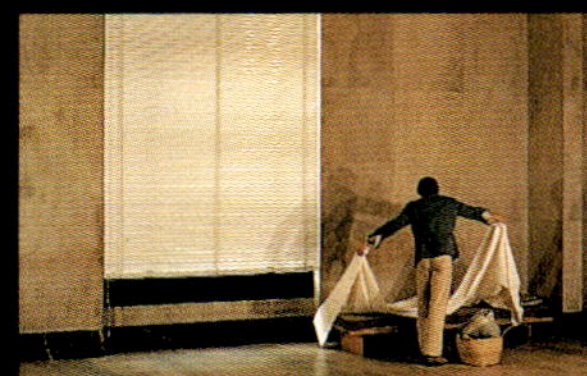

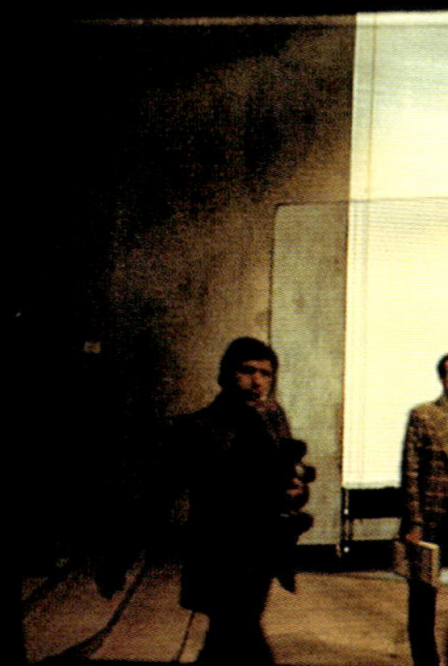

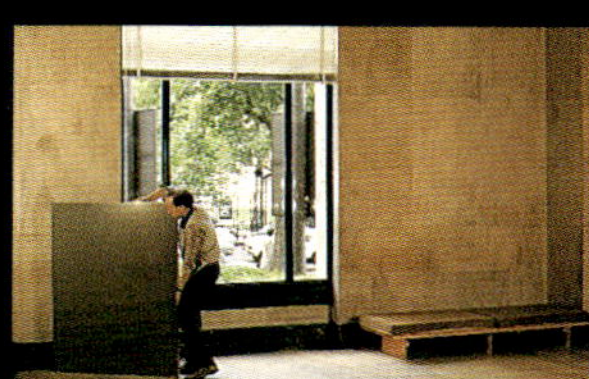

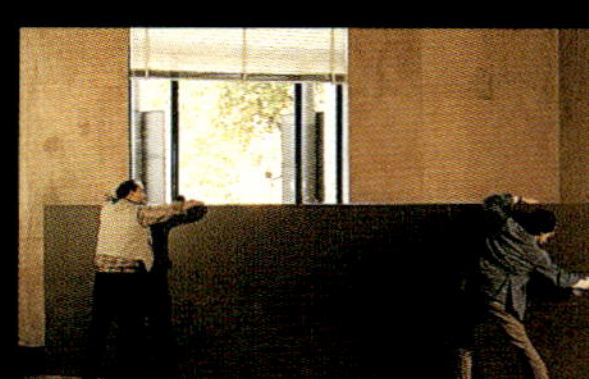

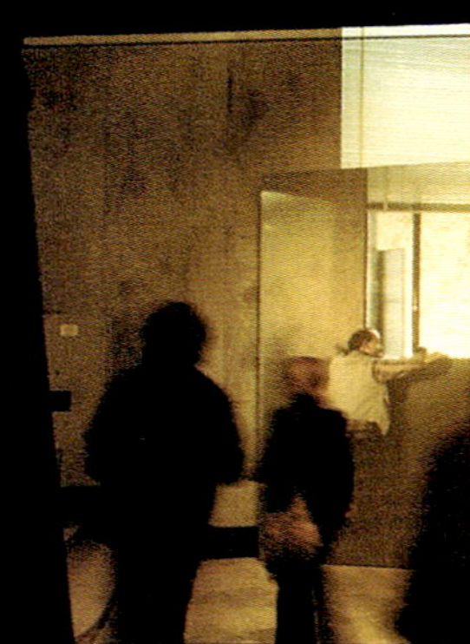

tionierte, ohne daß der Museumsraum abgedunkelt werden mußte, so daß eine kohärente Collage aus projizierten Bildern und realer Umgebung entstehen konnte. Darüberhinaus zeigten die Bilder exakt den Teil des Museumsraumes, der von der Leinwand verborgen wurde, so daß ein nahtloser Übergang zwischen virtuellem und realem Raum geschaffen wurde. Besucher, die an der Leinwand vorbeigingen, bemerkten nicht, daß sie die Installation betreten hatten und Teil des visuellen Raumes des projizierten Bildes geworden waren.

Zwölf verschiedene Szenen waren vor Beginn der Ausstellung im Museumsraum inszeniert und fotografiert worden. Sie waren als Diasequenzen programmiert, die eine synoptische Animation der Ereignisse herstellten. Während die optische Anordnung der Arbeit eine überzeugende illusorische Verbindung von realem und projiziertem Raum schuf, machte die Verwendung einer Diaprojektion (statt Film oder Video) eine klare Unterscheidung von tatsächlichen und projizierten Ereignissen möglich. Die physische Wiederherstellung vergangener Ereignisse in bloß dokumentarischen Fotosequenzen war sowohl überzeu-

events with documentary sequences of photographs was both persuasive and equivocal, as the forced concurrence of two time frames created a simultaneous congruity and contrariety of past and present situations.

Whenever a visitor stepped onto the base of the viewing console, one of the twelve slide sequences would be triggered. These projected events showed various occurrences in the museum such as a visitor who made a bed for himself on a museum bench and then went to sleep on it; the projection screen itself being built up and gradually blocking the view of the museum space behind it; a visitor who was seen walking up to the museum window and smashing it with a pickaxe; the venetian blind over the window being closed, blacking out only the projected part of the room; a museum guard pointing his gun at one of the visitors and robbing him; the projected colour image of the room crumpling like paper and leaving behind a black-and-white image of the room.

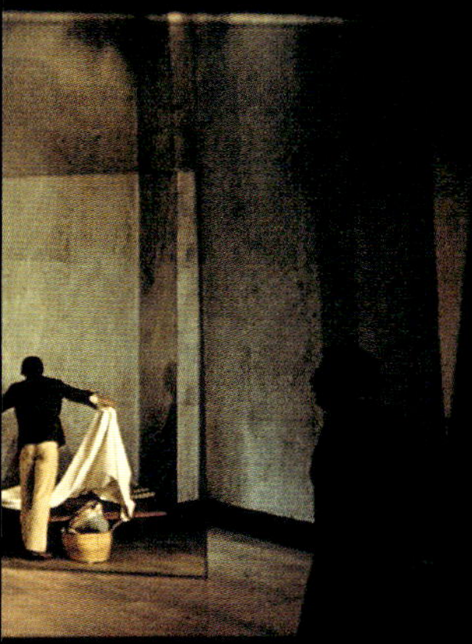

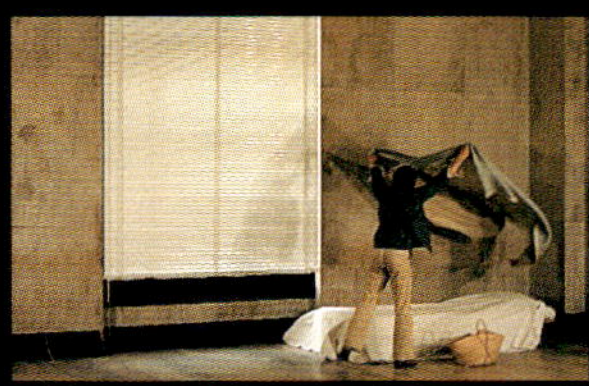

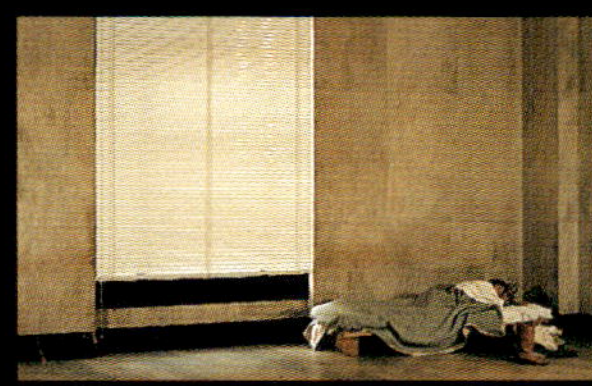

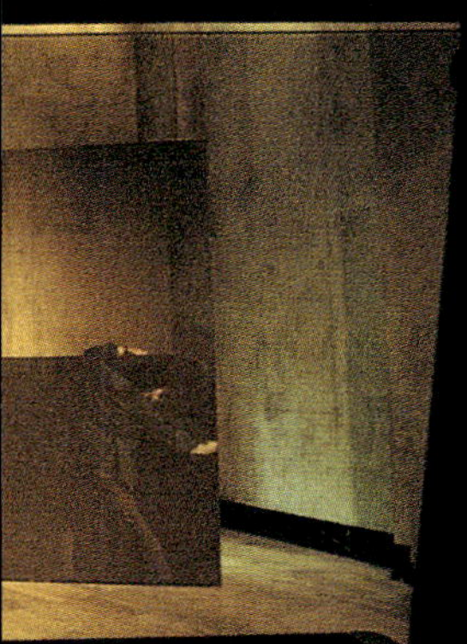

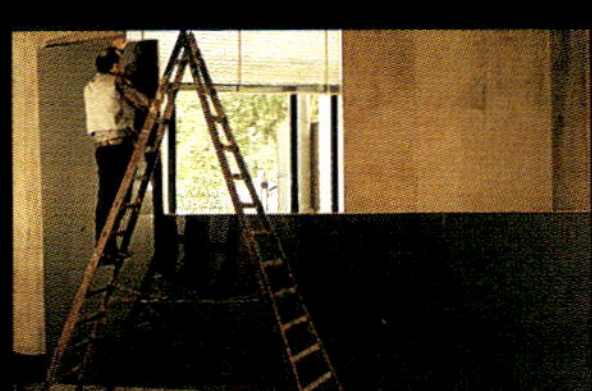

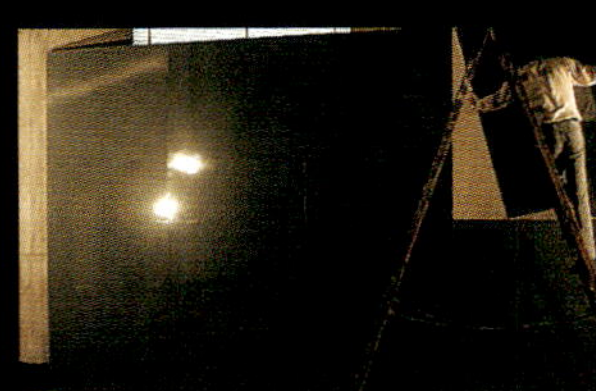

gend als auch zweideutig: durch das unnatürliche Zusammenfallen von zwei Zeitebenen erschienen vergangene und gerade stattfindende Ereignisse übereinstimmend und widersprüchlich zugleich.

Sobald ein Besucher den Boden der Sichtkonsole betrat, wurde eine der zwölf Diasequenzen ausgelöst. Die projizierten Szenen zeigten verschiedene Begebenheiten, die sich im Museum abspielten, wie beispielsweise einen Besucher, der sich auf einer Museumsbank sein Bett machte und sich dort schlafen legte; den Aufbau der Projektionsleinwand, die allmählich die Sicht auf den hinter ihr liegenden Museumsraum verstellte; einen Besucher, der zu einem der Fenster des Museums ging und es mit einer Spitzhacke einschlug; oder die Jalousie vor dem Fenster wurde heruntergelassen, wobei nur der projizierte Teil des Raumes abgedunkelt wurde; eine Museumsaufsicht richtete ihre Pistole auf einen Besucher und raubte ihn aus; das projizierte Farbbild des Raumes wurde wie ein Stück Papier zusammengeknüllt und ließ ein schwarzweißes Bild des Raumes zurück.

The Lamb Lies Down on Broadway

1975

Sequences of images were created that freely interpreted the themes of Peter Gabriel's song cycle to provide a continuous visual accompaniment to the live stage performance (Genesis world tour 1975). These slides were projected onto three screens installed over the full width of the stage behind the performers. A laser-beam wand which Peter Gabriel held in his hand to direct the laser projections around the auditorium and a number of inflatable eventstructures were also made for this performance.

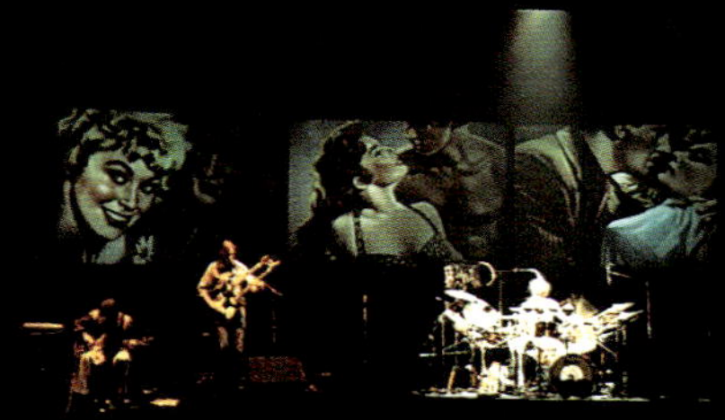

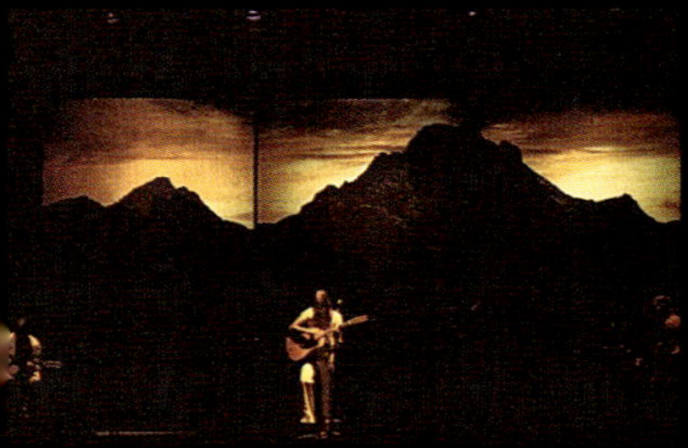

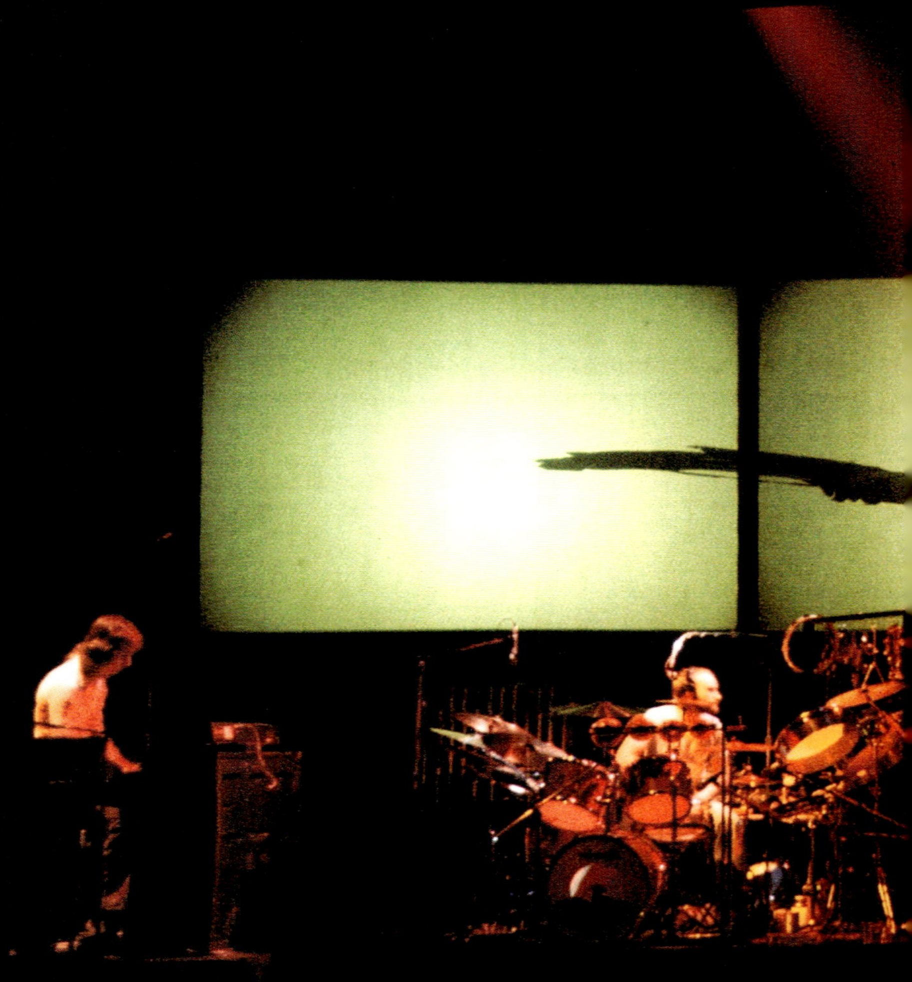

The Lamb Lies Down on Broadway

Das Lamm legt sich auf den Broadway 1975

Für die Genesis Welttournee (1975) wurden Bildsequenzen geschaffen, die die Themen von Peter Gabriels Songzyklen frei interpretierten und das Bühnengeschehen der Live-Konzerte kontinuierlich visuell begleiteten. Die Dias wurden auf drei Leinwände projiziert, die die ganze Breite des Bühnenraumes hinter den Musikern einnahmen. Für diese Performance wurden mehrere aufblasbare Strukturen und ein Laserstab entwickelt, den Peter Gabriel in der Hand hielt und mit dem er die Laserprojektionen durch den Zuschauerraum lenken konnte.

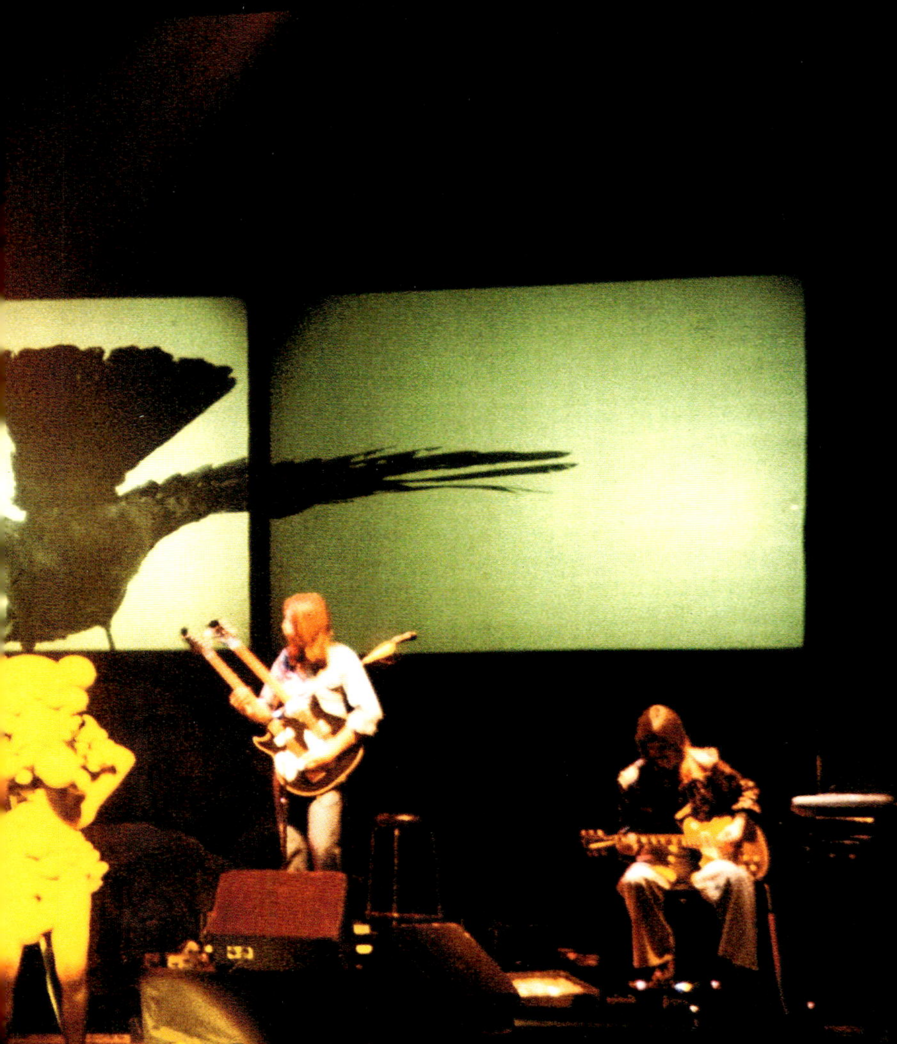

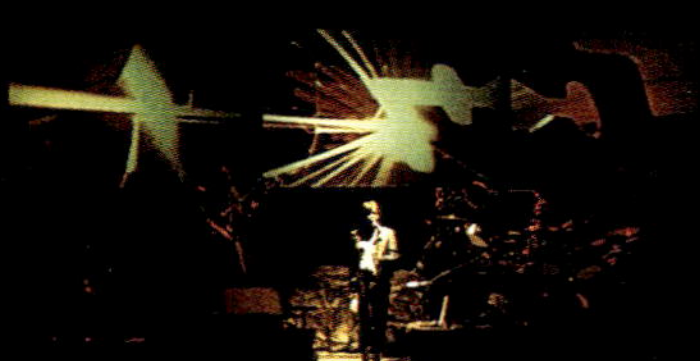

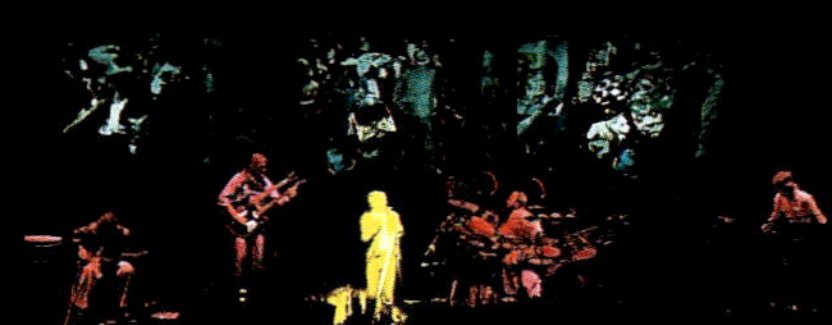

Kinetic Light and Mirror Sculture

1977

This sculpture enabled beams of light to be dynamically moved over Genesis's entire stage as well as out into the auditorium. It was constituted by six large mirrors which were all pivoted on two axes and could be rotated in all directions using computer-controlled servomotors. Suspended above the stage, these mirrors reflected beams of light from follow-spot projectors and during the performance were moved about according to programmed and improvised choreographies.

In certain positions these mirrors also offered the audience aerial views of the musicians (Genesis world tour, 1977).

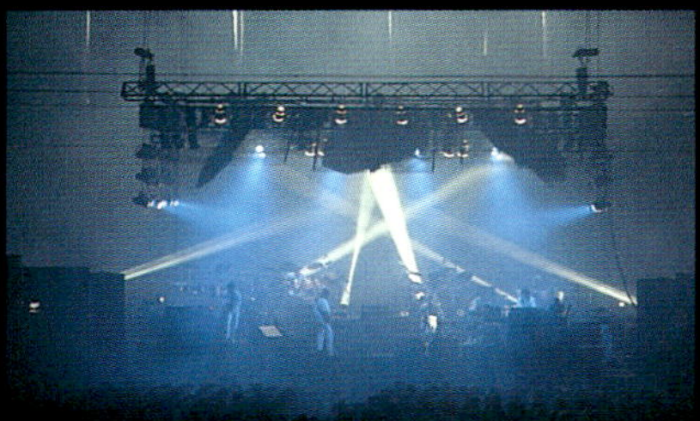

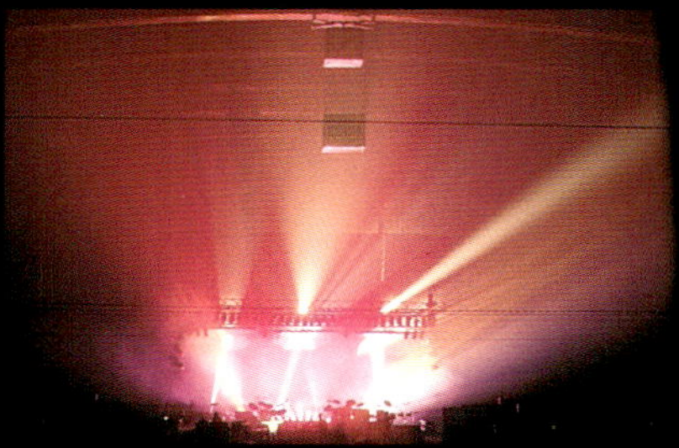

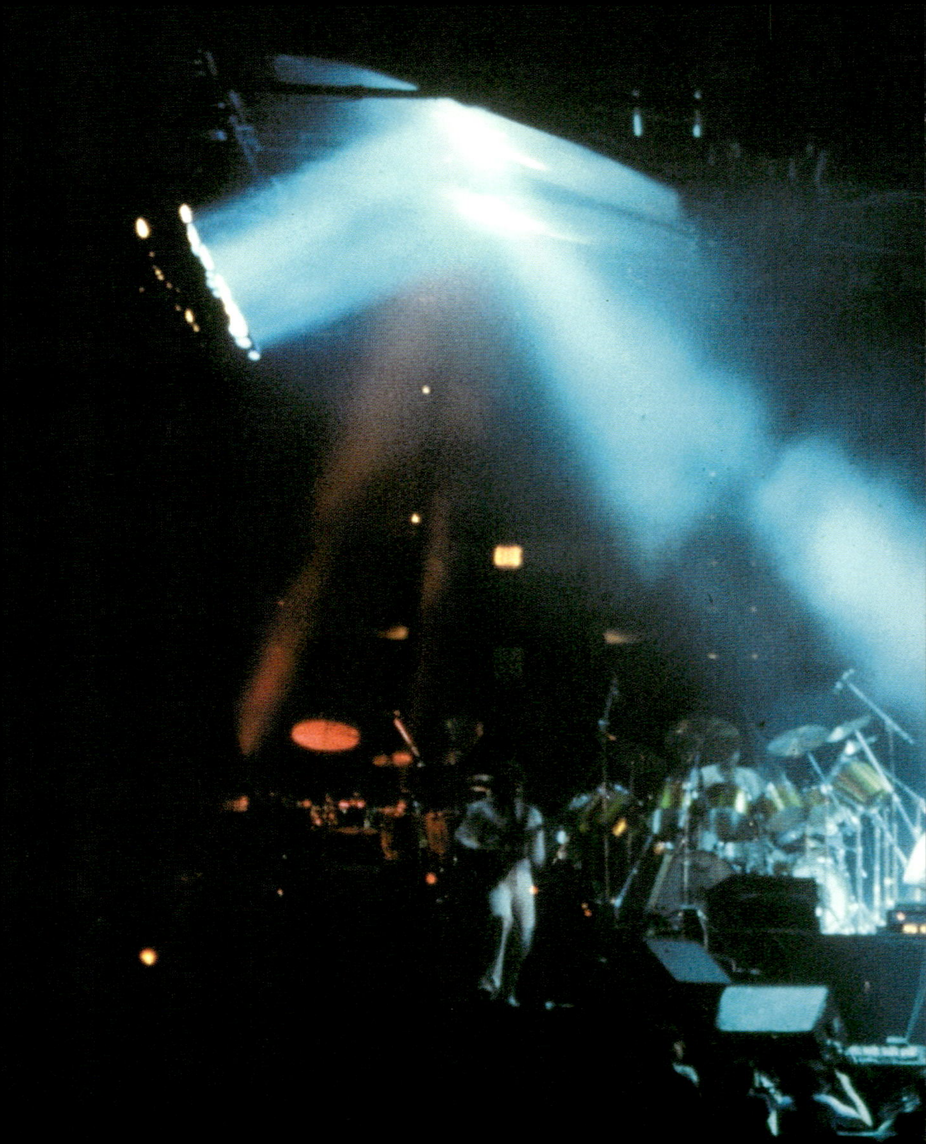

Kinetic Light and Mirror Sculpture

Kinetische Licht- und Spiegelskulptur 1977

Mit dieser Skulptur konnten Lichtstrahlen dynamisch über den ganzen Bühnenraum sowie in den Zuschauerraum bewegt werden. Sie bestand aus sechs großen Spiegeln, die sich um zwei Achsen drehten und über computergesteuerte Servomotoren in alle Richtungen rotiert werden konnten. Die Spiegel, die über der Bühne aufgehängt waren, reflektierten Lichtstrahlen von Verfolgerscheinwerfern und wurden während des Konzertes entsprechend der festgelegten bzw. improvisierten Choreographie gesteuert. In bestimmten Positionen zeigten die Spiegel dem Publikum die Musiker von oben (Genesis Welttournee ,1977).

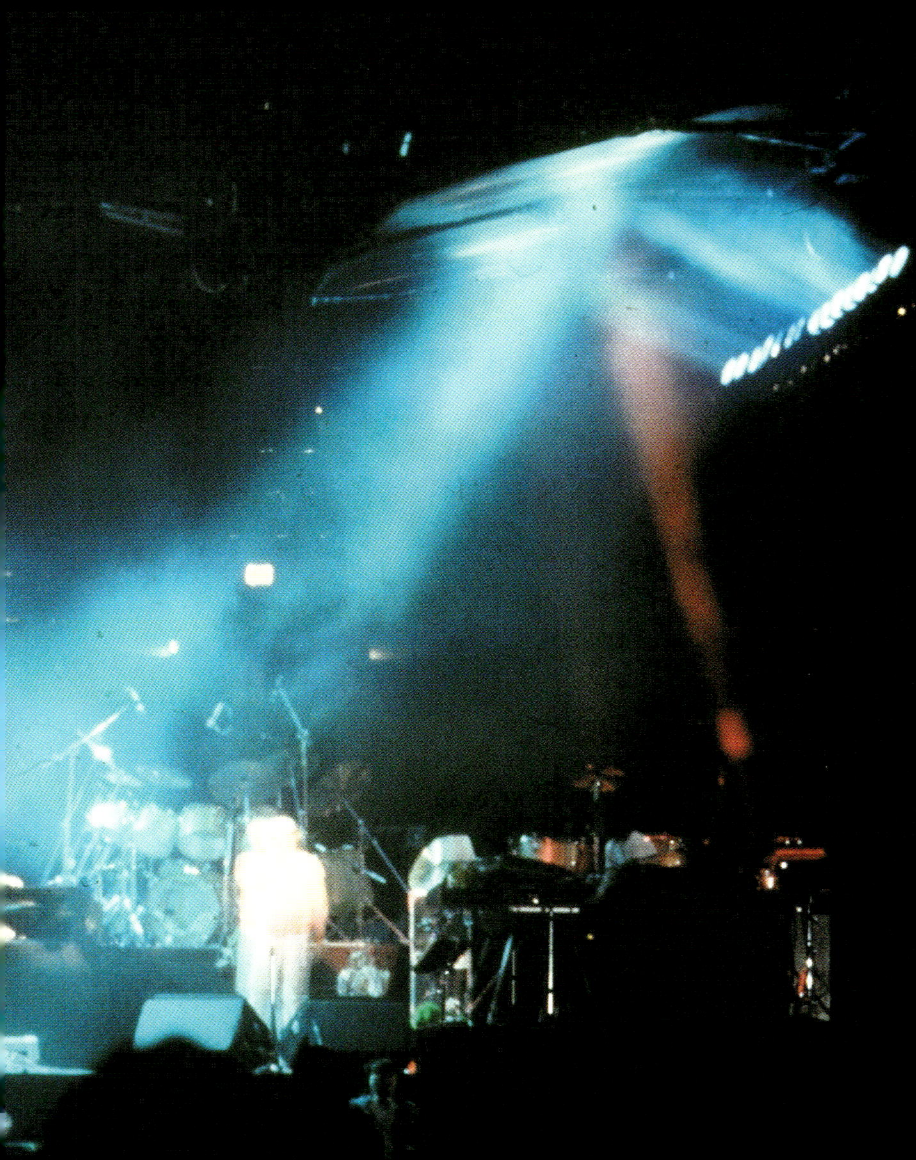

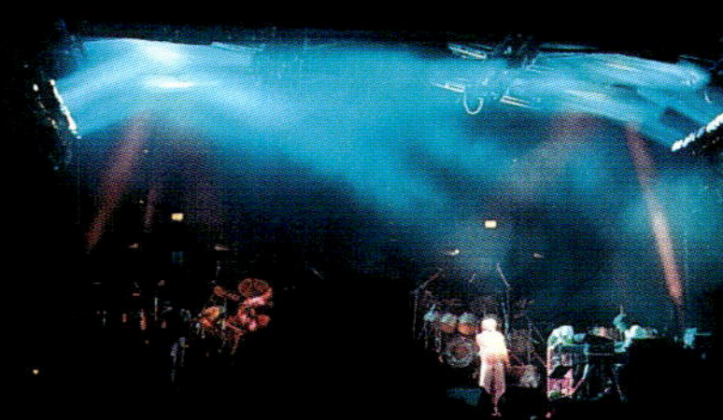

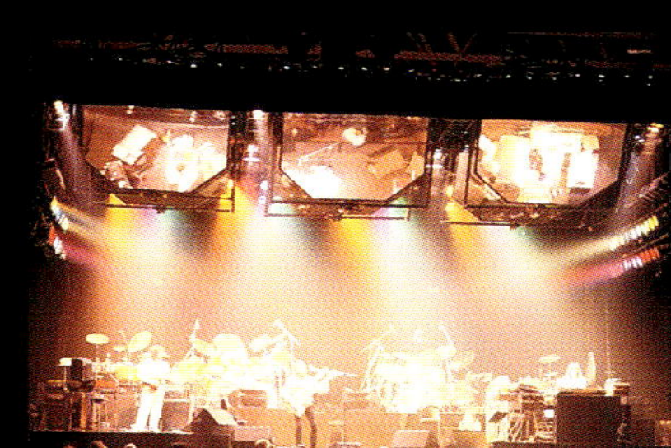

Laser installations and performances 1976–78

A custom laser scanning system was developed that could project the laser beam as shaped planes and cones of light in a full 360-degree space around the projector. Scanning and rotation

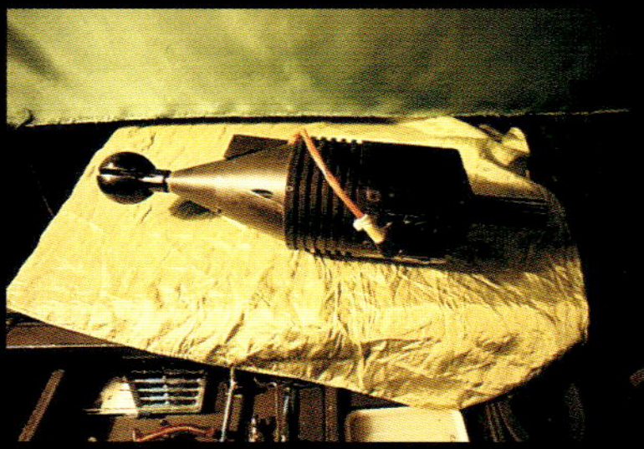

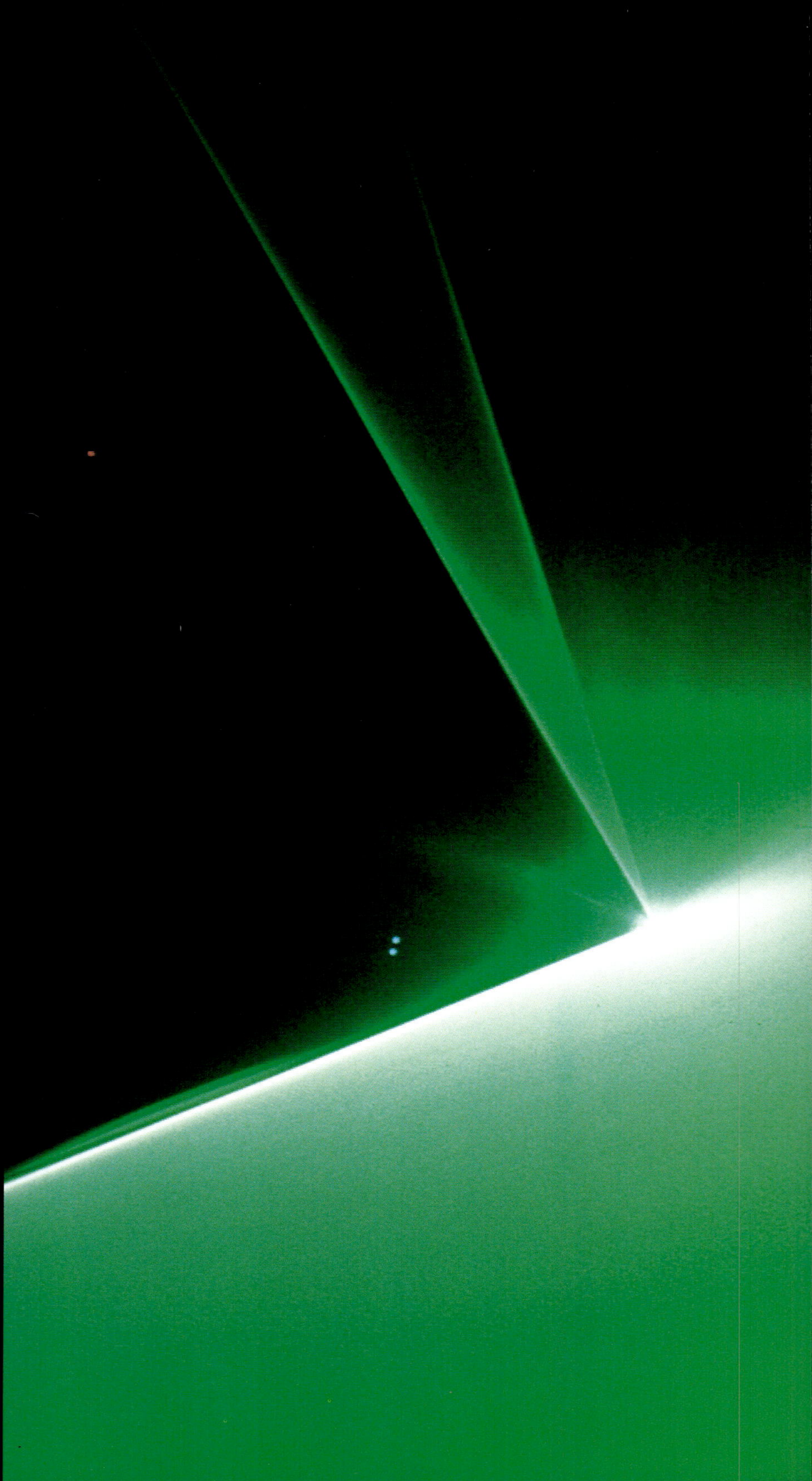

Laserinstallationen und -performances 1976–78

Es wurde ein spezielles System zur Steuerung des Lasers entwickelt, mit dem der Laserstrahl in unterschiedlich geformten Schichten und Lichtkegeln in einem Radius von 360 Grad um den Projektor geschwenkt werden konnte. Die Bewegung

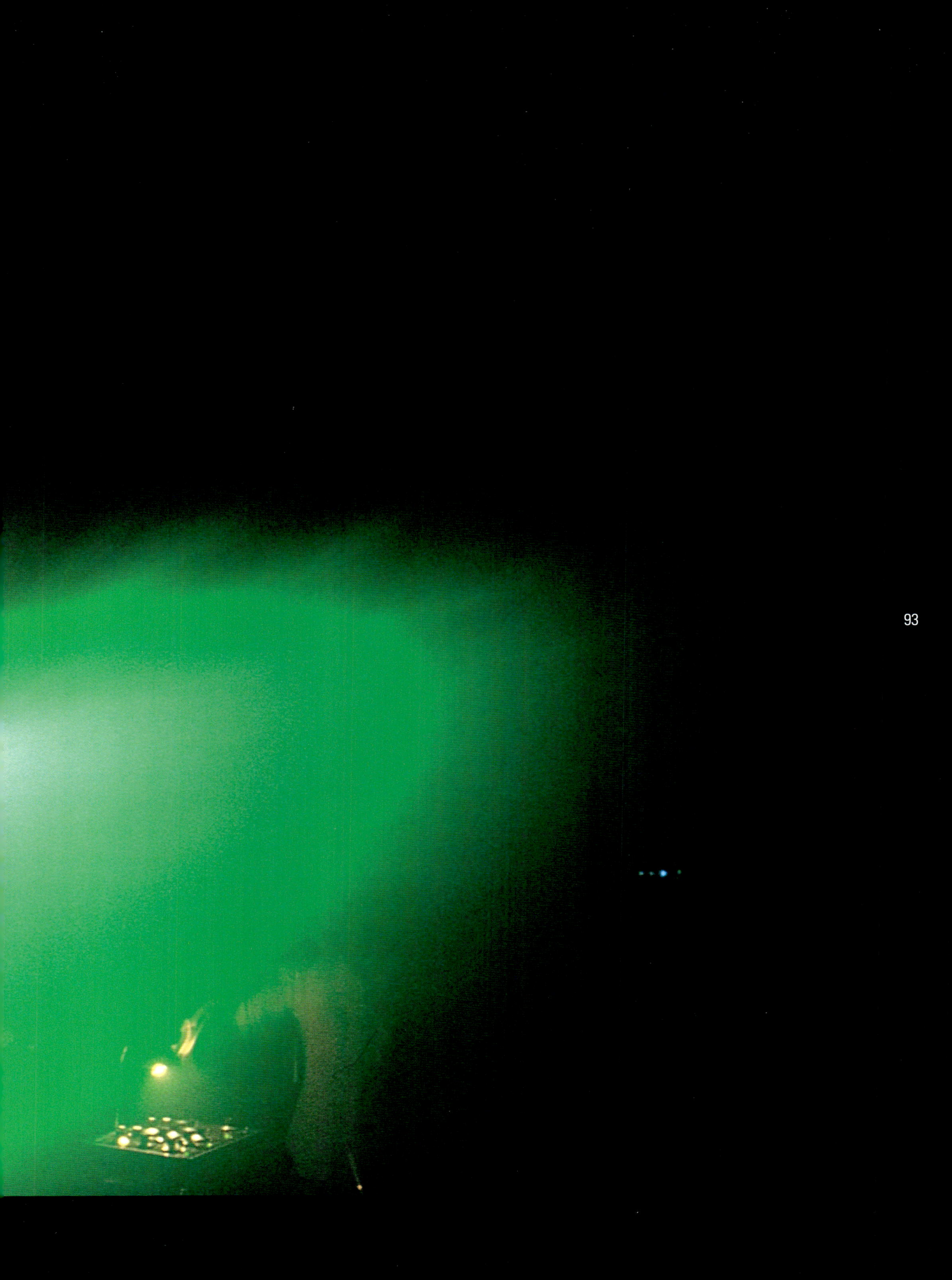

of the laser mirrors was controlled by a specially made analog synthesizer.

Materials such as smoke, water vapour and material particles were used to visualize the moving laser beam and so create immaterial kinetic architectures of light.

This technique was used for three Genesis concert tours (1976, 1977, 1978). The presentation at Stichting de Appel (Amsterdam, Netherlands, 1978) explored the possibilities of an interactive electronic connection between a live cello performance and the consequent articulation of laser-generated light forms.

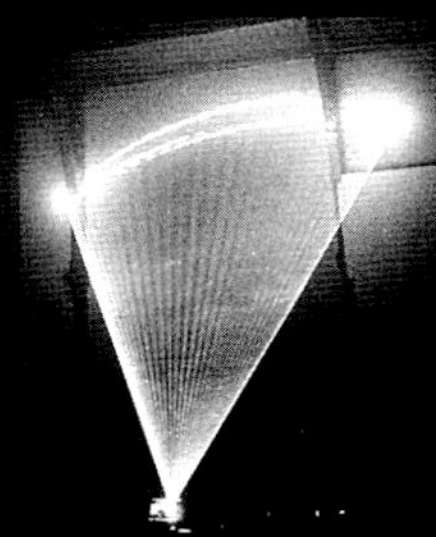

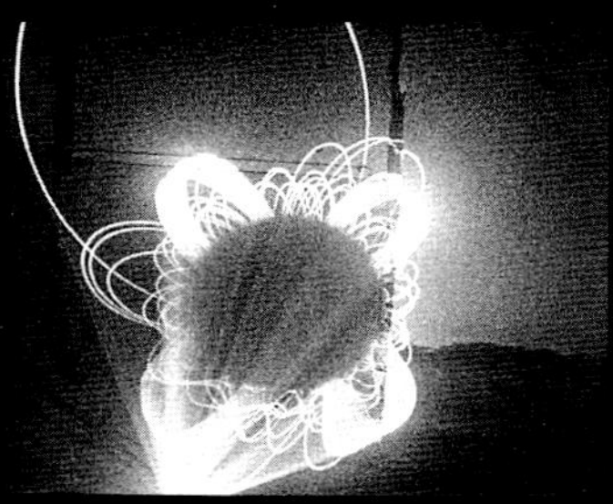

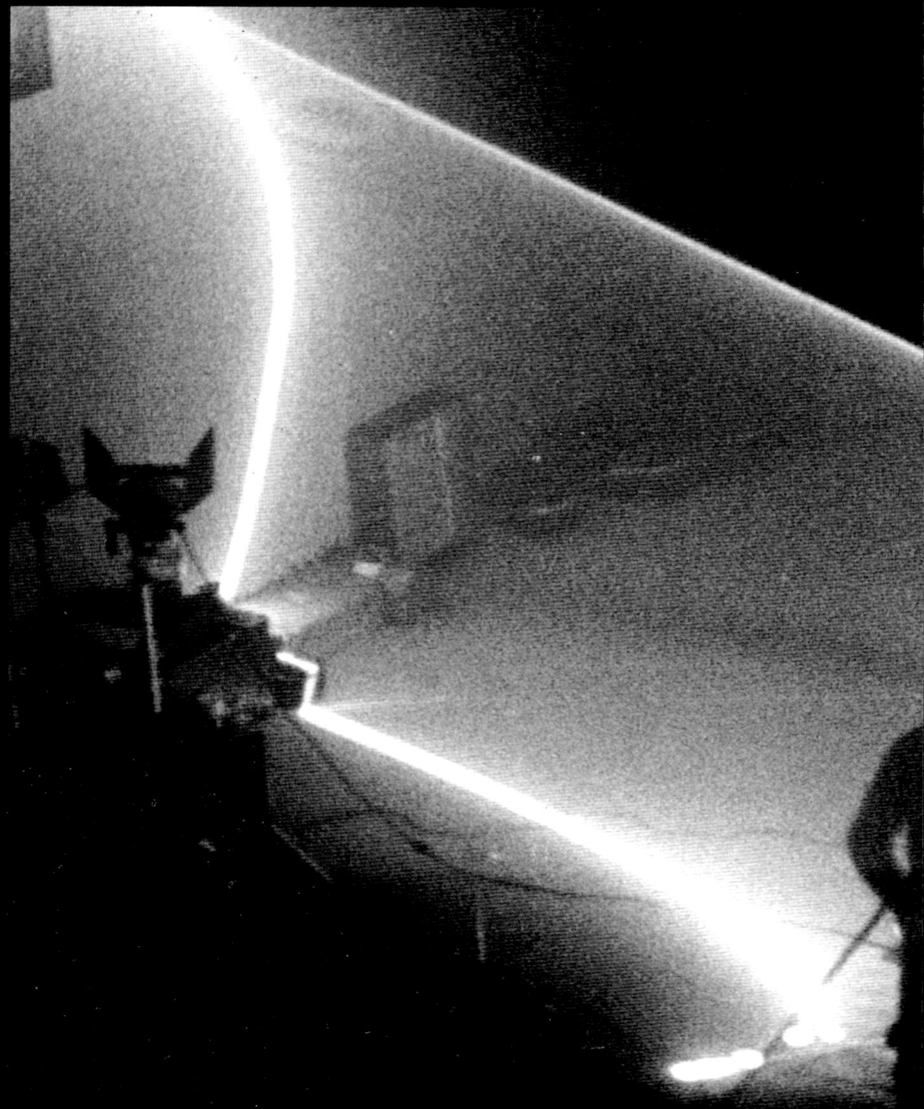

und Rotation der Laserspiegel wurde über einen speziell entwickelten analogen Synthesizer gesteuert. Der sich bewegende Laserstrahl wurde mit Hilfe von Rauch, Wasserdampf und anderen Substanzen sichtbar gemacht, so daß immaterielle kinetische Lichtarchitekturen entstanden.

Diese Technik wurde auf drei Konzerttourneen von Genesis (1976, 1977 und 1978) eingesetzt. Die Präsentation in Stichting de Appel (Amsterdam, Niederlande, 1978) erforschte die Möglichkeiten einer interaktiven elektronischen Verbindung zwischen einem Live-Cellokonzert und lasergenerierten Lichtformen.

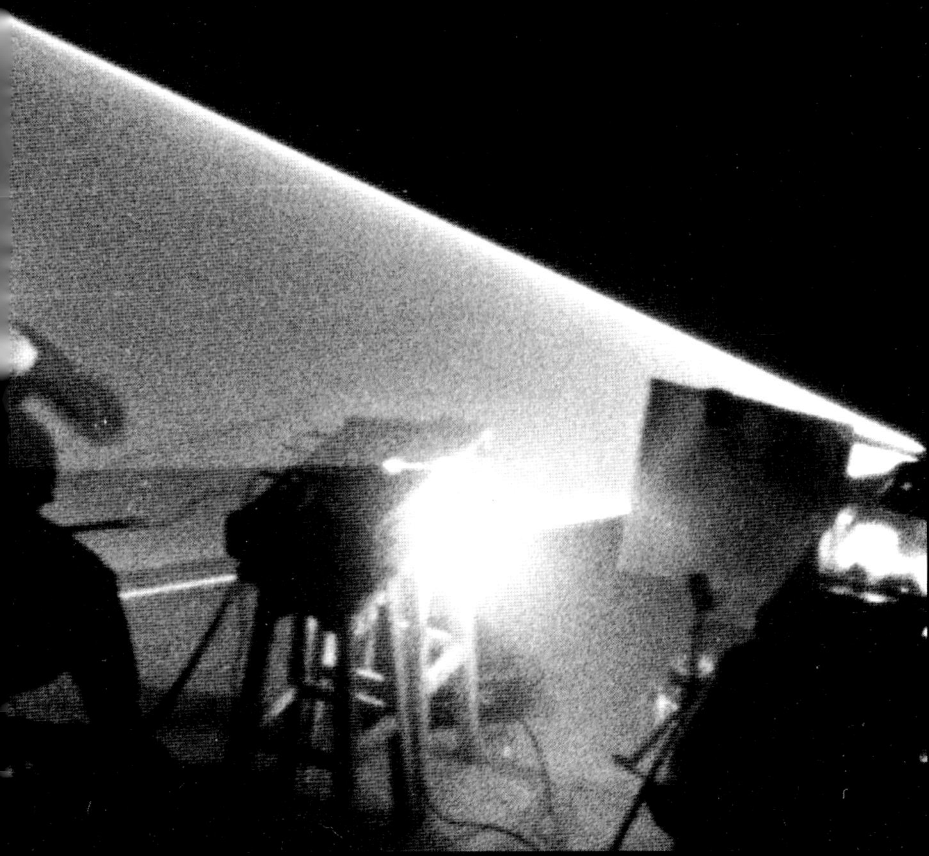

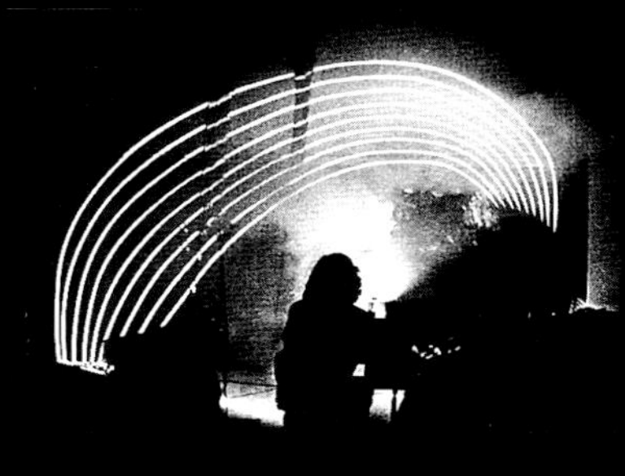

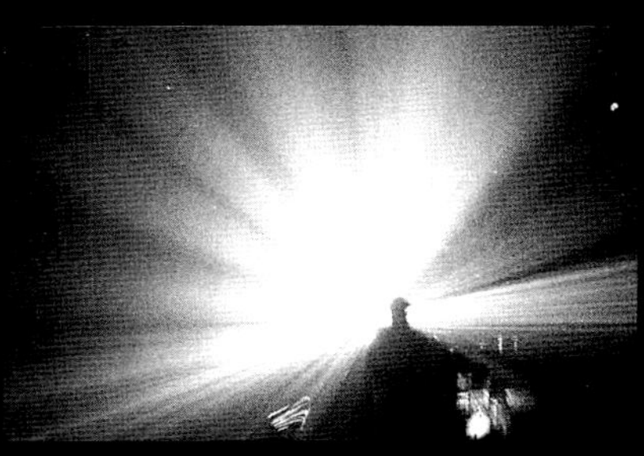

Interactive sculptures for public buildings Since 1979

Many large sculptural commissions were undertaken for public buildings where appropriate modalities of interactivity were sought within the constraints of these contexts. The *Neon Wave Sculpture* (Koopvaardersplantsoen, Amsterdam Noord, Netherlands, 1979), for instance, is a light sculpture that is interactively controlled by varying wind speeds. Mounted on the exterior wall of an apartment building, it is constituted by 48 sine-curved neon tubes. The light level in each tube can be electronically modulated so that an animated movement of waveforms appear to travel across the sculpture. Eight different patterns are interactively determined by the actual wind speed conditions metered on the roof of the building – these wave patterns relate directly and metaphorically to wind speeds ranging from calm to storm.

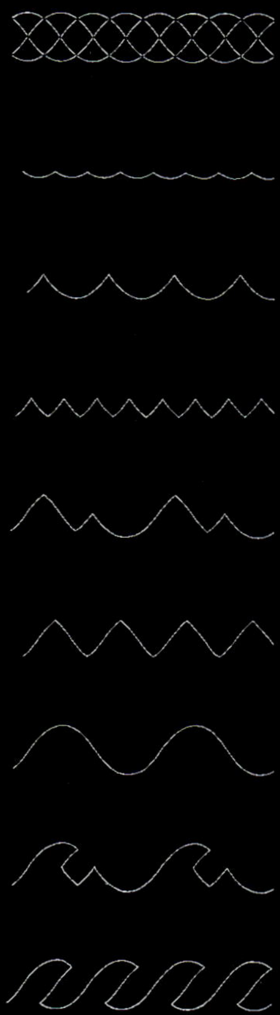

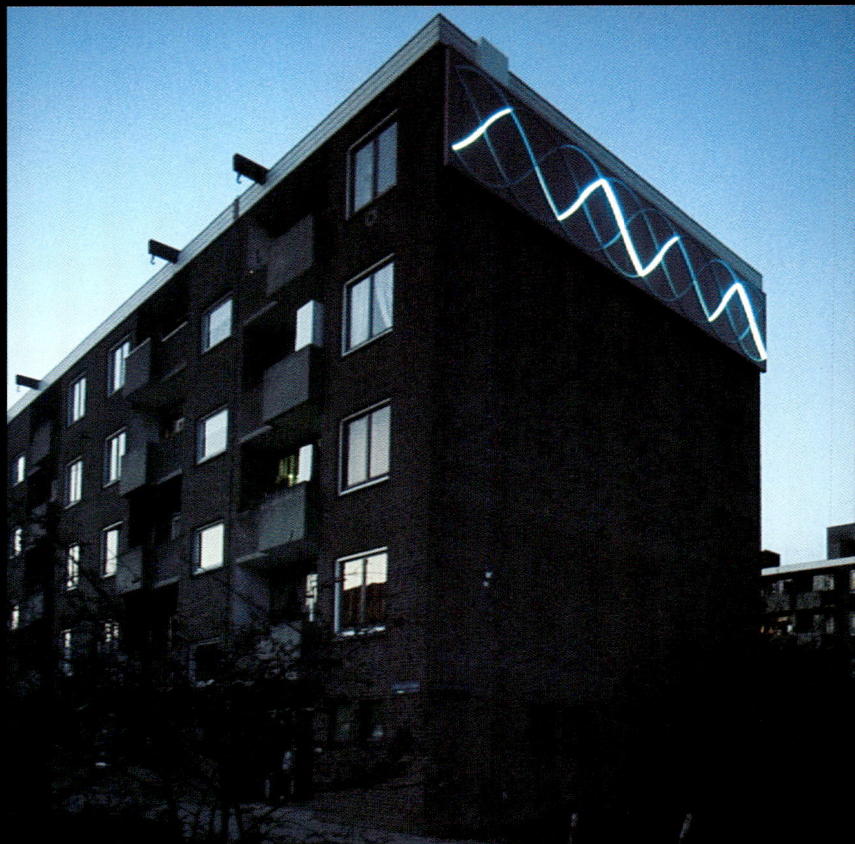

Interaktive Skulpturen für öffentliche Gebäude Seit 1979

Viele große skulpturale Auftragsarbeiten wurden für öffentliche Gebäude entwickelt, wobei nach adäquaten Formen von Interaktivität für den jeweiligen Kontext gesucht wurde. *Neon Wave Sculpture* (›Neonwellen-Skulptur‹, Koopvaardersplantsoen, Amsterdam, Niederlande, 1979) beispielsweise ist eine Lichtskulptur, die interaktiv über variierende Windgeschwindigkeiten gesteuert wird. Die an der Außenwand eines Appartementgebäudes angebrachte Skulptur besteht aus 48 sinuskurvenförmigen Neonröhren. Die Lichtstärke jeder Röhre kann elektronisch moduliert werden, so daß eine animierte wellenförmige Bewegung über die Skulptur zu wandern scheint. Acht verschiedene Muster können über die gerade herrschende Windstärke bestimmt werden, die auf dem Dach des Gebäudes gemessen wird. Diese Wellenmuster stehen in direkter und in metaphorischer Beziehung zur jeweiligen Windstärke.

In *Architext* (Stadstheater, Zoetermeer, Netherlands, 1992) large alphanumeric LED elements are mounted in 13 columns and nine rows on one side of the stage tower of the city theatre in Zoetermeer. Textual information is scrolled through the sculpture like in a traditional billboard, but because the illuminating elements are spaced far apart the projected information becomes abstracted into a more complex image – the words and sentences now appear to weave in and out of the wall of the building. This architectural permutation of the text is further articulated by the programming of various patterns and directions of movement of the letters. The sculpture is interactively programmed using titles and texts of performances taking place in the theatre. In this way the sculpture broadcasts fragments of texts from current stage productions to the viewers outside and makes the building porous for a visual transposition of information from interior to exterior.

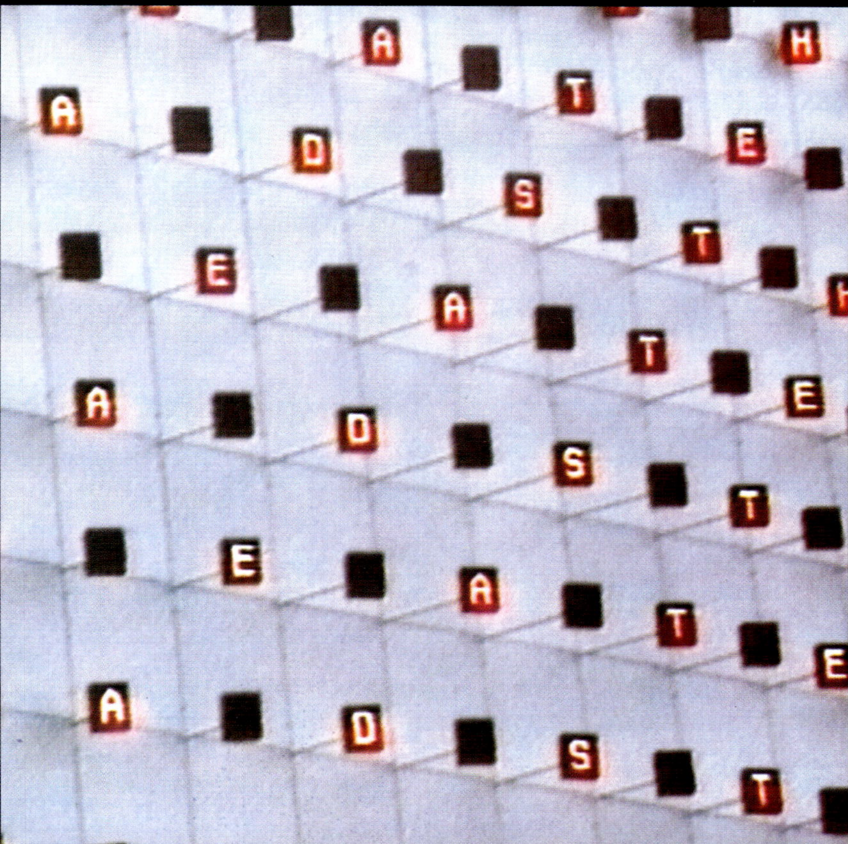

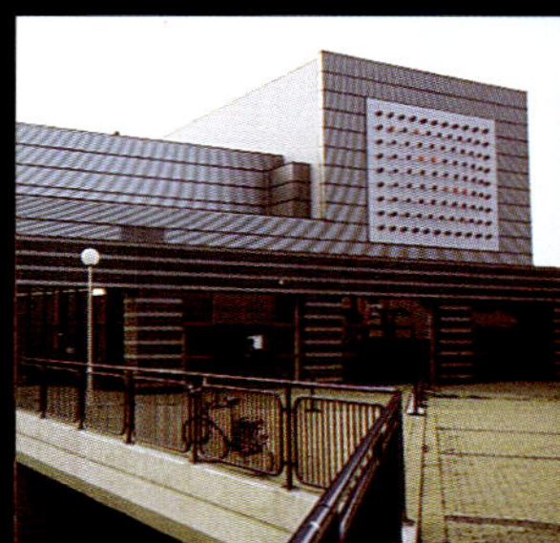

Architext (Stadstheater Zoetermeer, Niederlande, 1992) besteht aus großen alphanumerischen LED-Elementen, die in 13 Kolonnen und neun Reihen angeordnet sind und einen Teil der Außenwand des Stadttheaters Zoetermeer bedecken. Über die Skulptur werden, ähnlich wie bei herkömmlichen Reklametafeln, Texte gescrollt. Doch da die Leuchtelemente in weitem Abstand voneinander angebracht sind, wird die projizierte Information zu einem komplexeren Bild abstrahiert – es scheint, als schlängelten sich die Worte und Sätze in die Wand des Gebäudes hinein und wieder aus ihr heraus. Die architektonische Permutation des Textes wird noch verstärkt durch die Programmierung verschiedener Bewegungsmuster und -richtungen der Buchstaben. Die interaktiv programmierte Skulptur zeigt Titel und Texte von Aufführungen, die im Theater stattfinden. Auf diese Weise überträgt die Skulptur Textfragmente aus aktuellen Bühnenproduktionen zu den Betrachtern nach draußen und läßt das Gebäude durchlässig werden für eine visuelle Transposition von Informationen von innen nach außen.

Javaphile Productions 1977–79

Javaphile Productions created a number of theatrical performances and installations at various venues – salons, galleries, theatres – in the Netherlands. Founded by residents at the Javastraat in Amsterdam (Marga Adama, John Munsey and Jeffrey Shaw), they were joined for different performances by artists including Robert Hahn, Wendela Gevers-Deynoot, Carlyle Reedy, Lanny Harrison and Jenn ben Jakov.

Javaphile was a multi-disciplinary grouping that included actors, singers, poets, writers, painters, sculptors and media artists. Its composition determined the idiosyncratic conjunction of theatrical, musical, literary and visual art components that marked these performances. While all the pieces were ritualistic and symbolic in character, their speculative discourses were usually embodied in bizarre formations and grotesque actions.

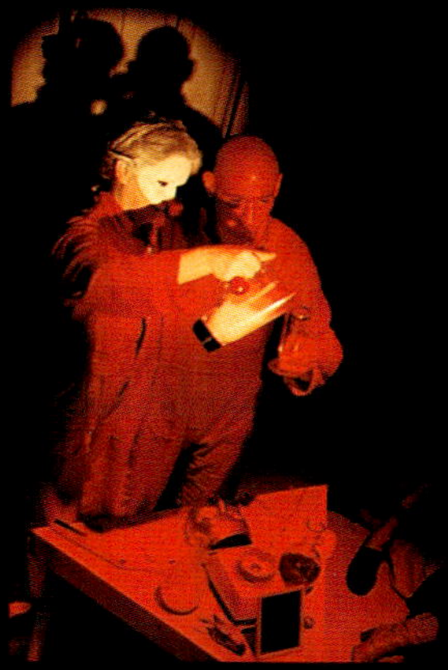

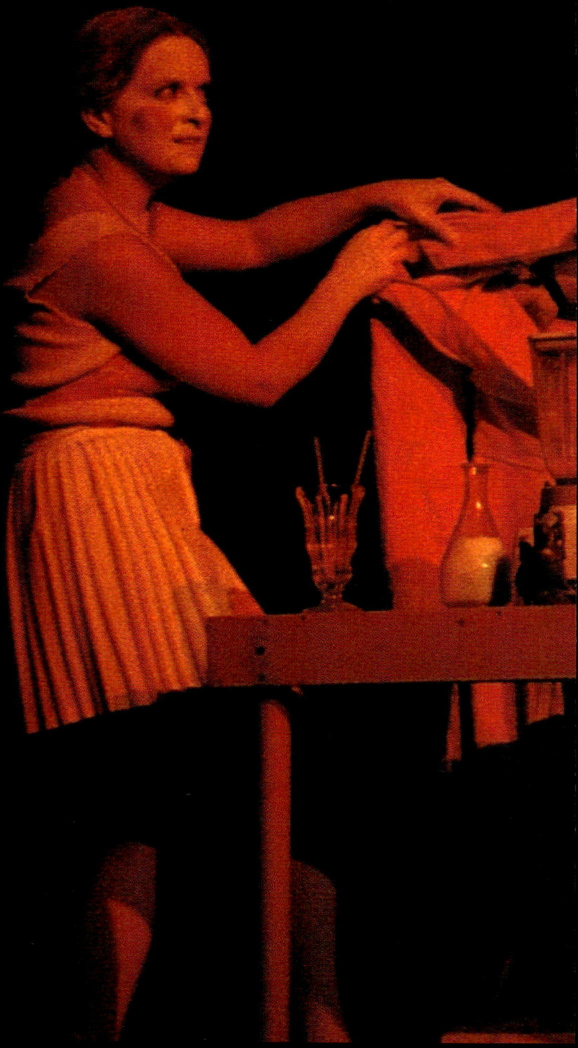

Javaphile Produktionen 1977–79

Zwischen 1977 und 1979 zeigte Javaphile eine Reihe von theatralen Performances und Installationen an verschiedenen Orten – Salons, Galerien, Theater – in den Niederlanden. Javaphile wurde von Bewohnern der Javastraat in Amsterdam (Marga Adama, John Munsey und Jeffrey Shaw) gegründet; an den verschiedenen Aufführungen beteiligten sich weitere Künstler – u.a. Robert Hahn, Wendela Gevers Deynoot, Carlyle Reedy, Lanny Harrison und Jenn ben Jakov.

Javaphile war eine multidisziplinäre Gruppierung von Schauspielern, Sängern, Dichtern, Schriftstellern, Malern, Bildhauern und Medienkünstlern. Diese Zusammensetzung bestimmte die idiosynkratische Verbindung von Elementen aus den Bereichen des Theaters, der Musik, der Literatur und der Bildenden Kunst, die diese Performances auszeichneten. Obwohl all diese Stücke rituellen und symbolischen Charakter hatten, enthielten sie auf der Ebene des spekulativen Diskurses meist bizarre Formationen und groteske Aktionen.

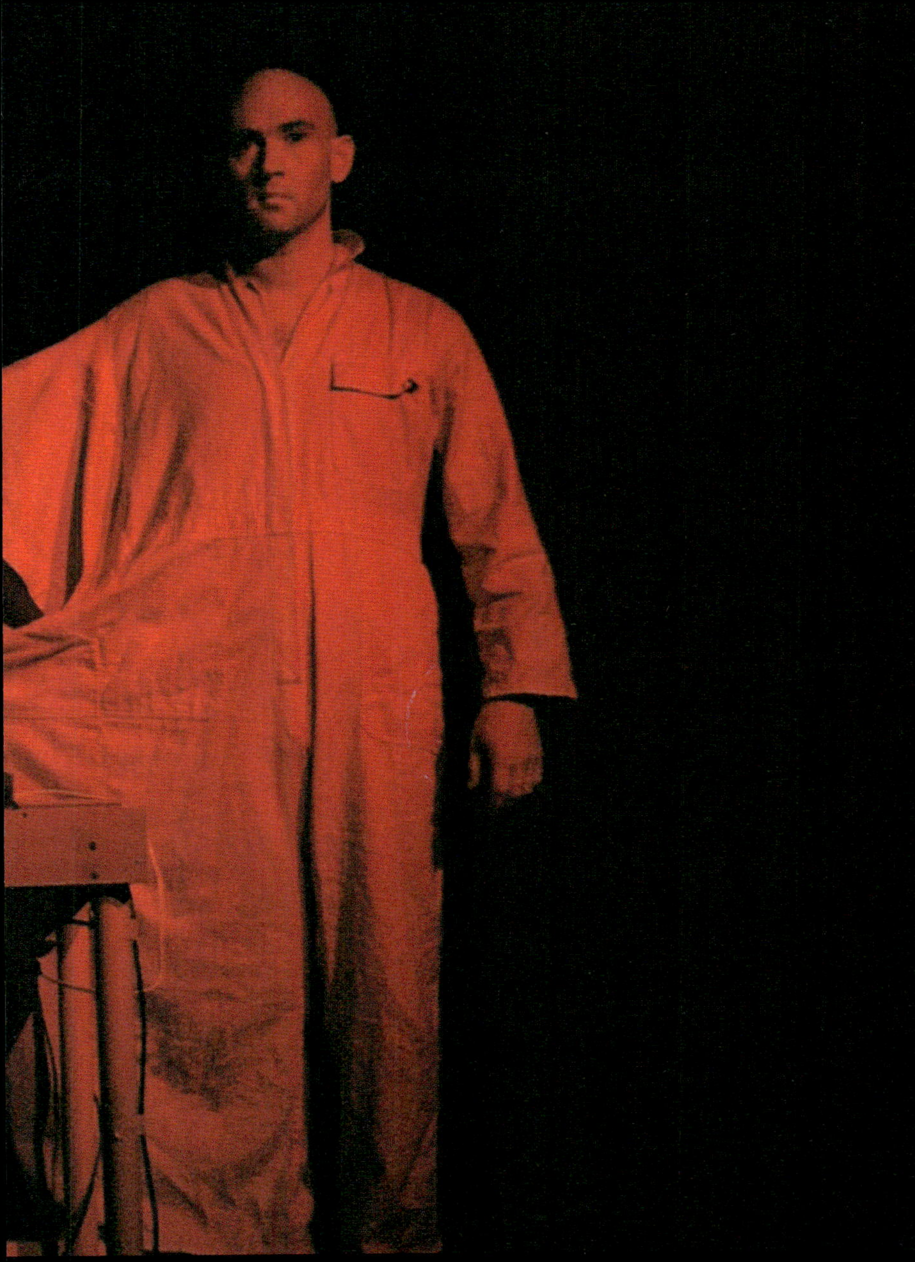
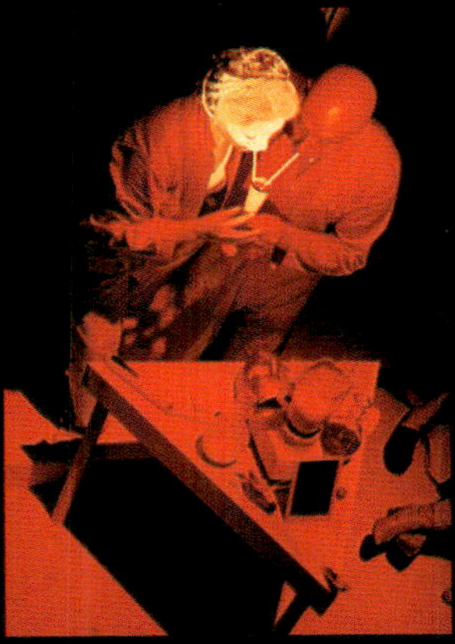

Virtual projection works

Experiments with computer-generated stereo imagery led to the development of optical devices that projected these images virtually. A virtual-reality type of apparatus was made where the viewer could rotate and tilt a monitor so that various simple computer-generated objects could be seen floating in different places in the real space (*Virtual Projection Installation*, Melkweg, Amsterdam, Netherlands, 1979).

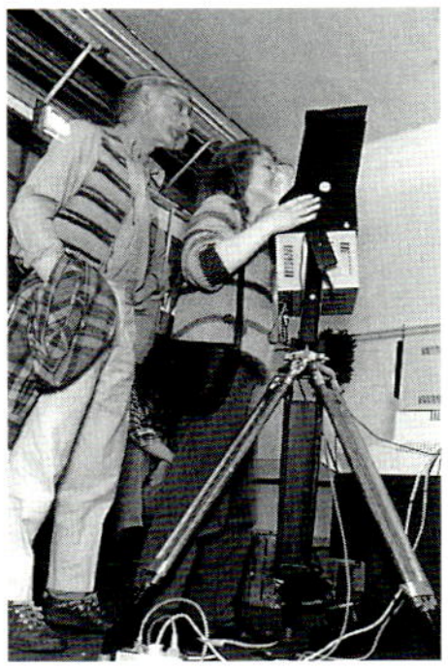

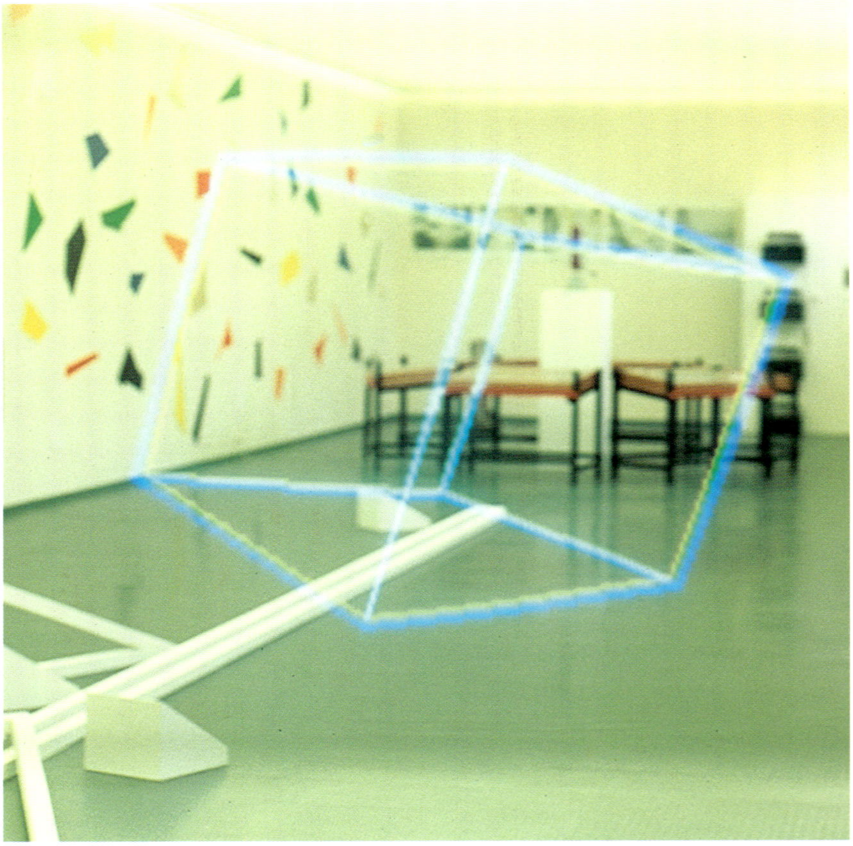

Arbeiten mit virtuellen Projektionen

Experimente mit computergenerierten Stereobildern führten zur Entwicklung von optischen Geräten, die diese Bilder virtuell projizierten. Hieraus entstand eine Art ›Virtual-Reality-Apparatur‹, mit der der Betrachter einen Monitor drehen und neigen konnte, so daß einfache, computergenerierte Objekte gesehen werden konnten, die im realen Raum an verschiedenen Stellen schwebten (*Virtual Projection Installation* (›Installation mit virtuellen Projektionen‹, 1979).

This kind of virtual projection technique was also used during a performance by Fabienne de Quasa Riera (*Virtual Projection Performance*, De Lantaren, Rotterdam, Netherlands, 1983) where the audience looking through a window saw a computer-animated swing superimposed over the performer seated on a real swing.

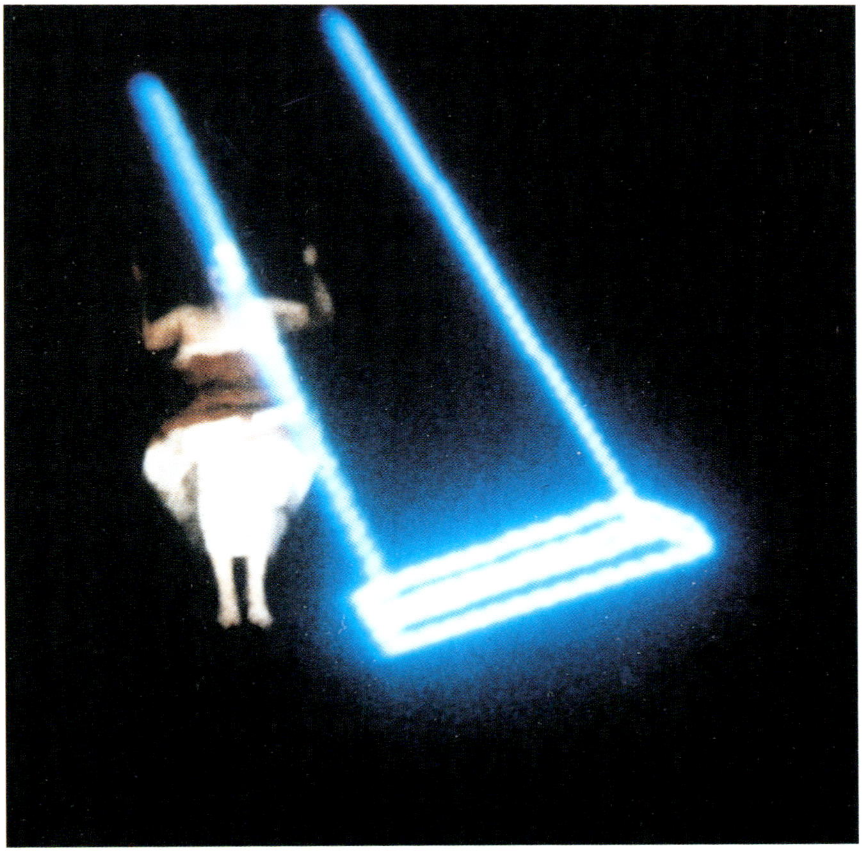

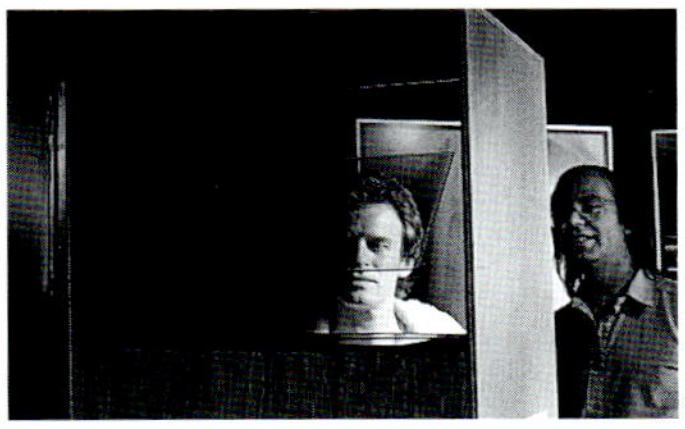

Diese Art der virtuellen Projektionstechnik wurde auch während einer Performance von Fabienne de Quasa Riera (*Virtual Projection Performance* ›Performance mit Virtuellen Projektionen‹), De Lantaren, Rotterdam, Niederlande, 1983) verwendet: Das Publikum schaute durch ein Fenster und sah eine computeranimierte Schaukel, die die reale Schaukel, auf der die Künstlerin saß, überlagerte.

Points of View 1983/84

Points of View was a 'theatre of signs' with both stage and protagonists constituted by a three-dimensional computer graphics simulation that was video-projected onto a large screen in front of a seated audience.

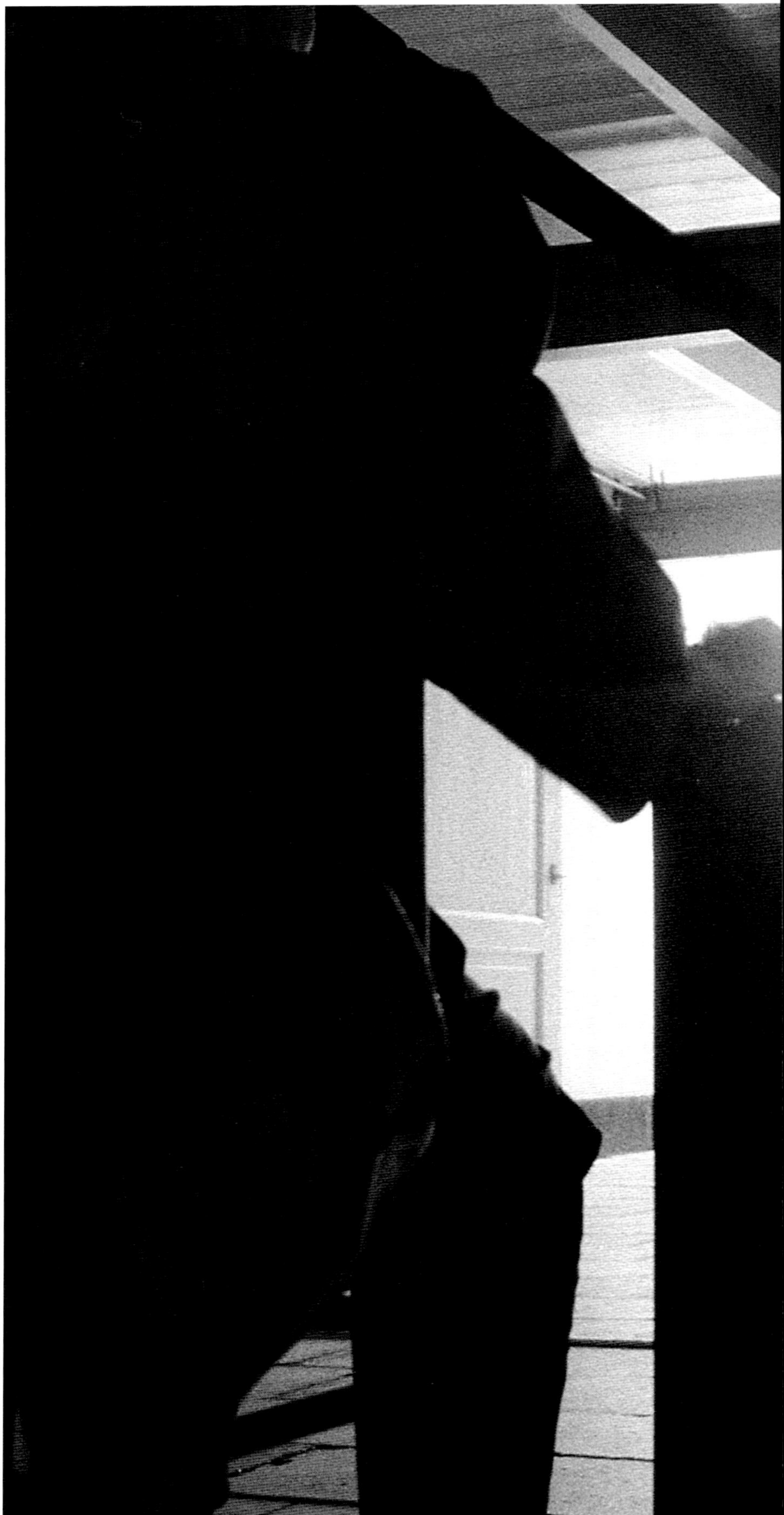

Points of View Standpunkte 1983/84

Points of View war ein ›Theater der Zeichen‹, dessen Bühne und Protagonisten in einer dreidimensionalen Computergrafiksimulation erzeugt und auf eine große Leinwand, die sich vor dem sitzenden Publikum befand, projiziert wurden.

Mit zwei speziell angefertigten Joysticks konnte

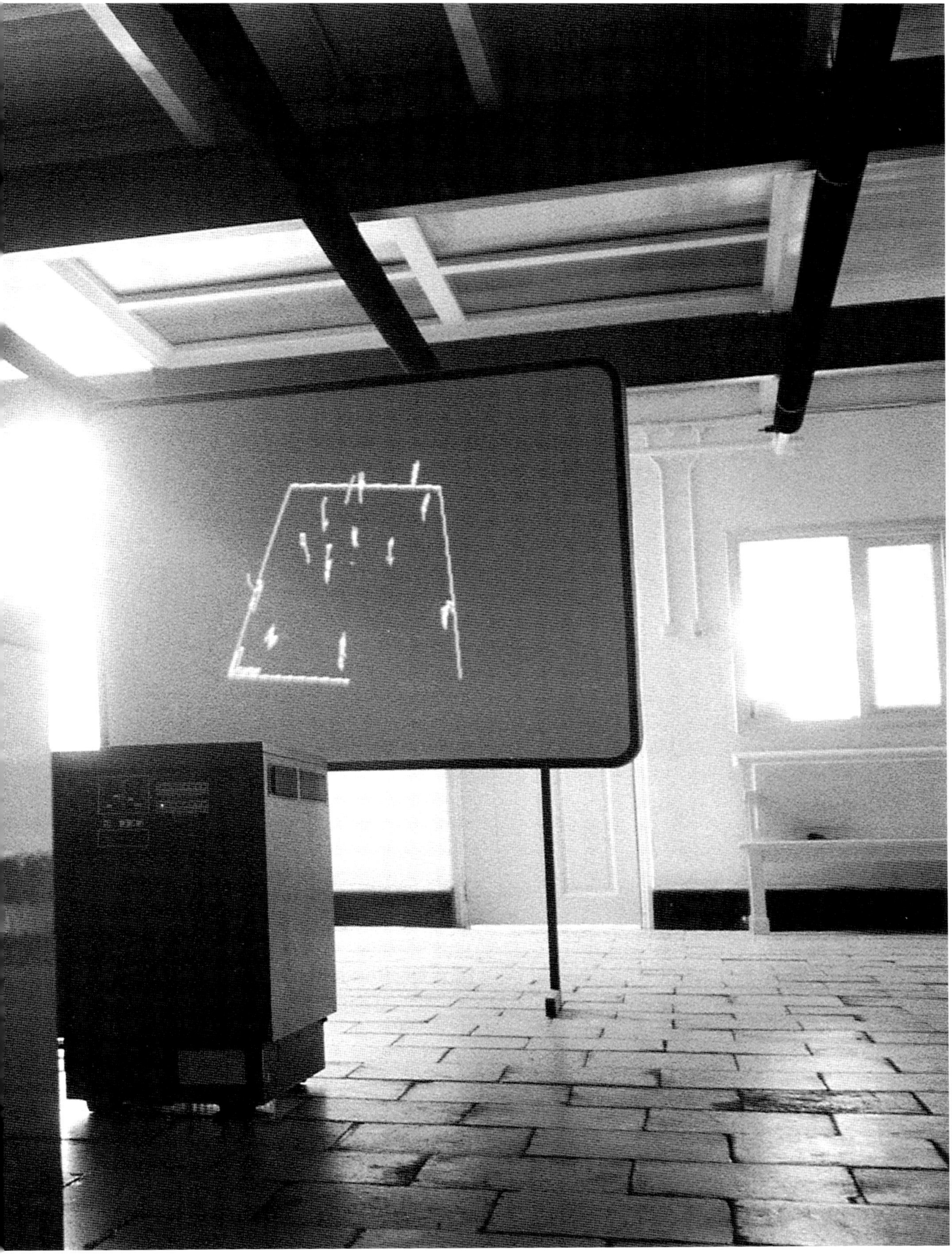

The action of the work was controlled by one member of the audience using two specially made joysticks. Embodying techniques developed for flight simulation, this work gave the operator the ability to interactively move his virtual point of view 360 degrees around the stage, 90 degrees up and down from ground level to aerial view, and forwards and backwards from a far distance to the centre of the stage.

The representation of the actors on the stage was derived from the ancient Egyptian alphabet and each figure was a hieroglyphic character. This constellation of signs was used to articulate a world model with an underlying set of physical and conceptual relationships. Sixteen sound tracks – mostly spoken texts – were interactively linked to the image via the same joystick that controlled the visual movements. Functioning like an audio mixer, this modulated the relative volume of the various voices with respect to the changing spatial positions taken by the viewer. Here again, an intrinsic conceptual structure

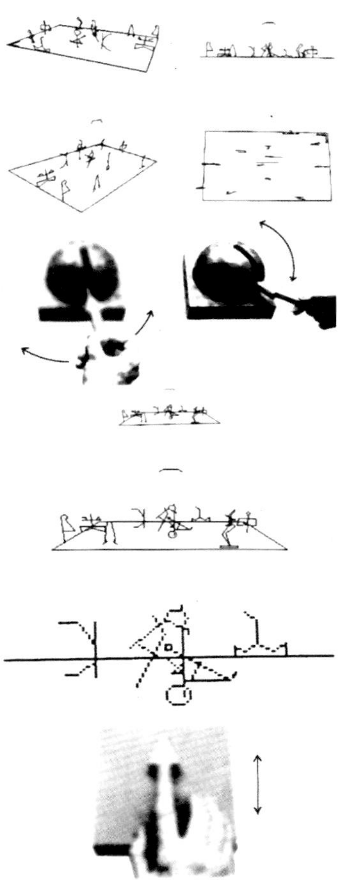

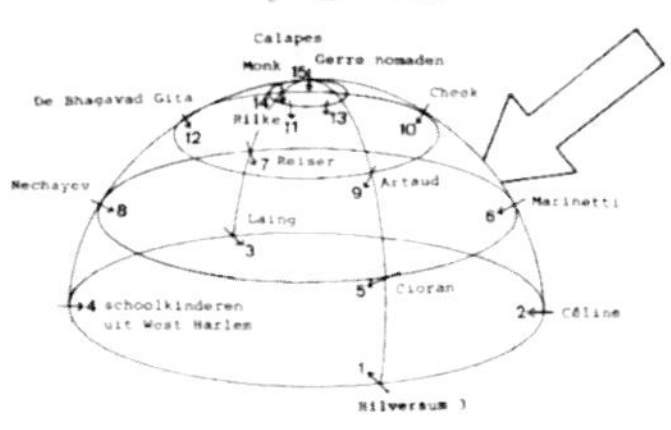

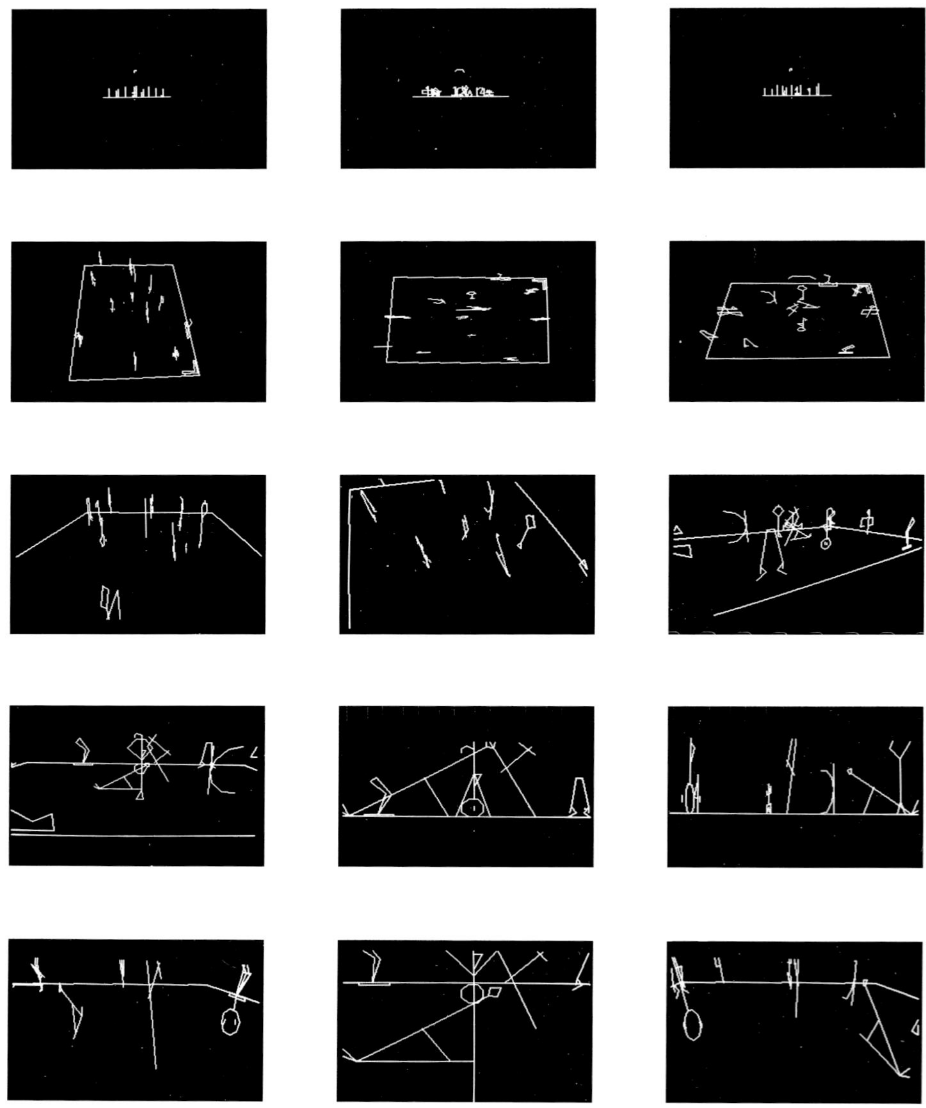

die Handlung von einem der Zuschauer gesteuert werden. Durch die Verwendung von Techniken aus dem Bereich der Flugsimulation war es möglich, daß der Benutzer seinen virtuellen Standpunkt interaktiv verändern konnte: in einem Radius von 360 Grad über die Bühne, von 90 Grad nach oben und unten (vom Boden bis zu einer Ansicht aus der Luft) sowie vor und zurück (zur Bühnenmitte hin und von ihr weg).

Die Schauspieler auf der Bühne wurden dargestellt als Zeichen, abgeleitet vom alten ägyptischen Alphabet – jede Figur war ein hieroglyphisches Zeichen. Diese Zeichenkonstellation wurde verwendet, um ein Weltmodell auszudrücken, dem eine Reihe physikalischer und konzeptueller Beziehungen zugrunde liegen. 16 Tonspuren – größtenteils gesprochene Texte – waren über den Joystick, der auch die visuellen Bewegungen kontrollierte und wie ein Audiomixer funktionierte, interaktiv mit dem Bild verbunden. Auf diese Weise konnte die Lautstärke der verschiedenen Stimmen entsprechend der wechselnden Positionen des Betrachters im Raum verändert werden. Auch hier wurde eine im wesentlichen konzeptuelle Struktur dargestellt durch die räumliche Verbindung der Tonspuren mit vier Standpunkten auf

was articulated in the spatial mapping of these sound tracks to four positions on four levels of a semi-sphere.

Two further installations were made using the same functional and iconographic elements as this work, but with differing contents. *Points of View II – Babel* (1983) addressed issues relating to the Falklands War. *Points of View III – A Three-Dimensional Story* (1984) explored the notion of an open art-work by inviting sixteen people to make narrative contributions which were then interactively linked to the visual scenography so that the viewer could navigate between parallel stories.

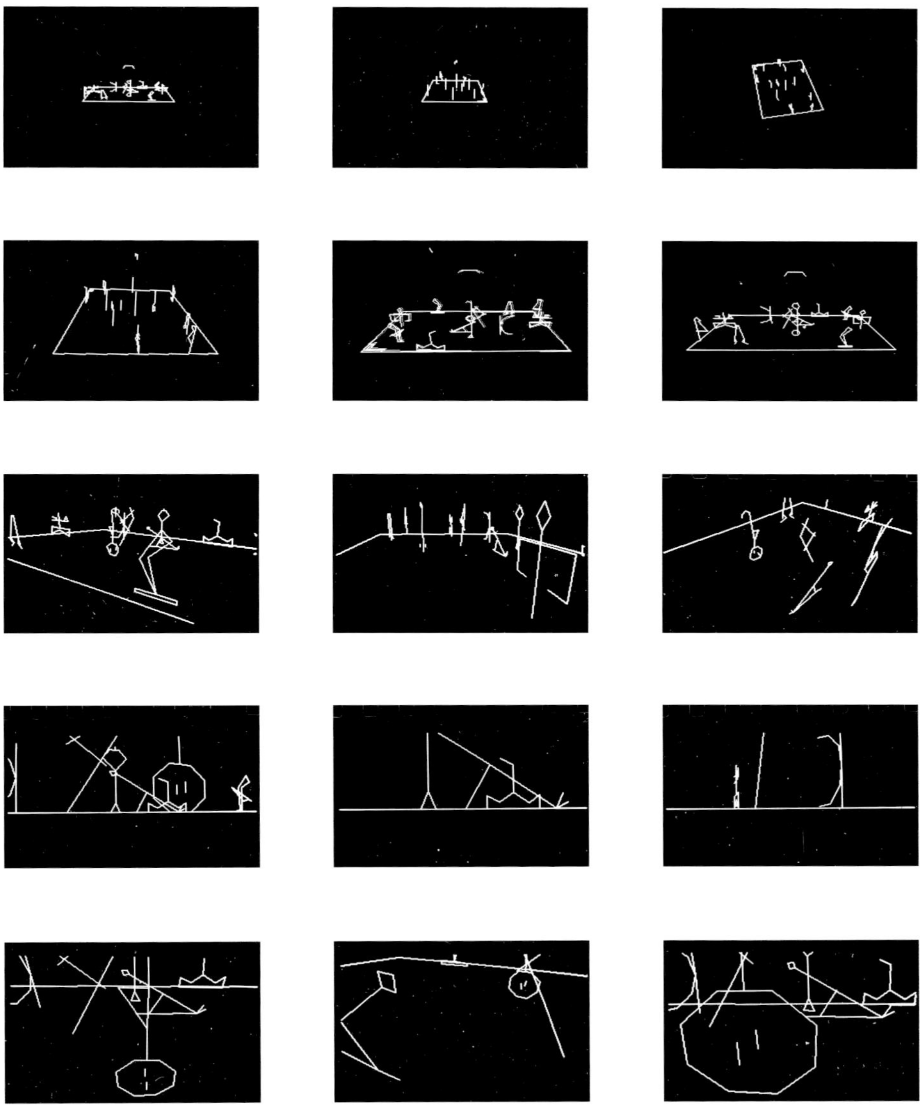

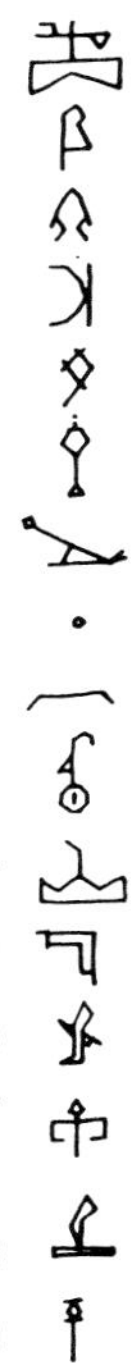

to balance	balancieren
what is true	was wahr ist
to be without	ohne etwas sein
to separate	trennen
to love	lieben
light	Licht
all that grows	alles was wächst
the underworld	die Unterwelt
what is above	was oben ist
time	Zeit
foreigner	Fremder
to hide	verstecken
to attack	angreifen
treasury/ 'white house'	Schatzkammer/ ›Weisses Haus‹
to possess	besitzen
sickness/death	Krankheit/Tod

vier Ebenen einer Semisphäre.

Zwei weitere Installationen wurden entwickelt, die dieselben funktionellen und ikonographischen Elemente verwendeten, aber unterschiedliche Inhalte besaßen. *Points of View II – Babel* (›Perspektiven II – Babel‹, 1983) setzte sich mit dem Falkland-Krieg auseinander. *Points of View III – A Three-Dimensional Story* (›Perspektiven III – Eine dreidimensionale Erzählung‹, 1984) versuchte, die Idee eines offenen Kunstwerks umzusetzen: Sechzehn Personen wurden eingeladen, sich mit erzählerischen Beiträgen zu beteiligen, die interaktiv mit der visuellen Ebene verbunden wurden, so daß der Betrachter zwischen parallel laufenden Erzählungen navigieren konnte.

The Narrative Landscape 1985/95

In this installation images are projected onto a large screen lying flat on the floor of the exhibition space. The spectators stand on a surrounding balcony where a joystick enables any one of them to interactively operate the work.

The images and spoken texts are digitally stored in a computer. The viewer uses the joystick to control panning in any lateral direction over the surface of these images and zooming in or out of a chosen part of an image. At the zoom extremes the joystick

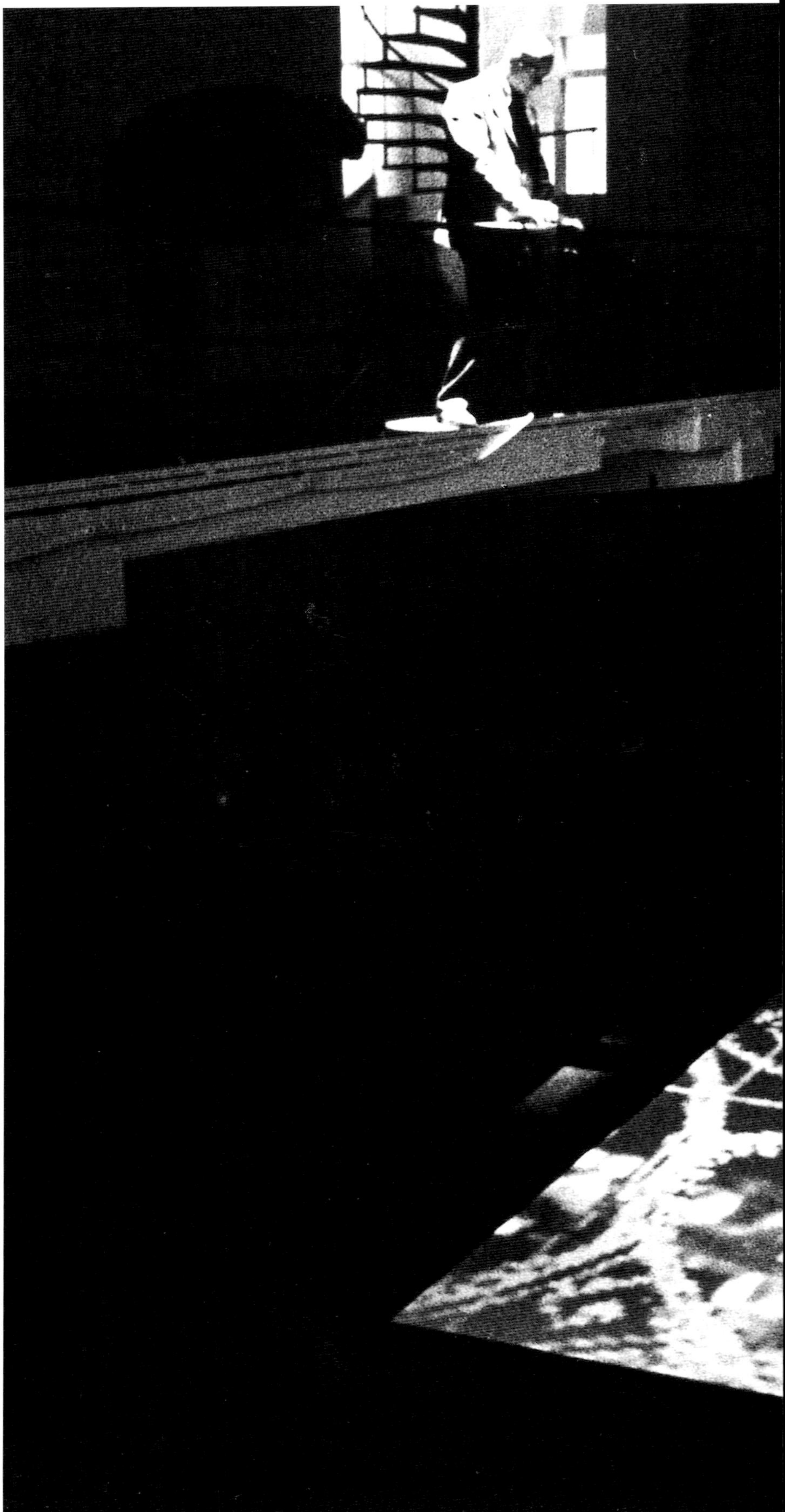

The Narrative Landscape

Erzählerische Landschaft 1985/95

In dieser Installation werden Bilder auf eine große Leinwand projiziert, die flach auf dem Boden des Ausstellungsraumes liegt. Die Zuschauer stehen auf einem umlaufenden Balkon, auf dem sich ein Joystick befindet, mit dem eine Person die Arbeit interaktiv bedienen kann.

Die Bilder und die gesprochenen Texte sind digital in einem Computer gespeichert. Der Betrachter benutzt den Joystick, um in jede beliebige Richtung über die Oberfläche der projizierten Bilder zu schwenken und um in einen ausgewählten Bildausschnitt hinein oder aus ihm heraus zu zoomen. Sobald die

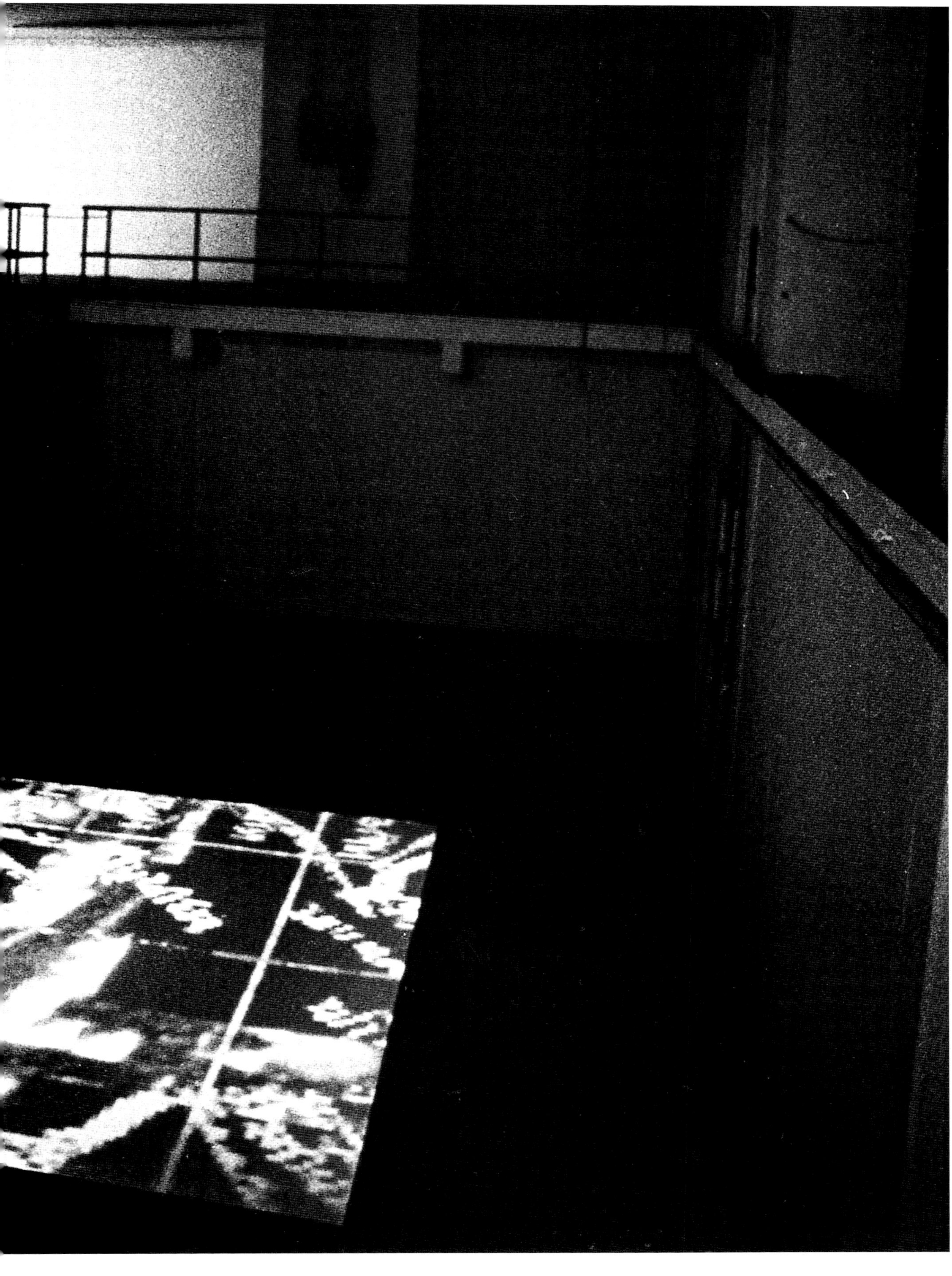

generates a digital transition to a new image – a process experienced by the viewer as breaking through from one image level to another. Most of the images in this work are derived from photographs that were digitized, collaged and electronically processed. Because these images are a digital raster, the action of zooming is also a process of increasing abstraction as the pixels become progressively larger. The different levels of representation induced by this digital deconstruction is a formal and conceptual attribute of this work.

The Narrative Landscape is constituted by twenty-eight images which are interelated by a specific spatial and conceptual architecture. The primary image (a satellite picture of earth inscribed with a Hebraic astrological chart) is divided by a grid of red lines into nine areas which define access to nine groups of three images. The three images in each group are arranged one below the other and the viewer can move up or down through these three levels. He can also go back to the primary image and then choose

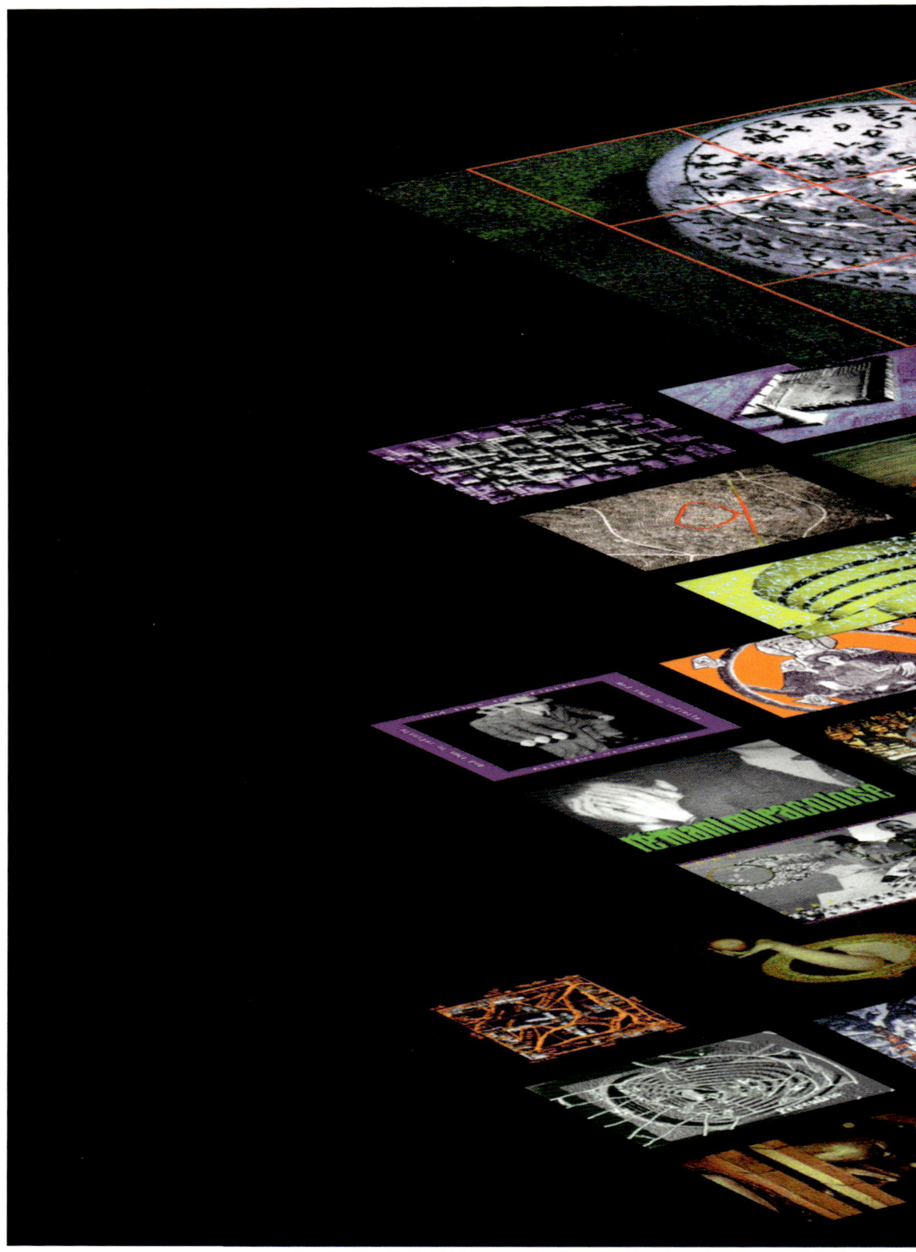

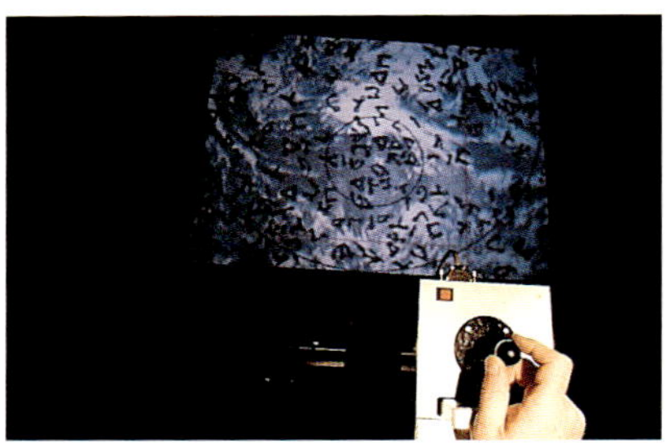

äußerste Zoomposition erreicht ist, generiert der Joystick einen digital gesteuerten Übergang zu einem neuen Bild – ein Vorgang, der den Betrachter von einer Bildebene zur nächsten ›durchbrechen‹ läßt. Die meisten Bilder dieser Arbeit entstanden aus Fotografien, die digitalisiert, collagiert und elektronisch bearbeitet wurden. Da diese Bilder aus einem digitalen Raster bestehen, bewirkt die Betätigung des Zooms gleichzeitig einen Prozeß zunehmender Abstraktion, da die Pixel immer größer werden. Diese verschiedenen, durch digitale Dekonstruktion entstandenen Darstellungsebenen stellen ein formales und konzeptuelles Merkmal dieser Arbeit dar.

The Narrative Landscape besteht aus 28 Bildern, die durch eine spezielle räumliche und konzeptuelle Architektur miteinander verbunden sind. Das erste Bild (eine Satellitenaufnahme der Erde, in die Symbole einer hebräischen astrologischen Karte eingeschrieben sind) ist durch ein Gitter roter Linien in neun Bereiche unterteilt, die den Zugriff auf neun Bildgruppen mit je drei Bildern markieren. Die drei Bilder jeder Gruppe liegen jeweils untereinander, und der Betrachter kann sich durch die drei Ebenen nach oben und unten bewegen oder zum Anfangsbild

another image group to zoom into.

All nine groups are structured as an iconographic triptych. The images on the first level represent a place; they have the scale of an aerial image of a city or landscape; the images on the second level indicate the body; they have the scale of human situations; the images on the third level show a figuration of signs that symbolically extend the themes expressed in the first two image levels of place and body. Each group of three images has a distinct narrative formation – the underlying metaphor is one of emblematic places whose typologies are articulated in the fate of their citizens.

The texts of *The Narrative Landscape* were written by Dirk Groeneveld and are conceived as nine distinct narrative poems interactively linked to the nine groups of three images.

In 1995 a compact CD-ROM version of this work was made. It uses a trackball as the interface and the imagery is shown on a monitor mounted with its screen facing upwards in a specially made table.

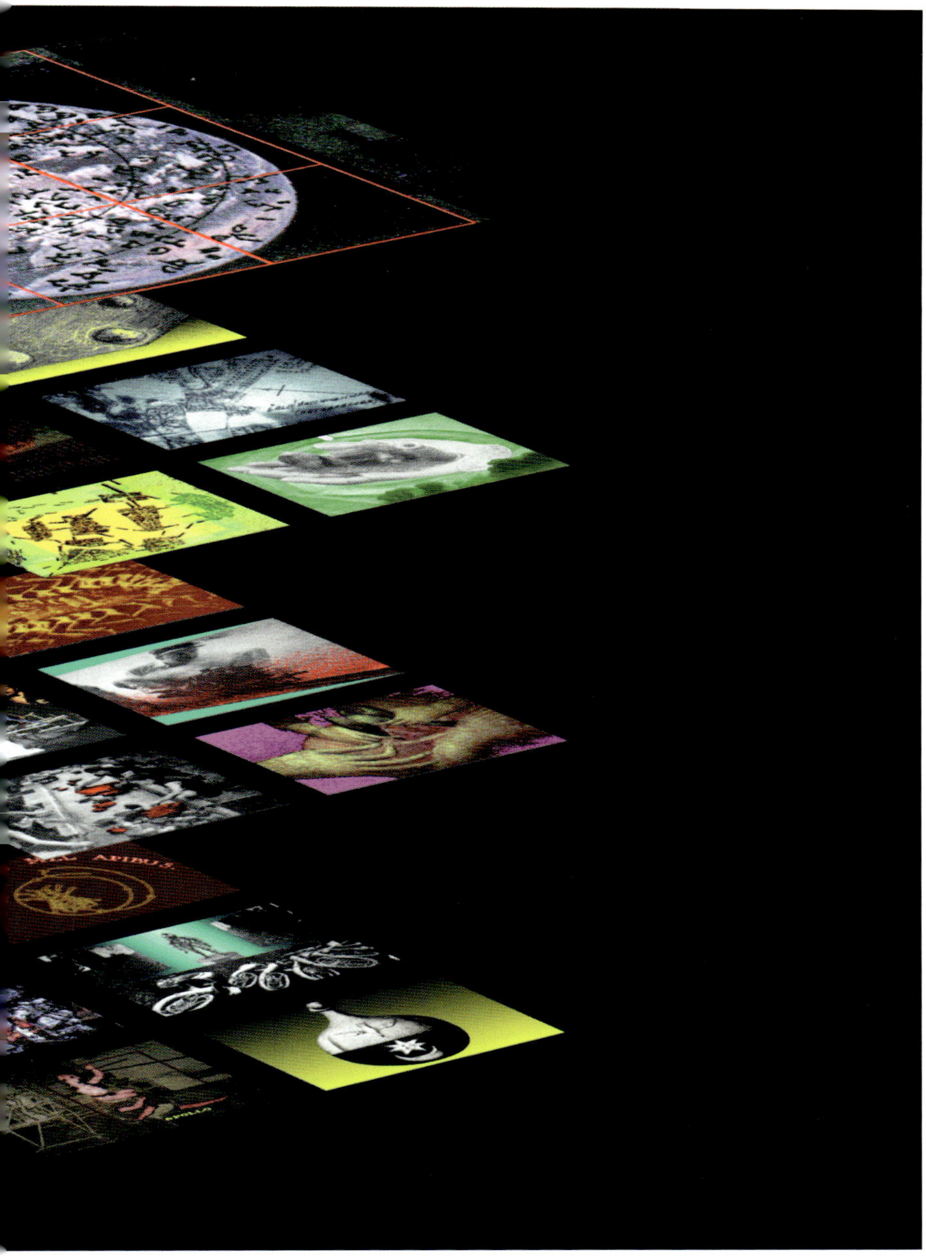

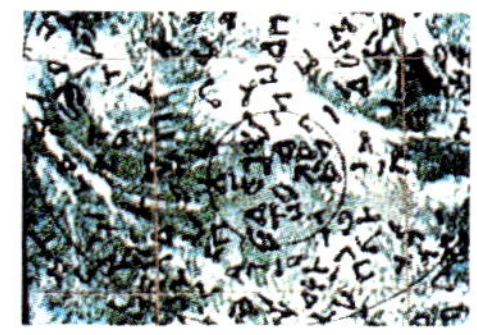

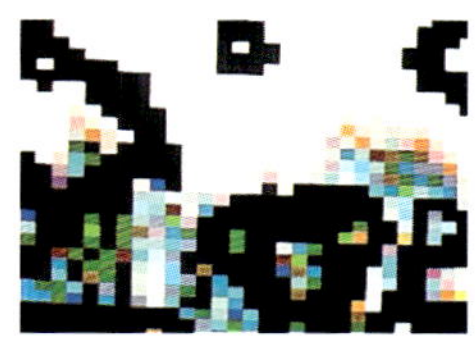

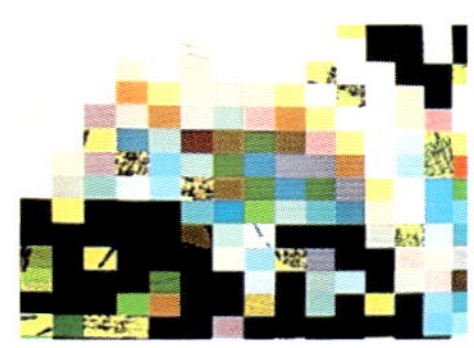

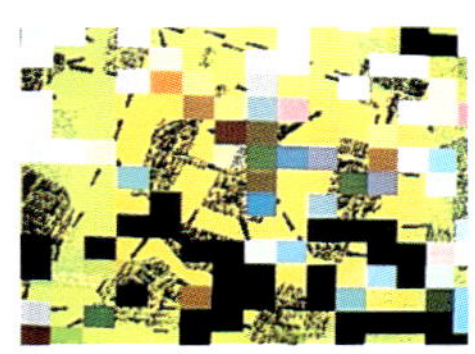

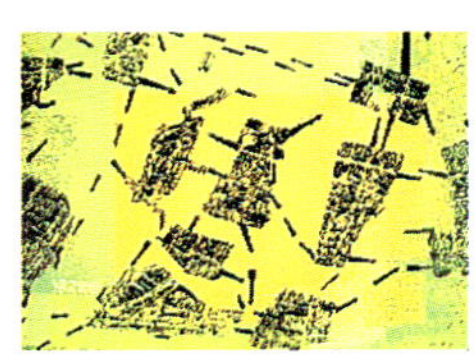

zurückgehen und eine andere Bildgruppe auswählen.

Jede der neun Bildgruppen ist wie ein ikonographisches Triptychon strukturiert. Die Bilder der ersten Ebene repräsentieren einen Ort; sie zeigen Luftaufnahmen einer Stadt oder einer Landschaft. Die Bilder der zweiten Ebene thematisieren den Körper; sie zeigen den Menschen in verschiedenen Situationen. Die Bilder der dritten Ebene zeigen eine Figuration von Zeichen, die die in den ersten beiden Bildebenen dargestellten Themen von Ort und Körper symbolisch erweitern. Jede aus drei Bildern bestehende Gruppe besitzt eine eigene erzählerische Gestaltung – zugrunde liegt die Metapher emblematischer Orte, deren Typologien sich im Schicksal ihrer Bewohner ausdrücken.

Die Texte für *The Narrative Landscape* wurden von Dirk Groeneveld geschrieben und in neun Prosagedichte gegliedert, die interaktiv mit den neun Bildgruppen gekoppelt sind.

1995 wurde eine CD-ROM-Version dieser Arbeit entwickelt. Ein Trackball dient als Schnittstelle, und die Bilder werden auf einem Monitor gezeigt, der mit nach oben ausgerichtetem Bildschirm in einen speziell angefertigten Tisch eingelassen ist.

Going to the Heart of the Center of The Garden of Delights 1986

The installation, which was made specifically for the neo-Gothic Vleeshal in Middelburg (Netherlands, 1986) consisted of a computer graphics video projection onto a large screen at the far end of the room opposite the entrance. Infra-red sensors and seven pairs of blue lights along the floor defined a path from the entrance area to the screen. The visitor walking towards the screen interactively controlled a sequence of transformations in the image and sound.

The sequence of digitally processed images was derived from works by Yves Klein, Nagisa Oshima and Hieronymus Bosch. A conjugation of the representational image and its underlying digital structure was articulated in the transformations of a frame from Oshima's film *In the Realm of the Senses* into a portion of Bosch's painting *The Garden of Delights*. The interactive sequence showed a progressive digital reduction of the Oshima image into a more and more abstract configuration, and out of this raster of picture elements the Bosch image gradually appeared. The sequence was reversed when the viewer walked away from the screen. The viewer's lone journey from the entrance up to the surface of the screen embodied a virtual journey through a set of images that had been architectonically mapped into the installation space. This convergence of an exoteric and an esoteric journey reiterated the conjunction of profane and sacred allusions presented in the work's iconographic structure.

In 1993 a new videodisk-based version of this work was made titled *The Royal Road*. No longer related to a particular architectural context, the viewer walks along a path marked by blue lights towards a large video monitor. In so doing he passes through a row of six virtual video monitors whose screens display the same sequence of images as the original work.

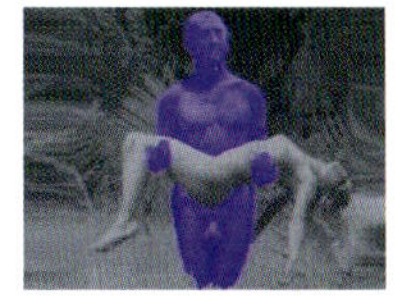

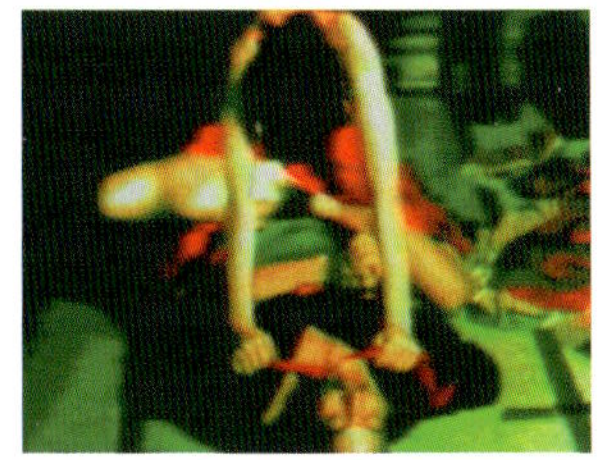

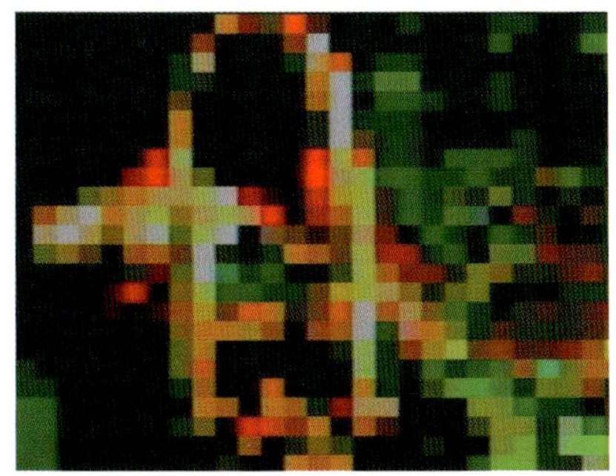

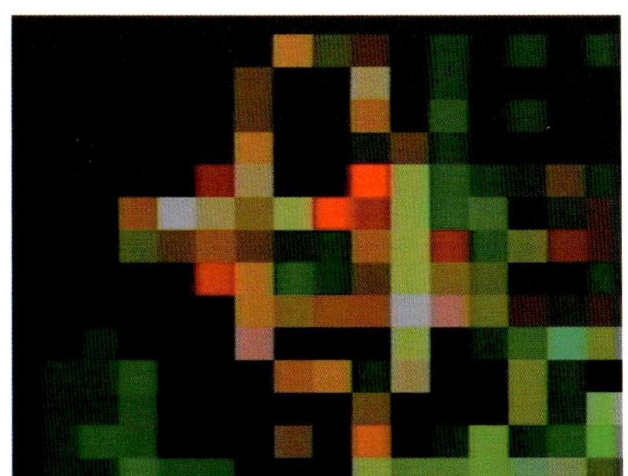

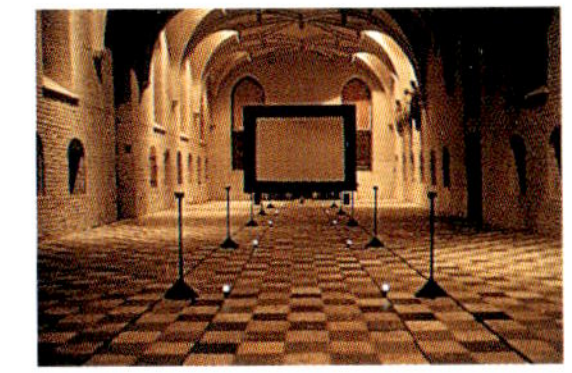

Going to the Heart of the Center of The Garden of Delights

Ins Herz des Zentrums des Gartens der Lüste gehen 1986

In dieser Installation, die für die Räume der neogotischen Vleeshal in Middelburg (Niederlande, 1986) entwickelt wurde, wurden Computergrafikbilder auf eine große Leinwand projiziert, die sich am hinteren Ende des Raumes, direkt gegenüber dem Eingang, befand. Infrarotsensoren und vierzehn paarweise am Boden angeordnete blaue Scheinwerfer definierten einen Weg vom Eingang zur Leinwand. Bewegte sich ein Besucher auf die Leinwand zu, steuerte er interaktiv eine Abfolge von Bild- und Tontransformationen.

Die digital bearbeiteten Bildsequenzen basierten auf Arbeiten von Yves Klein, Nagisa Oshima und Hieronymus Bosch. Die Verbindung des gegenständlichen Bildes mit der ihm zugrundeliegenden digitalen Struktur artikulierte sich in den Transformationen eines Einzelbildes aus Oshimas Film *Im Reich der Sinne* zu einem Ausschnitt aus Boschs Gemälde *Der Garten der Lüste*. Die interaktive Sequenz zeigte die fortschreitende, digital erzeugte Auflösung des Oshima-Bildes in eine immer abstrakter werdende Struktur gerasteter Bildelemente, aus denen sich allmählich Boschs Gemälde formte. Sobald sich der Betrachter von der Leinwand wegbewegte, kehrte sich die Sequenz wieder um. Der einsame Gang des Betrachters vom Eingang zur Leinwand verkörperte eine virtuelle Reise durch eine Bildfolge, die architektonisch in den Ausstellungsraum eingebunden war. Dieses Zusammentreffen einer exoterischen und einer esoterischen Reise wiederholte sich in der Verbindung profaner und sakraler Allusionen in der ikonographischen Struktur der Arbeit.

1993 wurde unter dem Titel *The Royal Road* (›Königsweg‹) eine neue Version dieser Arbeit entwickelt, die über Bildplatte gesteuert wird und nicht mehr in direkter Beziehung zu einem bestimmten architektonischen Kontext steht: Der Betrachter geht auf einem von blauen Lampen begrenzten Weg auf einen großen Videomonitor zu. Dabei durchläuft er eine Reihe von sechs virtuellen Bildschirmen, die die Sequenz der Ursprungsarbeit zeigen.

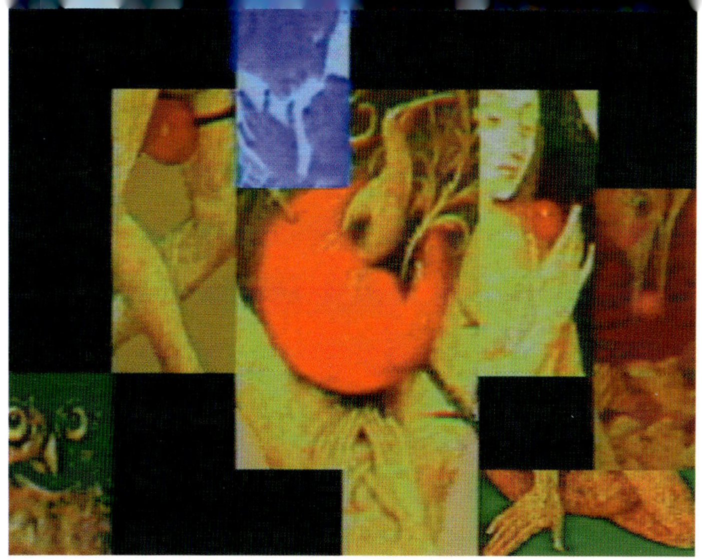

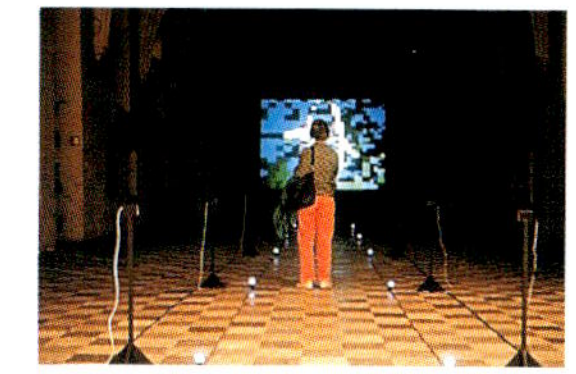

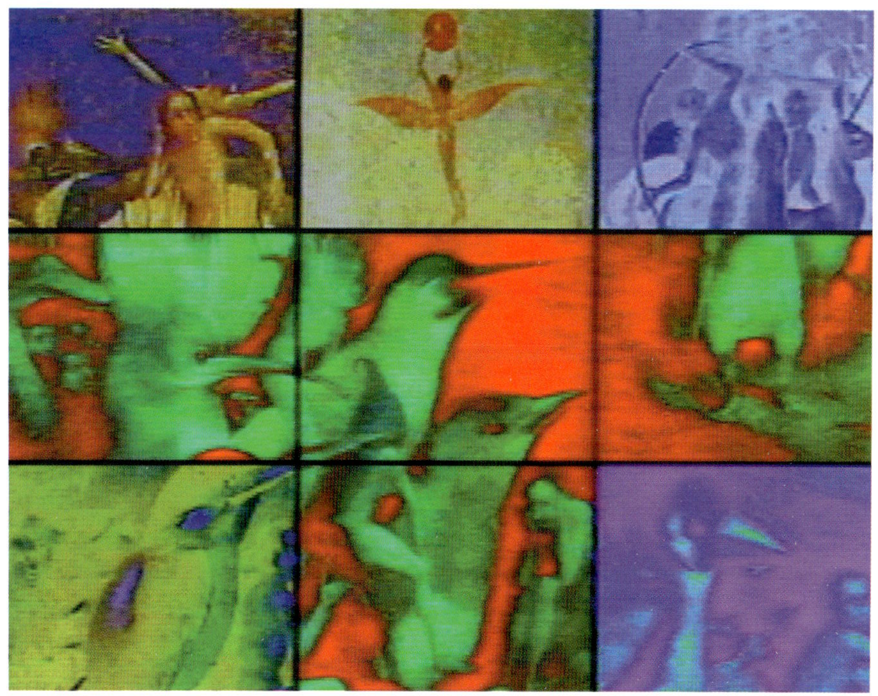

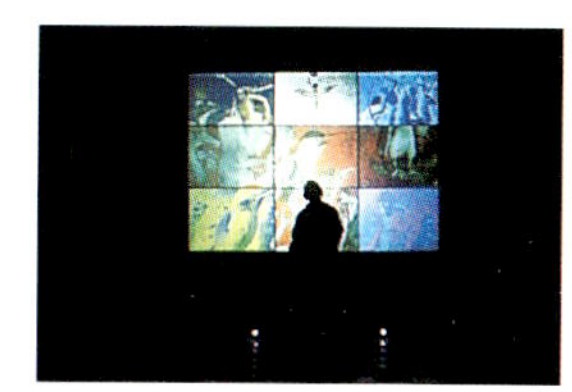

Inventer la Terre Inventing the World 1986

In this work a chrome-plated column stands on a round black terrazzo base inlaid with brass signs representing a Hebraic astrological map. This column has a viewing aperture, two controlling handles, and a pair of loudspeakers. Inside the column there is an

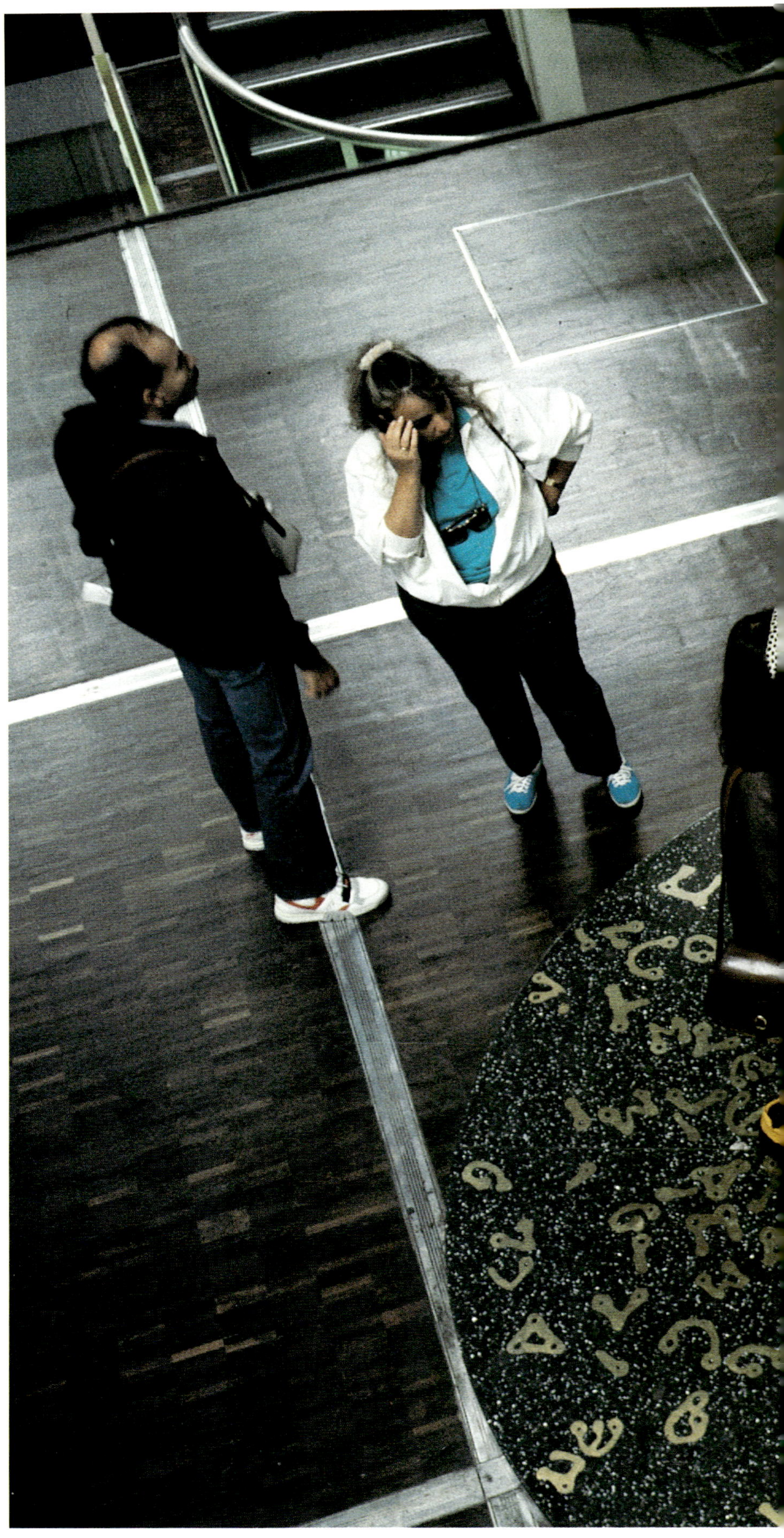

Inventer la Terre

Die Erfindung der Welt 1986

In dieser Arbeit steht eine verchromte Säule auf einer runden schwarzen Terazzounterlage, in die Messingzeichen, die eine hebräische, astrologische Karte darstellen, eingelegt sind. Diese Säule ist mit einem Sichtfenster, zwei Kontrollgriffen und zwei Lautspre-

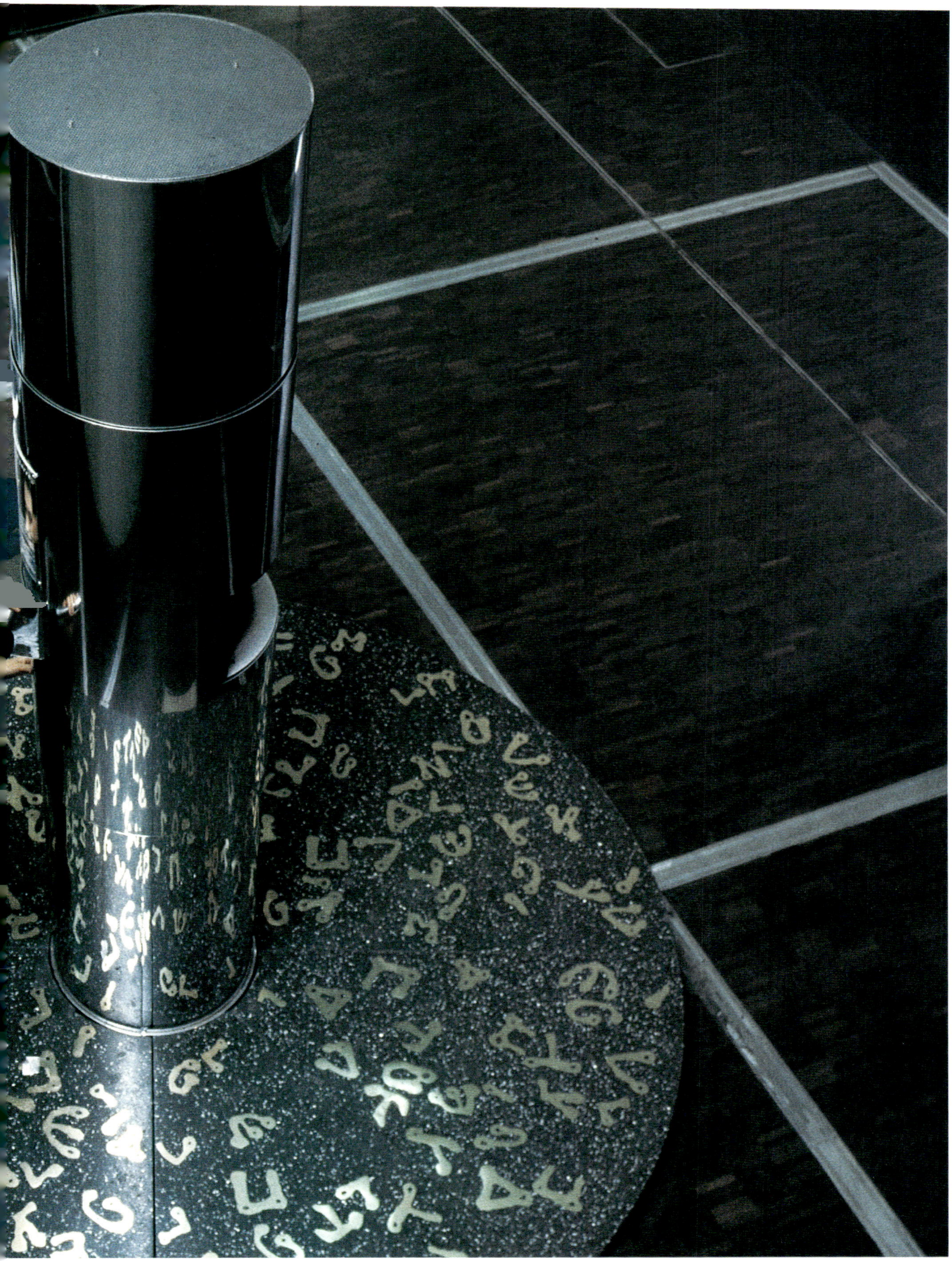

optical system constituted by a video monitor, a fresnel lens and a semi-transparent mirror. Looking through the opening in the column, the spectator sees a large virtual image projected into the museum space – this image is overlaid on his view of the real environment. By pushing the handles, the spectator can interactively control the rotation of the column and the movement of this virtual image. Sound and image are interactively accessed from two videodisk players and the virtual image is generated by the optical display system within the column.

Initially there is a 360-degree panorama representing six different symbolic sites in a landscape. As the spectator rotates the column, he moves his point of view in a panorama apparently floating all around him. The viewer can select one of the six sites by pressing a button on the column handle. Linked to each site is an approximately three-minute video sequence which articulates the specific themes embodied by that place. At the end of each video sequence, the viewer returns to the panorama and

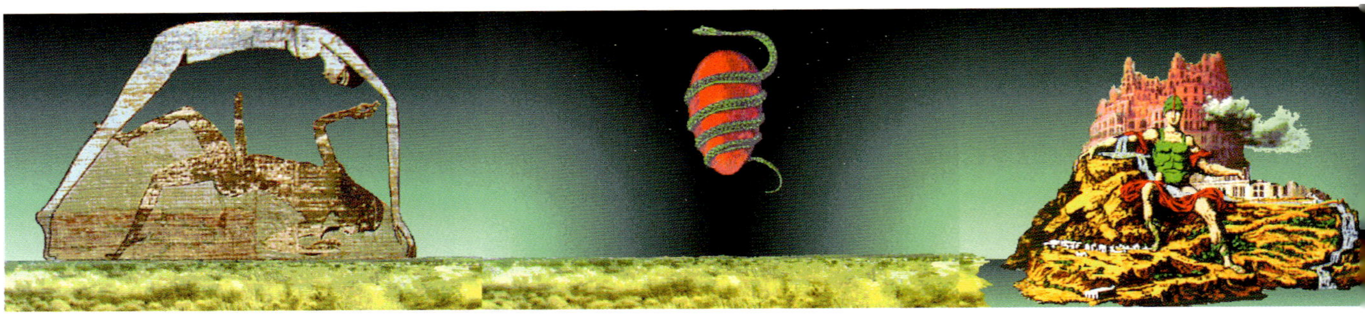

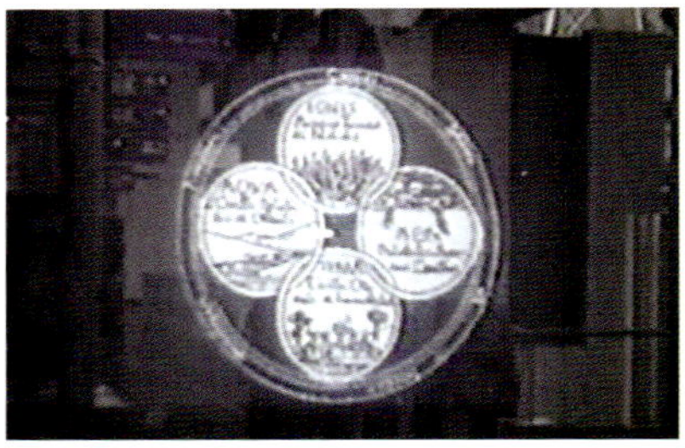

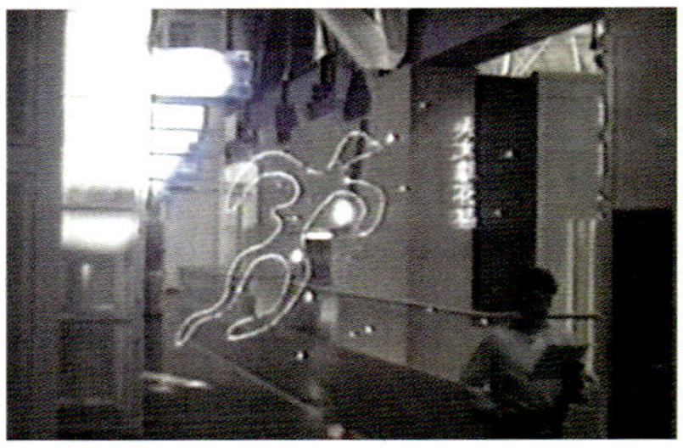

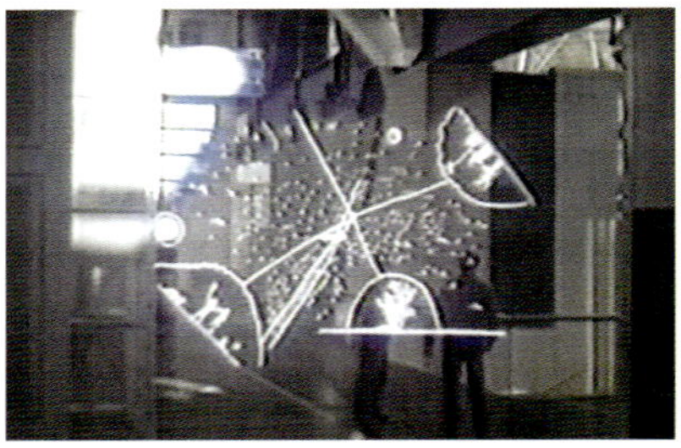

chern ausgestattet. Im Innern der Säule befindet sich ein optisches System, das aus einem Videomonitor, einer Fresnel-Linse und einem semitransparenten Spiegel besteht. Schaut der Betrachter durch die Öffnung der Säule, sieht er ein großformatiges virtuelles Bild, das in den Museumsraum projiziert wird und seinen Blick auf die reale Umgebung überlagert. Mit den Griffen kann der Betrachter die Rotation der Säule sowie die Bewegung des virtuellen Bildes interaktiv steuern. Ton und Bild werden von zwei Bildplattenspielern abgerufen; das virtuelle Bild wird vom optischen Displaysystem, das sich in der Säule befindet, generiert.

Anfangs ist ein 360-Grad-Panorama zu sehen, das sechs verschiedene symbolische Orte in einer Landschaft zeigt. Dreht der Betrachter die Säule, bewegt er seinen Standpunkt in ein Panorama, das um ihn herum zu schweben scheint. Der Betrachter kann einen der sechs Orte auswählen, indem er einen Knopf auf den Griffen der Säule drückt. Eine etwa dreiminütige Videosequenz ist mit jedem Ort verbunden, die bestimmte, von diesem Ort verkörperte Themen zeigt. Am Ende jeder Videosequenz kehrt der Betrachter zum Anfangspanorama zurück und kann

then, by turning the column, chooses another place to go to.

The title of this work – *Inventing the World* – refers to its central theme: the exemplification of archaic, mythological and esoteric world sciences. The form of the sculpture itself represents a conjunction of contemporary technology with the memory of archaic structures like the Megalithic stones. The six symbolic panoramic sites and their respective video sequences are each concerned with specific aspects of this overall subject – the totemic world, primal creation myths, astrology and astronomy, sacred geometry, hermetic geography, and the creation of fictional worlds in art and literature. Walter Maioli's soundtrack is composed from fragments of ethnic music from ancient cultures.

3-D image synthesis, digital image processing and digital post production techniques were used extensively in the visual sequences.

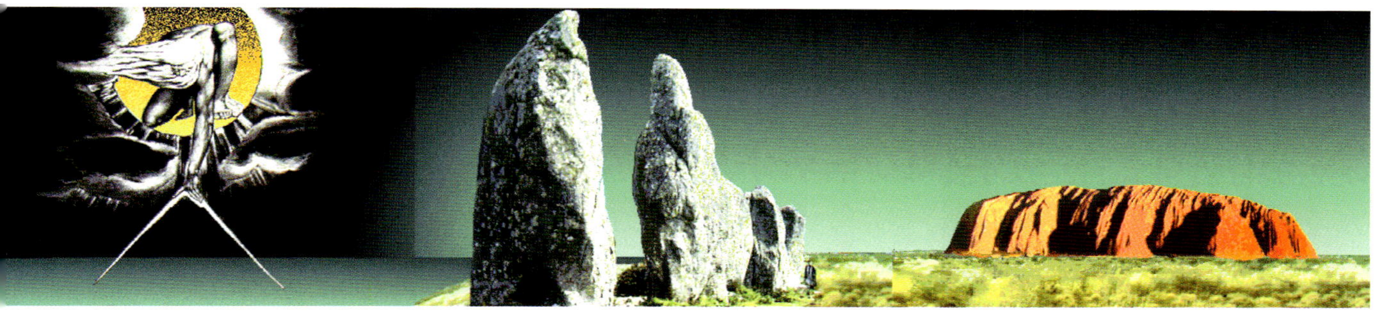

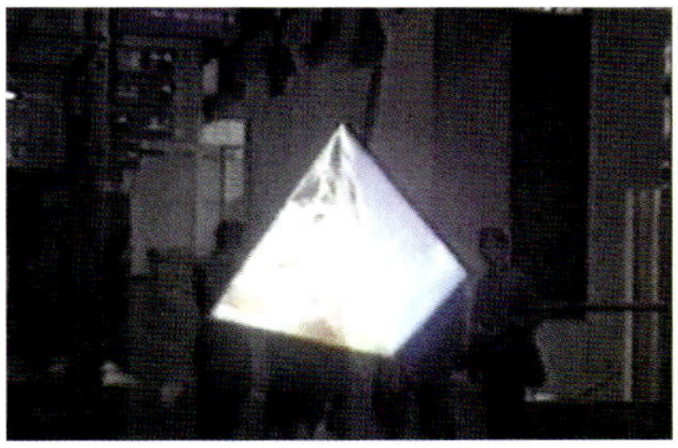

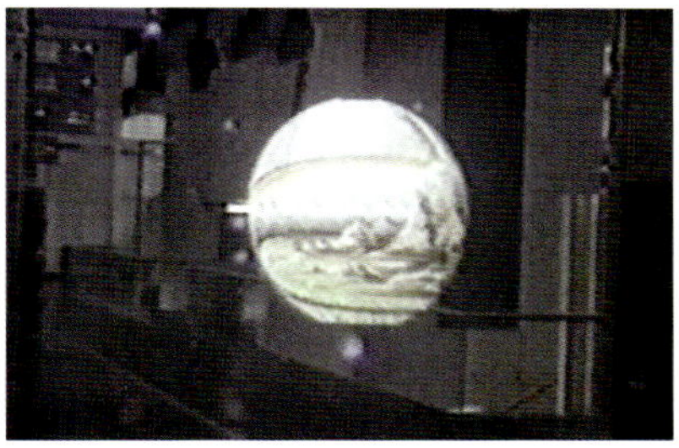

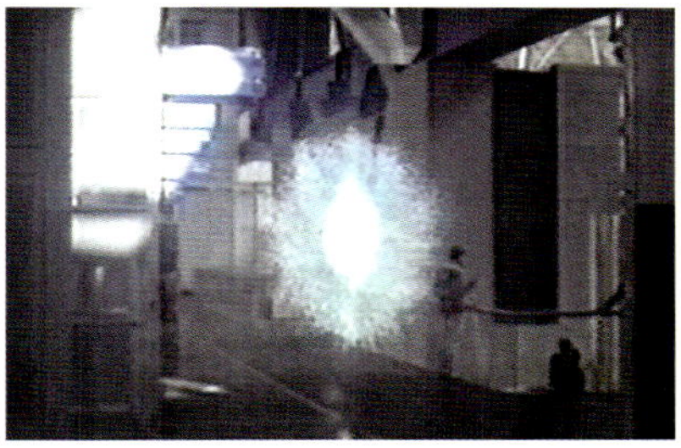

dann, indem er die Säule dreht, einen anderen Ort auswählen.

Der Titel dieser Arbeit – *Die Erfindung der Welt* – bezieht sich auf ihr zentrales Thema: die Veranschaulichung archaischer, mythologischer und esoterischer Weltlehren. Die Gestaltung der Skulptur selbst repräsentiert eine Verbindung von moderner Technologie und der Erinnerung an archaische Strukturen wie die Steinblöcke der Megalithkultur. Die sechs symbolischen Panoramen und die ihnen zugeordneten Videosequenzen beschäftigen sich mit bestimmten Aspekten des Gesamtthemas: Totemismus, Urmythen der Schöpfung, Astrologie und Astronomie, sakrale Geometrie, hermetische Geographie und die Schöpfung fiktiver Welten in Kunst und Literatur. Walter Maioli komponierte die Musik für diese Arbeit aus Fragmenten ethnischer Musik alter Kulturen.

In den Bildsequenzen wurden Techniken wie 3-D-Bild-Synthese, digitale Bildverarbeitung und -nachbearbeitung eingesetzt.

Heavens Gate 1986

Heavens Gate was first shown as a video installation in the neoclassical stairwell of Felix Meritis (Amsterdam, Netherlands, 1987). In other exhibition spaces the work usually occupies a specially constructed completely dark room. The video image is projected over the whole ceiling, and the floor is entirely covered by a mirror on which the visitors can stand and see both their own reflection and the reflection of the projected image on the ceiling. The otherwise total darkness of the space creates for the viewers a state of visual suspension between these two image planes.

The conceptual and iconographic references in this work are largely derived from Baroque ceiling paintings and aerial/satellite pictures of the surface of the earth. These images alternate in a computer-processed videographic morphology that deconstructs and manipulates the constituent pixels of the original images and then anamorphically reconfigures them in a virtual three-dimensional space. This digital tromp l'oeil characterizes the awesome contemporary view down from space which inverts the ecstatic Baroque gaze up to the heavens. Further iconographic references in this work conjoin these viewing extremities, for instance the Futurist embrace of the aerial point of view and the spatial apotheoses of El Greco, William Blake and Piero Manzoni.

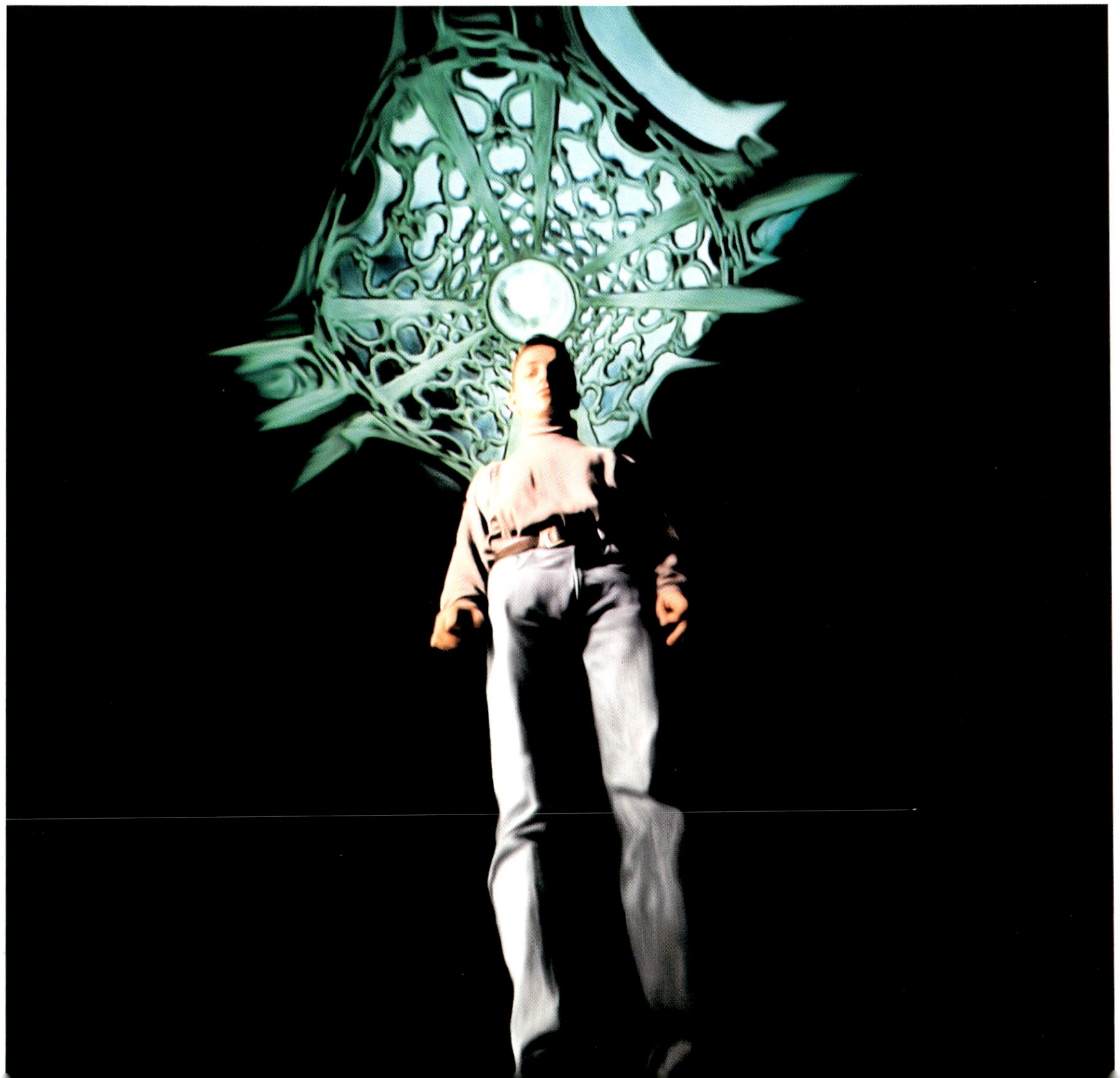

Heavens Gate Himmelstor 1986

Heavens Gate wurde als Videoinstallation erstmals im neoklassizistischen Treppenhaus des Felix-Meritis- Gebäudes (Amsterdam, Niederlande, 1987) gezeigt. In anderen Ausstellungsräumen ist die Arbeit meist in einem speziell angefertigten, abgedunkelten Raum installiert. Das Videobild wird an die Decke projiziert, und der Boden ist vollständig von einem Spiegel bedeckt, den die Besucher betreten können, so daß sie ihr eigenes Spiegelbild sowie die Reflektion des an die Decke projizierten Videobildes sehen können. Die ansonsten völlige Dunkelheit des Raumes läßt den Betrachter ein Gefühl des visuellen Schwebens zwischen diesen beiden Bildebenen erleben.

Die konzeptuellen und ikonographischen Allusionen stammen zum größten Teil von barocken Deckengemälden und Luft- und Satellitenaufnahmen der Erdoberfläche. Diese Bilder alternieren durch eine computerbearbeitete videographische Morphologie, die die aus Pixeln bestehenden Originalbilder dekonstruiert und manipuliert und sie anamorphotisch in einem virtuellen dreidimensionalen Raum neu anordnet. Dieser digitale Trompe-l'œil charakterisiert den zeitgenössisch-ehrfürchtigen Blick vom All auf die Erde, der eine Umkehrung des ekstatischen barocken Schauens hinauf zum Himmel darstellt. Weitere ikonograhische Bezüge der Arbeit verbinden diese beiden extremen Sehweisen, z. B. die futuristische Umarmung des Blicks aus der Luft und die Apotheosen eines El Greco, Wiliam Blake oder Piero Manzoni.

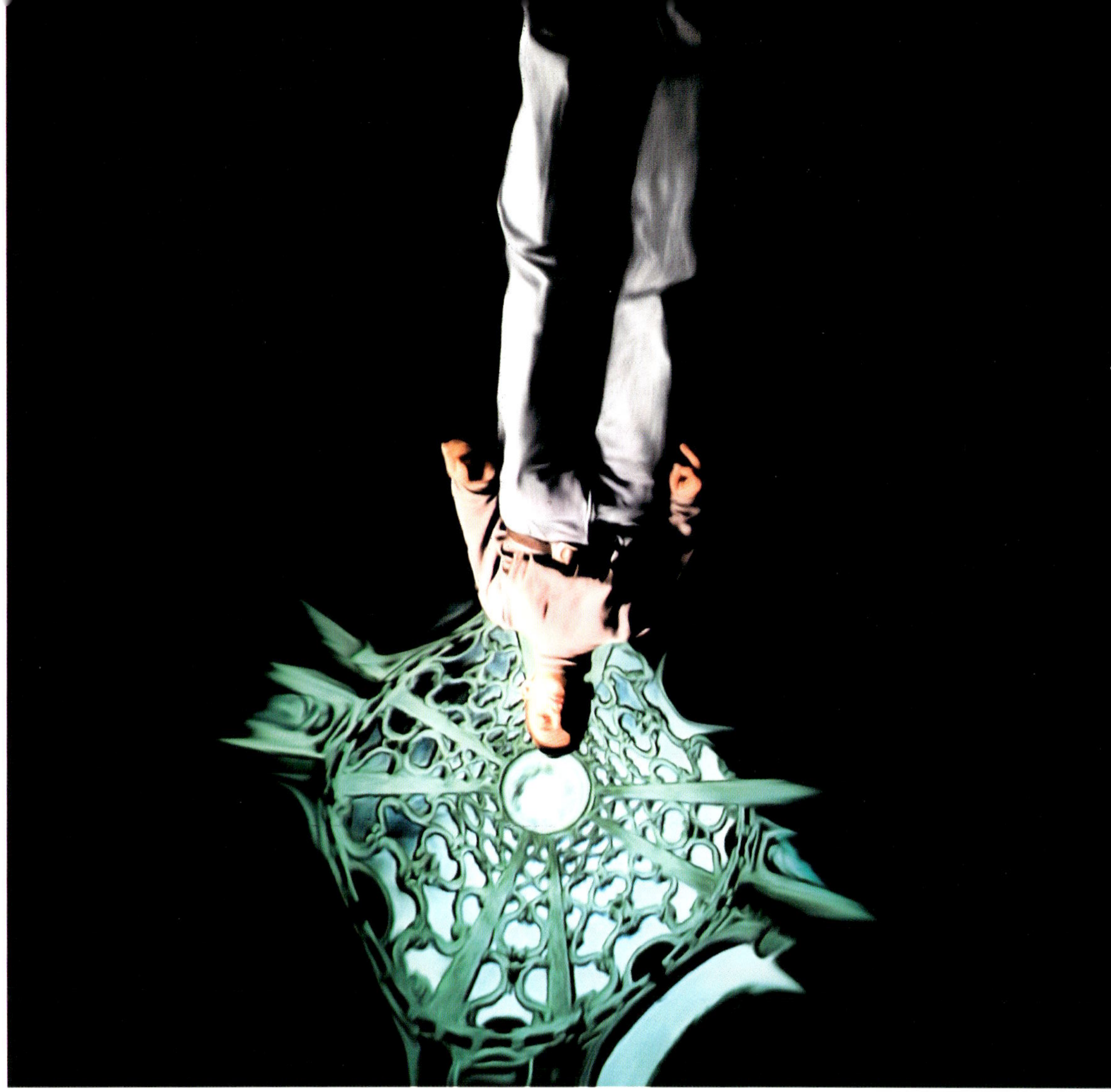

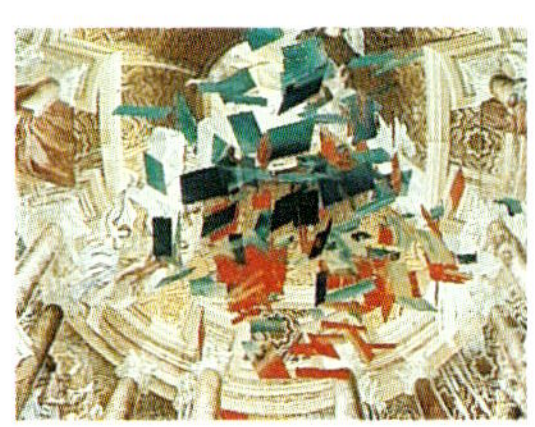

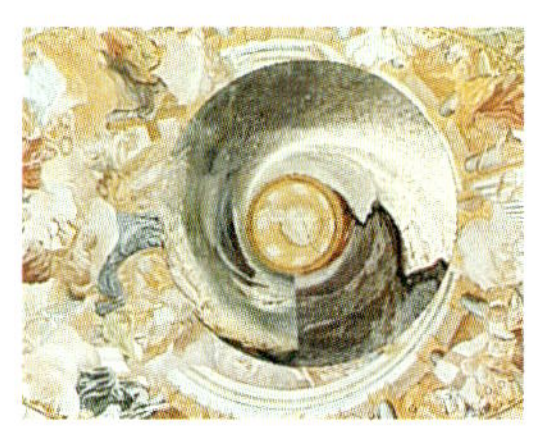

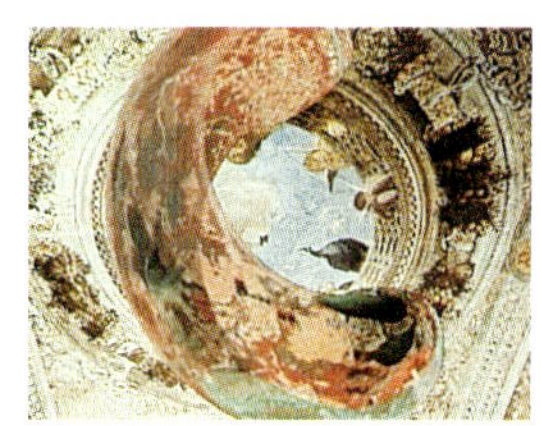

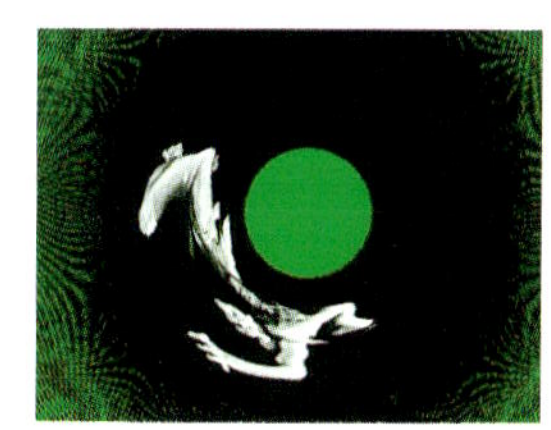

Infinity Divided by Sixteen 1987

In this interactive installation the visual and auditory components of the work were so closely interconnected as to constitute a form of 'visual music'. A perforated projection screen was visibly divided into sixteen sections. Behind each section was an independent speaker connected to its own amplifier and tape deck. Sixteen sound tracks were composed and recorded by Harry de Wit for this work. Each sound track was assigned to a specific position on the screen, and the volume of each of these sixteen spatially located sound tracks was modulated by a continual analysis of the changing light intensities of the images being projected onto the screen. In this way the interactively controlled movement of the imagery over the screen surface caused a simultaneous mixing of the sixteen sound channels, and the dynamics of this sound mix was determined by a shifting distribution of light intensities according to the viewer's manipulation of the images. The viewer

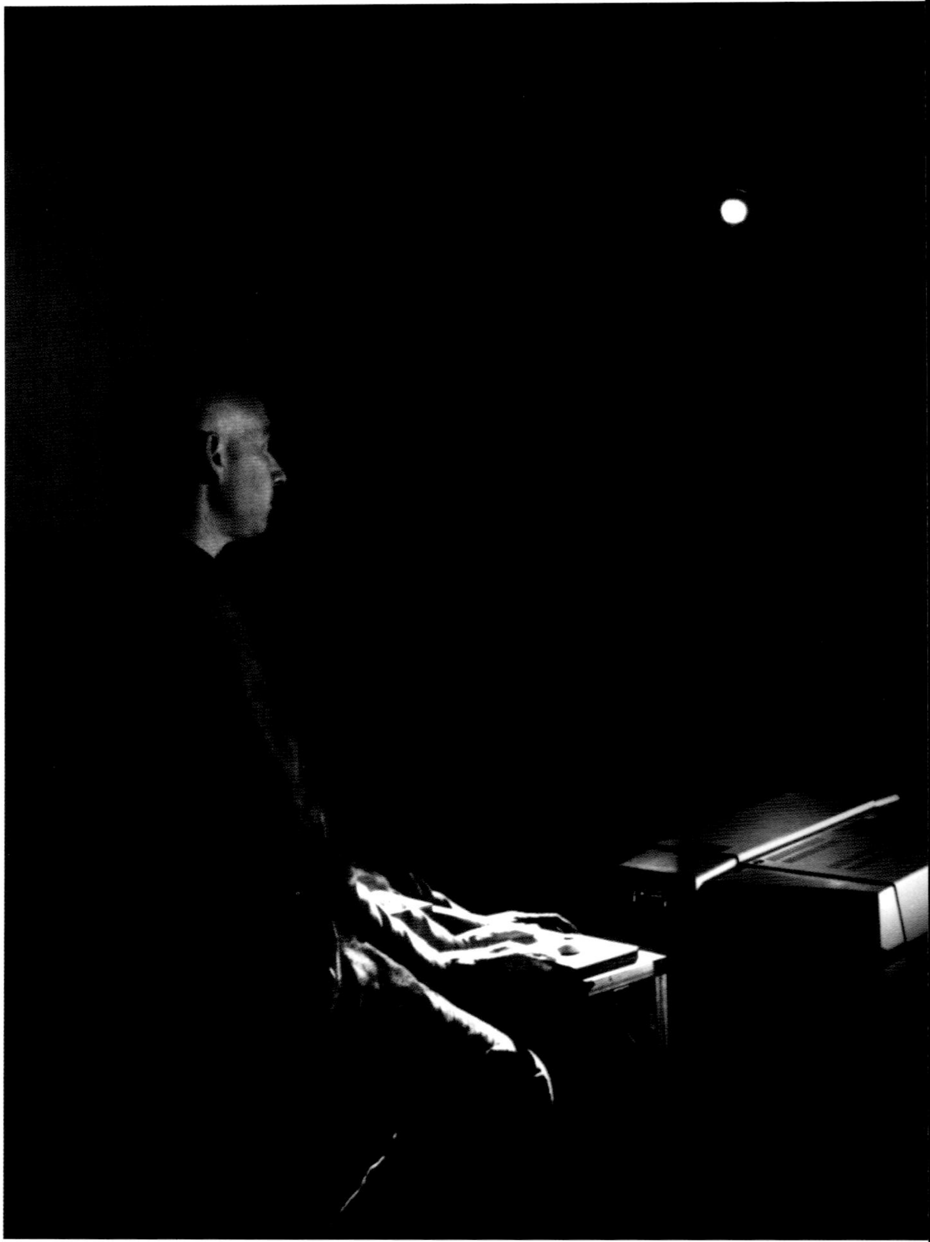

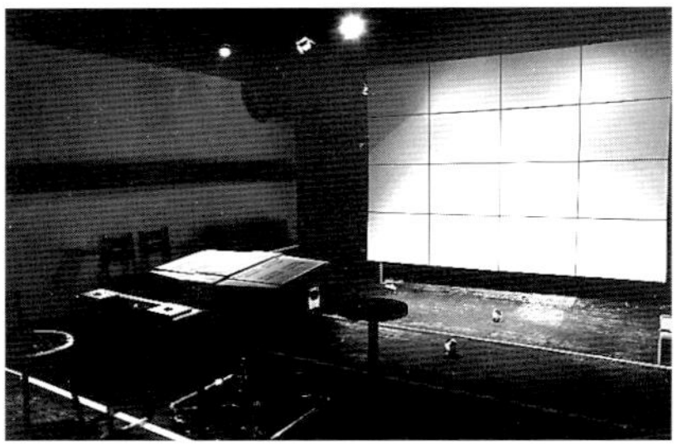

Infinity Divided by Sixteen

Unendlichkeit geteilt durch sechzehn 1987

In dieser interaktiven Installation wurden die Bild- und Tonkomponenten so eng miteinander verknüpft, daß eine Art ›visueller Musik‹ entstand. Eine perforierte Leinwand wurde deutlich sichtbar in sechzehn Bereiche unterteilt. Hinter jedem Bereich stand ein Lautsprecher, der mit jeweils einem Verstärker und einem Tonband verbunden war. Sechzehn Soundtracks wurden von Harry de Wit für diese Arbeit komponiert und aufgenommen. Jeder Soundtrack war einem bestimmten Bereich auf der Leinwand zugeordnet, und die Lautstärke jedes dieser sechzehn verorteten Stücke wurde durch eine kontinuierliche Analyse der wechselnden Lichtintensität der Bilder, die auf die Leinwand projiziert wurden, verändert. Auf diese Weise bewirkte die interaktiv gesteuerte Bewegung der Bilder über die Leinwand auch die Mischung der sechzehn Tonkanäle. Die Dynamik dieser Tonmischungen wurde von der sich verändernden Verteilung der Lichtintensität bestimmt, die der Betrachter durch die Manipulation der Bilder entsprechend steuerte. Der Betrachter konnte die Bewegung

controlled the movement of the projected imagery using two trackballs to pan left and right and up and down, and buttons to control zooming. The visual space was constituted by a network of interconnected pictorial images that were both conceptually and formally organised in relation to the sixteen-part division of the screen.

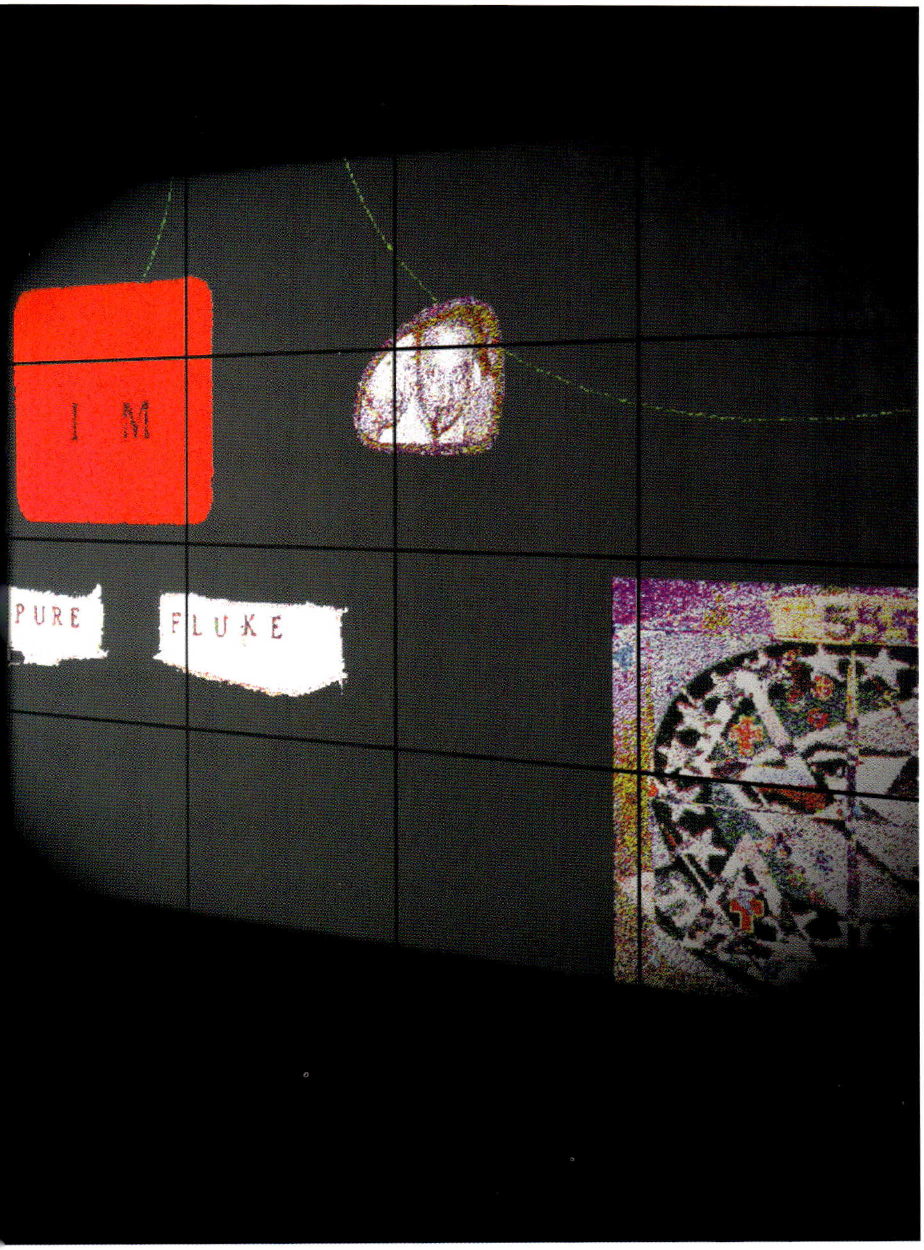

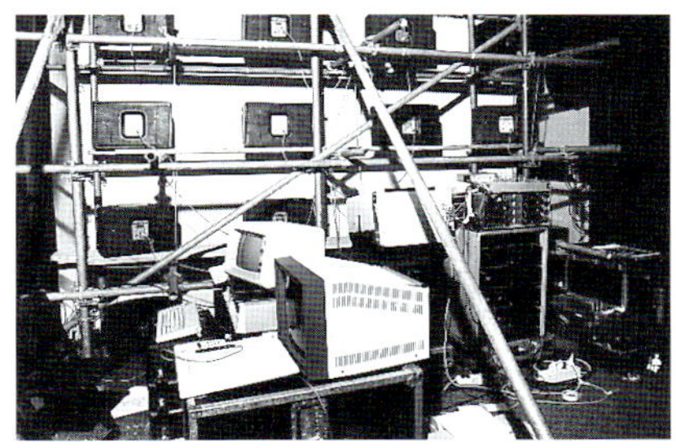

der projizierten Bilder nach links, rechts, oben oder unten mit zwei Trackballs steuern; den Zoomvorgang kontrollierte er mit separaten Tasten. Der visuelle Raum setzte sich aus einem Netzwerk miteinander verknüpfter, gegenständlicher Bilder zusammen. Die konzeptuelle und formale Anordnung der Bilder stand in direkter Beziehung zur Unterteilung der Leinwand in sechzehn Bereiche.

Anamorphoses of Memory 1986

For the exhibition Kunst Over de Vloer (Amsterdam, Netherlands, 1986) artists were invited to create works in the rooms of a private apartment building. *Anamorphoses of Memory* was located in a sparse and untidy student's bedroom. A monitor was placed on a mattress on the floor with its screen facing upwards. On the monitor screen moving rows of text were reflected onto a mirrored cylinder standing upright in the centre of the screen. These anamorphic texts moved outwards from the centre of the screen in concentric circles. Reflected on the cylinder, they became vertically scrolling sentences which could be read by the viewers. The texts were written specially by Dirk Groeneveld and evoked certain erotic contingencies projected into this bedroom.

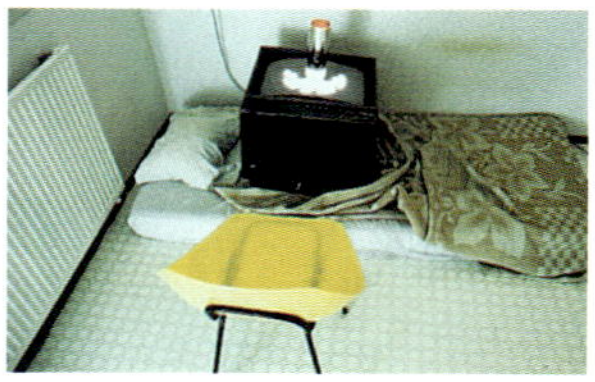

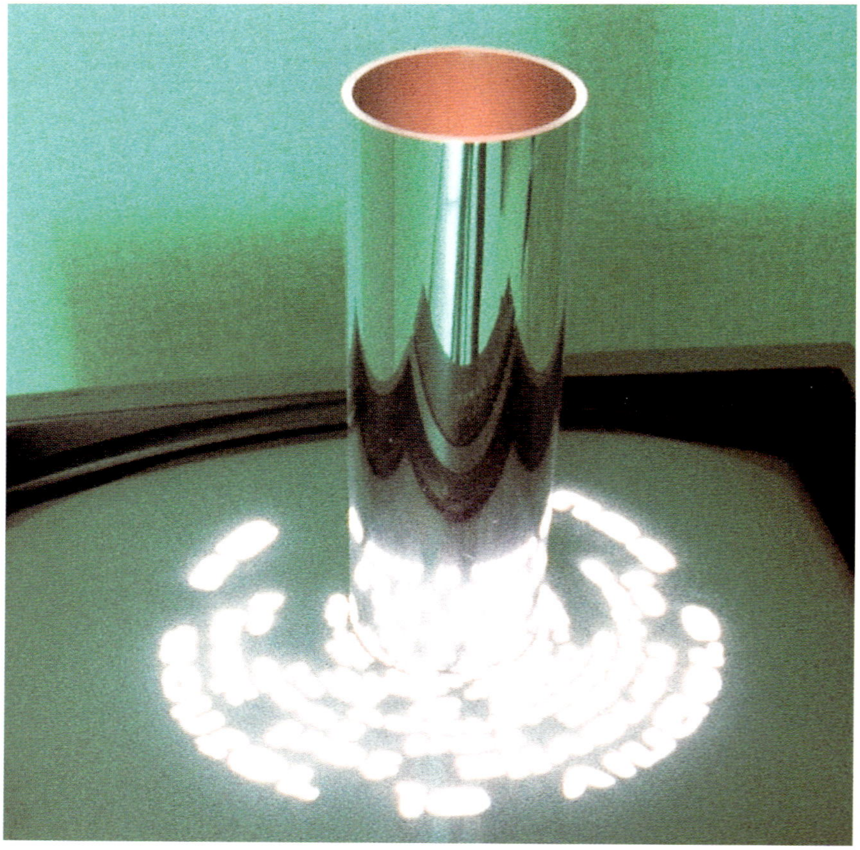

Anamorphoses of Memory

Anamorphosen der Erinnerung 1986

Für die Ausstellung Kunst Over de Vloer (Amsterdam, Niederlande, 1986) wurden Künstler eingeladen, Arbeiten in den Räumen eines privaten Appartementhauses zu entwickeln. *Anamorphoses of Memory* befand sich in dem spärlich möblierten, unordentlichen Schlafzimmer eines Studenten. Ein Monitor wurde mit dem Bildschirm nach oben auf einer Matratze plaziert, die auf dem Boden lag. Der Monitor zeigte fließende Textreihen, die auf einen verspiegelten Zylinder reflektiert wurden, der aufrecht in der Mitte des Bildschirms stand. Diese anamorphotischen Texte bewegten sich in konzentrischen Kreisen von der Bildschirmmitte nach außen. Durch die Reflektion auf den Zylinder wurden sie zu vertikal angeordneten Sätzen und konnten vom Betrachter gelesen werden. Die Texte, die von Dirk Groeneveld für diese Arbeit geschrieben worden waren, riefen bestimmte erotische Assoziationen hervor, die in das Schlafzimmer projiziert wurden.

Video Narcissus 1987

A transparent container filled with water stood on top of a video monitor placed on its back with screen facing upwards. Bubbles of air could be electronically released in this container, causing the water surface to ripple outwards in concentric circles. A video camera pointed up at the face of the spectator, whose image was digitally processed and displayed on the screen beneath the water. Whenever a spectator moved in front of the monitor a sensor detected his presence and a bubble of air was released into the water and the digital processing of the video image of the spectator's face began simultaneously. Starting at centre of the screen and moving outwards in a pattern of concentric circles, the computer created a digital reflection of the viewer that was visually analogous to the ripples in the water.

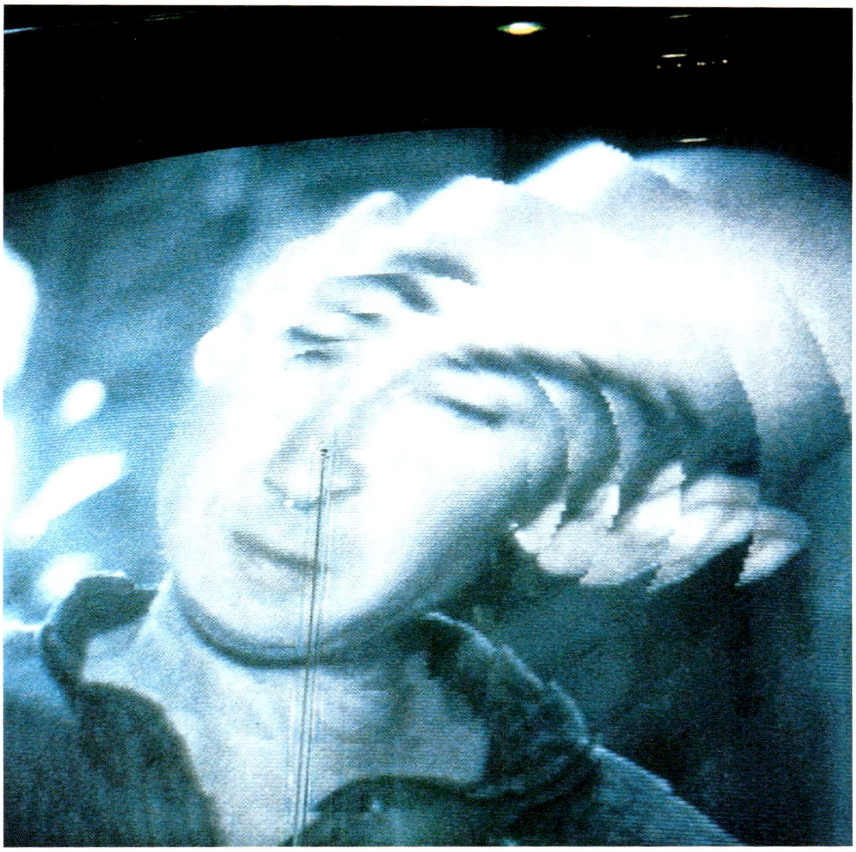

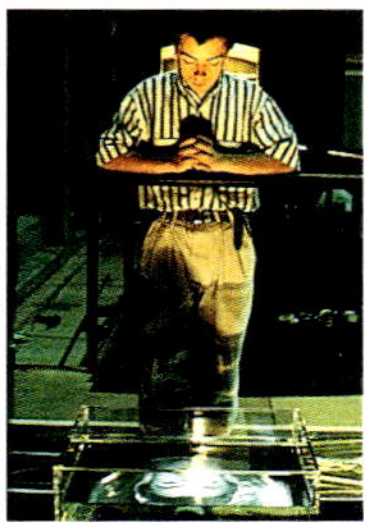

Video Narcissus Videonarziß 1987

Ein durchsichtiger, mit Wasser gefüllter Behälter war auf einem Videomonitor plaziert, der mit nach oben ausgerichtetem Bildschirm auf dem Rücken lag. In diesem Behälter konnten Luftblasen elektronisch erzeugt werden, wodurch sich kleine Wellen auf der Wasseroberfläche bildeten, die sich in konzentrischen Kreisen nach außen bewegten. Eine Videokamera nahm von unten das Gesicht des Betrachters auf, das digital bearbeitet auf dem Bildschirm unter dem Wasserbehälter wiedergegeben wurde. Sobald sich ein Besucher vor den Monitor stellte, wurde er von einem Sensor wahrgenommen und gleichzeitig eine Luftblase ins Wasser gelassen, während die digitale Bearbeitung des Videobildes vom Gesicht des Betrachters begann. Ausgehend von der Mitte des Bildschirms und sich in konzentrischen Kreisen nach außen bewegend, kreierte der Computer eine digitale Reflektion vom Gesicht des Betrachters, das in seiner bildlichen Form dem Kräuseln des Wassers entsprach.

An Imaginary Museum of Revolutions

1987–89

An Imaginary Museum of Revolutions was a proposed multimedia installation to commemorate the 200th anniversary of the French Revolution. The main components were a sculpture garden of replicas of 200 revolutionary monuments, a group of coin-operated dispensing machines where one could buy small replicas of these revolutionary monuments, and a set of multimedia terminals which when activated by the purchased revolutionary monument would allow the user to explore an audiovisual database concerning these 200 revolutions via three interconnected paths of navigation – 'space', 'time' and 'ideology'.

The following description accompanied the original proposal:'200 monuments, statues that are conveyors of information about 200 revolutions from the last three centuries from throughout the world are to be reproduced on slightly larger than human scale and assembled in one place. Lofty monuments made

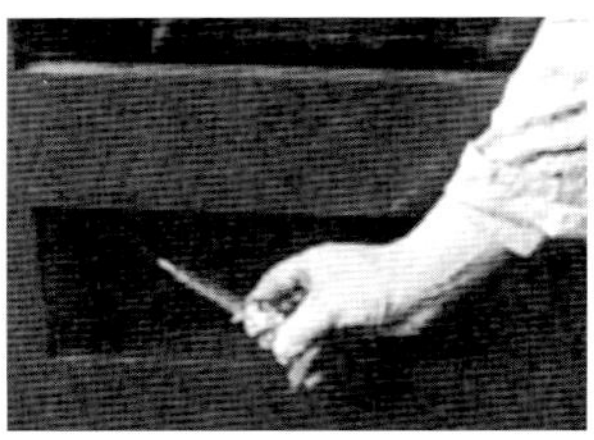

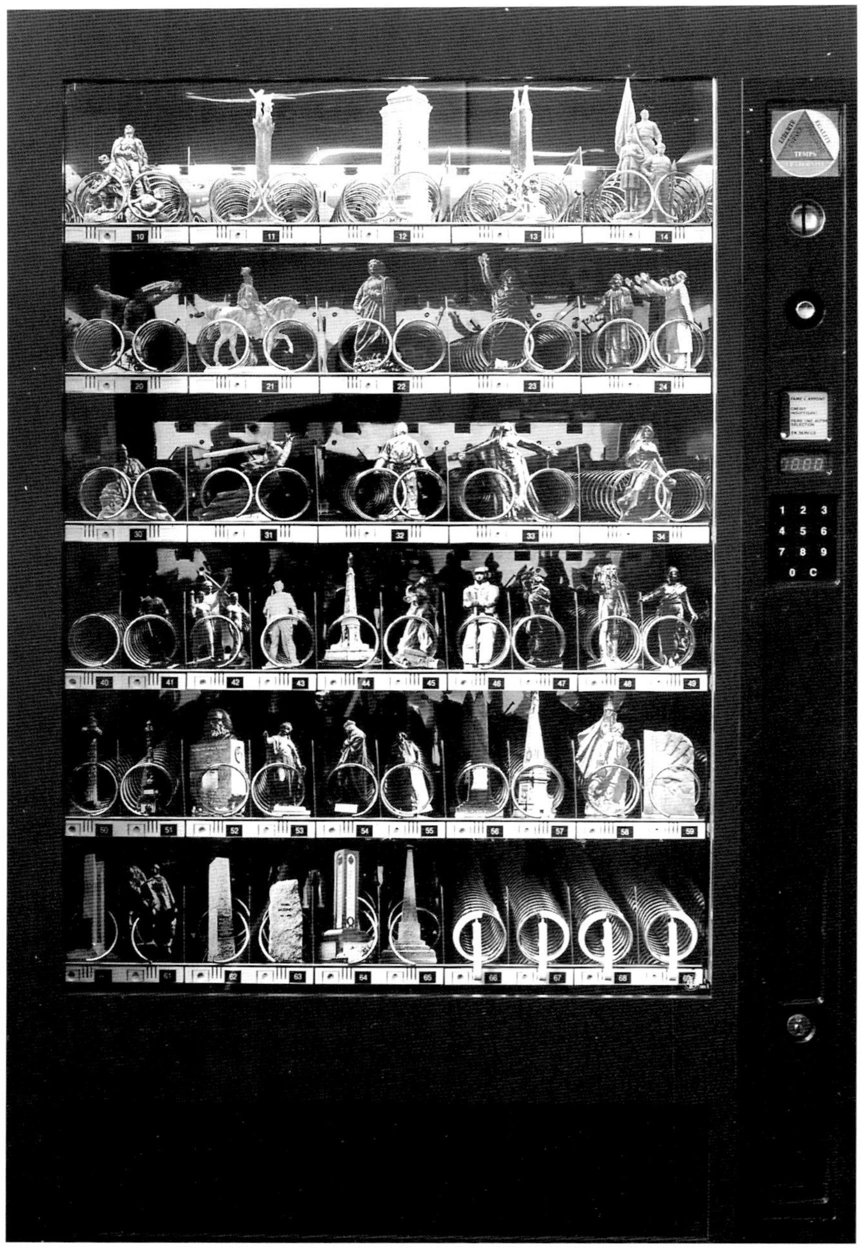

An Imaginary Museum of Revolutions

Ein imaginäres Revolutionsmuseum 1987–89

An Imaginary Museum of Revolutions war ein Entwurf für eine Multimedia-Installation anläßlich des 200. Jahrestages der Französischen Revolution. Die Arbeit setzte sich im wesentlichen aus folgenden Komponenten zusammen: ein Skulpturenpark mit Repliken von zweihundert Revolutionsdenkmälern, eine Gruppe von Münzautomaten, an denen man Miniaturrepliken jener zweihundert Skulpturen kaufen konnte und eine Reihe von Multimediaterminals, die der Benutzer mit der gekauften Statue aktivieren konnte, um durch eine audiovisuelle Datenbank zu navigieren, in der er über drei miteinander verbundene Ebenen – ›Raum‹, ›Zeit‹ und ›Ideologie‹ – auf Informationen zu den zweihundert Revolutionen zugreifen konnte.

Mit folgendem Text wurde der ursprüngliche Entwurf dieser Arbeit formuliert: ›Zweihundert Denkmäler – Statuen, die Informationen zu zweihundert Revolutionen weltweit aus drei Jahrhunderten vermitteln – werden in einem Maßstaß, der etwas über der menschlichen Größe liegt, reproduziert und in

intimate which can be touched and listened to, to rediscover forgotten meanings, and which are adjoined by miniature versions sold in vending machines which can be held and moved like chess pieces on the board of history. A game in space, time and ideology played on interactive videodisk installations with sounds and images of revolutions from countless archives, libraries and museums, their meanings heightened by electronic processes: a dramatized presentation of revolutionary moments from three centuries of world history with instant access by means of compact information carriers; a conjunction of library, museum and amusement arcade.'

While the project was never realized in this form, a number of installations and demonstrations were made which did embody many aspects of the proposal.

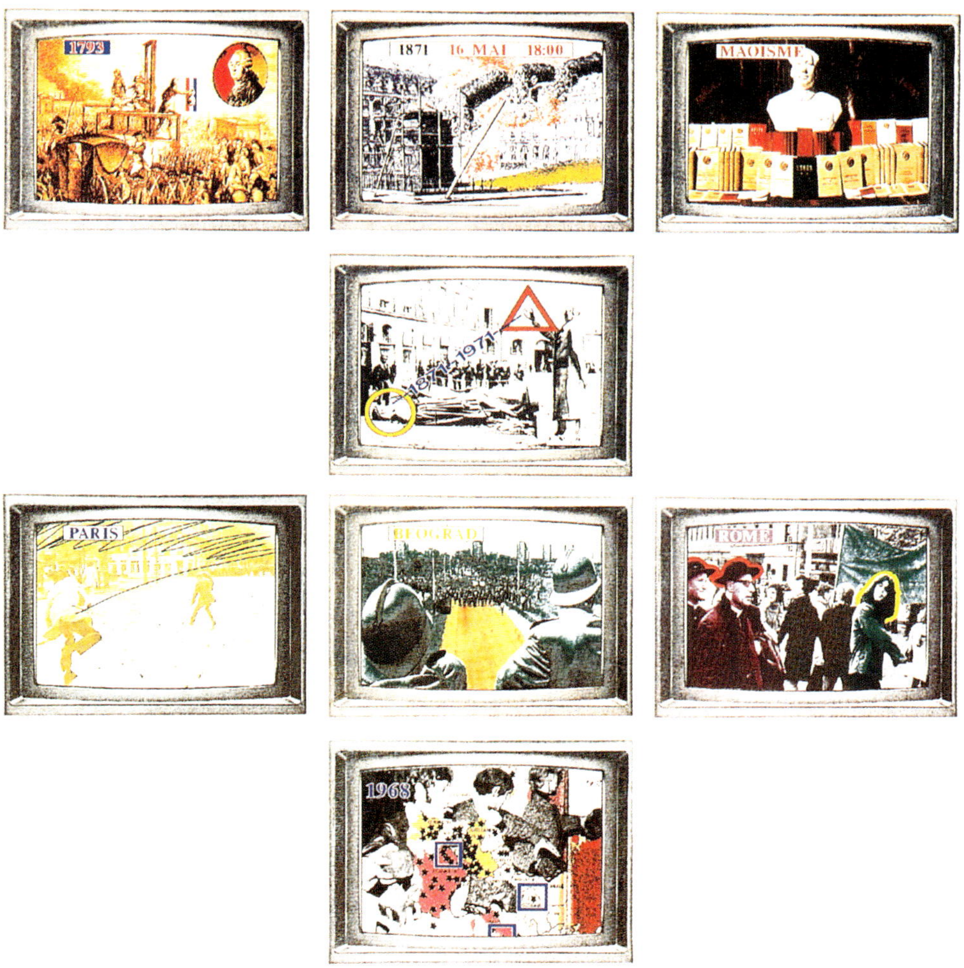

einem Raum gruppiert. Erhabene Denkmäler werden zu Vertrauten, die berührt werden können und denen man zuhören kann, um vergessene Bedeutungen wiederzuentdecken. Miniaturausgaben jener Denkmäler können an Automaten gekauft werden und wie Schachfiguren über das Spielbrett der Geschichte bewegt werden. Interaktive Installationen mit Liedern und Bildern von Revolutionen, die über Bildplatte abgerufen werden können und aus verschiedenen Archiven, Bibliotheken und Museen zusammengetragen wurden, laden ein zum Spiel durch Zeit, Raum und Ideologie, wobei die Bedeutung dieser Revolutionen durch die elektronische Bearbeitung verstärkt zum Ausdruck gebracht wird: eine Präsentation von Momenten von Revolutionen aus drei Jahrhunderten der Weltgeschichte, auf die mittels kompakter Informationsträger direkt zugegriffen werden kann; eine Verbindung von Bibliothek, Museum und Spielhalle.‹

Das Projekt wurde zwar in dieser Form nie realisiert, doch es wurden verschiedene Installationen und Präsentationen entwickelt, die viele Aspekte des Entwurfes beinhalteten.

Revolution 1990

In this interactive laserdisk-based work the viewer has to push a protruding steel bar to rotate a column-mounted monitor which in turn animates the images on its screen. A friction plate forces the viewers to make a strong physical effort. Turning the monitor in one direction, the viewer rotates a virtual millstone and grinds grain into flour. Pushing it in the other direction, he interactively moves through a large number of images that illustrate many of the major social uprisings and revolutions over the last 200 years worldwide. These images – all originally created for *An Imaginary Museum of Revolutions* (1987–89) – are digitally processed collages made from documentary photographic sources.

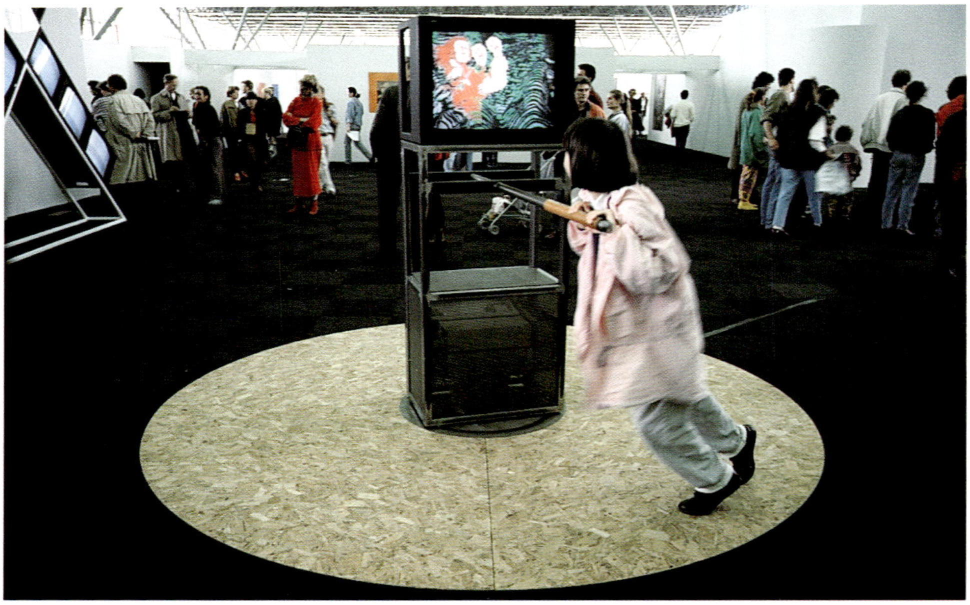

Revolution 1990

In dieser interaktiven Installation, die über Bildplatte gesteuert wird, muß der Betrachter einen vorstehenden Stahlarm bewegen, um einen in eine Säule eingelassenen Monitor drehen und dadurch die Bilder auf dem Bildschirm des Monitors animieren zu können. Eine Reibungsplatte erzeugt einen Widerstand bei der Rotation des Monitors und zwingt den Betrachter zu körperlicher Anstrengung. Dreht der Betrachter den Monitor in die eine Richtung, setzt er einen virtuellen Mühlstein in Bewegung und mahlt Korn zu Mehl. Dreht er ihn in die andere Richtung, durchläuft er eine Vielzahl von Bildern, die die wesentlichen sozialen Aufstände und Revolutionen weltweit aus den vergangenen zweihundert Jahren darstellen. Diese Bilder, die ursprünglich für *An Imaginary Museum of Revolutions* (1987–89) hergestellt worden waren, sind digital bearbeitete Collagen, basierend auf dokumentarischem Bildmaterial.

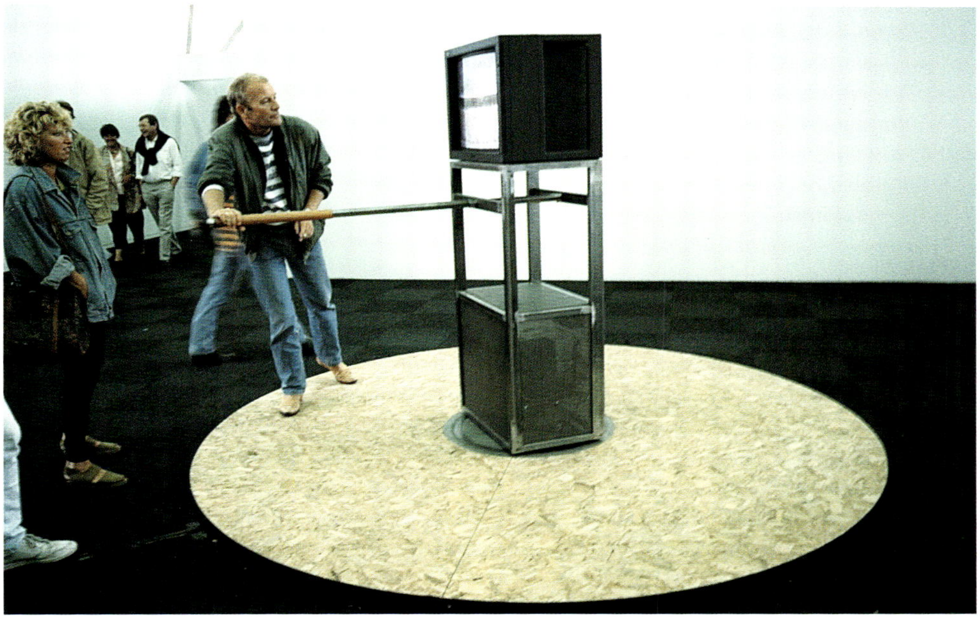

The Legible City 1988–91

The Legible City was first presented in 1988 (Bonnefantenmuseum, Maastricht, Belgium) as wire-frame graphics that were interactively operated by a joystick. This constituted a prototype for later implementations of this work using a bicycle as the viewer interface and more advanced computer visualization methods.

In *The Legible City* the visitor is able to ride a stationary bicycle through a simulated representation of a city that is constituted by computer-generated three-dimensional letters forming words and sentences along the sides of the streets. Using the ground plans of actual cities – Manhattan, Amsterdam and Karlsruhe – the existing architecture of these cities is completely replaced by a new architecture of letters and texts written and compiled by Dirk Groeneveld.

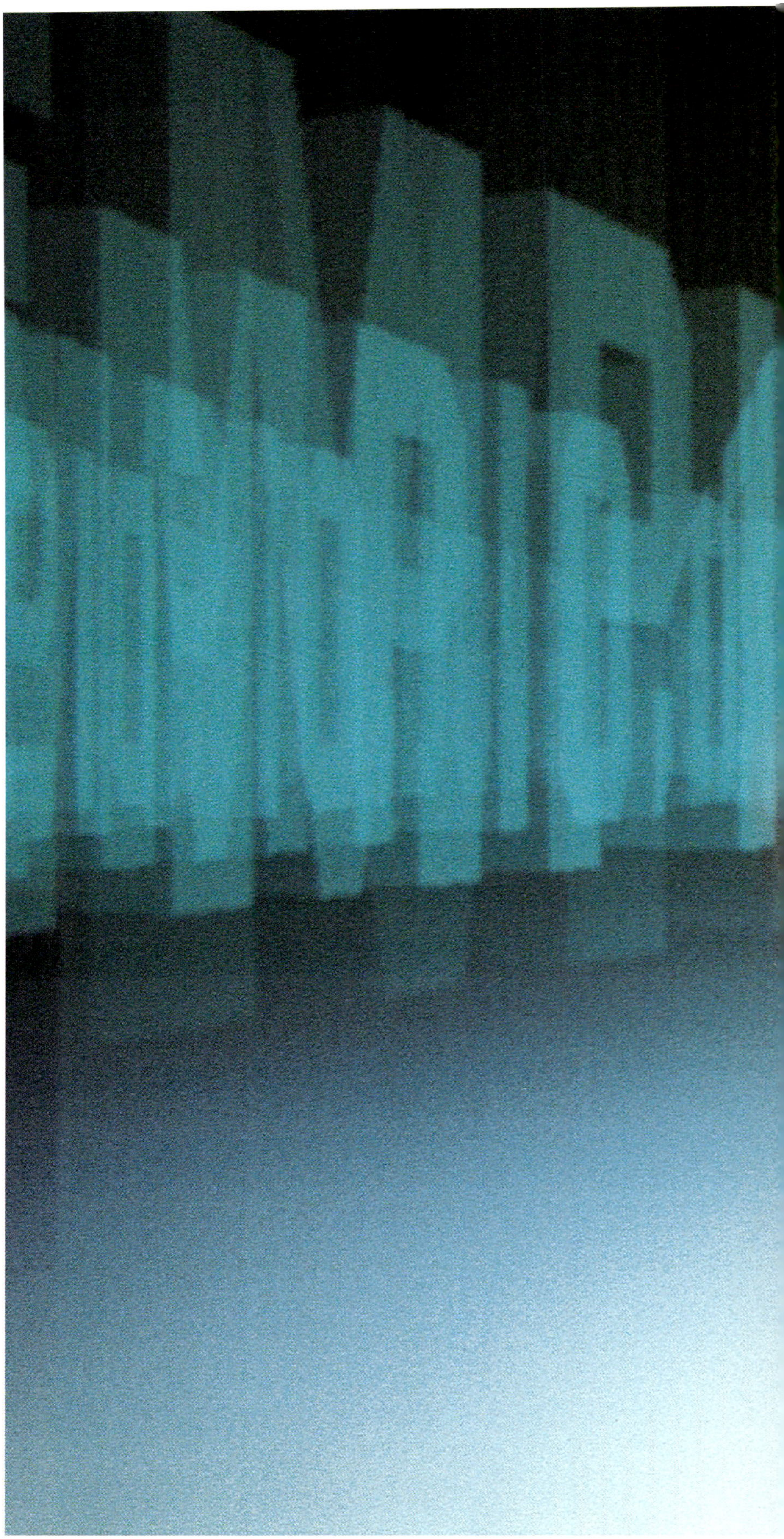

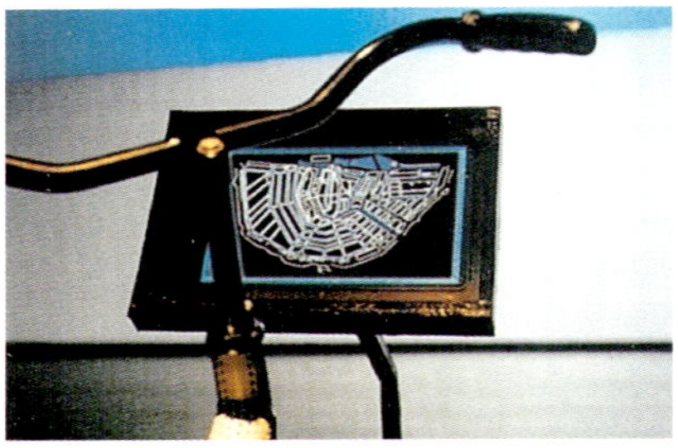

The Legible City Die lesbare Stadt 1988–91

The Legible City wurde erstmals 1988 (Bonnefantenmuseum, Maastricht, Belgien) als Drahtgittergrafik gezeigt und konnte über einen Joystick bedient werden. Dies war der Prototyp für die späteren Ausführungen der Arbeit, in denen ein Fahrrad als Interface und avanciertere Methoden computergestützter Visualisierung eingesetzt wurden.

Der Benutzer von *The Legible City* tritt die Pedale eines fest installierten Fahrrads und bewegt sich so durch die simulierte Darstellung einer Stadt aus computergenerierten dreidimensionalen Buchstaben, die sich – entlang der Straßen angeordnet – zu Worten und Sätzen verbinden. Die bestehende Architektur dreier Städte – Manhattan, Amsterdam und Karlsruhe – wird unter Verwendung ihrer Grundrisse ersetzt durch eine neue Architektur aus Buchstaben und Texten, die Dirk Groeneveld geschrieben und zusammengestellt hat.

Ein modifiziertes Klapprad dient als Schnittstelle

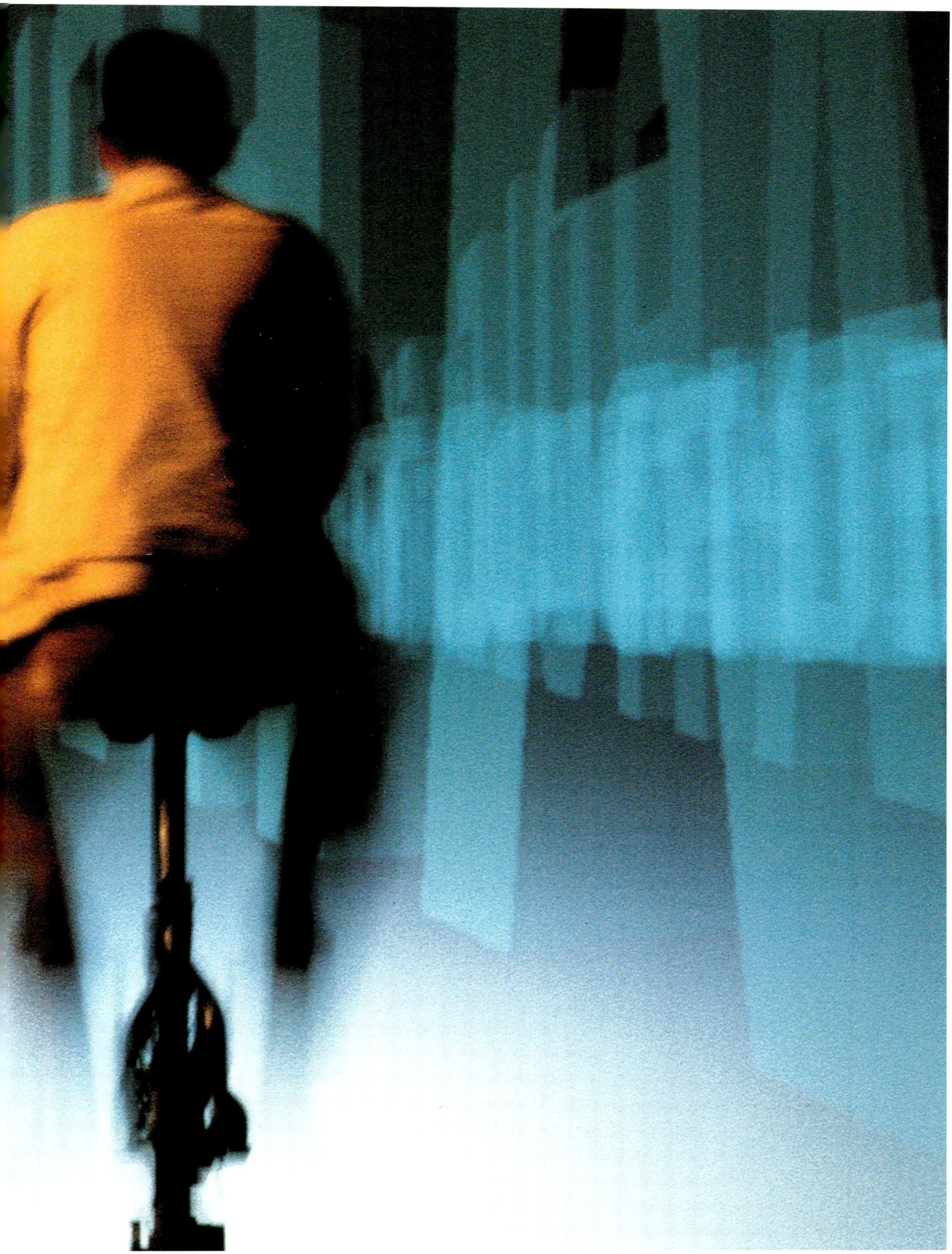

A modified folding bicycle is used as the interface between the viewer and the image. Its handlebar and pedals are linked to the computer, and give the viewer interactive control over direction of travel and speed. The physical effort of cycling in the real world is thus gratuitously transposed into this virtual world, affirming a conjunction of the active body in the virtual domain. A video projector is used to project the computer-generated image onto a large screen. Another small monitor screen in front of the bicycle shows a simple ground plan of each city with a moving dot to indicate the momentary position of the cyclist.

A city is simultaneously a tangible arrangement of forms and an immaterial pattern of experiences. Its architecture is a morphology of language, its ground plan a psycho-geographic network and its streets a labyrinth of narrative pathways. In *The Legible City* the viewer rides through a virtual city made up by an architecture of letters and texts. The bicycle trip through these cities of words is consequently a jour-

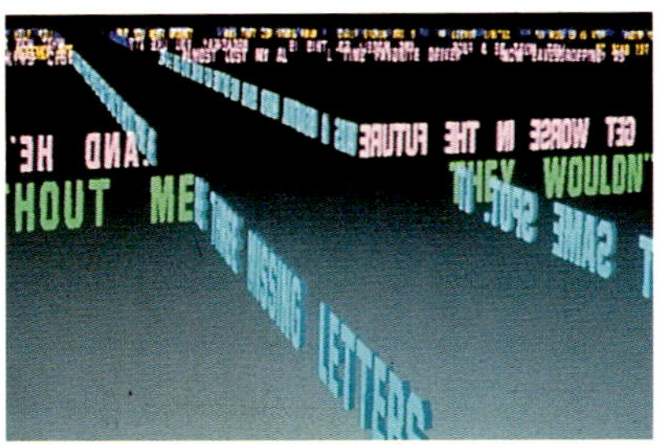

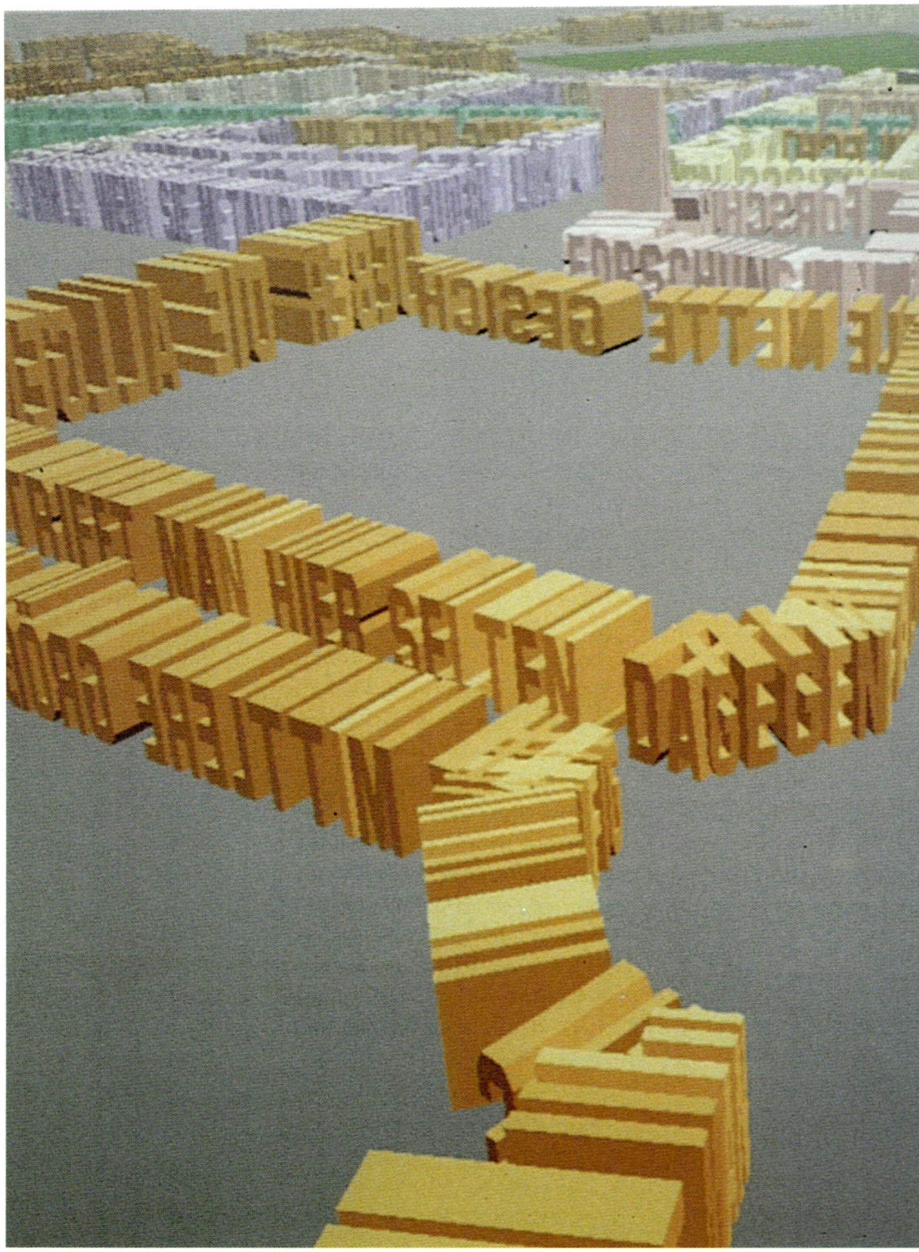

zwischen Bild und Betrachter. Die Lenkstange und die Pedale sind mit dem Computer verbunden, so daß der Betrachter die Richtung seiner Reise und die Geschwindigkeit interaktiv steuern kann. Die körperliche Anstrengung des Radfahrens in der realen Welt wird so in die virtuelle Welt übertragen, in der sie eigentlich überflüssig ist, und die Verbindung mit dem aktiven Körper wird im Reich des Virtuellen bestätigt. Das computergenerierte Bild wird von einem Videoprojektor auf eine große Leinwand projiziert. Ein kleiner Bildschirm vor dem Fahrrad zeigt einen einfachen Grundrißplan der jeweiligen Stadt, auf dem die Position des Radfahrers mit einem sich bewegenden Punkt markiert ist.

Eine Stadt ist reales Formgefüge und immaterielles Erfahrungsmuster zugleich. Ihre Architektur ist eine Morphologie der Sprache, ihr Grundriß ein psycho-geographisches Netzwerk und ihre Straßen sind ein Labyrinth aus Erzählsträngen. In *The Legible City* fährt der Betrachter durch eine virtuelle Stadt, deren Architektur aus Worten und Texten besteht. Die Fahrradfahrt durch diese ›Wortstädte‹ wird somit zu einer Lesereise. Einen bestimmten Weg einzuschlagen bedeutet, bestimmte Texte auszuwählen und sponta-

ney of reading. Choosing the path one takes is a choice of certain texts and their spontaneous juxtapositions. The identity of these new cities thus becomes the conjunction of the meanings these words generate as one travels freely around in this virtual urban space.

The Manhattan version (1989) of this work comprises eight separate fictional story lines in the form of monologues by ex-Mayor Koch, Frank Lloyd Wright, Donald Trump, a tour guide, a confidence trickster, an ambassador and a taxi-driver. Each story line has a specific lettering colour so that the bicyclist can choose one or another to follow the path of a particular narration. In the Amsterdam (1990) and Karlsruhe (1991) versions all the letters are scaled so that they have the same proportion and location as the actual buildings which they replace, resulting in a transformed representation of the actual architectural appearance of these cities. The texts for these two places are largely derived from archive documents that describe mundane historical events there.

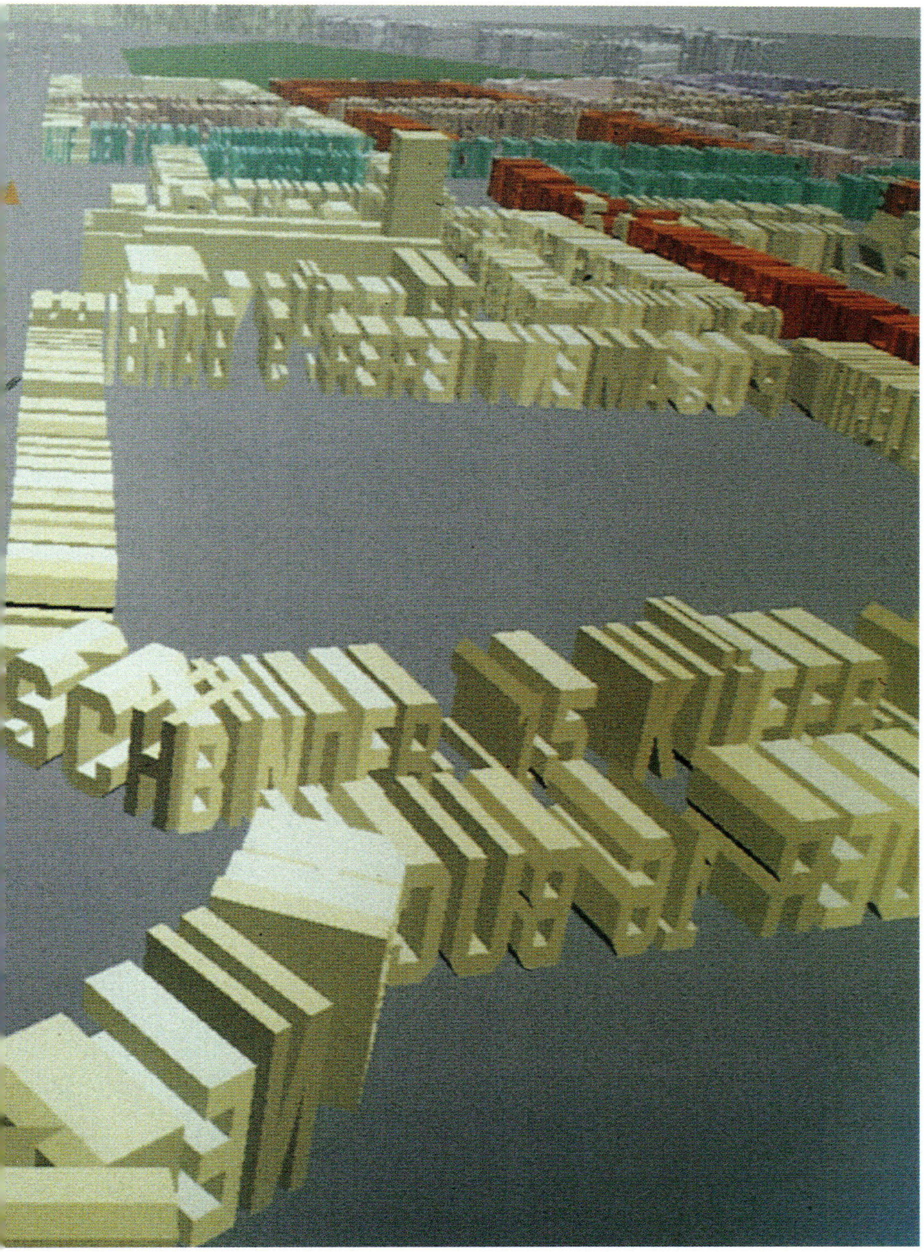

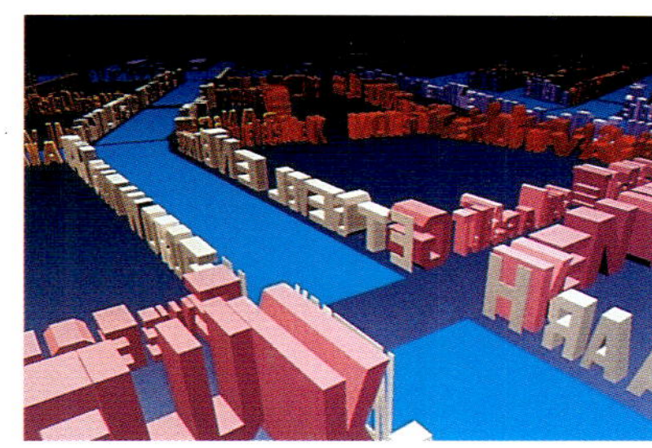

ne Kombinationen herzustellen. Die Identität dieser neuen Städte entsteht somit aus dem Zusammentreffen der Bedeutungen, die diese Worte evozieren, während man sich frei durch den virtuellen Stadtraum bewegt.

Die Manhattan-Version (1989) dieser Arbeit besteht aus acht verschiedenen fiktiven Erzählsträngen mit Monologen des Ex-Bürgermeisters von Manhattan, Koch, von Frank Lloyd Wright, Donald Trump, einem Reiseführer, einem Hochstapler, einem Botschafter und einem Taxifahrer. Die Buchstaben jedes Monologes haben eine andere Farbe, so daß der Radfahrer dem Weg der von ihm gewählten Erzählung entsprechend folgen kann. Für die Amsterdam- (1990) und die Karlsruhe-Version (1991) wurden alle Buchstaben maßstabsgetreu generiert, so daß sie dieselbe Größe und dieselbe Position haben wie die realen Gebäuden, die sie ersetzen – die reale architektonische Erscheinung dieser Städte wird somit in transformierter Weise dargestellt. Die Texte der Amsterdam- und der Karlsruhe-Version basieren größtenteils auf Archivmaterialien, die in nüchterner Form Ereignisse aus der Geschichte dieser Städte dokumentieren.

Alice's Room 1989

In this installation at the International Art & Science Exhibition (Kawasaki, Japan, 1989) a large, back-projected high-resolution monitor was mounted on a motorized turntable. An infra-red joystick controlled the 360-degree rotation of this screen and the synchronous rotation of the viewer's point of view in the computer-generated scene. This joystick also allowed the viewer to move his point of view forwards and backwards in the scene.

The computer-generated imagery showed a room that reproduced the appearance and proportions of the real room accommodating the installation. The virtual space (the image on the the screen) and the real space (the room) were optically aligned so that the viewer facing a door or a window in the real room would also be facing the same features in the simulated room. In this way *Alice's Room* set up a conjunction of virtual and actual spaces that enabled reality and fiction to be physically interpolated.

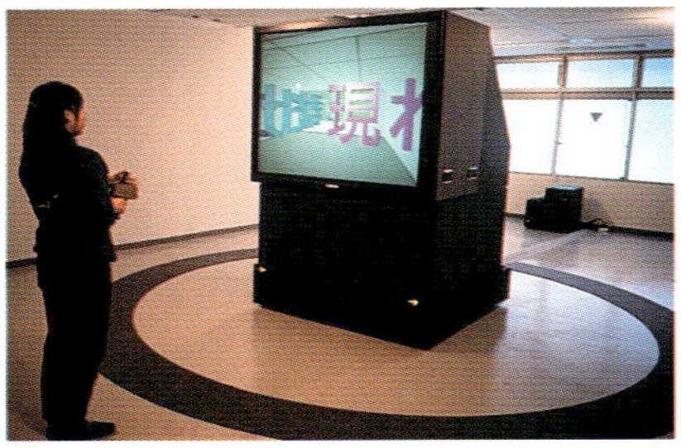

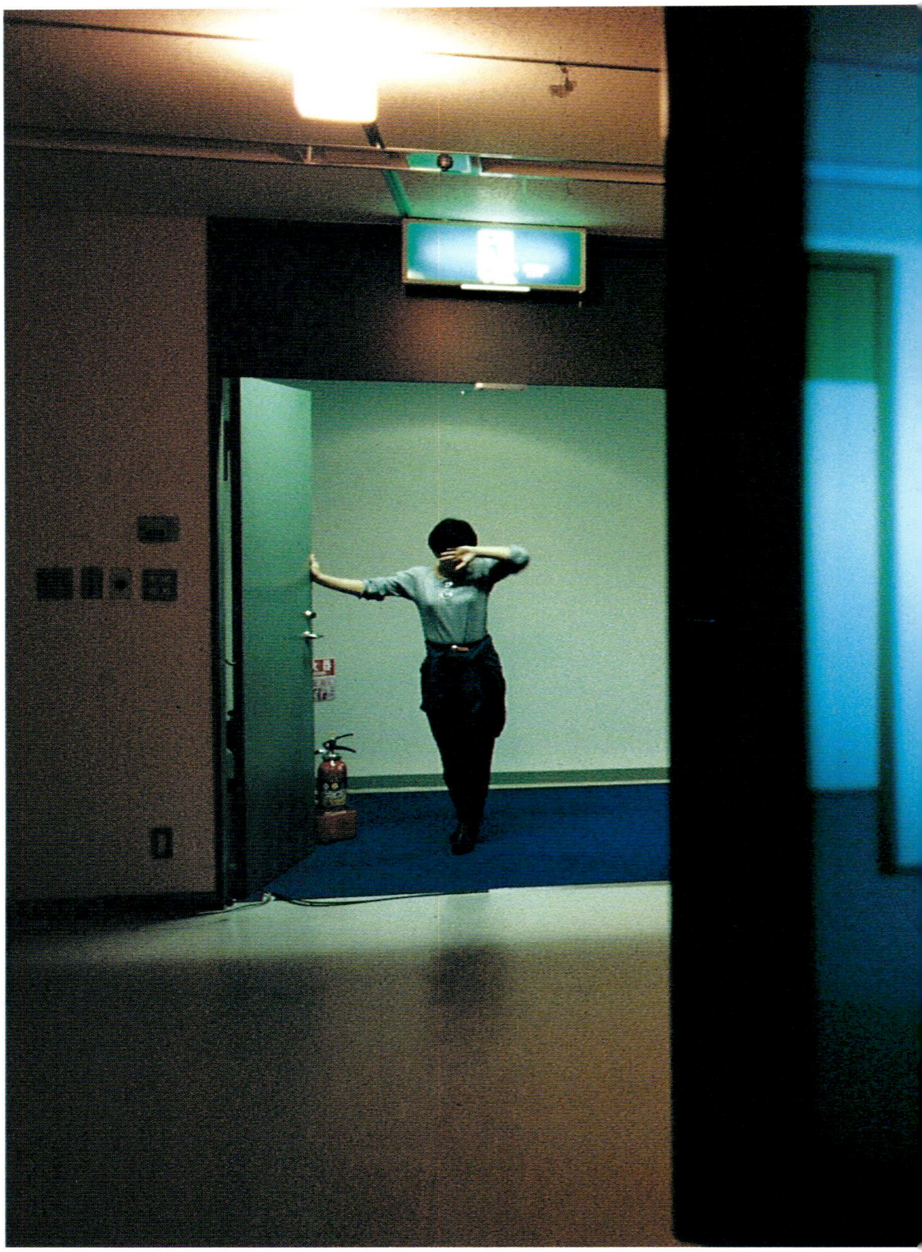

Alice's Room Alices Raum 1989

In dieser Installation, die während der internationalen Kunst- und Wissenschaftsausstellung (Kawasaki, Japan, 1989) gezeigt wurde, stand ein großer, hochauflösender Rückprojektionsmonitor auf einer motorisierten, drehbaren Plattform. Mit einem Infrarot-Joystick konnte die 360-Grad-Rotation des Bildschirms und die synchrone Rotation des Betrachterstandpunktes innerhalb der computergenerierten Szene gesteuert werden. Der Betrachter konnte über diesen Joystick auch seinen Standpunkt vor und zurück bewegen.

Das computergenerierte Bild zeigte einen Raum, der die Erscheinung und die Proportionen des realen Raumes, in dem sich die Installation befand, reproduzierte. Der virtuelle Raum (das Bild auf dem Monitor) und der reale Raum (der Ausstellungsraum) waren optisch aufeinander abgestimmt, so daß der Betrachter, der einer Tür oder einem Fenster im realen Raum gegenüberstand, sich auch im simulierten Raum diesen gegenüber befand. Auf diese Weise stellte *Alice's Room* eine Verbindung zwischen virtuellen und realen Räumen her; Realität und Fiktion wurden

Four computer-generated objects were added in this simulated environment – red, green, yellow and blue rectangular boxes in the corners of the room. When entered, each box became a room interior which looked exactly like the outer room while at the same time possessing unique characteristics. The first room showed the four coloured boxes in a continuous circulating process of splitting into thirty-two smaller boxes and then reassembling themselves. The second room showed two rows of large moving Japanese characters – a haiku written specially by Shuntaro Tanikawa. The third room contained a slowly rotating wire-frame hypercube. At the centre of the fourth room was a continuously turning replica of the actual video monitor. While this simulated monitor had a blank white screen, moving coloured reflections on the walls of the room conveyed the impression that it was being illuminated by images on this empty screen.

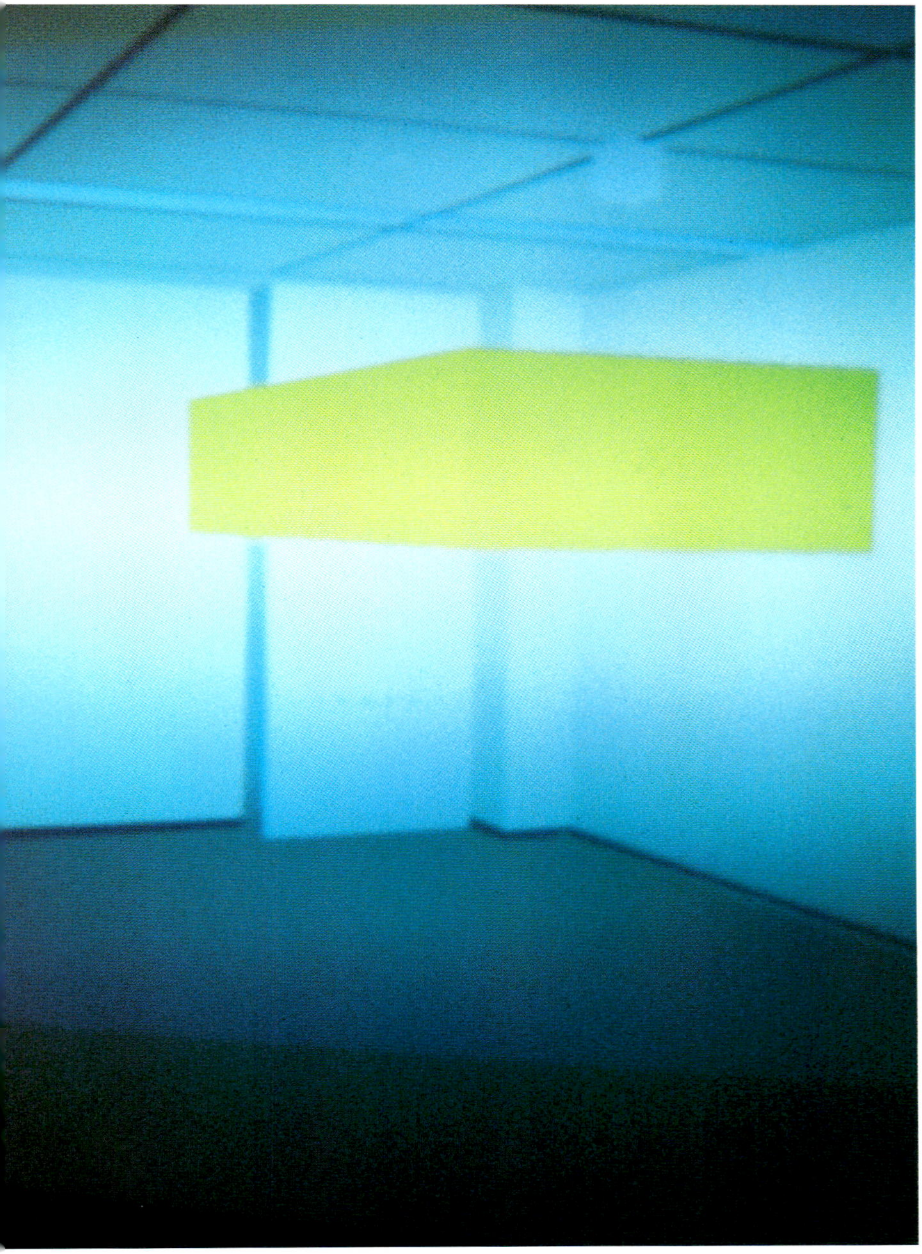

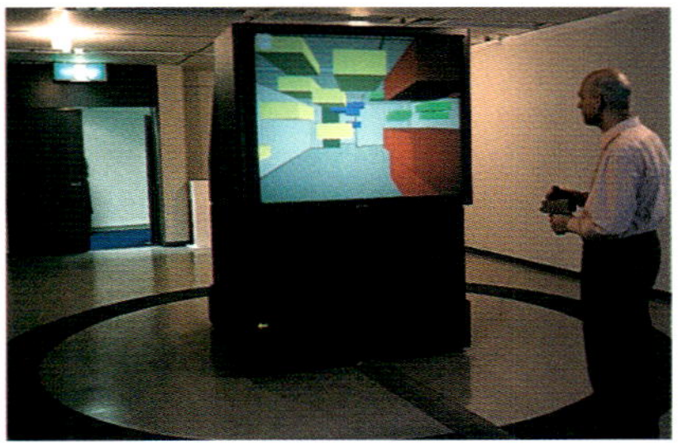

physisch ineinander gefügt.

Der simulierten Umgebung wurden vier computergenerierte Objekte hinzugefügt: in jeder Ecke des Raumes befand sich eine rechteckige Box, jede in einer anderen Farbe (rot, grün, gelb und blau). Betrat man eine Box, verwandelte sie sich in einen Innenraum, der den Außenraum exakt nachzeichnete, doch gleichzeitig über ganz eigene Charakteristika verfügte. Der erste Raum zeigte die vier farbigen Würfel in einem sich ständig wiederholenden Prozeß der Aufspaltung in 32 kleinere Boxen und der erneuten Zusammensetzung zu vier großen Boxen. Der zweite Raum zeigte zwei Reihen großer, vorbeiziehender japanischer Zeichen – ein Haiku, das von Shuntaro Tanikawa für diese Arbeit geschrieben wurde. Der dritte Raum enthielt ein langsam rotierendes Drahtgittermodell eines Hyperwürfels. In der Mitte des vierten Raumes befand sich eine Nachbildung des realen Videomonitors, die sich ununterbrochen um ihre eigene Achse drehte. Obwohl der Bildschirm dieses simulierten Monitors weiß und leer war, entstand durch sich bewegende Farbreflektionen auf den Wänden des Raumes der Eindruck, als würde der Raum durch Bilder vom Monitor erleuchtet.

The Virtual Museum 1991

The Virtual Museum is a three-dimensional computer-generated museum constituted by an immaterial constellation of rooms and exhibits. A round, motorized rotating platform is furnished with a large video projection monitor, a computer, and a chair from which the viewer interactively controls his journey through *The Virtual Museum*. Forwards and backwards movement of the chair causes corresponding motion by the viewer through the museum space represented on the screen. Turning the chair produces a rotation of this virtual image space, and also a synchronous physical rotation of the platform.

The *Virtual Museum* is made up by five rooms which have the same appearance as the real room in which the installation is located. This establishes a conjunction of the real and virtual spaces and a conjunction of the real and virtual modalities of travel for the viewer. To make this explicit, the first virtual room shows a representation of the installation itself. At

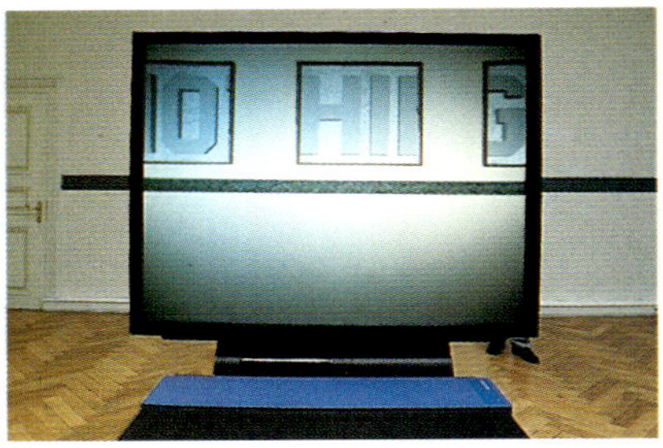

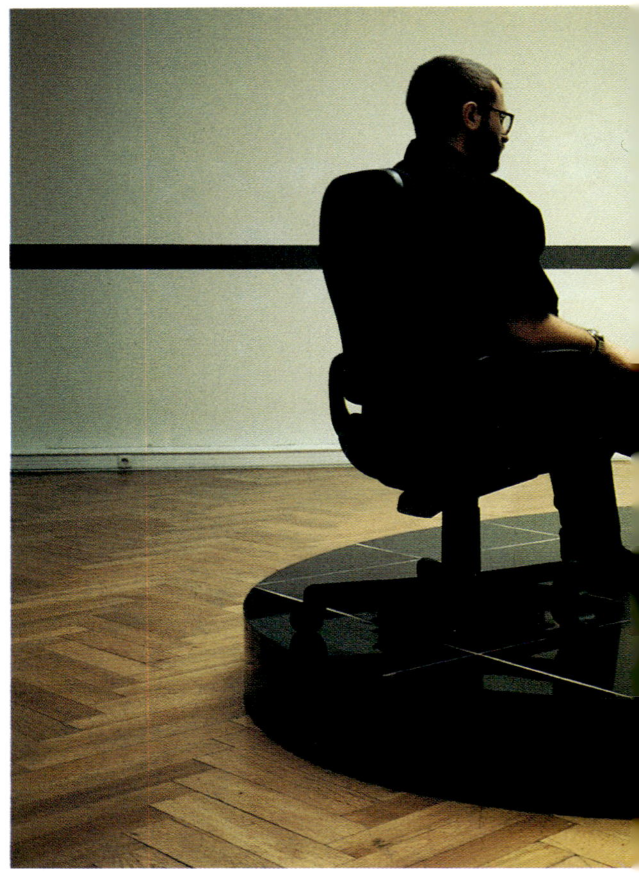

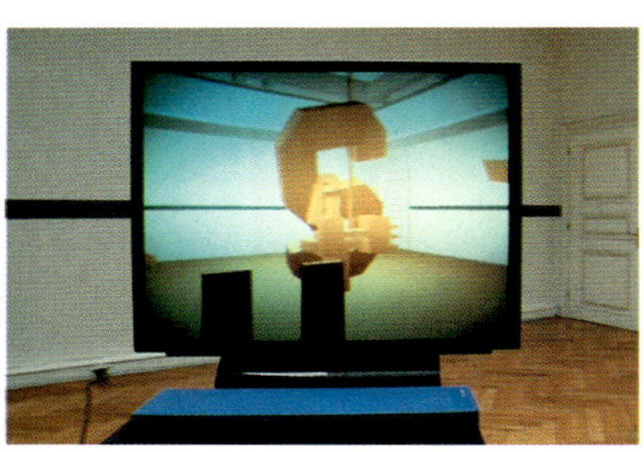

The Virtual Museum

Das Virtuelle Museum 1991

The Virtual Museum ist ein dreidimensionales computergeneriertes Museum, das durch die immaterielle Anordnung von Räumen und Ausstellungsobjekten entsteht. Auf einer runden, motorisierten, drehbaren Plattform befinden sich ein großer Videomonitor, ein Computer und ein Stuhl. Mit dem Stuhl kann der Betrachter seine Reise durch das virtuelle Museum steuern: Lehnt sich der Betrachter im Stuhl nach vorne oder hinten, erzeugt er eine synchrone Bewegung im virtuellen Museumsraum. Dreht er den Stuhl, dreht sich der virtuelle Bildraum und gleichzeitig auch die Plattform.

The Virtual Museum besteht aus fünf Räumen, die dieselbe Erscheinung haben wie der reale Raum, in dem sich die Installation befindet. Dadurch entsteht für den Betrachter eine Verbindung zwischen den realen und den virtuellen Räumen sowie zwischen realen und virtuellen Bewegungsformen. Um dies zu verdeutlichen, zeigt der erste der virtuellen Räume eine Darstellung der realen Installation. Der Betrachter sitzt gleichzeitig dem realen und dem virtuellen Bild-

first the viewer faces both the real and virtual monitor screens – the real and virtual realities are exactly aligned. The viewer moving through *The Virtual Museum* in effect transports himself out of this chair and can see the installation, with its vacated chair, as an object outside his virtual point of view.

The other four rooms are entered consecutively by passing through any of the immaterial walls of the room the viewer is in. Using alphabetic and textual forms, each room contains its own specific virtual 'exhibits'. The exhibits in the first three rooms are referential to existing genres – painting, sculpture and cinema. The exhibit in the fourth room describes the particularity of a wholly computer-generated environment – three randomly moving signs ('A', '2', 'Z') are primary-coloured light sources that disclose and irradiate the room.

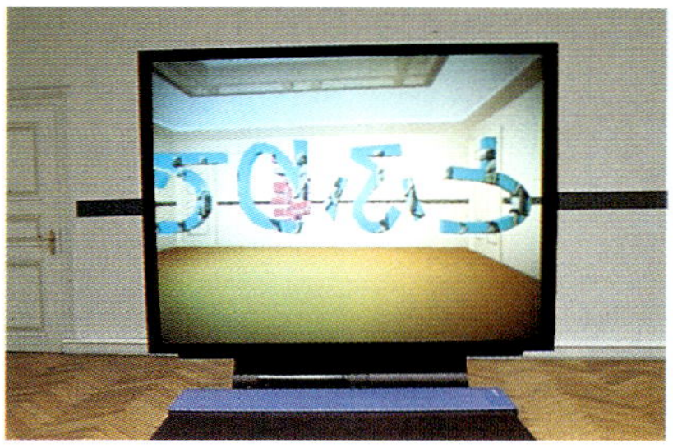

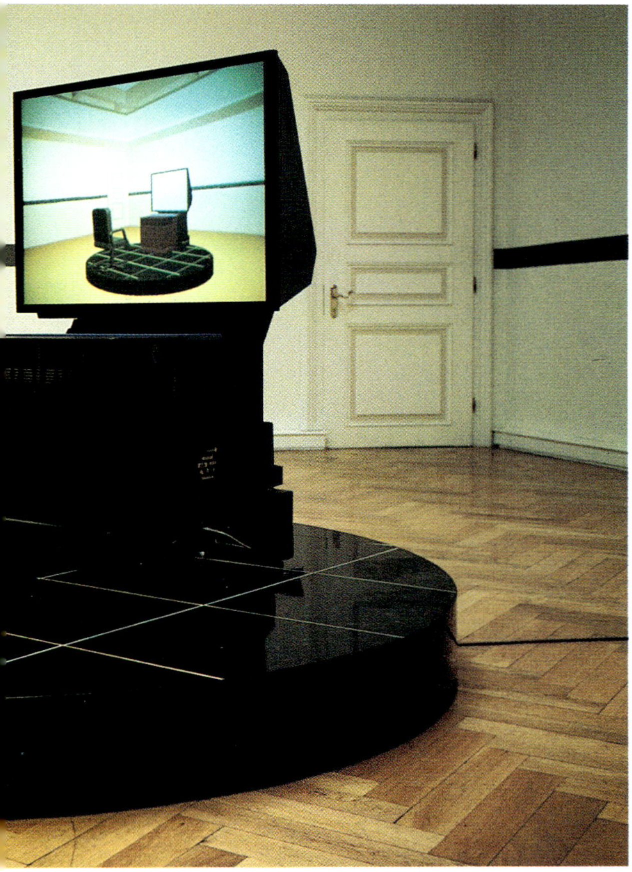

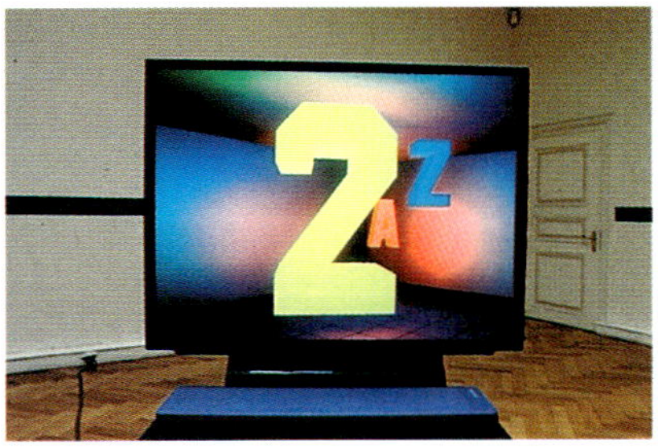

schirm gegenüber – reale und virtuelle Wirklichkeit sind exakt aufeinander ausgerichtet. Sobald sich der Betrachter durch das virtuelle Museum bewegt, manövriert er sich selbst aus dem Stuhl heraus und wird zu einem Objekt, das sich außerhalb seines virtuellen Standpunktes befindet und die Installation – mit dem leeren Stuhl – beobachten kann.

Die übrigen vier Räume können nacheinander betreten werden, indem der Betrachter durch eine der immateriellen Wände des Raumes, in dem er sich gerade befindet, hindurchgeht. Jeder Raum enthält bestimmte virtuelle ›Ausstellungsstücke‹, geformt aus Buchstaben und Texten. Die Ausstellungsobjekte in den ersten drei Räumen verweisen auf bestehende Kunstgattungen wie Malerei, Bildhauerei und Kino. Das Ausstellungsobjekt im vierten Raum beschreibt die Besonderheit einer vollständig computergenerierten Umgebung – drei sich ziellos bewegende Zeichen (›A‹, ›2‹, ›Z‹) in den Primärfarben sind Lichtquellen, die den Raum enthüllen und erleuchten.

Televirtual Chit Chat 1993

During Imagina '93 (Monte Carlo, Monaco, 1993) computer graphics installations in Monte Carlo and in Karlsruhe were connected by modem through a conventional telephone line. Facing large video screens, the two distant players each shared the same virtual image space. While manipulating their own graphic elements each person was at the same time seeing the result of the distant partner's actions on the screen in front of him.

Each player could choose letters from a simulated keyboard on their screen. Using a multi-axis 3-D mouse, the position, size and shape of each of these letters could be interactively manipulated over a rectangular plane that was divided like a game board into a grid of 64 squares. A map on surface of this game board showed Europe between Monte Carlo and Karlsruhe, representing the geographical distance between the two players.

Sharing a televirtual space of alphabetic forms,

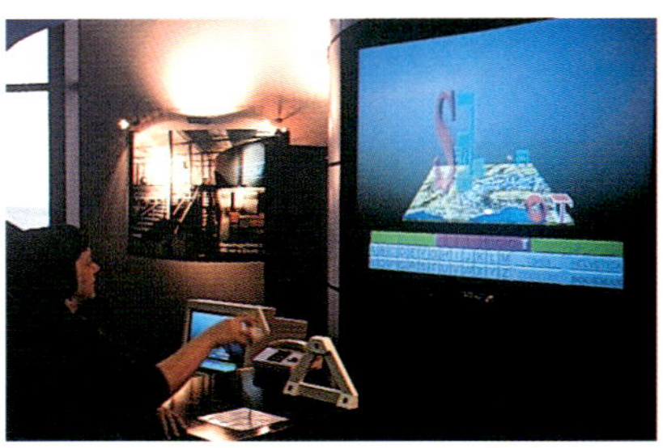

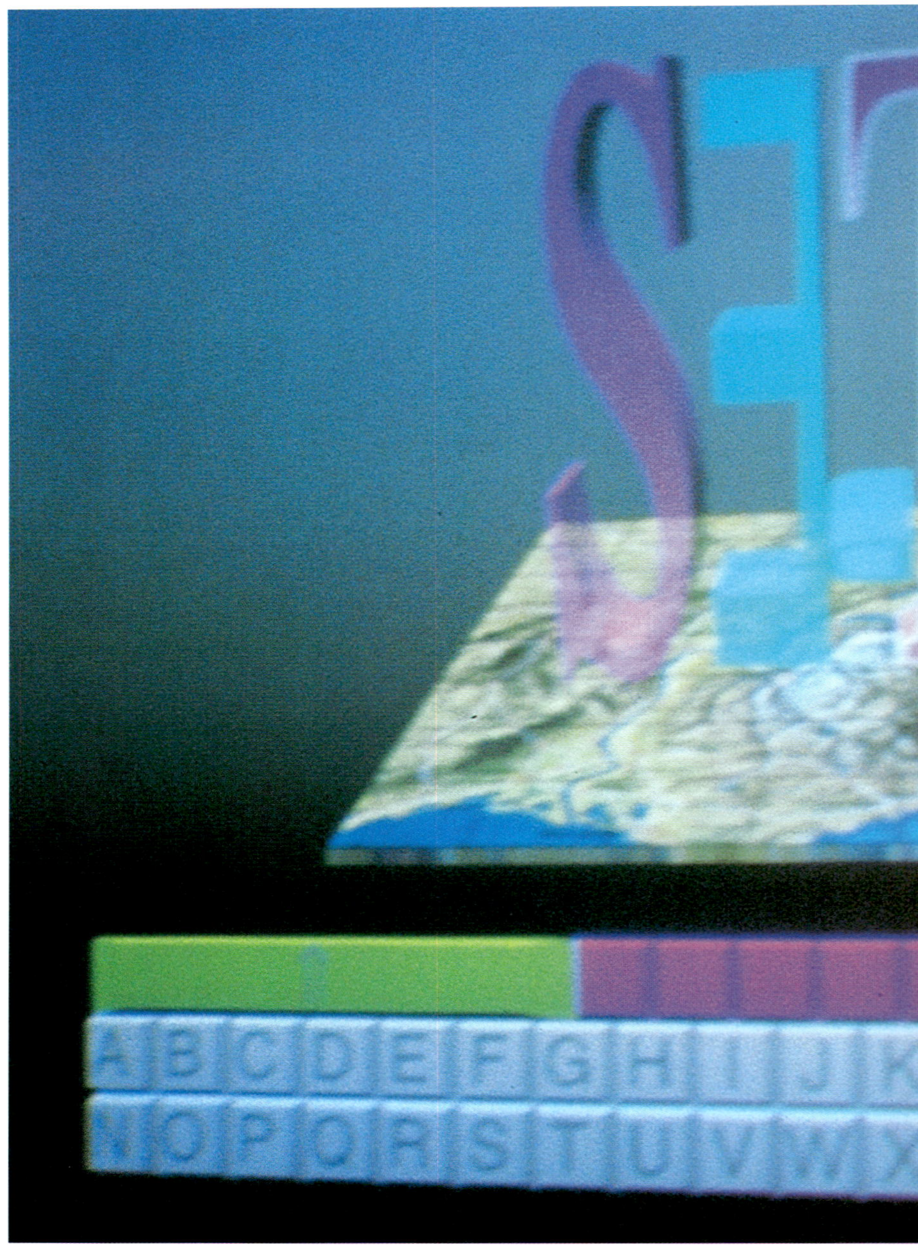

Televirtual Chit Chat

Televirtuelle Plauderei 1993

Je eine Computergrafikinstallation in Monte Carlo und in Karlsruhe wurden während der Imagina '93 (Monte Carlo, Monaco, 1993) per Modem über eine konventionelle Telefonleitung miteinander verbunden. Die beiden weit entfernt voneinander agierenden Spieler saßen jeweils einem großen Videomonitor gegenüber und sahen denselben virtuellen Bildraum. Während beide Personen jeweils ihre eigenen grafischen Elemente manipulierten, konnten sie gleichzeitig auf dem Bildschirm auch die Aktionen ihres Partners auf der anderen Seite verfolgen.

Jeder Spieler konnte Buchstaben von einer simulierten Tastatur auf dem Bildschirm auswählen. Mit einer multiaxialen 3-D-Maus konnten Position, Größe und Form jedes Buchstabens über ein rechteckiges Feld, das wie ein Spielbrett in ein Raster aus 64 Quadraten unterteilt war, interaktiv verändert werden. Eine Landkarte auf der Oberfläche dieses Spielbrettes zeigte Europa zwischen Monte Carlo und Karlsruhe und verdeutlichte so die geographische Entfernung zwischen den beiden Spielern.

the formal interaction of the two players was both a sculptural interplay of the letters as well as a tentative communication with words. Up to eight letters could be placed by each player on the board at one time, and each player's letters had a distinctive colour (magenta and cyan). These letters could be individually resized in width, height and depth, becoming more transparent as their size increased. Each letter could also be moved anywhere over and above the surface of the game board. After some time, letters that were not being manipulated would disappear from the game board area. Another function allowed each player to independently control their angle of view over the whole scene, and a voice phone connection between the two sites also allowed the players to speak to each other while manipulating these letters in the shared virtual space.

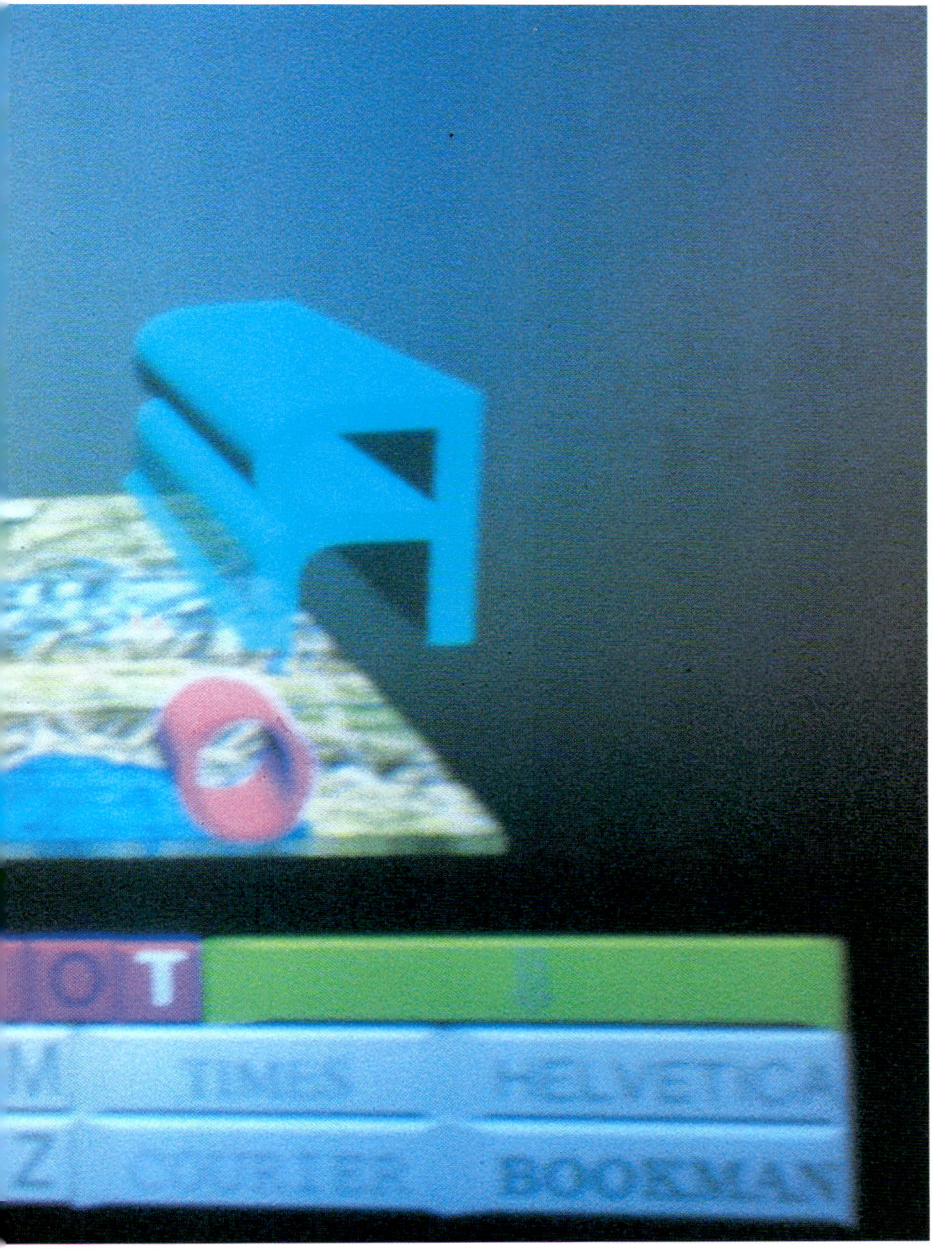

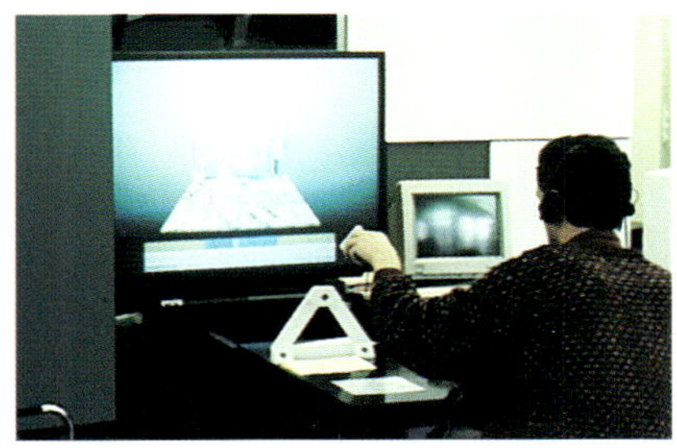

Indem die beiden Spieler einen televirtuellen Raum alphabetischer Zeichen miteinander teilten, bestand ihre formale Interaktion sowohl in einem skulpturalen Zusammenspiel der Buchstaben als auch in einer unverbindlichen Kommunikation mit Worten. Bis zu acht Buchstaben konnten von jedem Spieler auf dem Brett gleichzeitig plaziert werden; die Buchstaben der Spieler besaßen verschiedene Farben (magenta bzw. cyan). Ihre Breite, Höhe und Tiefe konnte individuell verändert werden; je größer sie wurden, umso durchsichtiger wurden sie. Jeder Buchstabe konnte an jede beliebige Stelle des Spielbretts und über dessen Oberfläche bewegt werden. Wurden Buchstaben eine Zeit lang nicht bewegt oder verändert, verschwanden sie vom Spielbrett. Eine weitere Funktion ermöglichte es den Spielern, ihren Blickwinkel auf den Schauplatz unabhängig voneinander zu verändern; über eine telefonische Sprechverbindung zwischen den beiden Orten konnten die beiden Spieler auch miteinander reden, während sie die Buchstaben im gemeinsamen virtuellen Raum manipulierten.

Disappearance 1993

In this work the movement of a large video monitor mounted on an industrial forklift truck creates a virtual representation of a larger-than-life ballerina. As the forklift moves the monitor up and down the ballerina is presented from head to toe, and as the forklift truck rotates the ballerina appears to turn. In this way the monitor functions as a window that gradually reveals the virtual presence of the ballerina, who is dancing in the same axis as the rotating forklift truck.

Visible inside the motor compartment of the forklift truck is a small rotating ballerina figurine in front of which a video camera moves up and down. This mechanism is electronically synchronized with the movement of the forklift itself and provides the closed-circuit source for the video image of the ballerina that is seen on the monitor screen.

Disappearance evokes and celebrates the memory of the ballerina on a music box (a first-generation robot) and generates her virtual reconstruction to the

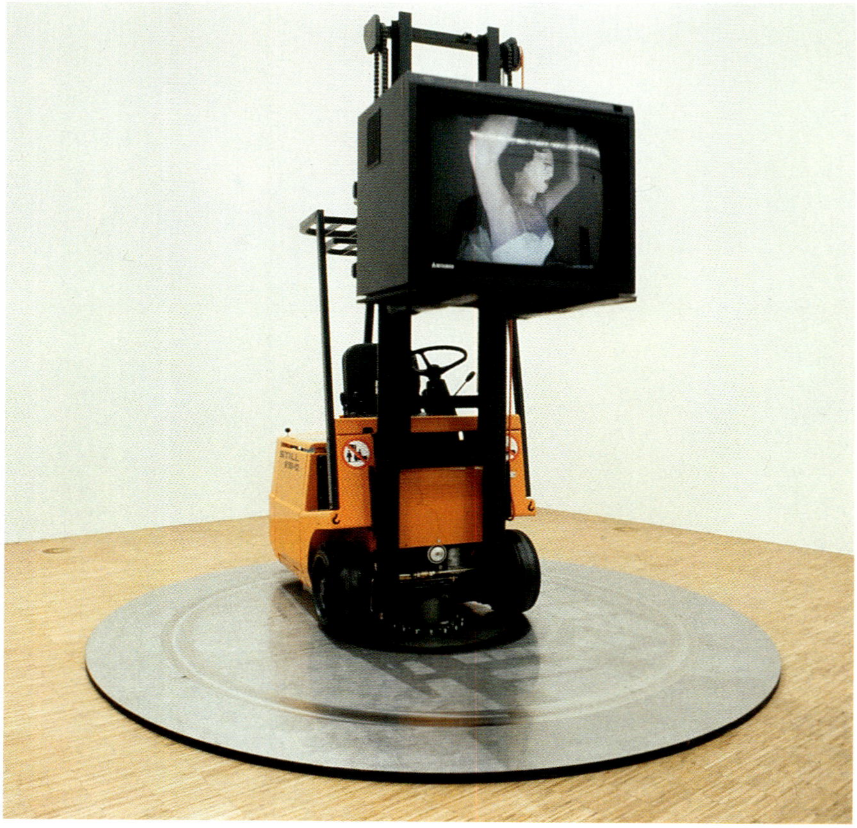

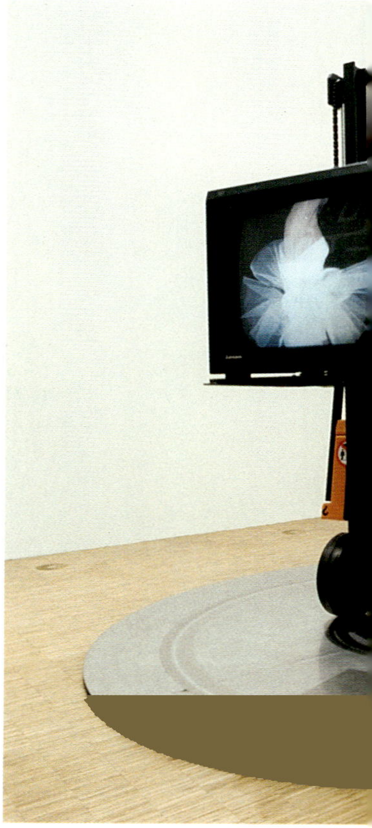

Disappearance Verschwinden 1993

In dieser Arbeit erzeugt die Bewegung eines großen Videomonitors, der auf einem Gabelstapler befestigt ist, eine virtuelle Repräsentation einer überlebensgroßen Ballerina. Die Gabel bewegt den Monitor auf und ab, wodurch die Ballerina nach und nach vom Kopf bis zu den Füßen auf dem Bildschirm erscheint; da sich der Gabelstapler dreht, scheint sich auch die Tänzerin zu drehen. So wird der Monitor zu einem Fenster, das allmählich die virtuelle Präsenz der Ballerina enthüllt, die um dieselbe Achse tanzt, um die sich der Gabelstapler dreht.

Im Motorraum des Gabelstaplers befindet sich – sichtbar– die Figur einer kleinen, sich drehenden Ballerina, vor der sich eine Videokamera auf- und abbewegt. Dieser Mechanismus ist elektronisch mit der Bewegung des Gabelstaplers synchronisiert und bildet die Quelle des ›Closed-Circuit‹ mit dem Videobild der Ballerina auf dem Bildschirm.

Disapppearance weckt und zelebriert die Erinnerung an die Ballerina auf der Jukebox (ein Roboter der ersten Generation) und treibt die virtuelle Rekonstruktion so weit, daß nun die Reproduktions-

extent that the machinery of reproduction itself now incarnates her pirouettes.

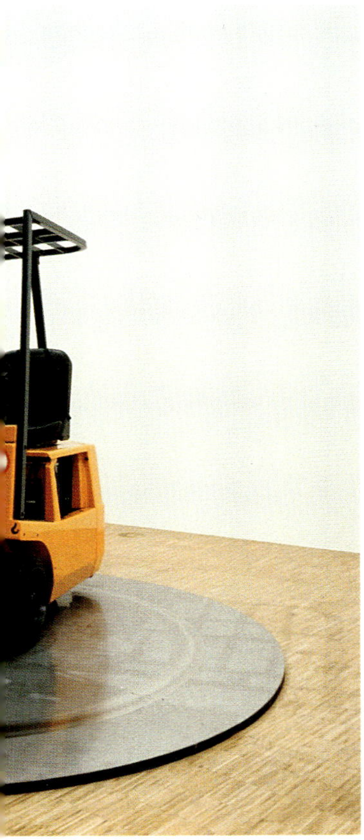

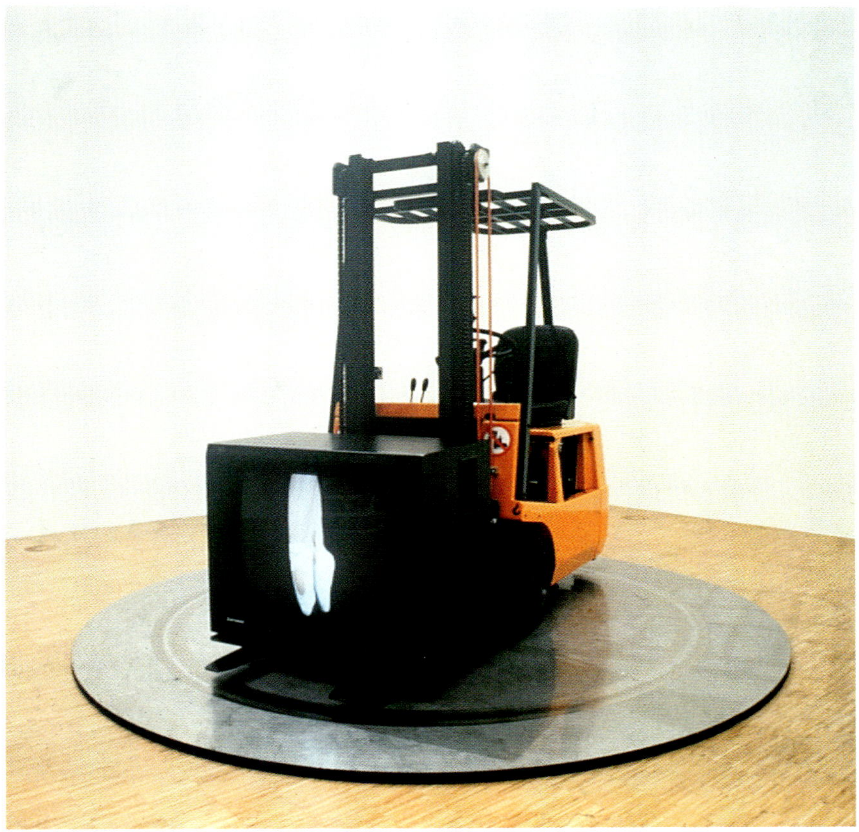

maschinerie selbst die Pirouetten der Ballerina verkörpert.

EVE (Extended Virtual Environment)

1993

EVE is a research and development project initiated at the ZKM Karlsruhe in cooperation with the Forschungszentrum Karlsruhe. It encompasses the conceptual and technical development of a new form of interactive immersive visualization environment and virtual-reality apparatus.

In the centre of a large inflatable dome, two video projectors are mounted on a motorized pan/tilt device (e.g. robot arm) which can move the projected image anywhere over the inside surface of the dome. The two video projectors present a stereo pair of images and the viewers wearing polarizing spectacles can see the projected imagery in three dimensions.

One of the visitors to *EVE* wears a helmet (or a 'miner's lamp') with an attached spatial tracking device that identifies the position and angle of his head. This controls the positioning of video projectors so that the projected image always follows the direc-

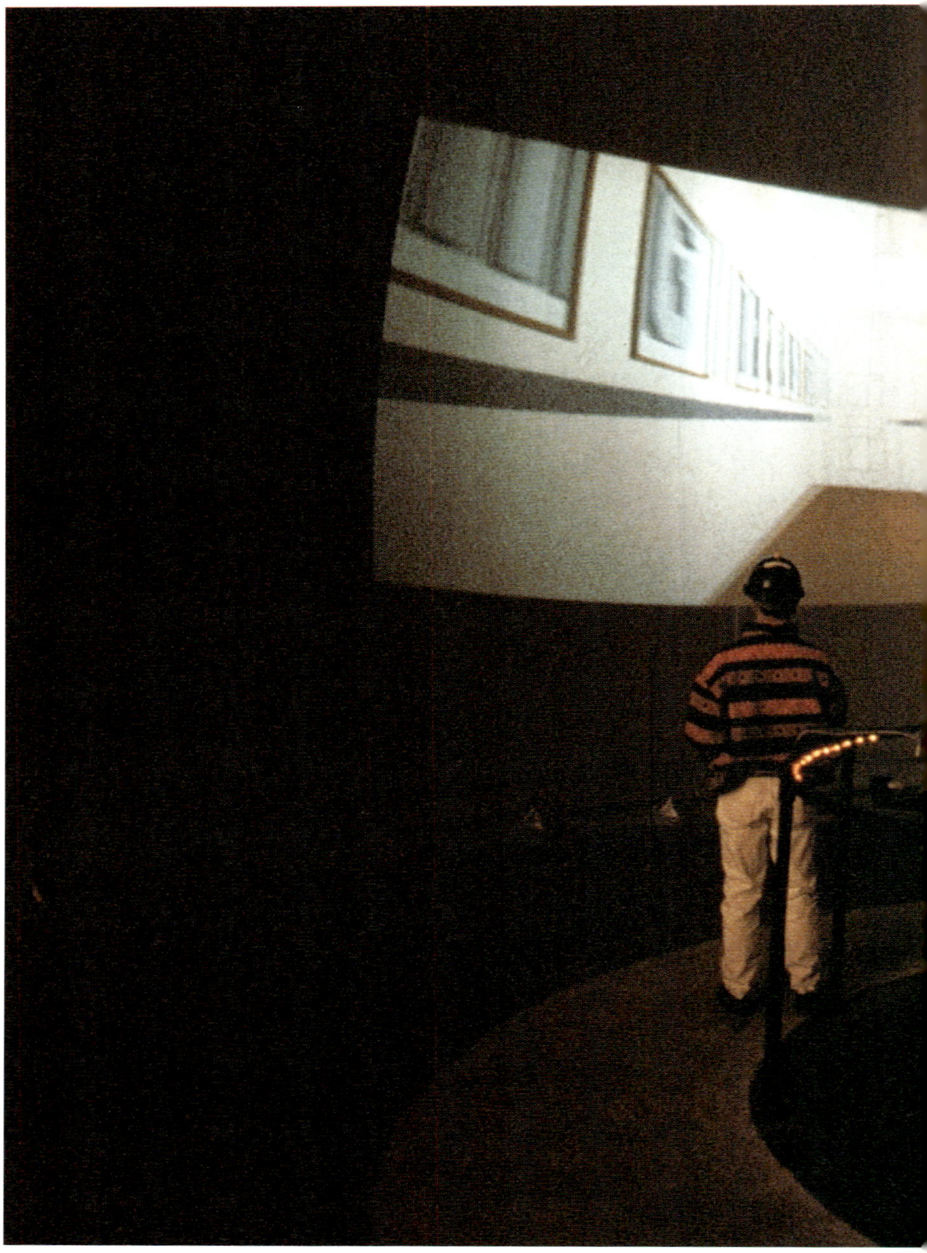

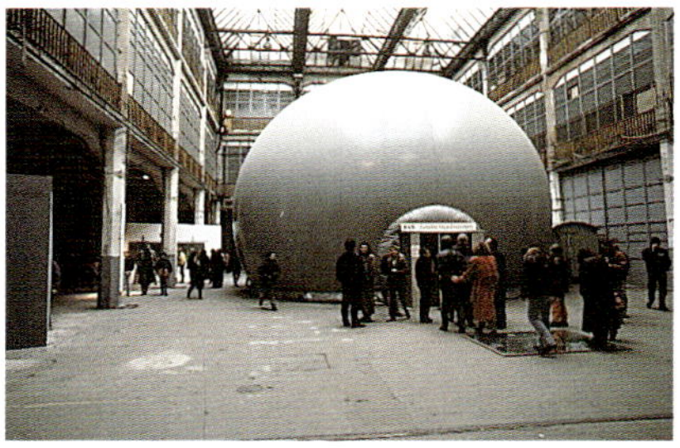

EVE (Erweiterte Virtuelle Umgebung)

1993

EVE ist ein am ZKM Karlsruhe in Kooperation mit dem Forschungszentrum Karlsruhe initiiertes Forschungs- und Entwicklungsprojekt. Es umfaßt die konzeptuelle und technische Entwicklung einer neuartigen interaktiven immersiven Visualisierungsumgebung und Virtual-Reality-Apparatur.

In der Mitte einer großen luftgetragenen Kuppel sind zwei Videoprojektoren auf einer Schwenk-Neige-Vorrichtung (z.B. einem Roboterarm) plaziert, die das projizierte Bild in alle Richtungen über die Innenseite der Kuppel bewegen kann. Die beiden Videoprojektoren projizieren stereoskopische Bilder, die von den Betrachtern, die Polarisationsbrillen tragen, dreidimensional gesehen werden können.

Einer der Betrachter trägt einen Helm (oder eine ›Grubenlampe‹) mit einem Positionsmesser, der Position und Blickwinkel des Betrachters erkennt. Dadurch wird die Bewegung der Videoprojektoren gesteuert, so daß das projizierte Bild immer der Blickrichtung des Betrachters folgt. Auf diese Weise kann der Betrachter das Bildfenster über die gesamte

tion of the viewer's gaze. In this way the viewer can move the picture frame over the entire dome surface and interactively explore the computer-generated virtual scenographies which are presented there. A joystick also allows the viewer to control his forwards and backwards movement in the surrounding virtual space.

In 1993 (MultiMediale 3, ZKM Karlsruhe, Germany) *The Virtual Museum* (1991) was adapted for presentation within *EVE*. In 1995 (MultiMediale 4, ZKM Karlsruhe, Germany) a new work titled *The Telepresent Onlookers* linked the movement of the interior video projectors to a stereo pair of video cameras mounted on another pan/tilt device situated outside the dome. As a result the exterior scene could be reconstituted within the dome, allowing the viewers inside to be vicariously telepresent in the outside space .

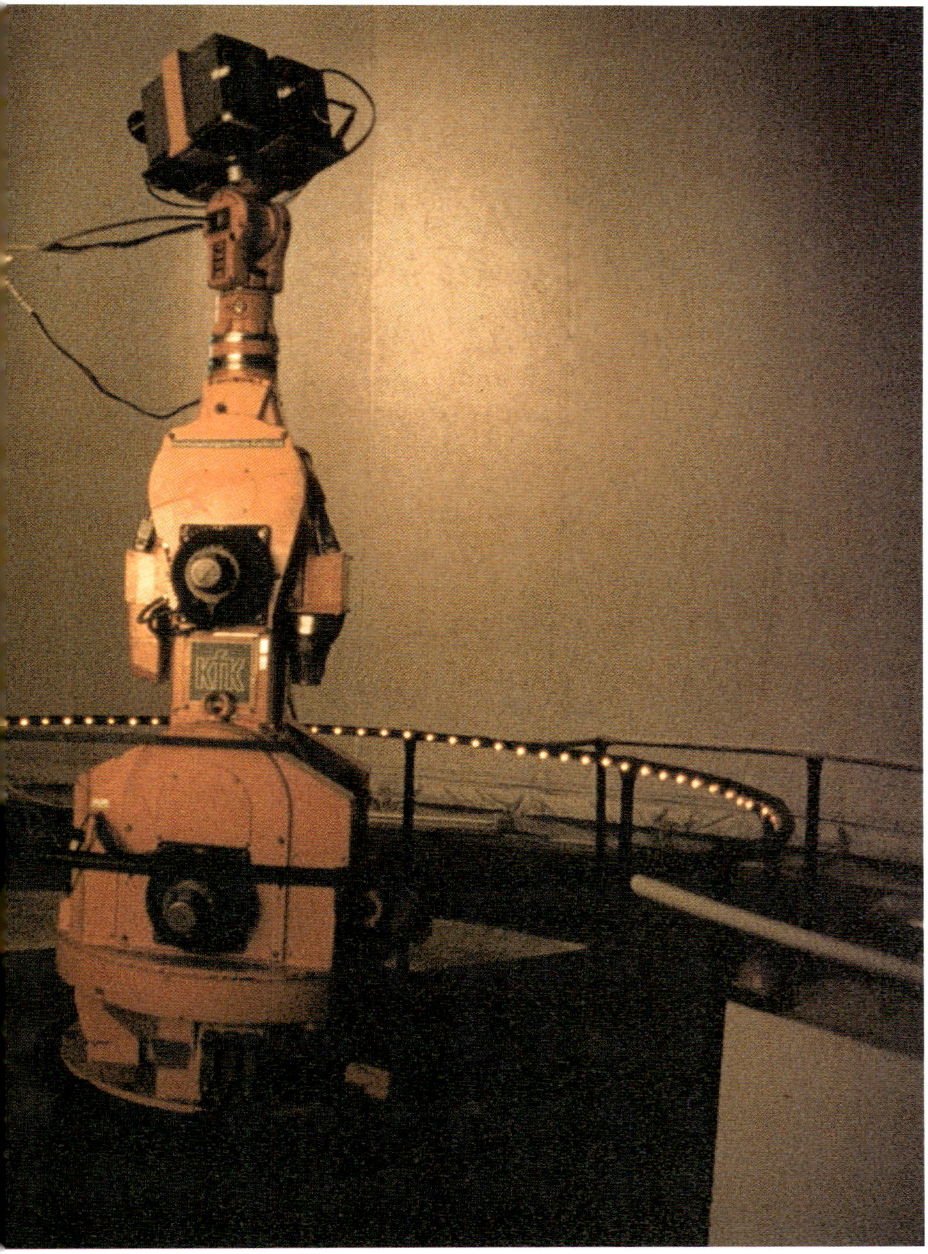

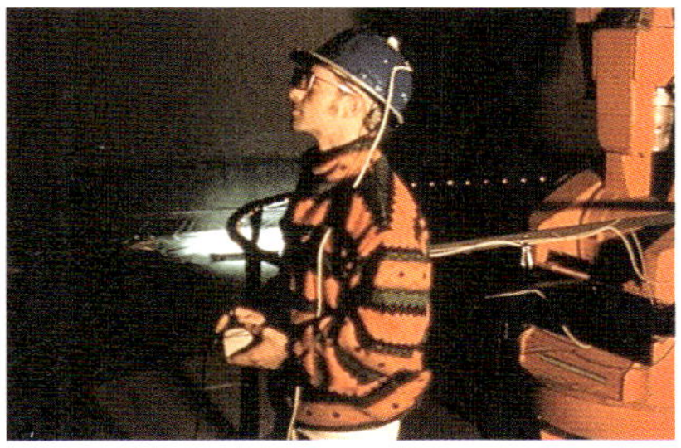

Innenfläche der Kuppel bewegen und interaktiv die projizierten computergenerierten virtuellen Räume erkunden. Mit einem Joystick kann er auch seine Vor- und Rückwärtsbewegungen innerhalb des virtuellen Raumes steuern.

1993 wurde *The Virtual Museum* für die Präsentation in *EVE* adaptiert (MultiMediale 3, ZKM Karlsruhe, Deutschland). 1995 wurde eine neue Arbeit mit dem Titel *Die telepräsenten Betrachter* (MultiMediale 4 , ZKM Karlsruhe, Deutschland) entwickelt: Die Bewegung der Videoprojektoren im Innern der Kuppel wurde mit zwei Videokameras verbunden, die auf einer weiteren Schwenk-Neige-Vorrichtung außerhalb der Kuppel befestigt waren. Der äußere Schauplatz konnte auf diese Weise in der Kuppel rekonstituiert werden und erlaubte es den Betrachtern im Innenraum, indirekt im Außenraum ›telepräsent‹ zu sein.

The Golden Calf 1995

This work is constituted by a white pedestal on which there is an LCD colour monitor connected to computing machinery by a cable running through the pedestal. The viewer picks up and holds this monitor in his hands. The screen shows a representation of the pedestal with a computer-generated image of a golden calf on top. By moving the monitor around the actual pedestal the viewer can examine this golden calf from above and below and all sides. Thus the monitor functions like a window that reveals a virtual object apparently located in the real space.

The golden calf has a shiny mirror-like surface in which the viewer sees reflections of the actual venue of the installation. These are previously digitized photographs of the room that are 'reflection-mapped' onto the calf's skin. While the viewer is not included in this digitized reflection of the environment, he does see himself reflected on the glass surface of the LCD screen.

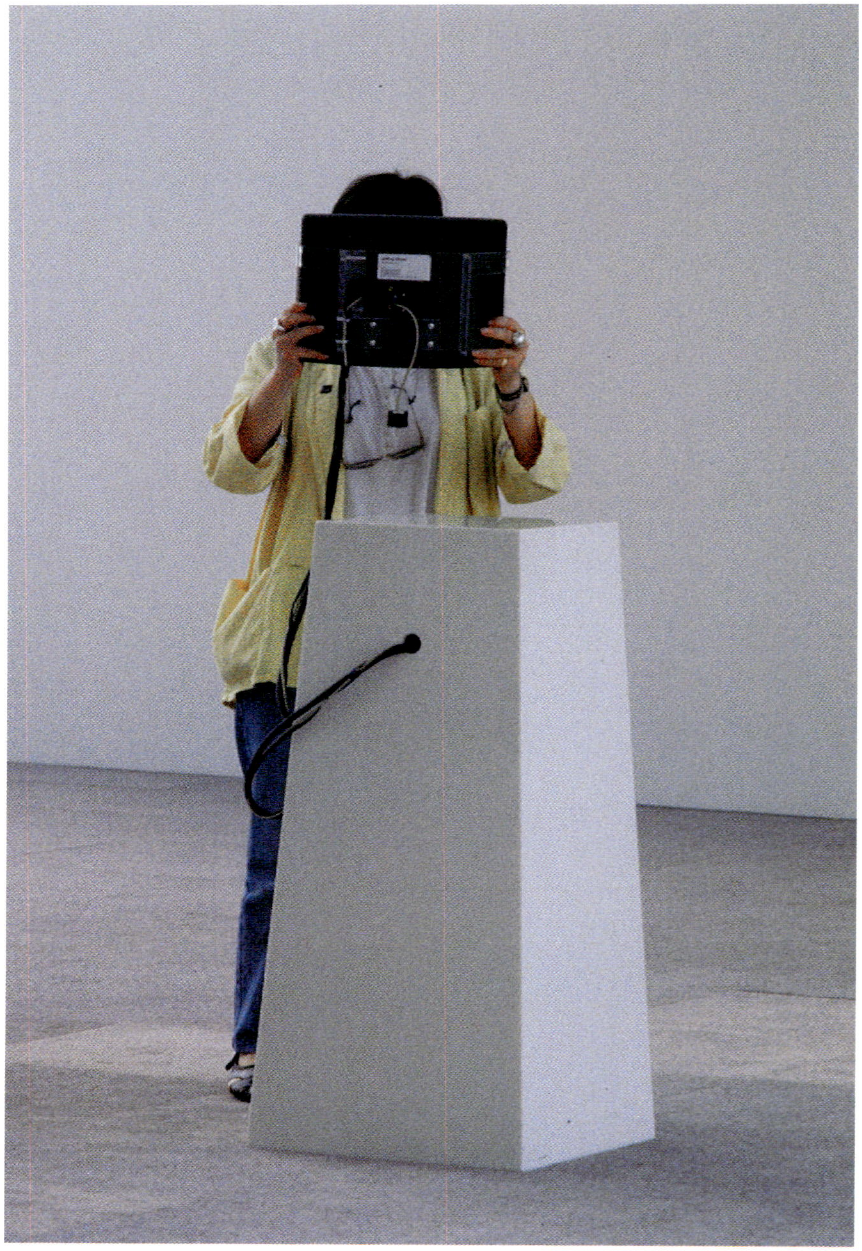

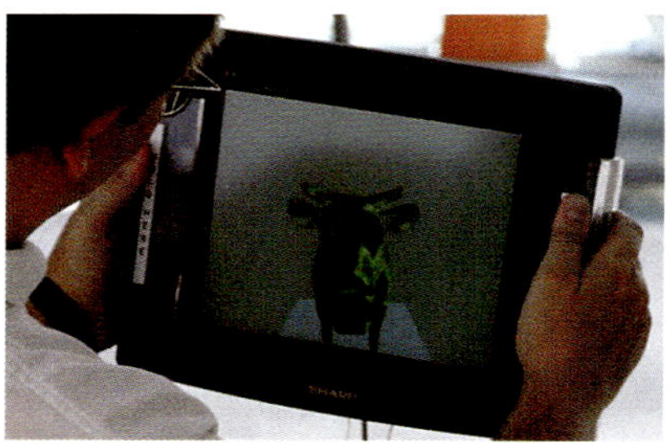

The Golden Calf Das goldene Kalb 1995

Diese Arbeit besteht aus einem weißen Podest, auf dem ein LCD-Farbmonitor liegt, der über ein durch die Säule laufendes Kabel mit einem Computer verbunden ist. Der Betrachter kann den Monitor vom Podest nehmen und in den Händen halten. Auf dem Bildschirm ist eine Darstellung des Podestes zu sehen, auf dem, als computergeneriertes Bild, ein goldenes Kalb erscheint. Bewegt sich der Betrachter mit dem Bildschirm um das reale Podest herum, kann er das goldene Kalb von oben, von unten und von allen Seiten betrachten. So wird der Monitor zu einem Fenster, das ein virtuelles Objekt enthüllt, das sich scheinbar im realen Raum befindet.

Das goldene Kalb hat eine glänzende spiegelähnliche Oberfläche, auf der der Betrachter Reflektionen des aktuellen, realen Ausstellungsraumes sehen kann. Es handelt sich hierbei um vor Beginn der Ausstellung digitalisierte Fotografien des Raumes, die als Reflexionen auf der ›Haut‹ des Kalbes programmiert wurden. Obwohl der Betrachter selbst nicht Teil jener digital erzeugten Spiegelungen ist, spiegelt er sich doch in der Glasscheibe des LCD-Monitors.

The immateriality of this golden calf is further emphasized by the fact that only its outer surfaces are modelled, so that if the viewer moves the monitor screen into the calf's body none of its interior surfaces are visible.

In *The Golden Calf* the body is no longer a corporeal object but the immaterial subject of a physical process of disclosure. When moving the monitor screen up, down and round the pedestal, the viewer performs what looks like a ceremonial dance around a technological pilaster construing an almost tangible phantasm.

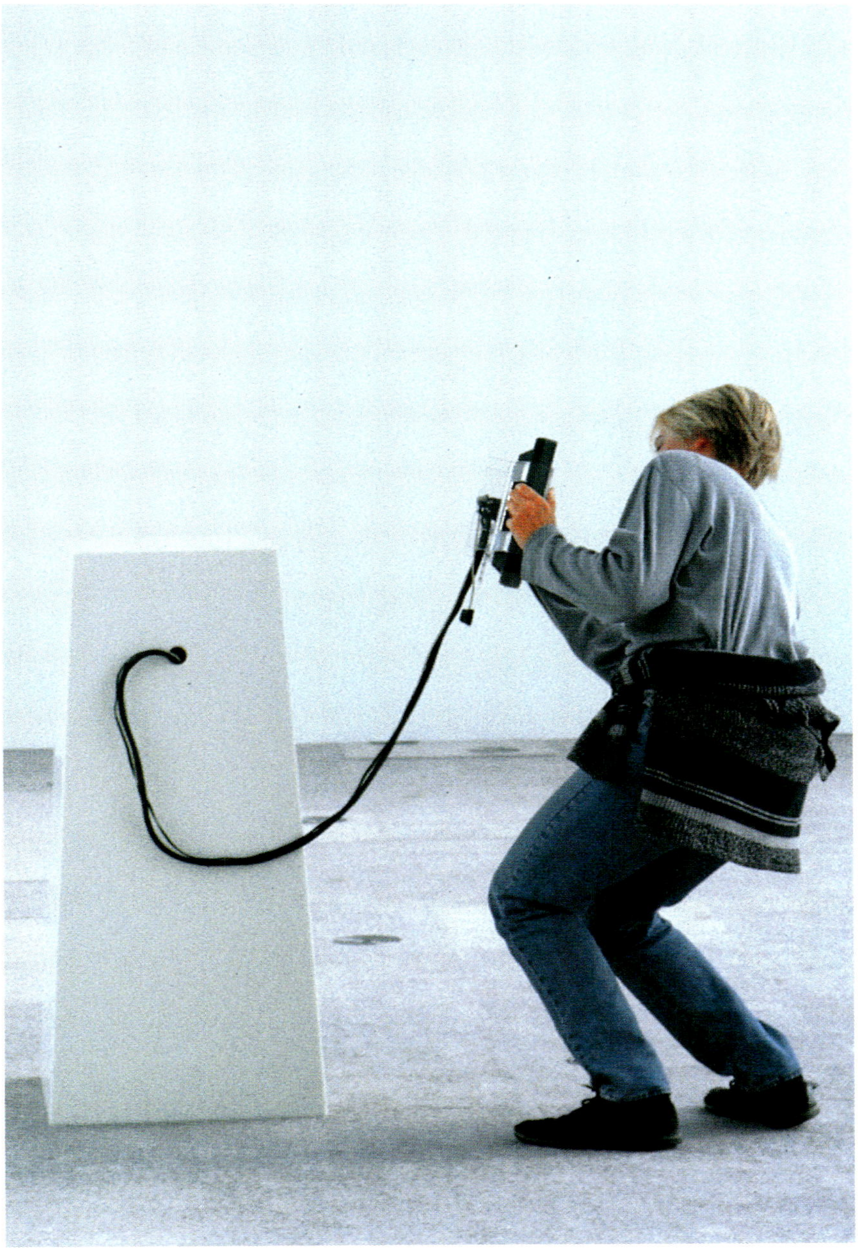

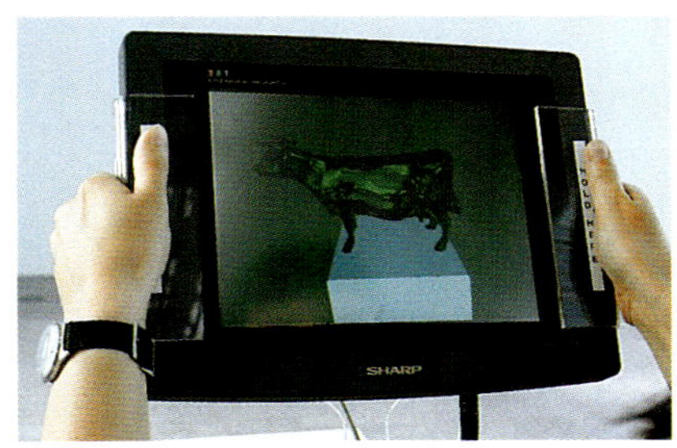

Die Immaterialität des goldenen Kalbes wird auch dadurch betont, daß lediglich seine äußere Oberfläche modelliert wurde: bewegt der Betrachter den Monitor in den Körper des Kalbes hinein, bleiben die Innenflächen unsichtbar.

In *The Golden Calf* ist der Körper nicht mehr länger ein materielles Objekt, sondern das immaterielle Subjekt eines körperbezogenen Enthüllungsprozesses. Bewegt der Betrachter den Bildschirm auf und ab und um die Säule herum, wird er zum Ausführenden einer Art zeremoniellen Tanzes um einen High-Tech-Pilaster, während er ein fast greifbares Phantasma erkundet.

Place – a user's manual 1995

This work extends the tradition of panorama painting, photography and cinematography in the vector of simulation and virtual reality. The viewer can interactively rotate a projected image around a circular screen and so explore a virtual three-dimensional space constituted by an emblematic constellation of panoramic photographic landscapes.

The installation has a large cylindrical projection screen. In its centre there is a round motorized platform with a computer and three video projectors which project onto a 120-degree portion of the screen. Continuous rotation of this viewing window around the screen reveals the full 360-degree computer-generated scene. While the work is controlled and generally viewed from within the circumference of the screen, the projected image can also be seen on its outside surface (together with the projected shadows of those spectators who are standing inside).

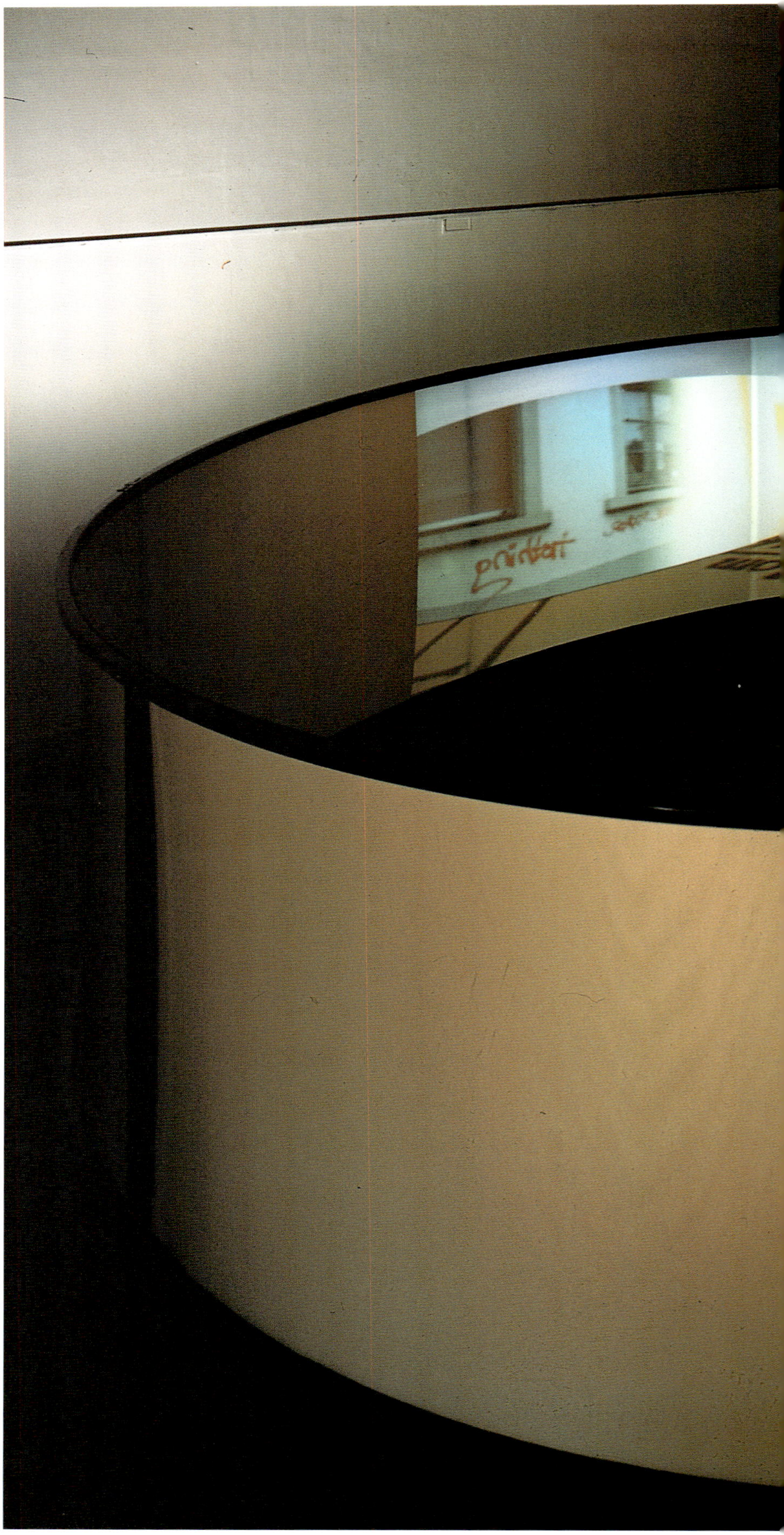

Place – a user's manual

Ort – eine Gebrauchsanweisung 1995

Die Tradition des Panoramas in Malerei, Fotografie und Kinematographie wird mit dieser Arbeit in den Bereich der Simulation und der virtuellen Realität ausgeweitet. Der Betrachter kann interaktiv ein projiziertes Bild über eine kreisförmige Leinwand bewegen und so einen virtuellen, dreidimensionalen Raum erkunden, der sich aus einer emblematischen Anordnung fotografierter Landschaftspanoramen zusammensetzt.

Die Installation besteht aus einer großen, zylinderförmigen Projektionsleinwand mit einer runden, motorisierten Plattform in der Mitte, einem Computer und drei Videoprojektoren, die das Bild auf einen 120 Grad umfassenden Bereich der Leinwand projizieren. Die kontinuierliche Rotation dieses Sichtfensters über die Leinwand enthüllt den gesamten 360 Grad umfassenden Radius des computergenerierten Schauplatzes. Obwohl die Arbeit innerhalb des die Leinwand einschließenden Bereiches gesteuert und zumeist auch betrachtet wird, kann das projizierte Bild auch auf der Außenfläche der Leinwand gesehen werden (überlagert von den projizierten Schatten der Besucher, die sich im Innenbereich aufhalten).

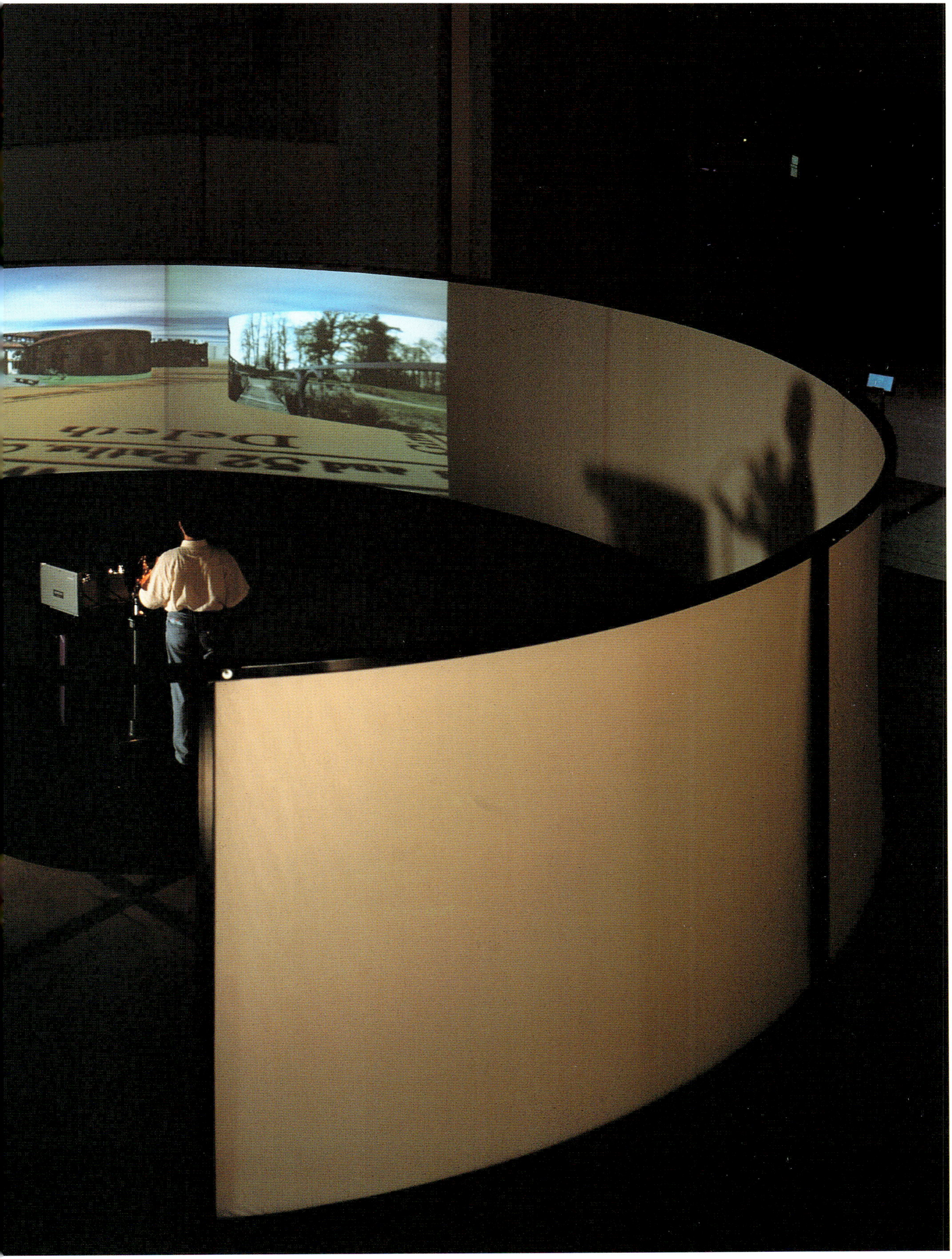

The interactive interface in this work is a video camera. By rotating this camera and using its zoom and play buttons, the viewer controls his forward, backward and rotational movements through the virtual scene, as well as the rotation of the platform and projected image around the circular screen.

The projected scenery is constituted by eleven cylinders showing landscape photographs taken by a special panoramic camera in various locations – Australia, Japan, La Palma, Bali, France, Germany, etc. Each of these virtual panoramic cylinders in the computer-generated landscape has the same height and diameter as the projection screen, so that when locating himself at the centre of these pictures the viewer can completely reconstitute the original 360-degree camera view on the screen. In this way the work locates the panoramic imagery in an architectonic framework that correlates the design of the virtual landscape with that of the installation itself, so making the virtual and actual spaces coactive on many levels of signification.

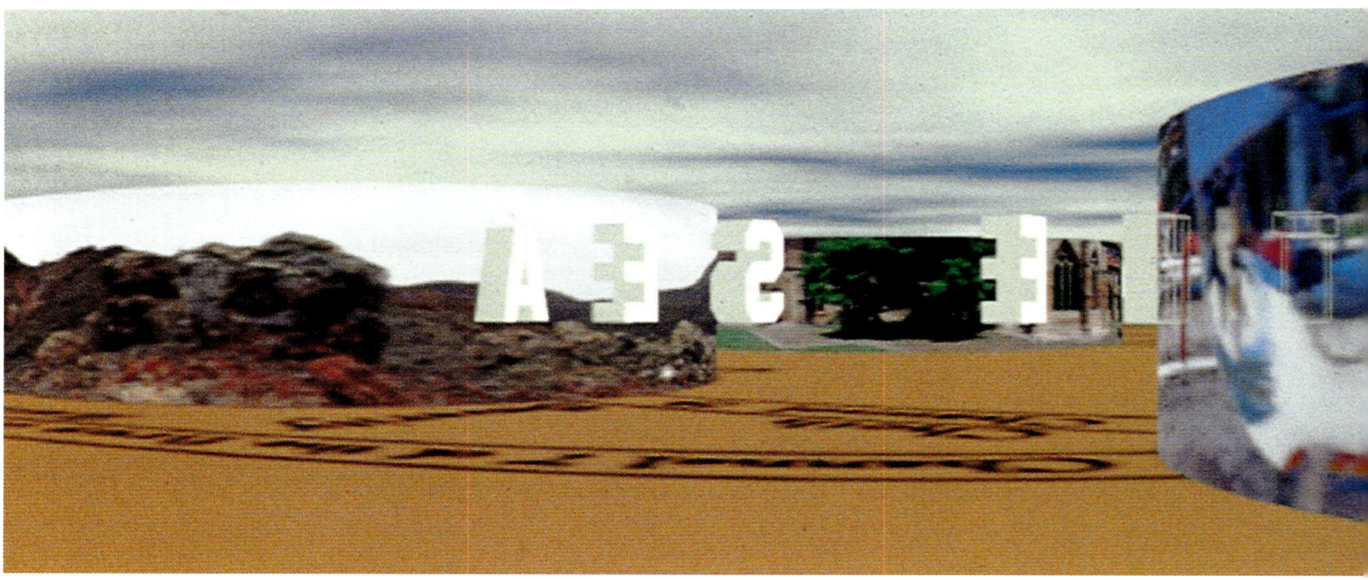

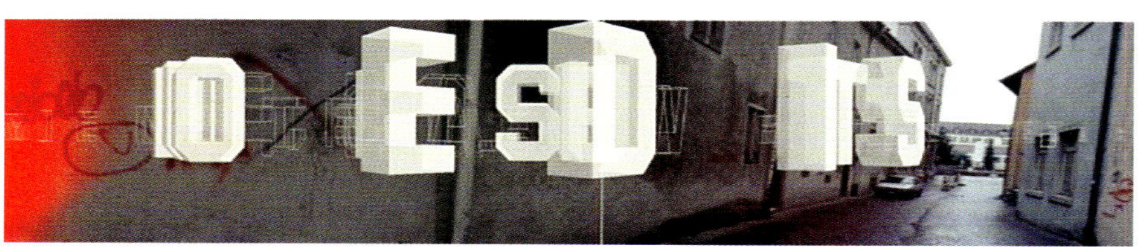

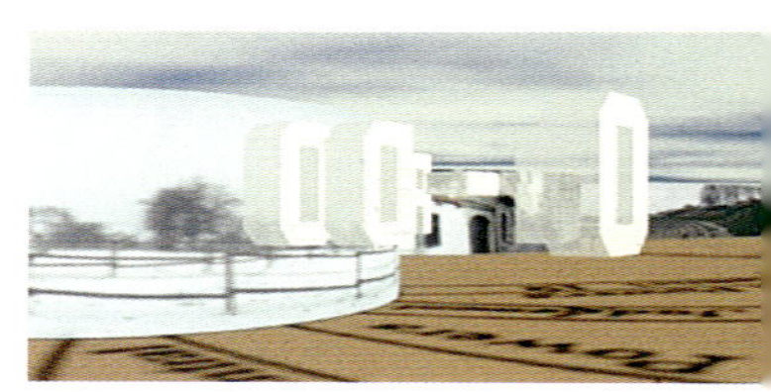

Als interaktives Interface dient eine Videokamera. Durch Rotation der Kamera und Betätigung ihrer Zoom- und Abspielknöpfe steuert der Betrachter seine Vor- und Rückwärtsbewegungen sowie die Rotation im virtuellen Raum und gleichzeitig die Rotation der Plattform sowie des projizierten Bildes über die Leinwand.

Der projizierte Schauplatz setzt sich aus elf Zylindern zusammen. Jeder dieser Zylinder zeigt Landschaftsaufnahmen, die mit einer speziellen Panoramakamera an verschiedenen Orten – Australien, Japan, La Palma, Bali, Frankreich, Deutschland etc. – fotografiert wurden. Jedes dieser virtuellen zylindrischen Panoramen in der computergenerierten Landschaft hat dieselbe Höhe und denselben Durchmesser wie die Leinwand: Bewegt der Betrachter seinen virtuellen Standpunkt genau in die Mitte eines dieser Panoramen, kann er den ursprünglichen 360-Grad-Kamerablick auf der Leinwand wiederherstellen. Auf diese Weise bindet die Arbeit das Panoramabild in eine architektonische Struktur ein, die die Gestaltung der virtuellen Landschaft in Beziehung setzt zu der Installation selbst und so den virtuellen und den realen Raum auf verschiedenen Bedeutungsebenen mit-

The ground surface on which these panoramas are positioned is marked by a diagram of a Sephirothic Tree – the placement of each panorama connects the visual identity of its scenery with the connotation of its symbolic location. The viewfinder on the interface camera shows an aerial view of this Cabbalist diagram, interactively centered on the viewer's actual position in the landscape.

A microphone on top of the interface camera picks up any sound that the viewer makes and this controls the release of travelling three-dimensional texts within the projected scene. Quoted from various sources, these texts offer a discourse around issues of place and language. Whilst the letters originate in the centre of the screen, their physical arrangement in the virtual space is dynamically determined by the viewer's movements. After some minutes these letters become more and more transparent until they disappear, forming a trace of something said that temporarily marks each viewer's presence in this work.

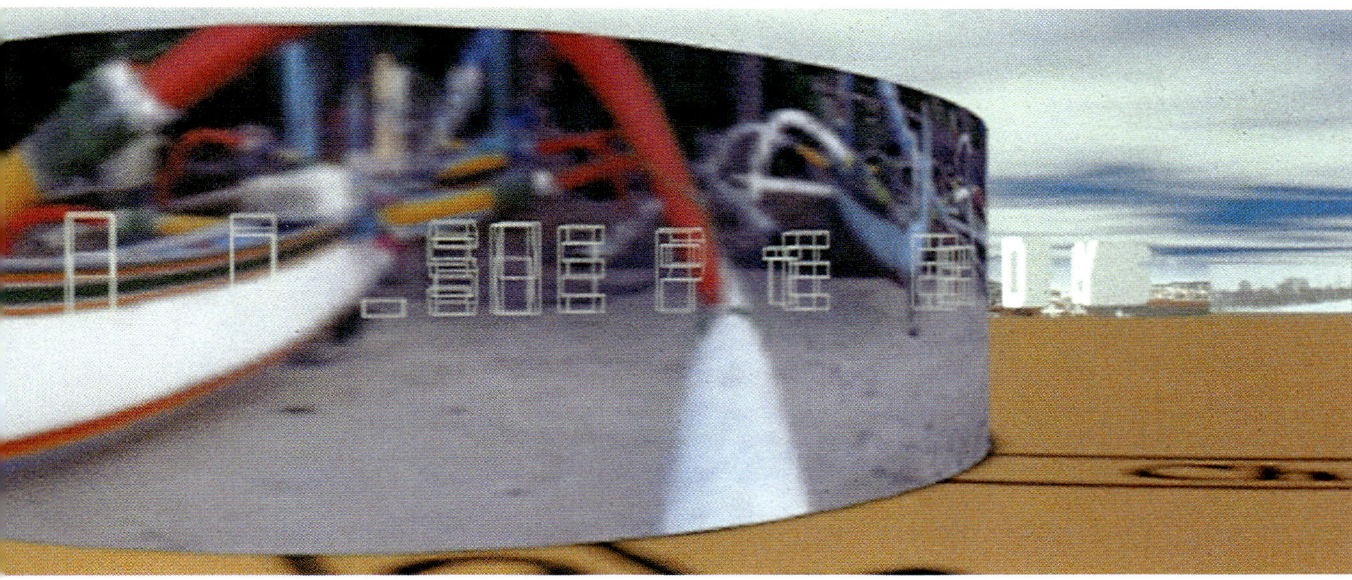

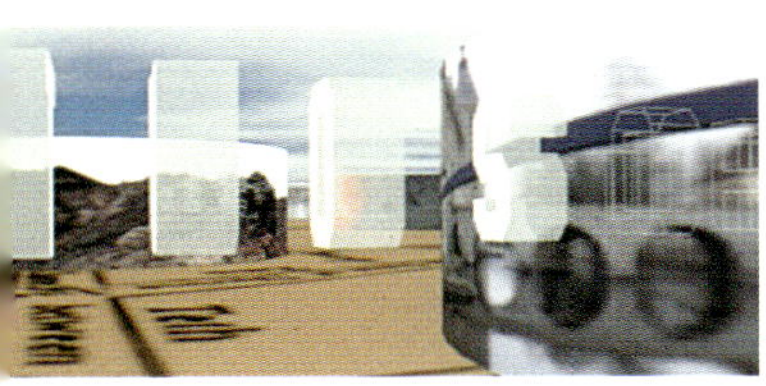

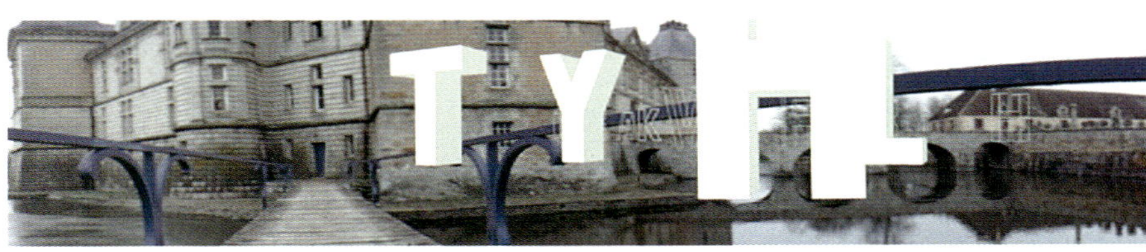

einander verbindet. Auf der Grundfläche, auf der sich diese Panoramen befinden, ist ein Diagramm eines Sephiroth-Baumes eingezeichnet – die Positionierung jedes Panoramas verbindet die visuelle Identität seiner Darstellung mit der Assoziation seines symbolischen Standorts. Auf dem Sucher der Interfacekamera ist eine Draufsicht dieses kabbalistischen Diagramms zu sehen, das interaktiv auf den momentanen Standort des Betrachters in der Landschaft zentriert wird.

Ein Mikrofon auf der Kamera nimmt sämtliche von den Betrachtern erzeugten Geräusche auf, wodurch dreidimensionale Texte, die sich über den projizierten Schauplatz bewegen, ausgelöst werden. Diese Texte – Zitate aus unterschiedlichen Quellen – bieten einen Diskurs zum Thema Ort und Sprache an. Die Buchstaben gehen von der Mitte der Leinwand aus und ihre physische Anordnung im virtuellen Raum wird dynamisch bestimmt von den Bewegungen des Betrachters. Nach einigen Minuten werden diese Buchstaben immer durchsichtiger, bis sie schließlich verschwinden – eine Spur des Gesagten hinterlassend, das für einen kurzen Augenblick die Präsenz jedes Betrachters in der Arbeit festhält.

Jeffrey Shaw: Texts

Jeffrey Shaw: Texte

Concepts for an Operational Art 1969

Art as that area of working with matter
that is not in the pay of the system in the sense that a 'job' is.
Rather, the work is self-regulating, demonstrating the capacity to make uselessly, i.e. to give form to an alternative and individuated system of usefulness and value. This does not mean art for art's sake. That formula has become abortive, embraced by the establishment for its decoration so as to rob the art project of its essential revolutionary function as a popular incitement to self-action and environmental transformation. With some exceptions, the predominant over-cultured esotericism of today's art forms and language is a shrinking away from this function.

Architecture as a multi-state
and responsive morphology of structure.
The environmental planning of an age is not neutral – rather it is the expression of the prevailing attitudes, and when in existence it reinforces those attitudes by structuring the basic elements (house, street, city, landscape) from which we infer the structure of the whole. One of the main features of the present environmental design programme is a monumental rigidity which precludes any significant role or identity of the user. It is the same third-rate democracy as the political structure as a whole – the range of freedom given (voting and furniture) is demeaning. To counteract this and again indicate to every individual his capacities as architect of the totality, an alternative form of environmental situation is envisioned which is in itself as undetermined as possible, depending for its life and forms on participant action and invention. Pneumatics seem at this moment to be one of the most useful means of realizing this programme. But not as a futuristic fantasy on paper, but as an event in operation *now*, confronting the institutional monolith in its midst.

Spectacle as a model of vitality for everyday.
Spectacle indicates the dynamic proportions by which the individual can mould his environment – it is the symbolic scale of excitement towards which the everyday yearns. Yet institutionalized spectacles (parades, festivals, displays etc.) fail because they are carefully circumscribed so as to disallow any inference or interference with the workday routine. The event is out of reach of the people's grasp – the role given them is that of passive consumer without identity. The problem now is to realize those new forms of spectacle which are non-alienated, reaching the individual and embedding that scale of excitement which puts in his grasp an expanded territory to act in. Some examples which come to mind are the outdoor projects of Yves Klein and Claes Oldenburg, Christo's wrapped buildings, and street happenings in general.

Konzepte für eine operative Kunst 1969

Kunst als ein Arbeitsbereich mit Materie, der sich für
das System nicht wie der ›Job‹ im herkömmlichen Sinne auszahlt.
Die Arbeit reguliert sich vielmehr selbst und zeigt das Vermögen zur Herstellung des Zweckfreien, d.h. das Vermögen, ein alternatives und individuiertes System des Nützlichen und Wertvollen zu gestalten. Das heißt aber nicht: l'art pour l'art. Diese Formel ist gescheitert, vereinnahmt vom Establishment wegen des Dekorativen, mit dem Ziel, das Kunstprojekt seiner essentiellen revolutionären Funktion – Aufwiegelung der Massen zu eigener Aktion und Umgestaltung der eigenen Umwelt – zu berauben. Mit Ausnahmen bedeutet doch die Vorherrschaft eines überzüchteten Esoterismus in den gegenwärtigen Formen der Kunst und ihrer Sprache ein Zurückweichen vor dieser Aufgabe.

Architektur als vielgestaltige
und reagierende Strukturmorphologie.
Wie eine Epoche ihre Umwelt gestaltet, ist kein neutraler Vorgang, sondern vielmehr der Ausdruck einer fortschreitenden Reihe von Geisteshaltungen. Im Zuge von Planung und Gestaltung werden diese Haltungen gestärkt durch die Strukturierung der Grundelemente (Haus, Straße, Stadt, Landschaft), woraus wir die Struktur des Ganzen ableiten. Einer der wichtigsten Punkte des gegenwärtigen Programms zur Gestaltung der Umwelt ist seine monumentale Starrheit, die dem Benutzer sowohl eine bedeutende Rolle als auch jegliche Form von Identität verweigert. Es ist dieselbe drittklassige Demokratie, die auch die politische Struktur im Ganzen aufweist – die Bandbreite der zugestandenen Freiheit (bei Wahlen oder bei der Möblierung) ist erniedrigend. Um das zu bekämpfen und jedem von neuem seine Fähigkeiten als Architekten des Ganzen zu verdeutlichen, wird eine alternative Form der Situation unserer Umwelt angestrebt, die so unbestimmt wie möglich sein muß und die in ihrer Lebendigkeit und in ihrer Gestalt abhängig ist von der Aktion und der Phantasie aller Beteiligten. Pneumatische Objekte (›Pneumatics‹) scheinen im Moment zu den tauglichsten Mitteln zu gehören, um dieses Programm zu verwirklichen. Aber nicht als futuristische Phantasie auf dem Papier, sondern als Ereignis, das *jetzt* stattfindet und den institutionellen Monolith ins Herz trifft.

Das Spektakel als Modell für einen lebendigen Alltag.
Das Spektakel setzt sich aus dynamischen Teilen zusammen, mit deren Hilfe das Individuum seine Umgebung formen kann – es verkörpert eine symbolische Skala der Spannung, auf die sich die Sehnsucht des Alltäglichen richtet. Bereits institutionalisierte Spektakel (Paraden, Festivals, Ausstellungen usw.) scheitern, weil sie sorgfältig eingegrenzt sind, um Schlußfolgerungen auf oder Einmischungen in die Routine des Arbeitstages zu verhindern. Das Ereignis läßt keinen Eingriff durch das Publikum zu – die Rolle, die ihm zugewiesen wird, ist die des passiven Konsumenten ohne Identität. Wir stehen jetzt vor dem Problem, neue Formen des

Technology as an open resource for the extraordinary.

While the capacities of technology are clearly phenomenal, at the same time its most advanced exercise – the moon project – is its greatest abuse. For in the context of poverty in half the world, this project becomes the symbol by which the system demonstrates to everyone that technology is beyond his understanding or control. It becomes another of the alienated consumer spectacles. Humbled by the complexity and scale of this resource, we begin to feel that the development of its forms – car, bomb, electric toothbrush, etc. – are determined virtually by force of nature. The system is thus able to recruit technology to its market principles with impunity. What is needed now are more and more demonstrations of technological application outside the dictates of the institutionalized programme. Such an open-ended exploitation of technological resources becomes the evidence for all people that it is there as an extension of their individual wills and freedom. Tingueley has been able to do this with the machine, Otto Mühl with food products, Nam June Paik with television, and John Latham with the book.

Conclusion:

Event as the articulation of communication through time.

The event we look for is when a particular structuring of art/architecture/spectacle/technology makes operational an expanded arena of will and action open to everyone.

Published in: *Art and Artists*, No. 10, January 1969, pp. 47–49.

Spektakels zu verwirklichen: nicht-entfremdete, den Menschen erreichende Formen, die die Skala der Spannung aufnehmen und den Menschen ein erweitertes Territorium zugänglich machen, in dem sie aktiv werden können. Einige Beispiele hierfür sind die ›Outdoor‹-Projekte von Yves Klein und Claes Oldenburg, Christos verhüllte Gebäude und die Straßen-Happenings im allgemeinen.

Technologie als freies

Produktionsmittel für das Außergewöhnliche.

Während die Möglichkeiten der Technologie ganz offensichtlich phänomenal sind, sind gleichzeitig ihre fortgeschrittensten Anwendungen – das Projekt Mond – auch ihr größter Mißbrauch. Vor dem Hintergrund von Armut in der halben Welt wird dieses Projekt zum Symbol, mit dem das System Jedermann demonstriert, daß sich die Technologie außerhalb seines Verstehens oder seiner Kontrolle befindet. Es wird zu einem weiteren entfremdeten Konsumenten-Spektakel. Gedemütigt von der Komplexität und dem Umfang dieser Ressource bekommen wir den Eindruck, die Entwicklung ihrer Anwendungen – Auto, Bombe, elektrische Zahnbürste etc. – sei praktisch durch Naturgewalt bestimmt. Dadurch kann das System ungestraft Technologie nach seinen Marktprinzipien einsetzen. Was wir jetzt brauchen, sind mehr und mehr Demonstrationen technologischer Anwendungen außerhalb des Diktates institutionalisierter Programme. Durch diese offene Nutzung technologischer Ressourcen wird es für alle Menschen offensichtlich, daß Technologie als Erweiterung ihres individuellen Willens und ihrer individuellen Freiheit existiert. Tinguely hat das mit der Maschine gezeigt, Otto Mühl mit Nahrungsmitteln, Nam June Paik mit dem Fernsehen und John Latham mit dem Buch.

Schlußfolgerung:

Das Ereignis als Ausdruck zeitübergreifender Kommunikation.

Das Ereignis, das wir suchen, entsteht, wenn eine bestimmte Zusamensetzung von Kunst/Architektur/Spektakel/Technologie eine erweiterte Arena des Willens und der Aktion, offen für Jedermann, in Betrieb nimmt.

Aus dem Englischen von Astrid Sommer. – Veröffentlicht in: *Art and Artists*, Nr. 10, Januar 1969, S. 47–49.

Virtual World Voyage 1990

In all my work there is a concern to give form to that fourth dimension which is the space between the work of art and the spectator. It is in this space that the art-work is transformed and recreated within the perception/experience of the viewer. In my early inflatable works this was a space of physical interaction – the spectator bodily entered and manipulated the air-filled plastic membranes. The audio-visual pieces used optical methods to create a paradoxical overlapping of the projected image space and the viewer's actual space. My recent computer works use the mechanisms of interactivity and simulation to create a virtual space of imagery (and sometimes sound) that the viewer can actually enter and explore.

Western culture has put all its bets on the efficacy of science and technology as a method of describing the world, and as a technique for materializing its desires. Traditionally it has been art that has been able to fulfill these ambitions, and with a remarkable economy of means (paint, stone, words, sounds, etc.). Science also yearns for the sublime and has come a long way since the primitivism of the industrial revolution. Relativity, quantum mechanics, chaos theory, etc. are are the modalities of our materialist ambitions today. Here is a complexity that begins to touch on a deeper understanding of the world – a new set of intellectual and material tools that is congruent with art's inner purpose and can serve and inspire the making of art. It is true that compared to paint or stone the new technological tools have no history, no traditions that spontaneously form the countless under-layers of meaning we are used to in art. But in a way this lack is also the power of these new tools – we are at a moment when history and tradition is being invented afresh. Photography and the cinema, for example, those prodigies of the industrial revolution, have certainly become the great artistic media of that era of invention. And now, the technologies of the cybernetic revolution are opening other new territories of expression to the artist, and of experience to the public.

The imaging technologies and products have been slow to evolve (compared with the electronic music technologies), and are still relatively complex and expensive. It was video technology that first became accessible as a tool, and in consequence there is already an important history of video art. In the last few years computer graphics equipment has been introduced at some art schools, and affordable image processing systems can be bought in stores. This means a new generation of artists will be more able to experiment with and explore the possibilities of these technologies. But a major hindrance to the application of new technology in the visual arts is the institutionalized identification of art with its traditional media and forms – painting, drawing, sculpture, etc. All the new technological media, e.g. photography, video, computer graphics,

Virtuelle Weltreise 1990

In all meinen Arbeiten liegt ein Bestreben, jene vierte Dimension zu gestalten, die den Raum zwischen Kunstwerk und Zuschauer einnimmt. In diesem Raum findet die Veränderung und Neuschaffung des Kunstwerks durch die Wahrnehmung/Erfahrung des Betrachters statt. In meinen frühen Arbeiten, in denen ich mit aufblasbaren Materialien arbeitete, war dies ein Raum der physischen Interaktion: das Publikum konnte die luftgefüllten Plastikmembranen tatsächlich betreten und sie manipulieren. Meine audio-visuellen Arbeiten nutzten optische Methoden, um ein paradoxes Überlappen von projiziertem Bildraum und realem Raum zu erzeugen. Meine jüngsten computergestützten Arbeiten bedienen sich der Mechanismen von Interaktivität und Simulation, um einen virtuellen Bildraum (oder auch einen Klangraum) zu schaffen, den der Betrachter tatsächlich betreten und erkunden kann.

Die westliche Gesellschaft hat ganz auf die Leistungsfähigkeit von Wissenschaft und Technologie gesetzt – als Methoden zur Erklärung der Welt und als Technik zur Verwirklichung ihrer Wünsche. Traditionellerweise war es die Kunst, der es möglich war, diese Wünsche zu erfüllen, und dies geschah mit einem bemerkenswert sparsamen Einsatz an Mitteln (Farbe, Stein, Worte, Töne etc.). Auch die Wissenschaft sehnt sich nach dem Sublimen und seit ihren primitiven Anfängen mit der industriellen Revolution hat sie einen weiten Weg zurückgelegt. Relativität, Quantenmechanik, Chaostheorie etc. – dies sind die Modalitäten unserer heutigen, materialistisch bestimmten Ziele. Hier offenbart sich eine Komplexität, die zu einem tieferen Verständnis der Welt vorzudringen beginnt. Neue intellektuelle und materielle Werkzeuge entsprechen der inneren Intention der Kunst und können dem Kunstschaffen dienen und es inspirieren. Es ist richtig, daß die neuen technologischen Werkzeuge im Vergleich zu Farbe und Stein keine Geschichte, keine Tradition haben, die spontan die zahllosen Bedeutungsschichten formen, die wir in der Kunst gewohnt sind. Doch in gewisser Weise stellt dieser Mangel auch die Stärke der neuen Werkzeuge dar – wir haben einen Punkt erreicht, an dem Geschichte und Tradition neu erfunden werden. Nehmen wir zum Beispiel Fotografie und Kino: diese Wunder der industriellen Revolution sind zum großen künstlerischen Medium jener Zeit der Erfindungen geworden. Und heute eröffnen die Technologien der kybernetischen Revolution dem Künstler neue Audrucksformen und dem Publikum neue Formen von Erfahrung.

Die Bildtechnologien und ihre Produkte haben sich (im Vergleich zu den Technologien der elektronischen Musik) nur langsam entwickelt und sind noch relativ komplex und teuer. Es war die Videotechnologie, die zuerst als Werkzeug zugänglich wurde, und als Konsequenz existiert bereits eine bedeutsame Geschichte der Videokunst. In den letzten Jahren begann man an einigen Kunstschulen mit Grafikcomputern zu arbeiten, und auf dem Markt sind bereits erschwingliche Bildverarbeitungssysteme erhältlich. So-

etc. have to fight for their authenticity as art and thus also for their economic viability in the art marketplace. And without the security of institutional and market approval, most artists will not risk working with the new technologies.

All art is language – and if art wanted for a while to forget this in its yearnings for a visual absoluteness, we are now back to conversation again, speaking to each other with images, objects, words, sounds, movements, etc. whose boundaries are all fluid. The immateriality of digital technology facilitates this radical exchange between all the forms within language and makes it ideal for expressing the sensibility of our time.

The museums of contemporary art are losing all their legitimacy as they capitulate to and reinforce the commercial/conservative strategies of the art market. Their mass-attraction exhibitions are just a last gasp attempt to justify their existence. So what is next? These museums of contemporary art are themselves ready to be put into a new museum, a museum of the history of art museums and of art's modalities of public consumption (and there we will be able to ponder the peculiar way Western cultures have given art its detached identity and functionality, so different to the way that art is anonymously woven into the fabric of everyday life in the non-Western cultures). The essential role of the traditional museum is to be a place of conservation and archival so that a culture can maintain a complete memory of what has already been achieved in its search for new meanings. On the other hand the museums of contemporary art can be replaced by a decentralized network of sites of artistic action where new modalities of interaction between art and public can evolve as an open marketplace of ideas. Certainly, the resources of the new media and telecommunication technologies will soon be available to give shape to such a network. And the active involvement of the industries producing those technologies is clearly a matter of self-interest, as artists will create the meaningful forms of the new technological culture.

The relationship of the 'real' and the 'virtual' is fundamental. The activity of both art and science has always been the interpretation and recreation of reality. It is an exercise of the human imagination, creating virtual realities which embody tentative structures of meaning. The world appears to us in the light of the fictions we project onto its surface. Whereas Eastern culture has always understood the primacy of this projection, Western culture has made an idolatory out of the virtual reality it has invented, calling it an 'objective' reality that is separate from the mind that projects it. Paradoxically, the new computer-generated 'virtual-reality' technologies are rooted in this Cartesian dualism. Our materialist culture had to create a technology able to conjure fiction with a materialistic 'realism' simulating the characteristics of that

mit wird es für eine neue Künstlergeneration einfacher, mit diesen Technologien zu experimentieren und deren Möglichkeiten zu erforschen. Der Hauptfaktor jedoch, der die Anwendung der neuen Technologien in der Bildenden Kunst verzögert, ist die institutionalisierte Identifikation der Kunst mit ihren traditionellen Medien und Formen wie der Malerei, der Zeichnung, der Skulptur etc. Alle neuen technologischen Medien wie Fotografie, Video, Computergrafik etc. müssen sowohl für ihre Berechtigung als Kunstgattung als auch für ihre ökonomische Lebensfähigkeit auf dem Kunstmarkt kämpfen. Und ohne die Sicherheit institutioneller und marktbezogener Anerkennung werden die meisten Künstler es nicht riskieren, mit den neuen Technologien zu arbeiten.

Jede Kunst ist Sprache – und wenn auch die Kunst diesen Anspruch durch ihr Streben nach visueller Absolutheit für einen Moment vergessen wollte, dann sind wir nun doch wieder zum Gespräch zurückgekehrt, sprechen miteinander mit Hilfe von Bildern, Objekten, Worten, Tönen, Bewegungen etc., deren Grenzen fließend sind. Die Immaterialität der digitalen Technologien erleichtert diesen radikalen Wechsel zwischen allen Sprachformen und bietet somit ausgezeichnete Möglichkeiten, um die Sensibilität unserer Zeit auszudrücken.

Museen für zeitgenössische Kunst werden ihre Legitimation verlieren, da sie vor den kommerziellen/konservativen Strategien des Kunstmarktes kapitulieren und ihn dadurch stärken. Ihre als Massenattraktion ausgelegten Ausstellungen sind lediglich ein letzter verzweifelter Versuch, ihre Existenz zu rechtfertigen. Was kommt aber danach? Die Museen für zeitgenössische Kunst haben sich bereits darauf vorbereitet, in ein neues Museum umgeformt zu werden: ein Museum der Geschichte der Kunstmuseen und der Modalitäten des öffentlichen Kunstkonsums (und dort werden wir darüber nachdenken können, warum die westliche Kultur der Kunst eine kühle und distanzierte Identität und Funktionalität gegeben hat, die sich von der unmerklich in das Gefüge des Alltagslebens eingebundenen Kunst nicht-westlicher Kulturen so sehr unterscheidet). Die wesentliche Rolle des traditionellen Museums ist es, einen Ort der Konservation und Archivierung zu schaffen, so daß eine Kultur sich ihre gesamte Erinnerung dessen erhalten kann, was sie auf der Suche nach neuen Bedeutungen bereits erreicht hat. Andererseits könnnen die Museen für zeitgenössische Kunst durch ein dezentralisiertes Netzwerk von Orten künstlerischer Aktion ersetzt werden, wo neue Formen von Interaktion zwischen Kunst und Öffentlichkeit entwickelt werden können – ein offener Marktplatz der Ideen. Sicherlich werden die Ressourcen der neuen Medien- und Telekommunikationstechnologien bald verfügbar sein und einem solchen Netzwerk Gestalt geben können. Und die aktive Beteiligung jener Industrien, die diese Technologien herstellen, liegt sicher auch in deren eigenem Interesse, da es die Künstler sind, die die Bedeutungsformen dieser neuen technologischen Kultur kreieren.

'objective' reality in which we so exclusively want to believe. Art has always struggled with/against this illusion of an objective reality (*This is not a pipe*, René Magritte). The simulational efficacy of the new technologies offers the artist an important new medium with which to further this discourse. Computer-generated virtual realities can be a persuasive new realm of fiction offering an apparent 'realism' as a gateway into a 'meta-realism' expressing the deeper immaterial dimensionality of reality.

All art is a labour of imaginative participation and re-creation on the part of the viewer. Art wakes us up, engages us in a discourse between all the dichotomies constituting the wholeness of reality. Is there something today that distinguishes a new 'trend' in art? Now that the disappointed illusions of Modernism have been replaced by a Postmodernist appetite for complexity and irony, we are also freed of old dogmas and simplistic fears concerning technology. What interests me is the trend in art that is inventing new meanings for technology, destructuring its materialism and creating poetry from its 'bits'. Of course, there will always be a place for the practice of art using the traditional media, because it is wonderful to inherit and add to the history of those sublime achievements already made with paint, pen, stone, wood, etc. But we should not confuse the identity of those traditional media with the actual identity and practice of art. Art is a broad mechanism of discourse that may use any medium to embody itself, and I believe it is specially effective and relevant when it adopts, transforms and instills meaning in those particular media that are contemporary in a society.

Extracts from an interview with Dorothy Hirokawa, published in: *BT Biyutsu Techno*, Vol. 42, No. 622, April 1990, pp. 117–131.

Das Verhältnis von ›Realem‹ und ›Virtuellem‹ ist von grundlegender Bedeutung. Der Schwerpunkt von Kunst und Wissenschaft liegt seit jeher auf dem Gebiet der Interpretation und der Neuschaffung von Realität. Die menschliche Vorstellungskraft übt sich in der Schaffung virtueller Realitäten, die vorläufige Bedeutungsstrukturen verkörpern. Die Welt erscheint uns im Licht dieser Fiktionen, die wir auf ihre Oberfläche projizieren. Während die östlichen Kulturen das Primat dieser Projektion immer verstanden haben, machte die westliche Kultur aus der von ihr erfundenen virtuellen Realität einen Götzendienst und nannte sie ›objektive‹ Realität, die sich vom Geist, der sie projiziert, unterscheidet. Paradoxerweiser wurzeln die neuen computergenerierten Technologien der virtuellen Realität in diesem kartesianischen Dualismus. Unsere materialistische Kultur mußte eine Technologie erschaffen, die in der Lage war, das Fiktive aus einem materialistischen ›Realismus‹ heraus zu beschwören, der die Charakteristika dieser ›objektiven‹ Realität, an die wir so ausschließlich glauben wollen, simuliert. Die Kunst hat immer mit/gegen diese Illusion einer objektiven Realität gekämpft (*Dies ist keine Pfeife*, René Magritte). Die simulative Wirksamkeit der neuen Technologien bietet dem Künstler ein bedeutsames neues Medium, mit dem er diesen Diskurs weiterführen kann. Computergenerierte virtuelle Realitäten können einen überzeugenden neuen Fiktionsraum schaffen, dessen scheinbarer ›Realismus‹ eine Tür zum ›Meta-Realismus‹ öffnen kann, der die tieferen immateriellen Dimensionen der Realität ausdrückt.

Jede Kunst ist ein Werk der phantasievollen Beteiligung und Neuschaffung durch den Zuschauer. Die Kunst rüttelt uns auf, verwickelt uns in einen Diskurs zwischen allen Dichotomien, die die Gesamtheit der Realität konstituieren. Können wir heute einen neuen ›Trend‹ in der Kunst erkennen? Jetzt, da die enttäuschten Illusionen der Moderne durch einen postmodernen Appetit auf Komplexität und Ironie ersetzt wurden, sind wir auch von den alten Dogmen und simplen Ängsten vor der Technologie befreit. Was mich interessiert, ist jene Kunstrichtung, die der Technologie neue Bedeutungsformen aufzeigt, ihren Materialismus zerstört und aus ihren ›Bits‹ Poesie schafft. Natürlich wird es immer einen Ort geben, wo Kunst mit Hilfe traditioneller Medien praktiziert wird. Schließlich ist es etwas Wunderbares, von der Geschichte jener sublimen Errungenschaften, die mit Farbe, dem Zeichenstift, Stein, Holz etc. gemacht wurden, zu erben und ihr etwas neues hinzuzufügen. Doch wir sollten die Identität jener traditionellen Medien nicht mit der gegenwärtigen Identität und Praxis der Kunst vermischen. Kunst ist ein breitgefächerter Mechanismus des Diskurses, die jedes Medium nutzen kann, um sich selbst zu verkörpern. Und ich glaube, daß Kunst besonders wirksam und wichtig ist, wenn sie Inhalte annimmt, verändert und sie gerade jenen zeitgenössischen Medien einflößt, die eine Gesellschaft prägen.

Aus dem Englischen von Manuela Abel. – Auszüge aus einem Interview mit Dorothy Hirokawa, veröffentlicht in: *BT Biyutsu Techno*, Bd. 42, Nr. 622, April 1990, S. 117–131.

Modalities of Interactivity and Virtuality 1992

The research and development of various mechanisms and codes of spatial representation has been a basic preoccupation throughout the history of Western art. The formulation of a set of spatial coordinates provides an underlying aesthetic and existential paradigm within which a culture achieves tentative representation (and thus comprehension) of its desires. The recently developed digital imaging technologies offer the artist new methods and new paradigms which extend the spatial identity of the art-work. And not just in terms of the structure of the image itself, but also in terms of a space of interaction between the image and the spectator.

Painted images hang on walls or rest in storage; bringing them into view is a question of material handling. Digital pictures reside immaterially inside the computer, and the computer screen functions like a window through which the viewer chooses what to look at. Furthermore, the computer screen functions like a cinema camera, because the viewer can pan in any direction over the surface of an image and zoom into the details. These characteristics offer the possibility of creating a virtual space of imagery wherein a three-dimensional structure of relationships between two-dimensional images can be defined. This can then constitute an interactive space which the viewer explores by utilizing some kind of interface device.

The interactive structure of *The Narrative Landscape* shows that the spatial boundaries of the digital image do not have to be defined by the traditional perimeter of a 'picture frame'. Instead, a virtual image space of any dimension can be created, and the viewer can explore it by moving his 'viewing window'. And like in the cinema, the externalization of the image is always referential to the activity of the viewer's eye (the 'camera'). This location of the viewer at the focal plane of an extended virtual space of imagery is likewise the modality of *Going to the Heart of the Center of The Garden of Delights* and *Inventer la Terre*. All three works demonstrate modalities for the location of two-dimensional digital imagery in a virtual three-dimensional space. *The Narrative Landscape* has a specific structure of image levels set behind the plane of the projection screen. *Going to the Heart of the Center of The Garden of Delights* implicitly brings these levels out in front of the screen and into the room where the viewer is walking. *Inventer la Terre* can dispense with the screen surface altogether and achieve an explicit optical conjunction of the virtual image space and the physical museum space surrounding the viewer.

If we describe the two-dimensional digital image as a planar raster of numeric values, then the three-dimensional digital image is a volumetric raster of numeric values. The viewer's eye position inside that volumetric space determines each momentarily displayed ordering of that raster. Thus, it is possible to create a three-dimensional virtual image which always reveals itself interactively

Formen von Interaktivität und Virtualität 1992

Die westliche Kunst hat sich im Laufe ihrer Geschichte immer wieder und grundsätzlich mit der Erforschung und Entwicklung verschiedenster Mechanismen und Zeichensysteme räumlicher Darstellung beschäftigt. Mit der Formulierung eines Sets räumlicher Koordinaten steht eine grundlegende Ästhetik und ein existentielles Paradigma zur Verfügung, wodurch eine Kultur die unverbindliche Darstellung (und damit das Verstehen) ihrer Wünsche erreicht. Die jüngsten Entwicklungen im Bereich der digitalen Bildbearbeitungstechnologien bieten dem Künstler neue Methoden und neue Paradigmen, die die räumliche Identität des Kunstwerks erweitern. Das gilt nicht nur für die Struktur des Bildes selbst, sondern auch für den Raum der Interaktion zwischen Bild und Betrachter.

Gemalte Bilder hängen an Wänden oder werden in Lagern aufbewahrt; sie sichtbar zu machen, ist immer mit einer physischen Tätigkeit verbunden. Digitale Bilder residieren immateriell im Innern des Computers, und der Bildschirm fungiert als Fenster, mit dessen Hilfe der Betrachter auswählen kann, was er sich ansehen möchte. Darüberhinaus ist der Bildschirm aber auch eine Art Filmkamera, denn der Betrachter kann in jede Richtung über die Oberfläche des Bildes schwenken oder in Details des ausgewählten Bildes zoomen. Diese Eigenschaften ermöglichen es, einen virtuellen metaphorischen Raum zu kreieren, in dem eine dreidimensionale Struktur von Beziehungen zwischen zweidimensionalen Bildern definiert werden kann. Dies kann dann einen interaktiven Raum konstituieren, den der Betrachter mit Hilfe eines Gerätes, das ihn mit dem Computer verbindet (›Interface-Device‹), erforschen kann.

Die interaktive Struktur von *The Narrative Landscape* zeigt, daß die räumlichen Grenzen des digitalen Bildes nicht unbedingt durch die traditionellen Grenzen des ›Bildrahmens‹ definiert werden müssen. Stattdessen kann ein virtueller Bildraum beliebiger Größe geschaffen werden, den der Betrachter durch Bewegen des ›Schaufensters‹ erforscht. Und wie im Kino steht die Externalisierung des Bildes immer in Beziehung zur Tätigkeit des Auges des Betrachters, der ›Kamera‹. Die Position des Betrachters in der Brennebene eines erweiterten virtuellen Bildraumes ist gleichfalls Bedingung für *Going to the Heart of the Center of The Garden of Delights* und *Inventer la Terre*. Alle drei Arbeiten zeigen die Bedingungen für die Positionierung zweidimensionaler digitaler Bilder innerhalb eines dreidimensionalen Raumes. In *The Narrative Landscape* gibt es eine spezielle Struktur verschiedener Bildebenen, die hinter/unter der Leinwand verborgen sind. *Going to the Heart of the Center of The Garden of Delights* bringt diese verschiedenen Ebenen indirekt vor die Leinwand und in den Raum, in dem sich der Betrachter bewegt. *Inventer la Terre* kann ganz auf die Oberfläche der Leinwand verzichten und stellt eine explizite optische Verbindung her zwischen dem virtuellen Bildraum und dem tatsächlichen Museumsraum, der den Betrachter umgibt.

Wenn wir das zweidimensionale digitale Bild als planes Raster numerischer Werte beschreiben, dann ist das dreidimensionale digitale Bild ein volumetrischer Raum numerischer Werte. Die

in relation to the viewer. The virtual-reality technologies allow a heightened degree of viewer 'immersion' in such a virtual image space – they can simulate the sensual coordinates of the real world in a new arena of fictional visualization.

The Legible City is a three-dimensional digital image whose virtual size was approximately six square kilometres. The viewer can interactively travel through this space by riding a stationary bicycle in front of a large video projection screen. The 'real-time' interaction of the bicycle and the computer-generated image allows the bicyclist complete freedom to move anywhere in this virtual image space. In *The Legible City* the space of visualization is virtually located beyond the surface of the projection screen and thus outside the actual room where the cyclist is situated. In *Alice's Room* and *The Virtual Museum* the virtual imagery is physically located in the same room as the viewers. Such a digital conjunction of virtual and actual space evokes a Mannerist ambiguity – different orders of simulation are located in a meta-dimensional structure that mirrors a confluence of the real and the fictional. This location of the virtual space in a contiguous relationship with the real space establishes a discourse in that fine zone between the virtual and the actual resembling what Duchamp called 'the inframince'. Here I believe the most interesting and challenging opportunities for artistic formulations exist.

The traditional activity of art has been the representation of reality – manipulating materials to create tangible mirrors of our experience and desire. With the mechanisms of the new digital technologies, the art-work can now become itself a simulation of reality – an immaterial digital structure encompassing synthetic spaces we can literally enter. Here the viewer is no longer consumer in a mausoleum of objects but traveller and discoverer in a latent space of sensual information, whose aesthetics are embodied both in the coordinates of its immaterial form and in the scenarios of its interactively manifest form. In this temporal dimension the interactive art-work is each time re-structured and re-embodied by the activity of its viewers.

Extract from a lecture at XXVIII. International Conference on Art History, Berlin, Germany, 1992. Published in: *Artistic Exchange*, Ed. Thomas W. Gaehtgens, Berlin, 1993, pp. 295–300.

Position des Auges des Betrachters innerhalb dieses volumetrischen Raumes bestimmt die jeweils angezeigte Anordnung dieses Rasters. Somit kann ein virtueller Bildraum geschaffen werden, der sich Schritt für Schritt interaktiv in Beziehung zum Betrachter enthüllt. Die Virtual-Reality-Technologien erlauben in verstärktem Maß die ›Immersion‹, das ›Eintauchen‹ des Betrachters in solche virtuellen Bildräume. Diese Räume können die sinnlichen Koordinaten der wirklichen Welt in einer neuen Arena fiktionaler Visualisierungen simulieren.

The Legible City ist ein dreidimensionales digitales Bild, dessen virtuelle Größe etwa sechs Quadratkilometer beträgt. Der Betrachter kann interaktiv durch diesen Raum reisen, indem er auf einem Fahrrad fährt, das sich vor einer großen Videoleinwand befindet. Die Interaktion von Fahrrad und computergeneriertem Bild in ›Echtzeit‹ gibt dem Radfahrer völlige Bewegungsfreiheit innerhalb des virtuellen Bildraums. In *The Legible City* befindet sich der Raum der Visualisierung scheinbar jenseits der Oberfläche der Leinwand und damit außerhalb des wirklichen Raums, in dem sich der Radfahrer bewegt. In *Alice's Room* und *The Virtual Museum* befindet sich der virtuelle Bildraum innerhalb des tatsächlichen Raumes, in dem der Betrachter steht. Eine solche digitale Verbindung von virtuellem und wirklichen Raum evoziert eine manieristische Doppeldeutigkeit – Simulationen in unterschiedlichen Anordnungen befinden sich in einer meta-dimensionalen Struktur, die das Zusammenfließen von Wirklichem und Fiktionalem spiegelt. Diese Position des virtuellen Raumes in enger Beziehung zum wirklichen Raum etabliert einen Diskurs in der schmalen Zone zwischen dem Virtuellen und dem Tatsächlichen, die dem ähnelt, was Duchamp ›Inframince‹ nannte. An dieser Stelle befinden sich, so meine ich, die interessantesten und herausfordernsten Möglichkeiten für künstlerische Formulierungen.

Das traditionelle Betätigungsfeld der Kunst war die Darstellung der Realität – das Manipulieren von Materialien, um greifbare Spiegel unserer Erfahrungen und Wünsche zu schaffen. Mit den Mechanismen der neuen digitalen Technologien kann das Kunstwerk selbst eine Simulation der Realität werden – eine immaterielle digitale Struktur, die synthetische Räume hervorruft, die wir tatsächlich betreten können. Hier ist der Betrachter nicht mehr Konsument in einem Mausoleum der Objekte, sondern wird vielmehr zum Reisenden und Entdecker in einem verborgenen Raum der sinnlichen Information, dessen Ästhetik verkörpert wird sowohl in den Koordinaten seiner immateriellen Gestalt als auch in den Szenarien seiner sich interaktiv manifestierenden Gestalt. In dieser zeitlichen Dimension wird das Kunstwerk jedesmal neu strukturiert und neu verkörpert durch die Aktivität seiner Betrachter.

Aus dem Englischen von Astrid Sommer. – Aus einem Vortrag, gehalten beim XXVIII. Internationalen Kongreß für Kunstgeschichte, Berlin, 1992. Veröffentlicht in: *Künstlerischer Austausch*, Hg. Thomas W. Gaehtgens, Berlin, 1993, S. 295–300.

The Dis-Embodied Re-Embodied Body 1995

The history of art exemplifies a complex set of negotiations between body and space – negotiations between the actual domain of the viewer's real body and the real space he inhabits as well as between the virtual domain of the represented body and represented spaces. The contemporary body in space is no longer the classical model. Ours is a vertiginous location – suspended upside down (Georg Baselitz), launched into space (Yves Klein), declared as obsolete (Stelarc) and now seemingly superhumanly re-embodied in cyberspace and suprahumanly re-united in netspace.

In the 1960s and 1970s the evolution of mixed-media and intermedia research made it clear that the exigencies of the body were a focal issue. The artist's performative body and the spectator's participatory body together constituted the notion of a body that was being increasingly 'immersed' in the dialectics of mediated experience. Today the protagonist body plugged into virtual reality is a perspicuous extension of this conjunction.

Body and space are at the root of all extensions. The narrative extension is the temporal body in space. The ritual extension is the liturgical body in sacred space. The interactive extension is the body affecting space. Then there are the multifarious iconoclastic extensions which suppress either the body or space so as to elevate the predominance of one over the other. And nowadays there is the virtual extension of mediated bodies and hyperspaces.

All extensions of the body/space conjunction struggle with a basic disjunction within our attitude to the body itself. On the one hand, the sensual body constitutes our very being; on the other hand, the mortal body is what sentences us to non-being. This unbearable contradiction evokes a simultaneous affirmation and denial of the body, a contradiction that has historically and in many cultures an important focus of art's speculative and iconographic concerns.

Clearly the current euphoric embrace of the virtualized body can also be traced to our disavowal of the mortal 'obsolete' body. At the same time, the latter is counterbalanced by the sensuous assertion of the performative and 'interactive' body. Such a paradoxical conjunction of denial and affirmation is characteristic of our present mediated condition. Energetically disembodied, we see ourselves as a pataphysical species, suspended in a vertiginous axis stretching seamlessly between the actual and the virtual.

The following works trace an idiosynchratic set of body/space relationships. Opposing that bourgeois paralysis of art exemplified by the passive gazing body of the cultural consumer, the various modalities of interactivity in these works call for a new level of exchange between the viewer and the art-work – an interplay of many energies. They also embody a discourse around the evolving technological incarnation of our being in the virtual (which is possibly also a virus of the virtual within our being).

Der entkörperte und wiederverkörperte Leib 1995

Die Kunstgeschichte gibt eine komplexe Reihe von Beispielen für die Beziehungen zwischen Körper und Raum – Beziehungen zwischen dem wirklichen Bereich des realen Körpers des Zuschauers und dem realen Raum, in dem er sich befindet, und dem virtuellen Bereich des repräsentierten Körpers und der repräsentierten Räume. Der gegenwärtige Körper im Raum entspricht nicht mehr dem klassischen Modell. Unser Körper ist ein schwindelerregender Ort – kopfüber aufgehängt (Georg Baselitz), in den Raum gestoßen (Yves Klein), als veraltet bezeichnet (Stelarc) und jetzt anscheinend übermenschlich wiederverkörpert im Cyberspace und übermenschlich wiedervereinigt im Netzraum.

In den sechziger und siebziger Jahren ließ die Evolution von Mixed-Media- und Inter-Media-Experimenten es deutlich werden, daß die kritische Situation des Körpers ein zentrales Thema war. Der performative Körper des Künstlers und der partizipierende Körper des Zuschauers ergaben zusammen den Begriff eines Körpers, der zunehmend in die Dialektik der mediatisierten Erfahrung ›eingetaucht‹ war. Der heute an die virtuelle Realität angeschlossene Körper des Protagonisten ist eine klare Erweiterung dieser Verbindung.

Körper und Raum befinden sich an der Wurzel aller Erweiterungen. Die narrative Erweiterung ist der zeitliche Körper im Raum. Die rituelle Erweiterung ist der liturgische Körper im sakralen Raum. Die interaktive Erweiterung ist der vom Körper beeinflußte Raum. Schließlich gibt es die mannigfaltigen Erweiterungen, die entweder den Raum oder den Körper unterdrücken, um die Vorherrschaft des einen über den anderen zu fördern. Und heute gibt es die virtuelle Erweiterung der mediatisierten Körper und Hyperräume.

Alle Erweiterungen der Körper-Raum-Verbindung kämpfen mit einer fundamentalen Trennung in unserer Haltung gegenüber dem Körper selbst. Einerseits ist der fleischliche Körper die Grundlage unseres Seins, andererseits verurteilt uns der sterbliche Körper zum Nicht-Sein. Dieser unerträgliche Widerspruch führt zu einer gleichzeitigen Affirmation und Ablehnung des Körpers. Es ist ein Widerspruch, der historisch und in vielen Kulturen einen entscheidenden Kern kunsttheoretischer und ikonographischer Interessen darstellt.

Es ist offensichtlich, daß die gegenwärtige Aufnahme des virtualisierten Körpers auch auf unsere Nichtanerkennung des sterblichen ›veralteten‹ Körpers zurückgeführt werden kann, die gleichzeitig durch die sinnenfreudige Hinwendung zum performativen und ›interaktiven‹ Körper ausgeglichen wird. Eine solche paradoxe Verbindung von Ablehnung und Affirmation ist für unsere gegenwärtige mediatisierte Situation charakteristisch. Energetisch entkörpert sehen wir uns selbst als eine pataphysische Gattung, aufgehängt an einer schwindelerregenden Achse, die sich nahtlos zwischen dem Wirklichen und dem Virtuellen erstreckt.

Die folgenden Arbeiten markieren ein idiosynkratisches Muster von Körper-Raum-Beziehungen. Im Gegensatz zur bürgerlichen Starrheit der Kunst, die sich im passiv blickenden Körper des Kul-

In *MovieMovie* a horizontal inflatable projection screen allows the spectators to physically enter and transform the cinematic space. Saturated with various forms of projected imagery, the customary taut membrane here becomes a soft osmotic surface where the action of the viewers' bodies interpolates the space of fiction and the space of the actual.

In the *Waterwalk* the body of the user/viewer is encapsulated in a dematerialized sculpture – a tranparent air-filled plastic skin. The body becomes the force that puts this sculpture into motion, and in turn the sculpture enables that body to 'walk on water'. The prodigious capabilities of such an art-work brings the body into a new condition – as an operative, as opposed to speculative, expression of new values.

In *The Legible City* the viewer rides a bicycle through a virtual city constituted by an urban architecture of letters and texts. The physical effort of cycling in the real world is gratuitously transposed over this interface into the virtual world, affirming the absurd yet euphoric conjunction of the zealous body in the virtual domain. This may be compared with the conventional interfaces – keyboard, mouse, joystick, etc. – which transpose minimal displacements of the body into media coordinates. Our presence in the virtual domain is afforded by a growing range of delicate prostheses that give us pseudo-tactile access to what is untouchable.

In *Revolution* the viewer has to continuously push a protruding steel bar to rotate and animate the image changes on a monitor screen. Turning the monitor in one direction, the viewer grinds virtual grain under a virtual millstone; pushing it in the other direction, he provokes images of the last 200 years of political revolutions. Thus the viewer's body, straining with effort, is an essential component of the formal, conceptual and functional figuration of this sculpture. Two expenditures of energy are conjoined, one actual, the other analogous, and the viewer revolves and is revolved in the orbit of this mundane wheel of mediated revolutions.

In *The Virtual Museum* the viewer's seated body moves itself effectively in the virtual space by simply shifting its balance in the chair forwards or backwards, to the left or right. The rotating platform on which he is seated forces the viewer's body to accompany the perambulations of his mobile virtual eye. Looking into the virtual museum, the viewer sees the chair he is seated in is empty and thus he confronts his paradoxical loss of physical body in the virtual domain. In exchange he gains in this virtual environment an omniscient disembodied presence which the art-work then strives to annex to his actual body. Here, the crucial issue of annexation of experience from within the virtual towards the actual and vice versa emerges once more. It is appropriate that *The Virtual Museum* is an 'art' museum – a paradigmatic space for such an undertaking.

In *Disappearance* the combined up and down movements of a video monitor mounted on a rotating forklift truck generate the

turkonsumenten ausdrückt, verlangen die verschiedenen Modalitäten der Interaktivität bei diesen Arbeiten eine neue Ebene des Austausches zwischen dem Betrachter und dem Kunstwerk – ein Zusammenspiel vieler Kräfte. Sie verkörpern auch einen Diskurs über die entstehende technologische Inkarnation unseres Seins im Virtuellen (was möglicherweise auch ein Virus des Virtuellen in unserem Sein ist).

In *MovieMovie* ermöglicht den Zuschauern eine horizontale aufblasbare Projektionsleinwand, den kinematischen Raum körperlich zu betreten und zu verändern. Erfüllt von verschiedenen Formen projizierter Bilder wird die normalerweise straff gespannte Membran hier zu einer weichen osmotischen Oberfläche, auf der die körperliche Aktion der Zuschauer den Raum der Fiktion mit dem Raum des Wirklichen verbindet.

In *Waterwalk* ist der Körper des Benutzers/Zuschauers in eine entmaterialisierte Skulptur eingeschlossen: in eine durchsichtige, luftgefüllte Haut. Der Körper wird zur Kraft, die diese Skulptur in Bewegung versetzt, und im Gegenzug erlaubt die Skulptur dem Körper, ›auf dem Wasser zu gehen‹. Die wunderbaren Möglichkeiten eines solchen Kunstwerks stellen den Körper in eine neue Situation – nicht als ein spekulativer, sondern als ein operativer Ausdruck neuer Werte.

In *The Legible City* fährt der Betrachter auf einem Fahrrad durch eine virtuelle Stadt, die durch eine urbane Architektur aus Buchstaben und Texten dargestellt wird. Die körperliche Anstrengung, in der realen Welt Fahrrad zu fahren, wird über die Schnittstelle in die virtuelle Welt übertragen, in der sie eigentlich überflüssig ist, und die absurde, jedoch euphorische Verbindung mit dem aktiven Körper wird im Virtuellen bestätigt. Das kann mit gewöhnlichen Schnittstellen – Tastatur, Maus, Joystick etc. – verglichen werden, die minimale Verschiebungen des Körpers in mediale Koordinaten übersetzen. Unsere Präsenz im Virtuellen wird durch eine wachsende Zahl empfindlicher Prothesen unterstützt, die uns einen pseudotaktilen Zugang zum Unberührbaren eröffnen.

In *Revolution* muß der Betrachter kontinuierlich einen herausragenden Stahlarm drücken, um die Bilder auf einem Monitor zu drehen und zu animieren. Dreht der Zuschauer den Monitor in eine Richtung, zermahlt er mit einem virtuellen Mühlstein virtuelles Korn. Dreht er ihn in die andere Richtung, sieht er Bilder von politischen Revolutionen aus den letzten 200 Jahren. So ist der Körper des Zuschauers, der Kraft aufwenden muß, eine wesentliche Komponente der formalen, konzeptuellen und funktionalen Figuration dieser Skulptur. Zwei Kraftaufwendungen werden miteinander verbunden – eine wirkliche und eine analoge – und der Zuschauer dreht sich und wird gedreht im Kreislauf dieses Weltrades mediatisierter Revolutionen.

In *The Virtual Museum* bewegt sich der sitzende Körper des Zuschauers im virtuellen Raum, indem er einfach seinen Schwerpunkt im Stuhl nach vorwärts oder rückwärts, links oder rechts verlagert. Die rotierende Plattform, auf der er sitzt, zwingt den Körper des Zuschauers, den Bewegungen seines mobilen virtuellen Auges zu folgen. Wenn er in das virtuelle Museum hineinsieht,

virtual representation of a larger-than-life ballerina. This work signals the incarnation of automata in this present era of technological exteriorization of desire. It takes a first-generation robot – the ballerina on a music box – and then generates her virtual reconstruction to the extent that the machinery of presentation itself now incarnates her pirouettes. While proclaiming a more radical exegesis of the body, such a simulational strategy also heralds the fact that deconstruction and restitution are the trenchant modalities of our cybernetic 'age of reproduction'.

In *The Golden Calf* the viewer holds a monitor screen in his hands, and by moving it around a bare pedestal sees a virtual golden calf standing on this pedestal. The body is no longer a corporeal idolotrous object; it has become an intangible subject of fascination. We dance around the high-tech pilaster construing this almost tangible phantasm. Representation is, and always was, the domain of both our embodied and disembodied yearnings. It is in the friction of this conjunction that we experience the euphoric dislocation of our present condition. Like Duchamp's 'inframince', this is an insubstantial zone of disillusion where, after all is said and done, there remains only an imperceptible yet ubiquitous plenitude of being.

The technologies of immaterial representation have opened a Pandora's Box of new relationships between the viewer and the art-work. The desire for the dissolution (and disillusion) of the corporeal art-work seems to be consistent with the avant-gardist ambition for the convergence between 'art and life'. In Guy Debord's words: 'Life can never be too disorientating'.

A new aesthetics comes to the fore. The art-work is more and more embodied in the interface, in the articulation of a space of meeting between the art-work and the viewer, and even in the articulation of a space where the art-work as an artifact seems to disappear altogether and only communication between the viewers remains.

While the success of an interface is constituted simply by its efficacy as a mechanism of conjunction, the artistic quality of an interface is the extent to which this conjunction embodies new cultural values. The interest now focusing on the raw creative modalities of interactivity, virtual reality, hypermedia, telepresence and networking comes from a recognition of the implicit shift in cultural paradigms these techniques embody. But the liability is of course an enthusiasm that merely articulates the metaphoric and anecdotal values of these techniques. In this situation, the poetic and conceptual rigour of traditional art practice may remain exemplary for all our efforts in the digital domain.

Published in: *Kunstforum. Die Zukunft des Körpers I*, Vol. 132, November 1995–January 1996, pp. 168–171.

bemerkt der Zuschauer, daß der Stuhl, auf dem er sitzt, leer ist und wird so mit dem paradoxen Verlust des körperlichen Leibes im Virtuellen konfrontiert. Im Austausch dafür gewinnt er in dieser virtuellen Umgebung eine allwissende entkörperte Präsenz, die das Kunstwerk versucht, auf seinen wirklichen Körper zu übertragen. Auch hier ist das zentrale Thema die Übertragung der Erfahrung aus dem Virtuellen in die Wirklichkeit und umgekehrt. Es scheint angemessen zu sein, *The Virtual Museum* als ein ›Kunst‹-Museum zu bezeichnen, weil es ein paradigmatischer Ort für ein derartiges Unternehmen ist.

In *Disappearance* erzeugen die kombinierten Auf- und Abbewegungen eines Videobildschirms, der auf einem rotierenden Gabelstapler plaziert ist, die virtuelle Darstellung einer überlebensgroßen Tänzerin. Diese Arbeit weist auf die Inkarnation der Automaten im gegenwärtigen Zeitalter der technologischen Veräußerung des Begehrens hin. Eingesetzt wird ein Roboter der ersten Generation – die Tänzerin auf einer Musikbox – und dann wird deren virtuelle Rekonstruktion bis zu einem Punkt generiert, an dem die Maschinerie der Darstellung nun selbst ihre Pirouetten verkörpert. Eine solche Strategie der Simulation stellt mit einer radikaleren Exegese des Körpers auch den Sachverhalt heraus, daß Dekonstruktion und Wiederherstellung die einschneidenden Modalitäten in unserem kybernetischen ›Zeitalter der Reproduktion‹ sind.

Bei *The Golden Calf* hält der Zuschauer mit seinen Händen einen Monitor. Geht er damit um ein leeres Podest herum, sieht er ein virtuelles goldenes Kalb, das sich auf dem Podest befindet. Der Körper ist nicht mehr ein materielles Objekt der Verehrung, sondern ist zu einem unberührbaren Subjekt der Faszination geworden. Wir tanzen um den High-Tech-Pilaster, der dieses fast berührbare Phantasma erzeugt. Repräsentation ist – und war dies immer – der Bereich unserer verkörperten und entkörperten Sehnsüchte. Durch die Reibung in dieser Verbindung erfahren wir die euphorische Dislokation unserer gegenwärtigen Lage. Wie Duchamps ›Inframince‹ ist dies ein nicht-substantieller Bereich der Desillusion, in dem – nachdem alles gesagt und getan worden ist – nur eine nicht wahrnehmbare, aber allgegenwärtige Seinsfülle zurückbleibt.

Die Technologien der immateriellen Repräsentation haben eine Büchse der Pandora mit neuen Beziehungen zwischen dem Zuschauer und dem Kunstwerk eröffnet. Das Verlangen nach der Auflösung (und der Desillusionierung) des materiellen Kunstwerks scheint mit der avantgardistischen Intention nach einer Verschmelzung von ›Kunst und Leben‹ übereinzustimmen. ›Das Leben kann‹, um es mit Guy Debords Worten zu sagen, ›niemals zu verwirrend sein‹.

Eine neue Ästhetik bildet sich heraus. Das Kunstwerk wird mehr und mehr in der Schnittstelle verkörpert – in der Artikulation eines Begegnungsraumes zwischen Kunstwerk und Betrachter und sogar in der Artikulation eines Raumes, wo das Kunstwerk als ein Artefakt ganz zu verschwinden scheint und nur die Kommunikation

zwischen den Zuschauern übrigbleibt.

Während der Erfolg einer Schnittstelle nur auf ihrer Wirksamkeit als Mechanismus der Verbindung beruht, so begründet sich die künstlerische Qualität einer Schnittstelle auf dem Ausmaß, in dem diese Verbindung neue kulturelle Werte verkörpert. Das Interesse, das sich jetzt auf einfache Modalitäten von Interaktivität, virtueller Realität, Hypermedia und Telepräsenz richtet, entsteht aus der Erkenntnis der impliziten Veränderung kultureller Paradigmen, die diese Techniken verkörpern. Aber diese Tendenz ist eine Begeisterung, die lediglich die metaphorischen und anekdotischen Werte der Techniken zum Ausdruck bringt. In dieser Situation kann die poetische und konzeptuelle Strenge der traditionellen Kunst vorbildhaft für alle Arbeiten im digitalen Bereich bleiben.

Aus dem Englischen von Florian Rötzer. – Veröffentlicht in: *Kunstforum. Die Zukunft des Körpers I*, Bd. 132, November 1995–Januar 1996, S. 168–171.

Appendix

Anhang

Biography

1944 Born in Melbourne, Australia
1962–64 Studies in architecture and art history at the University of Melbourne, Australia
1965 Studies in sculpture at the Accademia di Belli Arti di Brera, Milan, Italy
1966 Post-graduate studies in sculpture at St. Martin's School of Art, London, UK
1966 Participation in Sigma Projects, Amsterdam, Netherlands, with Pieter Boersma, Theo Botschuijver, Willem Breuker, John Latham, Nico Nijland, Graham Stevens and Tjebbe van Tijen
1967 Formation of the Eventstructure Research Group (ERG) in Amsterdam, Netherlands, with Theo Botschuijver and Sean Wellesley-Miller. Other persons associated with ERG on special projects included Hanni van de Dop, Lex de Groot, Robert Hahn, Klaas de Poel, Rob van de Poel, Kirsty Sorenson and Tjebbe van Tijen
1968 Formation of the Artist Placement Group (APG) in London, UK, with Stuart Brisley, Barry Flannagan, David Hall, John Latham, Ian Macdonald Monro and Barbara Steveni
1970–90 Diverse stipends and production grants from the Dutch Ministry of Culture
1977 Formation of Javaphile Productions in Amsterdam, Netherlands, with Marga Adama and John Munsey
1989 Teaching position at the Rotterdam Academie van Beeldende Kunsten, Netherlands
1990 Teaching position at the Gerrit Rietveld Academie, Amsterdam, Netherlands and at the Städelschule, Institut für Neue Medien, Frankfurt-on-Main, Germany
Since 1991 Director of the Institute for Visual Media at the ZKM/Center for Art and Media Karlsruhe, Germany
Since 1995 Professor of media arts at the Hochschule für Gestaltung, Karlsruhe, Germany
1995 First retrospective exhibition: 'Place – a user's manual. Jeffrey Shaw: Interaktive Computerinstallationen 1985–1995', Trigon-Personale '95, Neue Galerie am Landesmuseum Joanneum, Graz, Austria

Prizes:
1990: L'Immagine Elettronica, Ferrara, Italy;
Prix Ars Electronica, Linz, Austria, in the category interactive art

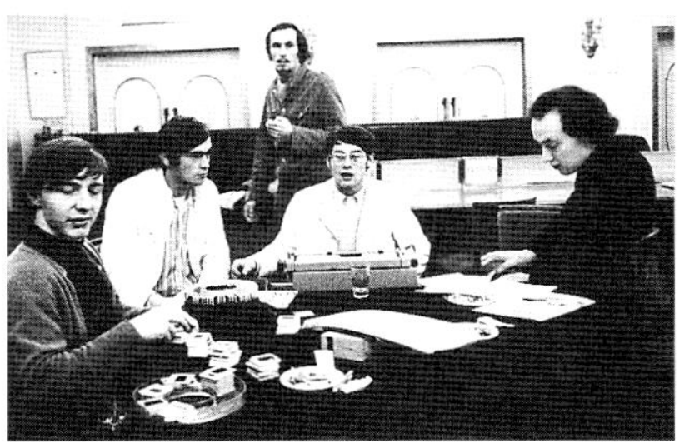
From left to right: Tjebbe van Tijen, Klaas de Poel, Sean Wellesley-Miller, Theo Botschuijver, Jeffrey Shaw. Amsterdam, Netherlands, 1967. Photo: Pieter Boersma.

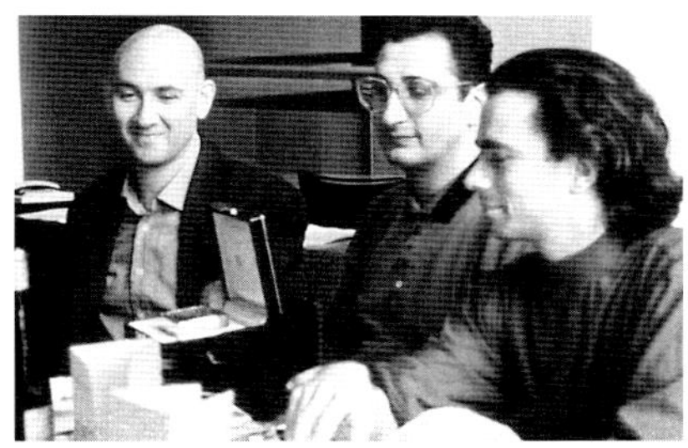
From left to right: Jeffrey Shaw, Dirk Groeneveld, Gideon May. Ferrara, Italy, 1990.

Biographie

1944 Geboren in Melbourne, Australien
1962–64 Studium der Architektur und Kunstgeschichte an der Universität von Melbourne, Australien
1965 Studium der Bildhauerei an der Accademia di Belli Arti di Brera, Milano, Italien
1966 Fortsetzung des Studiums an der St. Martin's School of Art, London, UK
1966 Zusammenarbeit mit Sigma Projects in Amsterdam, Niederlande mit Pieter Boersma, Theo Botschuijver, Willem Breuker, John Latham, Nico Nijland, Graham Stevens und Tjebbe van Tijen
1967 Gründung der Eventstructure Research Group (ERG) in Amsterdam, Niederlande mit Theo Botschuijver und Sean Wellesley-Miller; an den verschieden Projekten der ERG waren u.a. beteiligt: Hanni van de Dop, Lex de Groot, Robert Hahn, Klaas de Poel, Rob van de Poel, Kirsty Sorenson und Tjebbe van Tijen
1968 Gründung der Artist Placement Group (APG) in London, UK mit Stuart Brisley, Barry Flannagan, David Hall, John Latham, Ian Macdonald Monro und Barbara Steveni
1970–90 Mehrere Stipendien vom Kultusministerium der Niederlande
1977 Gründung von Javaphile Productions in Amsterdam, Niederlande mit Marga Adama und John Munsey
1989 Lehrauftrag an der Academie van Beeldende Kunsten, Rotterdam, Niederlande
1990 Lehrauftrag an der Gerrit Rietveld Akademie, Amsterdam, Niederlande und an der Städelschule, Institut für Neue Medien, Frankfurt a. M, Deutschland
Seit 1991 Leiter des Instituts für Bildmedien am ZKM/Zentrum für Kunst und Medientechnologie Karlsruhe, Deutschland
Seit 1995 Professor für Medienkunst an der Hochschule für Gestaltung Karlsruhe, Deutschland
1995 Erste retrospektive Einzelausstellung: ›Ort – eine Gebrauchsanweisung. Jeffrey Shaw: Interaktive Computerinstallationen 1985–1995‹, Trigon-Personale '95, Neue Galerie am Landesmuseum Joanneum Graz, Österreich

Auszeichnungen:
1990 L'Immagine Elettronica, Ferrara, Italien;
Auszeichnung im Bereich Interaktive Kunst des Prix Ars Electronica, Linz, Österreich

Selected Works and Exhibitions 1966–96

Werke und Ausstellungen 1966–96 (Auswahl)

1966

1 *The Dante Cupboard*
Group exhibition with Denis Masi, Claudio Martinenghi, Franco Mazzucchelli and Tjebbe van Tijen
This mixed-media sculpture extended over the gallery floor so that the viewers had to walk over it.
Centro Culturale San Fedele, Milan, Italy.

Continuous Sound and Image Moments
16 mm animated film
with Tjebbe van Tijen
Music: Willem Breuker
Collection of the Netherlands Film Museum, Amsterdam, Netherlands.
1966: Kasteelhoeve Beek en Donk, Netherlands; Better Books, London, UK. – 1967: 26 Kingly Street Gallery, London, UK; *Corpocinema*, Amsterdam, Rotterdam, Netherlands; *MovieMovie*, Knokke-le-Zoute, Belgium. – 1983: Film en Kunst, t'Hoogt, Utrecht, Netherlands.

2 *Disillusionary Homage to Clovis Trouille*
Expanded cinema installation and performance
with Tjebbe van Tijen
Slides of Clovis Trouille's paintings were projected over a sculpted replica of one of his figures and also onto a paper projection screen which was torn open by inflatable tubing during the performance.
1966: Kasteelhoeve Beek en Donk, Netherlands. – 1967: 26 Kingly Street Gallery, London, UK.

Emergences of Continuous Forms
Expanded cinema installation and performance
with Tjebbe van Tijen
Better Books, London, UK.

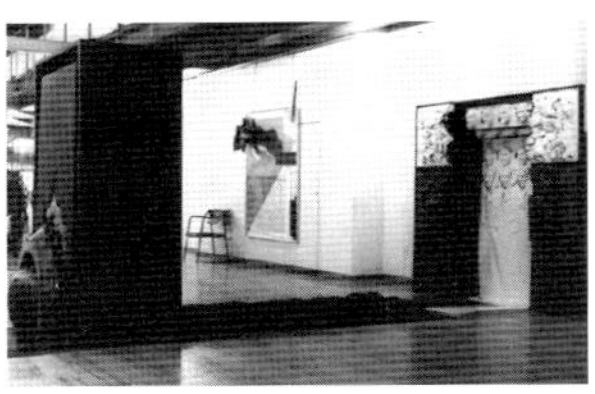

1

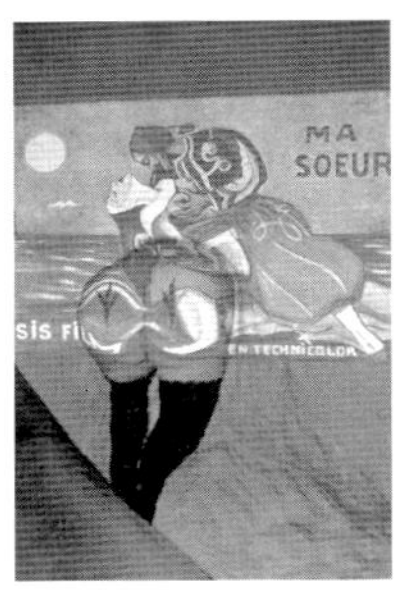

2

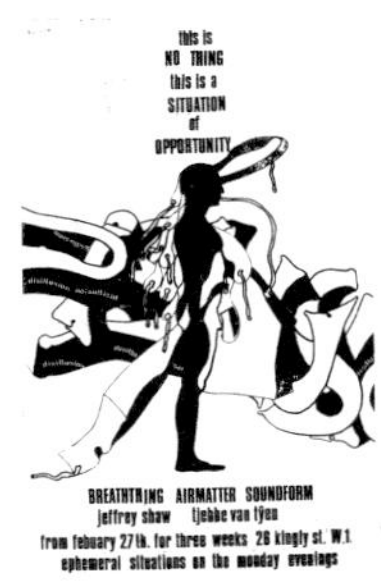

3

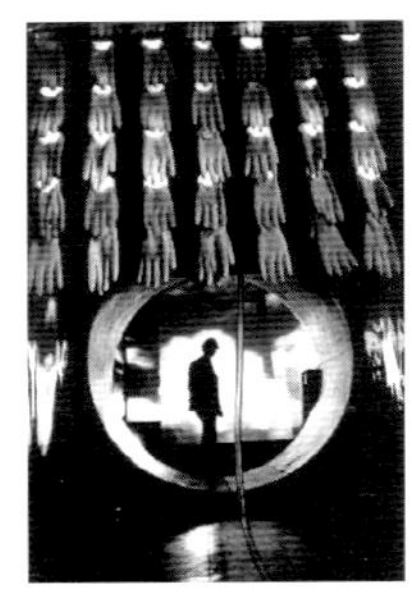

4

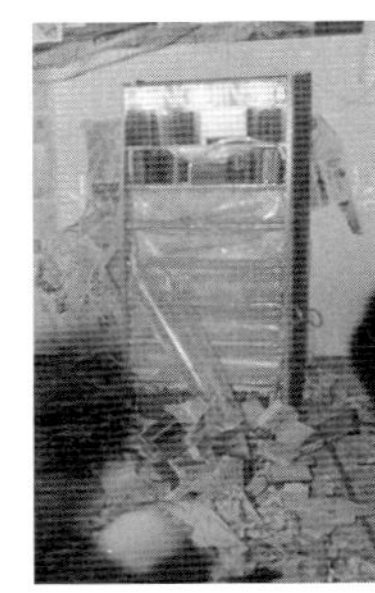

5

1968

Disillusion of Women Wrestling
Expanded cinema performance
The film *Continuous Sound and Image Moments* (1966) was projected onto a live performance of professional female mud wrestlers.
Theatre Royal Stratford, London, UK.

6 *Airground*
Pneumatic eventstructure
with Theo Botschuijver
1968: Brighton Festival, Brighton, UK; City of London Festival, London, UK.

Alpevent
Pneumatic eventstructure
with Theo Botschuijver
50 Jahre Kunsthalle Bern, Kornhauskeller, Bern, Switzerland.

7 *Octopus*
Pneumatic eventstructure
with Theo Botschuijver
A large inflatable structure in the form of an octopus was inflated inside the museum – the people there dragged about and entangled themselves in its long tentacles.
Stedeljik Museum, Amsterdam, Netherlands.

Structures Gonflables
Documentary Exhibition
with Theo Botschuijver
Structures Gonflables, Musée d'Art Moderne de la Ville de Paris, Paris, France.

8 *Pneutube*
Pneumatic eventstructure
with Theo Botschuijver
A large transparent inflatable tube the public could enter and which, depending on the context of showing, functioned as an expanded cinema and performance environment, playful interactive space, and architectural corridor.
1968/69: Environments, Rijksuniversiteit, Utrecht, Netherlands. – 1969: Kinetische Objektenshow, Franz-Hals-Museum, Haarlem, Netherlands; Six Events in Amsterdam, Amsterdam, Netherlands; Institute of Contemporary Art, London, UK.

9 *Black Airground*
Pneumatic eventstructure
with Theo Botschuijver and performance by Peter Dockley
A row of three large black parachutes were fixed around their perimeter to the floor and continuously inflated with air. A light bulb above each parachute was the only illumination in the installation, and they were individually activated by the pitch and volume of sounds the visitors made.
Museum of Modern Art, Oxford, UK.

1967

3 *This is No Thing – This is a Situation of Opportunity*
Expanded cinema installation
with Tjebbe van Tijen
26 Kingly Street Gallery, London, UK.

Disillusion of a Fish Pond
Expanded cinema performance
26 Kingly Street Gallery, London, UK.

4 *Glove Screen*
Interactive expanded cinema sculpture
Viewers could interactively control the inflation and deflation of translucent white surgical gloves built into a rectangular panel. The film *Continuous Sound and Image Moments* (1966) was projected from behind the panel into these gloves.
26 Kingly Street Gallery, London, UK.

Disillusion of Striptease Films
Expanded cinema performance
Striptease films were projected onto a woman as she struggled to remove her clothes while tightly encapsulated inside an inflatable structure.
1967: 26 Kingly Street Gallery, London, UK. – 1968: Palais de Sports, Paris, France.

Corpocinema
Expanded cinema eventstructure
with Theo Botschuijver, Sean Wellesley-Miller, Tjebbe van Tijen
1967: Rotterdam, Netherlands; Sigma Projects, Amsterdam, Netherlands

5 *Book Plumbing*
Mixed-media installation and performance
with John Latham
The centerpiece of the performance was a Penguin bookcase in which all the books were embedded in jelly. The gradual inflation of plastic tubing forced each consecutive row of books and jelly to slide out of its shelf and fall onto the floor.
Better Books, London, UK.

MovieMovie
Expanded cinema eventstructure
with Theo Botschuijver, Sean Wellesley-Miller, Tjebbe van Tijen
Music: Musica Elettronica Viva
Lightshow: The Overheads
Production: Sigma Projects, Amsterdam, Netherlands.
1967: 4th International Experimental Film Festival, Knokke-le-Zoute, Belgium. – 1969: St. George's Arts Centre, Liverpool, UK.

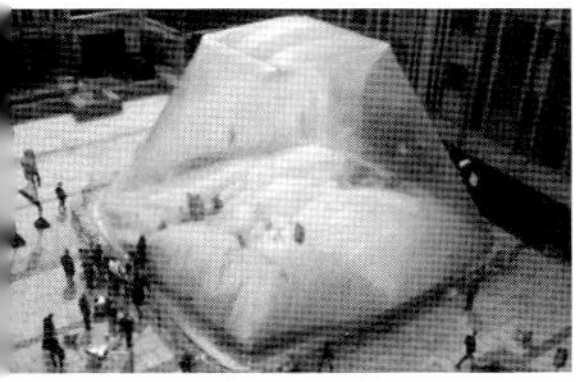
6

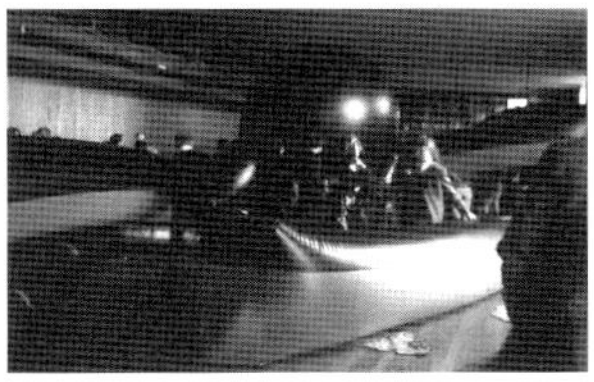
7

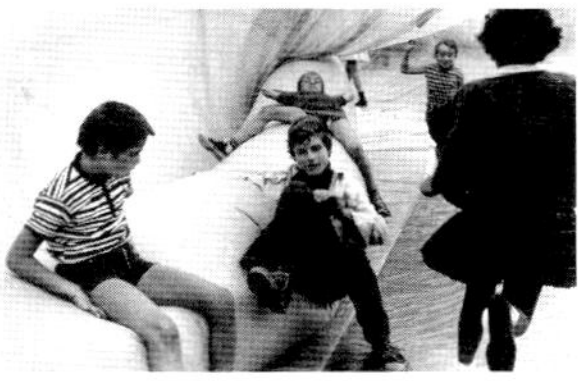
8

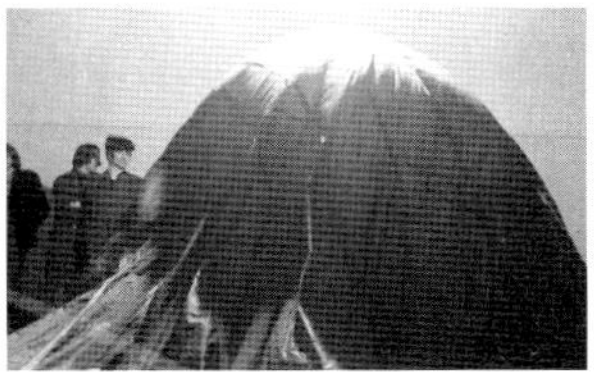
9

10 *Supertube*
Pneumatic eventstructure
with Theo Botschuijver
A high volume of air blown from below into a long open-ended plastic tube caused it to flap around wildly in the sky. Smoke and confetti could be added to the air stream.
Ouderkerk a/d Amstel, Netherlands.

1969

11 *Artificial Landscapes*
Photographic collages
with Theo Botschuijver
1969: Art After Plans, Kunsthalle, Bern, Switzerland. – 1970: Kunsthalle, Hamburg, Germany.

Wind and Rain
Disillusionary event
Sigma 5, Bordeaux, France.

12 *Grassroll*
Pneumatic eventstructure
with Theo Botschuijver
An air-inflated tube covered with synthetic grass.
Six Events in Amsterdam, Amsterdam, Netherlands.

Totems
Pneumatic eventstructure
with Theo Botschuijver
Air-inflated tubes printed with water texture were floated as vertical columns in a lake.
Six Events in Amsterdam, Amsterdam, Netherlands.

13 *Cushion*
Pneumatic eventstructure
with Theo Botschuijver
Six Events in Amsterdam, Amsterdam, Netherlands; Camden Arts Festival, London, UK.

Dragon
Inflatable creature
with Theo Botschuijver
An air-inflated dragon was commissioned for William Klein's film *Mr. Freedom*.

14 *Brickhill*
Pneumatic eventstructure
with Theo Botschuijver
An air-inflated cone-shaped structure printed with a brick pattern.
Six Events in Amsterdam, Amsterdam, Netherlands; Environments Reversal, Camden Arts Centre, London, UK.

The Pneu-Written
Expanded cinema performance
with Theo Botschuijver
and John Latham
Elements of the *MovieMovie* (1967) were merged with a performance scenography made by John Latham.
St. George's Arts Centre, Liverpool, UK.

Waterwalk
Pneumatic eventstructure
with Theo Botschuijver
The original *Waterwalk* was a closed tetrahedron-shaped balloon with a watertight zip. Later versions used air-inflated tubes and cylindrical compartments allowing it to be open at the sides.
1969: Six Events in Amsterdam, Amsterdam, Netherlands.
– 1970: Brighton Festival, Brighton, UK; Holland Pop Festival, Kralingen, Netherlands.
– 1971: National Gallery of Victoria, Melbourne, Australia.
– 1972: Moomba Festival, Melbourne, Australia.

Sandquake
Pneumatic eventstructure
with Theo Botschuijver
Long lengths of polythene tubing were buried in the sand at a beach in the Camargue in France. This tubing was then slowly inflated so that it gradually rose up and erupted out of the sand.
TV Gallery Gerry Schum, Camargue, France.

Smokescreen
Pyrotechnic event
1969: Swansea Art Festival, Swansea University, Wales.
– 1970: Holland Pop Festival, Kralingen, Netherlands.

1970

Cloud (of daytime sky at night)
Pneumatic structure
with Theo Botschuijver
Stedelijk Museum, Amsterdam, Netherlands.

Waterquake
Pneumatic eventstructure
with Theo Botschuijver
Assen, Netherlands.

15 *Walterwalk Tube*
Pneumatic eventstructure
with Theo Botschuijver
1970: Straßenkunstfestival, Hanover, Germany. – 1972: Groningen, Netherlands.

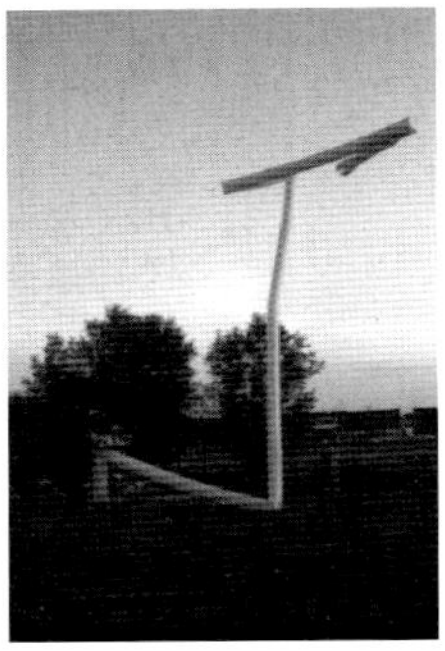
10

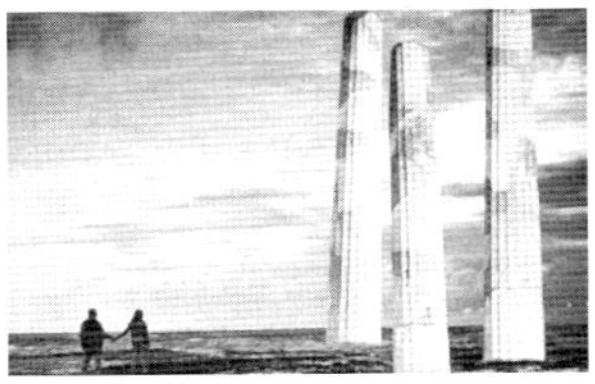
11

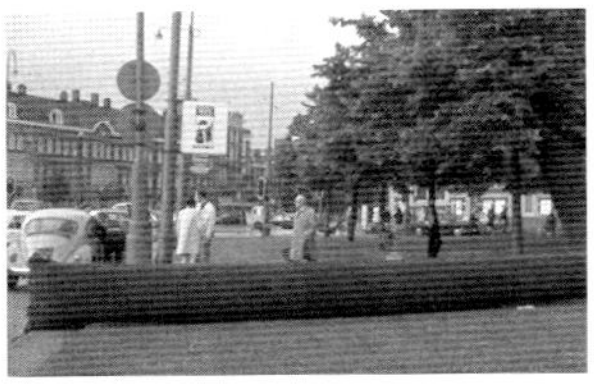
12

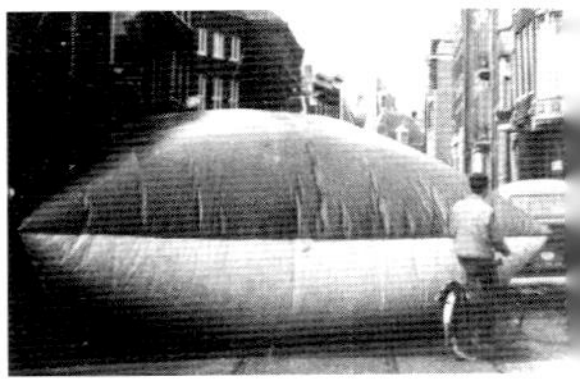
13

20 *Information Pavilion:* an air supported semi-sphere covered with synthetic grass.
Sonsbeek buiten de perken, Arnheim, Netherlands.

21 *Homage to Bladen*
Pneumatic eventstructure with Theo Botschuijver
Inflatable replica of an exhibited sculpture by Ronald Bladen which the visitors could play with.
Sonsbeek buiten de perken, Arnheim, Netherlands.

1972

Aqua-Airground
Pneumatic eventstructure
with Theo Botschuijver
Floriade Kind en Leefmilieu Festival, Amsterdam, Netherlands.

22 *Centipede*
Inflatable creature
with Theo Botschuijver
An inflatable centipede whose feet were constituted by the people who carried it through the streets.
Moomba Festival, Melbourne, Australia.

23 *More & Less*
Pneumatic eventstructure.
with Theo Botschuijver and John Latham
An installation in two rooms. One was filled with an inflatable structure that was slightly smaller than the room – visitors had to squeeze between it and the walls. In the other room the structure was larger than the room and so covered all its surfaces – here the visitors entered inside the structure.
British Avantgarde, Gallery House, London, UK.

24 *Rainbow*
Pneumatic eventstructure
with Theo Botschuijver
An large inflatable arch in rainbow colours from which a fine spray of water fell, creating real rainbows.
Melbourne, Australia.

16 *No Thing*
Sculpture
with Theo Botschuijver
A monumental sculpture proposed for the Schouwburgplein in Rotterdam and constituted by massive letters forming the words NO THING.
C '70, Schouwburgplein, Rotterdam, Netherlands.

Airground Mattress
Pneumatic eventstructure
with Theo Botschuijver
1970: Tomorrow's World, BBC TV, London, UK. – 1974: Tabarka Festival, Tabarka, Tunisia. – 1975: Speelruimte, Dordrechts Museum, Dordrecht, Netherlands.

17 *Televents*
Video performances
with Theo Botschuijver
Numerous disillusionary manipulations of domestic TV sets were made for television broadcasting by the V.P.R.O. For instance, the TV screen was replaced with a white painted black balloon on which film was projected – when the balloon was inflated the screen image cracked apart and burst.
V.P.R.O. Television, Amsterdam, Netherlands.

1971

Hayward Gallery Projects
Two concepts for the Hayward roof terrace: the roof filled with a heap of giant inflatable potatoes, and an inflatable dome covered with film projection which constituted a sphere of daytime sky during the night.
Photographic collages with Theo Botschuijver
1971: Inno '70, Hayward Gallery, London, UK; Between 5, Kunsthalle, Düsseldorf, Germany.

18 *Scottish Sorrow*
Mobile pneumatic eventstructure
with Theo Botschuijver
A tall van was completely covered in tartan printed plastic. It drove nightly through Edinburgh broadcasting classical bagpipe music and projecting tartan patterns onto the city's buildings.
Edinburgh Festival, Edinburgh, UK.

Three Pavilions
Pneumatic structures
with Theo Botschuijver
Auditorium Pavilion: a two-level air-supported structure (see page 81)
19 *Video Pavilion*: a tensile structure stretched over three large air-inflated arches.

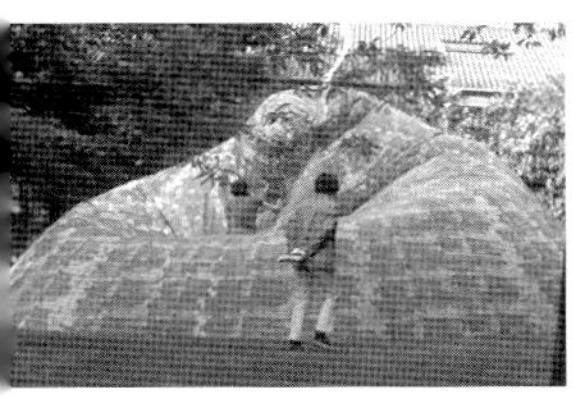

14

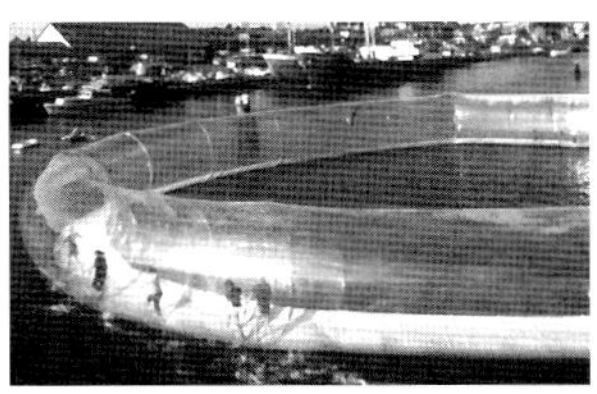

15

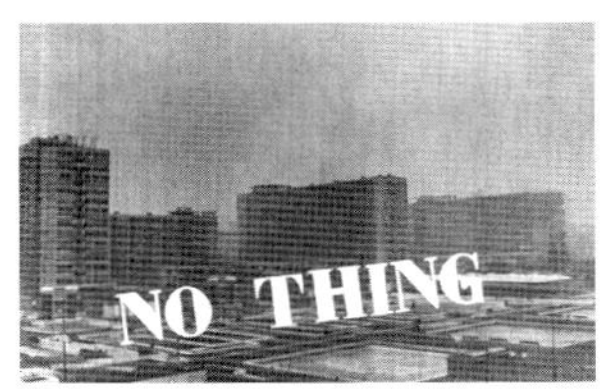

16

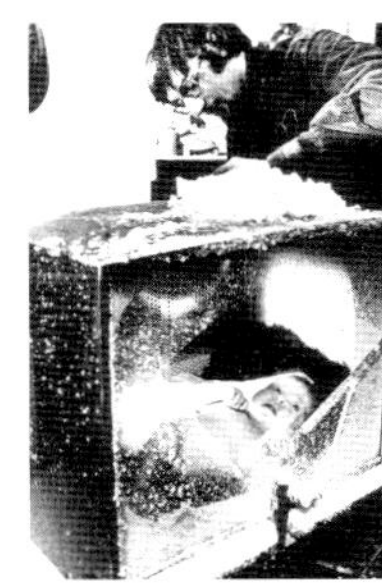

17

1973

25 *Projections*
Inflatable objects and photographic works
with Theo Botschuijver
Series of photographic prints on linen with specific functionalities: a table cloth with the image of a dinner serving, a window curtain with the image of a venetian blind, a sheet hanging on a line with the image of bedsheets hanging to dry. The interactive inflatable objects included a simulated brick wall which expanded out towards the viewer.
Pinacotheca and Tolarno Galleries, Melbourne, Australia; Museum Fodor, Amsterdam, Netherlands.

1974

Diadrama
Slide projection installation
with Theo Botschuijver
Universiteits Theater, Amsterdam, Netherlands;
De Lantaren, Rotterdam, Netherlands.

26 *Staircase*
Slide projection installation
with Theo Botschuijver
A sequence of photographs was taken of people using the central staircase in the Stedelijk Museum. This scene was then virtually re-constructed by projecting these images full-scale onto two contiguous projection screens – one hanging vertically on the wall and the other lying horizontally on the floor.
Stedelijk Museum, Amsterdam, Netherlands.

1975

Viewpoint
Interactive slide projection installation
with Theo Botschuijver
9th Biennale de Paris, Musée d'Art Moderne de la Ville de Paris, Paris, France.

The Lamb Lies Down on Broadway
Slide projections, laser performance and inflatable structures
with Theo Botschuijver
Genesis world tour.

1976

Laser installations and performances
with Theo Botschuijver
1976–78: Genesis world tours.
– 1978: Stichting de Appel, Amsterdam, Netherlands (performance with Ernst Reijseger, cello).

Sesamstraat (1976–79)
with Theo Botschujiver
A number of film and video items were produced for this children's television series. An early form of virtual studio was created using chroma-key and camera-synchronized movement of panoramic photographs.
NOS Television, Netherlands.

27 *Pig*
Inflatable creature
with Theo Botschuijver
A helium-inflated pig was specially made for the cover of Pink Floyd's *Animals* album.
Battersea Park, London, UK.

1977

Kinetic Light and Mirror Sculpture
with Theo Botschuijver
Genesis world tour.

Fort van Sjakoo
Opening event for this bookshop
with Theo Botschuijver
Inflatable tubing burst through a wall of brick-printed plastic that covered the shop window. This tubing was then taken into the street and used to signal the boundaries of the planned urban renewal in this area.
Jodenbreestraat, Amsterdam, Netherlands.

Tearfall
Pneumatic eventstructure
with Theo Botschuijver and Javaphile Productions performance
with Marga Adama and John Munsey
A large air-inflated teardrop hung from a crane proclaimed the theme of the festival as well as the Javaphile performance.
Festival van de Ongelukkige Liefde, De Lantaren, Rotterdam, Netherlands.

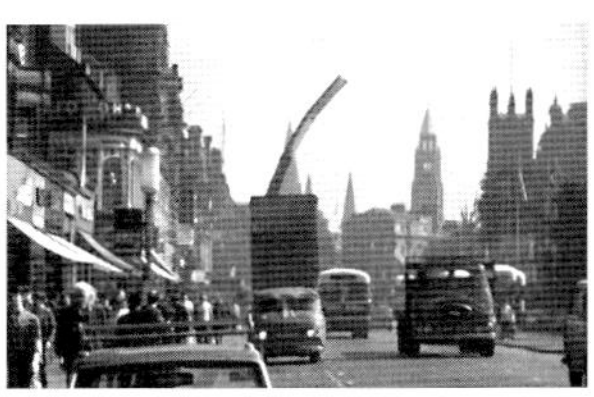
18

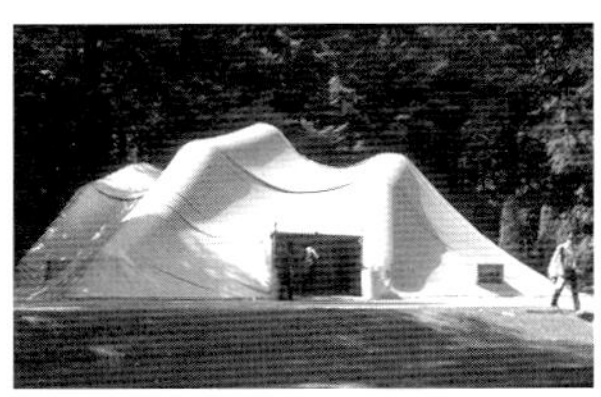
19

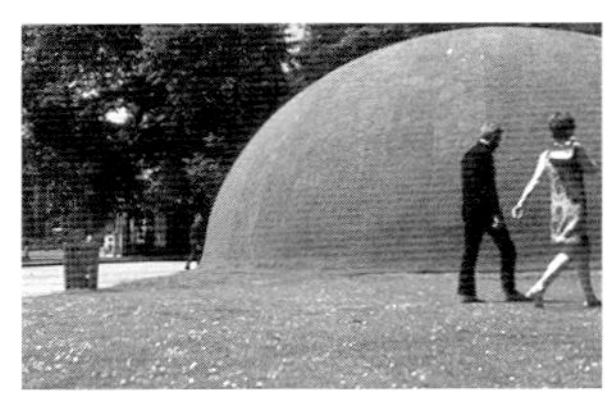
20

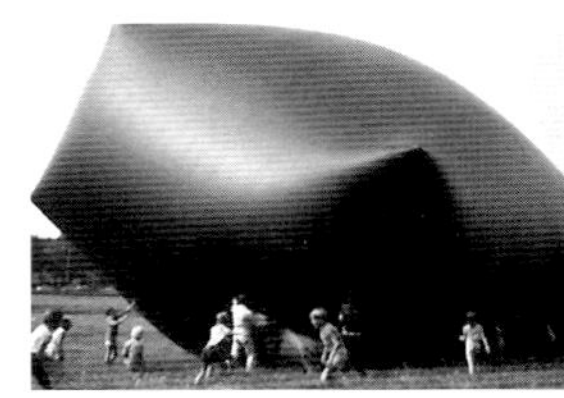
21

Once upon a time ...
Javaphile Productions performance
with Robert Hahn, John Munsey and Carlyle Reedy
One World Poetry Festival, Melkweg, Amsterdam, Netherlands; Gallery Bedaux, Amsterdam, Netherlands.

Documentation of ERG early works
Actie, Werkelijkheid en Fictie in de Kunst van de Jaren '60 in Nederland, Boymans-van-Beuningen Museum, Rotterdam, Netherlands.

1980

30 *Video Ball Sculpture*
Permanent interactive sculpture
with Theo Botschuijver
Images created by the viewers on a touchscreen are displayed by an electro-mechanical process of sorting and positioning thousands of blue and yellow balls.
Scholengemeenschap Quirijn, Tilburg, Netherlands

Stichting Stroombeeld (Current Image Foundation)
with Theo Botschuijver
Formal proposal to the Dutch Ministry of Culture for the creation of an art and technology research and production centre in Amsterdam, Netherlands.

1981

One plus Two in 3-D
Javaphile Productions performance
with Marga Adama, Wendela Gevers Deynoot, Robert Hahn, Jenn ben Jakov, Dea Kourt and John Munsey
Stadsschouwburg, Groningen, Netherlands.

1982

31 *Corrida – Logique de la Perception*
Digital video performance
with Fabienne de Quasa Riera and Shusaku Takauchi.
1982: World Wide Video Festival, Kijkhuis, The Hague, Netherlands.
– 1983: Gallery Menz, Amsterdam, Netherlands.– 1984: De Meervart, Amsterdam, Netherlands.

1978

28 *Suncycle*
Javaphile Productions
performance
with Marga Adama and John Munsey
Lucht, Stedelijk Museum, Schiedam, Amsterdam, Netherlands.

Fire and Ice
Javaphile Productions
performance
with Marga Adama, Lanny Harrison and John Munsey
Melkweg, Amsterdam, Netherlands.

Virtual Projection Installation
with Theo Botschuijver
Melkweg, Amsterdam, Netherlands.

Poetry in Performance
Javaphile Productions
performance
with Marga Adama, Robert Hahn, Jenn ben Jakov, Wendela Gevers Deynoot, Charly Jungbauer and John Munsey.
One World Poetry Festival, Melkweg, Amsterdam, Netherlands.

Slapstick
Pneumatic eventstructure
with Theo Botschuijver
Inflatable tube indicating the height of the planned new town hall.
Anti-City Circus, Amsterdam, Netherlands.

1979

Neon Wave Sculpture
Permanent interactive sculpture
with Theo Botschuijver
Koopvaardersplantsoen, Amsterdam, Netherlands.

29 *Bubble Wall*
Permanent interactive sculpture
with Theo Botschuijver
People walking in front of a liquid-filled wall interactively triggered patterns of air bubbles.
Swimmingpool de Hoogeberg, Velsen, Netherlands.

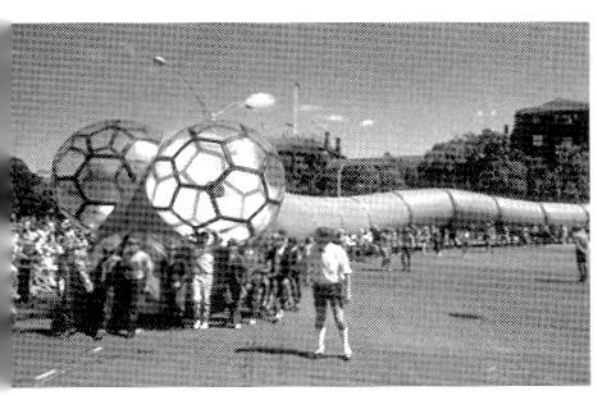

22

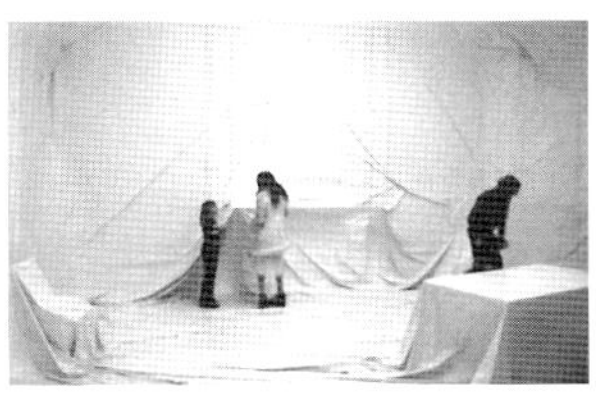

23

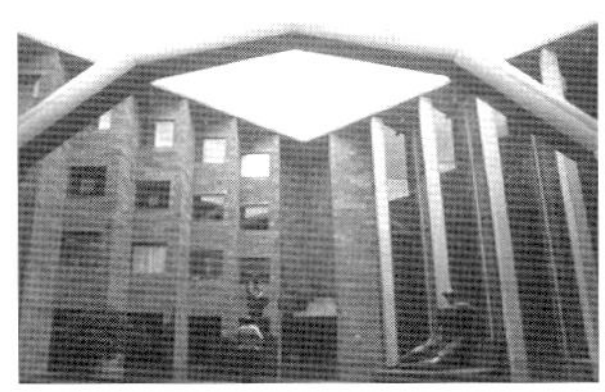

24

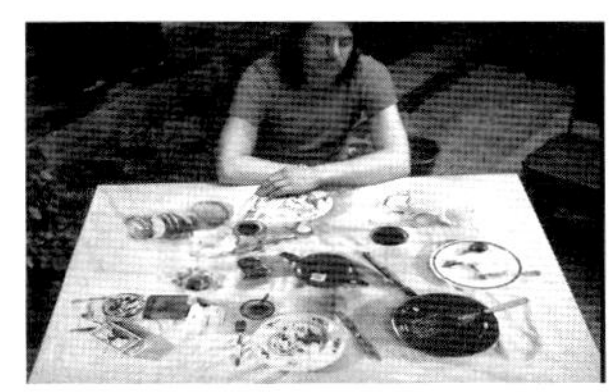

25

1983

Virtual Projection Performance
with Fabienne de Quasa Riera
De Lantaren, Rotterdam, Netherlands.

Dell'Inferno di Dante
Mixed-media installation
with Fabienne de Quasa Riera and M. Beatriz, C. Linaris-Couridou, R. Nottrot, C. Hartmann, C. Petit, J. Verburg
Aorta, Amsterdam, Netherlands.

Points of View I
Interactive computer graphics installation
Software: Larry Abel
Hardware: Tat van Vark and Charly Jungbauer
produced under the auspices of the Mickery Theater, Amsterdam, Netherlands.
1983: Mickery Theater, Amsterdam, Netherlands; Kijkhuis, The Hague, Netherlands; Centrum t'Hoogt, Utrecht, Netherlands; De Lantaren, Rotterdam, Netherlands. – 1983/84: Apollohuis, Eindhoven, Netherlands.

32 *Points of View II – Babel*
Interactive computer graphics installation
Software: Larry Abel
Hardware: Tat van Vark and Charly Jungbauer
Mickery Theater, Amsterdam, Netherlands.

1984

Points of View III – A Three-Dimensional Story
Interactive computer graphics installation
Software: Larry Abel
Hardware: Tat van Vark and Charly Jungbauer
Computer Festival, De Meervaart, Amsterdam, Netherlands.

1985

33 *Jules Verne*
Installation for an opera
A virtual projection installation created the illusion of looking through the theatre entrance doors at fictional scenes situated in the real space outside the theatre.
Stadsschouwburg, Groningen, Netherlands

The Narrative Landscape (1985/95)
Interactive computer graphics installation
with Dirk Groeneveld
Software: Larry Abel (1985)
Revised software: Gideon May (1992)
Hardware: Tat van Vark and Charly Jungbauer
CD-ROM version: Volker Kuchelmeister (1995)
Produced under the auspices of Stichting de Appel, Amsterdam, Netherlands.
1985: Aorta, Amsterdam, Netherlands; Siggraph '85 Art Show, Exploratorium, San Francisco, United States; De Lantaren, Rotterdam, Netherlands; Performancetage, Moltkerei-Werkstatt, Cologne, Germany. – 1986: Festival des Arts Electroniques, Rennes, France. – 1989: 25 Jahre Video-Skulptur, DuMont Kunsthalle, Cologne, Germany; 39. Berliner Festwochen, Berlin, Germany; Kunsthaus, Zürich, Switzerland. – 1992: The Robots, Nagashima Spaland, Nagoya, Japan. – 1995: Trigon-Personale '95, Neue Galerie am Landesmusuem Joanneum, Graz, Austria.– 1995/96: Fotografie nach der Fotografie, Siemens Kulturprogramm, Munich, Germany: Aktionsforum Praterinsel, Munich, Germany; Kunsthalle, Krems, Austria; Städtische Galerie, Erlangen, Germany; Brandenburgische Kunstsammlungen, Cottbus, Germany; Museet for Fotokunst, Odense, Denmark.

1986

Anamorphoses of Memory
Video installation
with Dirk Groeneveld
Software: Gideon May
Collection of Stedelijk Museum, Amsterdam, Netherlands
1986: Kunst Over de Vloer, Entrepotdok, Amsterdam, Netherlands. – 1987: Municipal Art Acquisitions, Fodor Museum, Amsterdam, Netherlands.

The Literary Psychogeography of Amsterdam
Pilot for an interactive multimedia work
with Tjebbe van Tijen
Various multimedia and hyper-

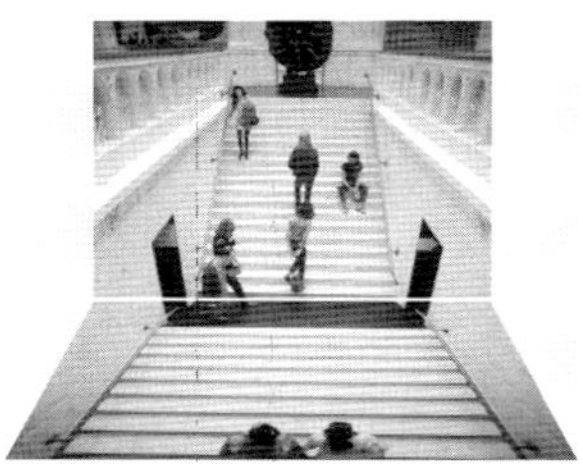

26

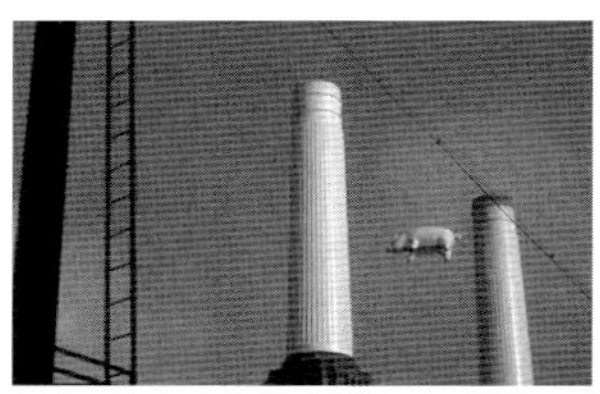

27

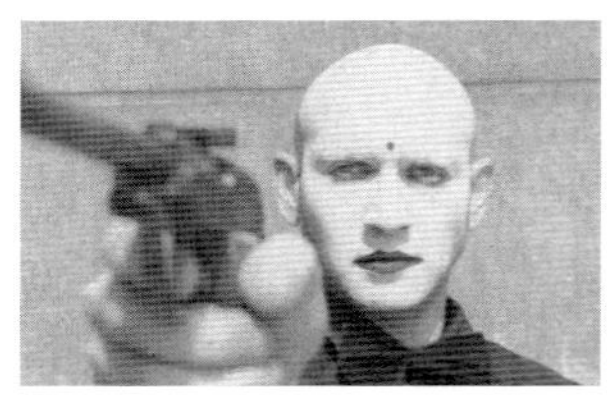

28

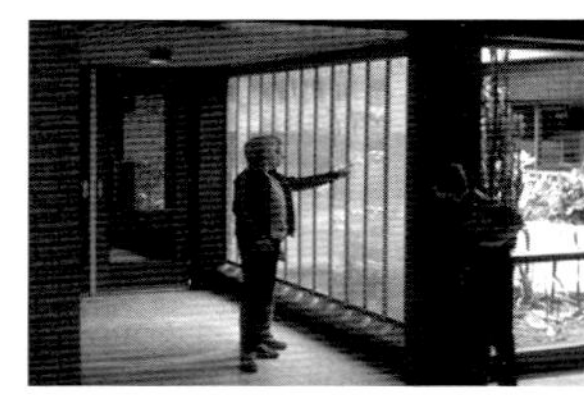

29

1987

34 *Sonus Lux*
35 Interactive 'son et lumiere' installation
with Harry de Wit
A computer-programmed lighting installation articulated the neoclassical features of this building. Transparent acoustic panels allowed the public to listen to music as if it were emanating from the walls of the building.
Felix Meritis 1787–1987 Festival, Shaffy Theater, Amsterdam, Netherlands.

Infinity Divided by Sixteen
Interactive computer graphics and sound installation
with Harry de Wit
Software: Larry Abel
Hardware: Charly Jungbauer
1987: Image and Sound Festival, Haags Filmhuis, The Hague, Netherlands; Manifestation for the Unstable Media, V2, Den Bosch, Netherlands.

Video Narcissus
Interactive computer graphics installation
Software: Gideon May
Lo Specchio e Il Doppio, Mole Antonelliana, Turin, Italy.

36 *An Imaginary Museum of Revolutions* (1987–89)
Interactive multimedia installation
with Tjebbe van Tijen
Software: Gideon May
Design and production: Curt Adelbert, Gijs Bakker, Bas van den Berg, Pieter Boersma, Hans Derks, Josien Eissens, Fred Gales, Marijke Griffioen, Marise Knegtmans, Hanns 't Mannetje, Bas Moreel, Willem van Oosterwijk, Bas van Tol and Mazdak Wahedi.
1988: De Haagse Zomer, The Hague, Netherlands. – 1989: Inventer 89, La Villette, Cité des Sciences et de l'Industrie, Paris, France; Zyklus Arbeit '89, Brucknerhaus, Linz, Austria; Tekens van Verzet, Museum Fodor, Amsterdam, Netherlands; IS in de HAL, KunstHal, Rotterdam, Netherlands.

1988

37 *Propagation of the Luminous Word*
Interactive sculpture
Software and hardware: Charly Jungbauer
An LED text display shows the keywords that are being requested from the library's computer database. These words are then converted into binary code and displayed on LED light elements attached to the ceiling.
LBC Landelijk Bibliotheekcentrale, Almere, Netherlands.

textual strategies were defined to interactively link historical and contemporary narratives about Amsterdam with computer-transformed images of that city.
Het IJ geopend de binnenstad gedicht, Amsterdam, Netherlands.

Going to the Heart of the Center of The Garden of Delights
Interactive computer graphics installation
Software: Larry Abel
Hardware: Charly Jungbauer
de Vleeshal, Middelburg, Netherlands.

Inventer la Terre
Interactive videodisk sculpture
Sound: Walter Maioli
Collection of La Villette, Cité des Sciences et de l'Industrie, Paris, France.

Heavens Gate
Video installation
Production: Video Hilversum, Netherlands
1986: Image and Sound Festival, Haags Filmhuis, The Hague, Netherlands. – 1987: Stipendia 85–86, Y-Tech, Amsterdam, Netherlands; PC RAI, Amsterdam, Netherlands; Felix Meritis 1787–1987 Festival, Shaffy Theater, Amsterdam, Netherlands. – 1988: The Third Australian Video Festival, Powerhouse, Sydney, Australia. – 1991/92: Outer Space: 8 Photo & Video Installations, South Bank Centre, UK; Laing Art Gallery, Newcastle-upon-Tyne, UK; Ferens Art Gallery, Hull, UK; Camden Arts Centre, London, UK; Arnolfini Gallery, Bristol, UK.– 1992: Fotografie Biennale Rotterdam III, Rotterdam, Netherlands; Der entfesselte Blick, Kunstmuseum Bern, Seedamm-Kulturzentrum, Bern,Switzerland. – 1993: InterCommunication '93 Media Passage, InterCommunication Center, BEAM Theater, Shibuya, Tokyo, Japan. – 1994: Technoart: An Interactive New Media Exhibition, Ontario Science Centre, Toronto, Canada. – 1995: MultiMediale 4, ZKM Karlsruhe, Karlsruhe, Germany; Arslab, Turin, Italy; Trigon-Personale '95, Neue Galerie am Landesmuseum Joanneum, Graz, Austria. – 1996: The Butterfly Effect, Soros Center for Contemporary Arts, Budapest, Hungary; Interaktive Objekte und Kunstwerke, Landeskunstwochen Ettlingen, Museum Ettlingen, Ettlingen, Germany.

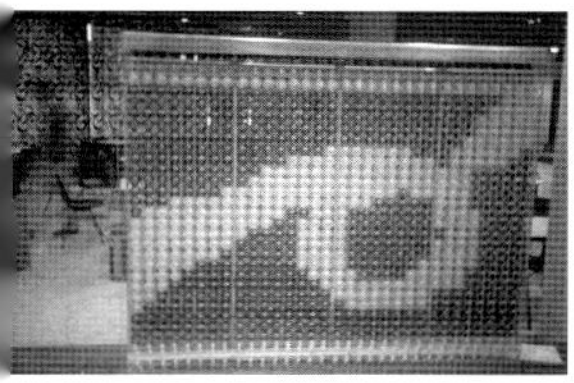
30

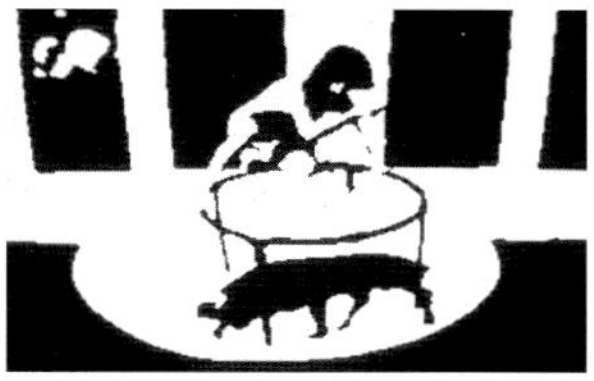
31

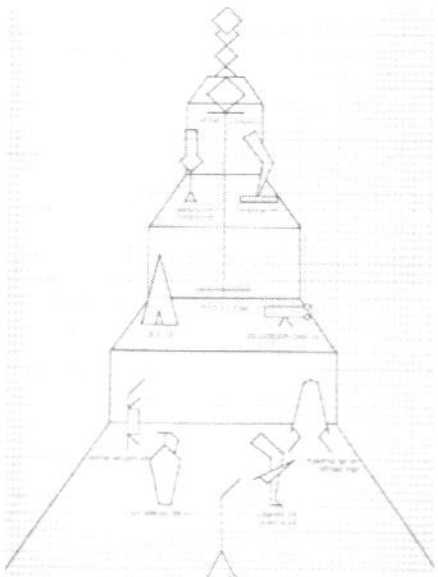
32

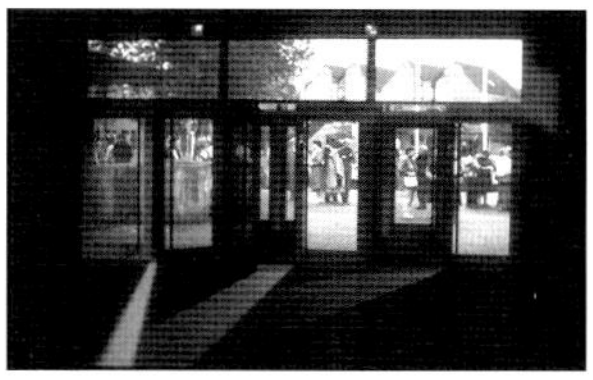
33

Self-Portrait with Eiffel Tower
Interactive computer graphics installation
Circular-patterned digitizing of the viewers' movements was conjoined with the static recording of a large model of the Eiffel Tower.
Manifestation for the Unstable Media, V2, Den Bosch, Netherlands.

38 *The Legible City (prototype)*
39 Interactive computer graphics installation with Dirk Groeneveld
Software: Gideon May and Lothar Schmitt
1988/89: Het Postmoderne aan kinderen verklaard, Bonnefantenmuseum, Maastricht, Belgium; MUseum van Hedendaagse Kunst, Antwerp, Belgium.

1989

The Legible City (1989–91)
Manhattan version (1989)
Amsterdam version (1990)
Karlsruhe version (1991)
Interactive computer graphics installation
with Dirk Groeneveld
Software: Gideon May
and Lothar Schmitt
Hardware: Tat van Vark
and Charly Jungbauer
Collection of ZKM/Medienmuseum, Karlsruhe, Germany
1989: Artec 89, The 1st International Biennale in Nagoya, Japan; Siggraph '89 Art Show, Boston, United States; Ars Electronica: Im Netz der Systeme, Brucknerhaus, Linz, Austria. – 1990: Time Space Light, Academie Minerva, Groningen, Netherlands; artifices, Saint-Denis, France; artware. Kunst und Elektronik, CeBIT, Hanover, Germany; Interface 1, Museum für Kunst und Gewerbe, Hamburg, Germany; Dernieres Visites Avant Travaux, Le Fresnoy, Tourcoing, France; De Balie Theater, Amsterdam, Netherlands; L'Immagine Elettronica, Chiesa di San Romano, Ferrara, Italy; Les Artistes et la Lumiere, Centre National Art et Technologie, Reims, France. – 1990/91: Vom Verschwinden der Ferne, Telekommunikation und Kunst, Deutsches Postmuseum, Frankfurt-on-Main, Germany.
– 1991: MuuMedia Festival, Galleria Otso, Espoo, Finland; MultiMediale 2, ZKM Karlsruhe, Karlsruhe, Germany; Imago: Fin de siècle in Dutch Contemporary Art, Video Art Festival, Locarno, Switzerland; El Art, Retretti Art Center, Retretti, Finland; Stanford Conference on Design, Stanford, California, United States. – 1992: Moving Image – Electronic Art, Fundació Joan Miro, Barcelona, Spain; Virtual World Voyaging: Agnes Hegedüs and Jeffrey Shaw, Art Gallery, Fukuoka, Japan; Manifestation for the Unstable Media, V2, Den Bosch, Netherlands.
– 1992/93: The Boundary Rider, 9th Biennale of Sydney, Sydney, Australia.
– 1993: Die Sprache der Kunst. Die Beziehung von Bild und Text in der Kunst des 20. Jahrhunderts,

Kunsthalle, Vienna, Austria. – 1995: Art and Electronics, Hong Kong Arts Centre, Hong Kong; Trigon-Personale '95, Neue Galerie am Landesmuseum Joanneum, Graz, Austria. – 1995/96: 3e Biennale d'art contemporain de Lyon, Musée d'art contemporain, Lyons, France. – 1996: Mediascape, Guggenheim Museum SoHo, New York, United States.

Alice's Room
Interactive computer graphics installation
with Gideon May
Software: Gideon May
Hardware: Huib Nelissen and Floris van Manen
1989: Kanagawa International Art & Science Exhibition, Kanagawa Science Centre, Kawasaki-shi, Japan.

40 *Word Play*
Permanent interactive sculpture with Dirk Groeneveld
Hardware and software: Novamatic, Eich, Germany
Two LED text displays are moving 'windows' that reveal a virtual space of randomly juxtaposing texts derived from well-known theatre plays.
Schouwburg, Arnheim, Netherlands

1990

Revolution
Interactive videodisk sculpture with Tjebbe van Tijen
Software: Gideon May
Hardware: Huib Nelissen, Charly Jungbauer and Bas Bossinade
Collection of Dutch Arts Council, Netherlands
1990: Imago: Fin de Siècle in Dutch Contemporary Art, Kunst Rai, Amsterdam, Netherlands; Video Art Festival, Locarno, Switzerland. – 1991: Imago: Fin de siècle in Dutch Contemporary Art, Kulturni Dom, Bratislava, Czechoslovakia. – 1992: Imago: Fin de siècle in Dutch Contemporary Art, Palao de la Virreina, Barcelona, Spain; Edificio de Alfandega do Porto, Oporto, Portugal; World Expo, Seville, Spain. – 1993: Mediale, Deichtorhallen, Hamburg, Germany. – 1994: Tart '94, Mens en cyberspace, De Vrijhof Universiteit, Twente, Netherlands, Imago: Fin de siècle in Dutch Contemporary Art, Hara Arc Museum, Gunma, Japan; Fine Arts Museum, Taipei, Taiwan. – 1995: Kwangju Biennale '95, Seoul, Korea.

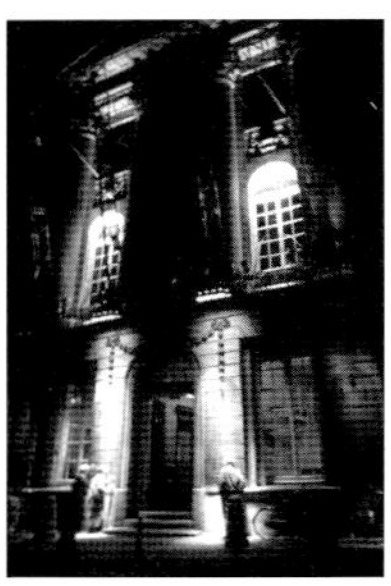

34

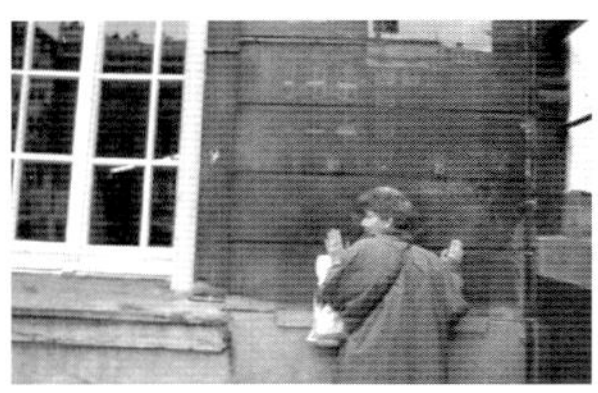

35

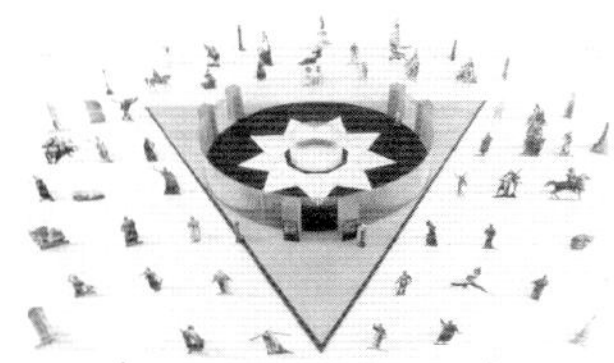

36

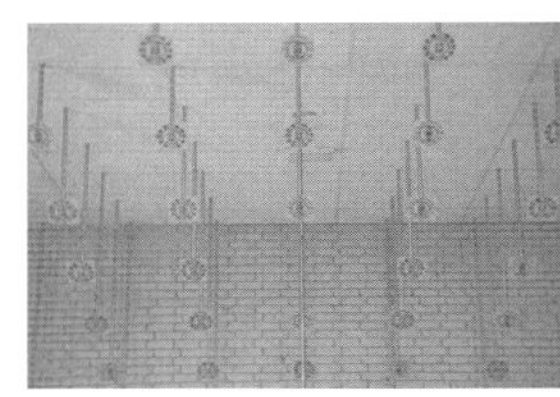

37

1993

Disappearance
Video sculpture
Hardware: Huib Nelissen and Bas Bossinade
Collection of the ZKM/Medienmuseum, Karlsruhe, Germany
1993: Binaera: 14 Interaktionen – Kunst und Technologie, Musée Communal d'Ixelles, Brussels, Belgium; Kunsthalle, Vienna, Austria. – 1994: Automata, World Festival Exposition MIE '94, Nagoya, Japan; MultiMediale 3, ZKM Karlsruhe, Germany.

EVE (Extended Virtual Environment)
Cooperative project between ZKM and Forschungszentrum Karlsruhe
Project leader: Ralph Gruber
Software: Gideon May
1993: MultiMediale 3, ZKM Karlsruhe, Germany. – 1994: Le Métafort, d'Aubervilliers, France. – 1995: Acciona Museo Interactivo de la Cienca, Madrid, Spain. – 1995: MultiMediale 4, ZKM Karlsruhe, Germany.

Televirtual Chit Chat
Interactive telematic computer graphics installation
Software: Gideon May
Imagina '93, Monte Carlo, Monaco and Karlsruhe, Germany.

The Royal Road
Interactive videodisk installation
Hardware: Huib Nelissen and Bas Bossinade
3-D animation: Tamás Waliczky
Collection of Institut für Auslandsbeziehungen, Stuttgart, Germany.
1993: Multimediale 3, ZKM Karlsruhe, Germany. – 1994–96: Videoskulptur seit 1963, Institut für Auslandsbeziehungen, Stuttgart: Kunsthalle, Rostock, Germany; Hong Kong Arts Centre, Centrum f. beeldende Kunst, Groningen, Netherlands; World Wide Video Center, The Hague, Netherlands; Museum van hedendaagse Kunst, Ghent, Belgium.

1994

The Golden Calf
Interactive computer graphics installation
Software: Gideon May
1994: Ars Electronica 94: Intelligente Ambiente, Brucknerhaus Linz, Austria. – 1995: The Interaction 95, International Academy of Media Arts and Sciences (IAMAS), Gifu, Japan; Trigon-Personale '95, Neue Galerie am Landesmuseum Joanneum, Graz, Austria. – 1996: Artifices 4, Saint-Denis, France.

The Spatial Pendulum
Interactive sculpture
Software: Charly Jungbauer
A large steel ball hangs from four cables and motorized pulleys within the atrium. Connected to the centre's computer network, anyone there can interactively program its movement paths.
Vrije Universiteit, Centre for Mathematics and Computer Science, Amsterdam, Netherlands.

1991

The Virtual Museum
Interactive computer graphics installation
Software: Gideon May
Hardware: Huib Nelissen and Bas Bossinade.
Produced under the auspices of the Städelschule, Institut für Neue Medien, Frankfurt-on-Main, Germany.
Collection of ZKM/Museum für Gegenwartskunst, Karlsruhe, Germany
1991: Das Belebte Bild. Interaktive Computer Installationen, Art Frankfurt, Frankfurt-on-Main, Germany; Machines à Communiquer, La Villette, Cité des Sciences et de l'Industrie, Paris, France. – 1992: The Robots, Nagashima Spaland, Nagoya, Japan; Ars Electronica: Die Welt von Innen – Endo & Nano, Brucknerhaus, Linz, Austria; Revue virtuelle, Centre Georges Pompidou, Paris, France. – 1993: Künstliche Spiele, Medienlabor, Munich, Germany. – 1994: Arte Virtual, Communidad de Madrid, Madrid, Spain; Interactive Media Festival, Los Angeles, United States.

1992

41 *Architext*
Permanent group of interactive sculptures
Hardware and software: Novamatic, Eich, Germany
Positioned on the highway, a tall column with nine rotating LED text displays announces the entrance to Zoetermeer. Another arrangement of LED displays is attached to the stage tower of the Stadstheater (see page 97). Acoustic panels on the exterior and interior front windows of this theatre bring the actual sounds from the stage out onto the street, and the live sounds from the street into the theatre.
Stadstheater and Europaweg, Zoetermeer, Netherlands.

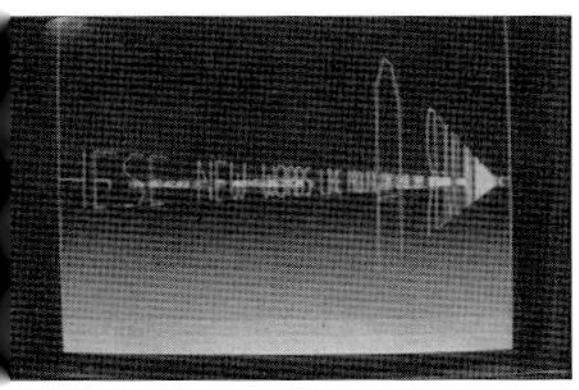

38

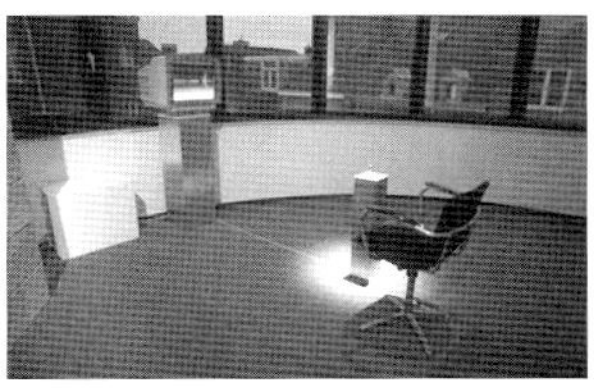

39

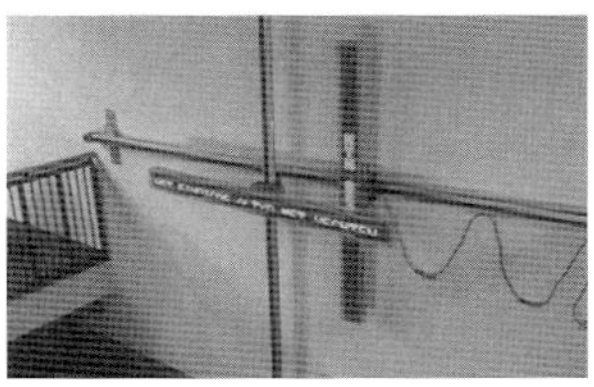

40

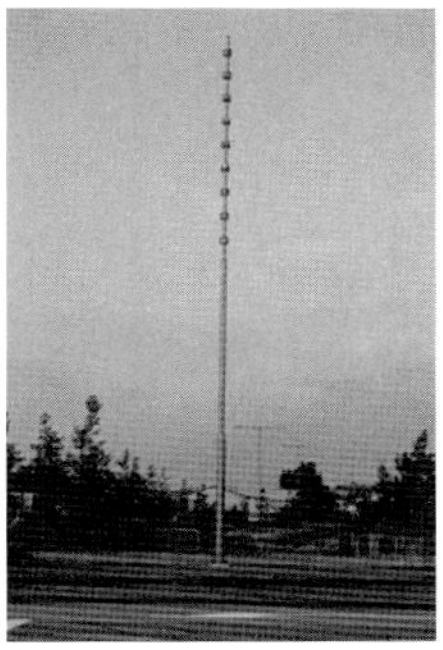

41

Three Signifiers
Permanent neon and video installation
Hardware and software: Bas Bossinade
The work is constituted by three components: a blue neon ladder going through the ceiling, a red neon wire-frame representation of the space, and closed-circuit video that transmits turning images of the space synchronized to and seen within a revolving door.
Central station, Utrecht, Netherlands.

1995

Place – a user's manual
Interactive computer graphics installation
Software: Adolf Mathias
Hardware: Huib Nelissen and Bas Bossinade
2-D graphics: Tamás Waliczky
Consultant: Rufus Camphausen
Produced under the auspices of the Neue Galerie am Landesmuseum Joanneum, Graz, Austria.– 1995: Trigon-Personale '95, Neue Galerie am Landesmuseum Joanneum, Graz, Austria – 1996: Under Capricorn, Stedelijk Museum, Amsterdam, Netherlands; Artifices 4, Saint-Denis, France; La Villette, Cité des Sciences et de l'Industrie, Paris, France.

Selected Bibliography

Auswahlbibliographie

Articles by Jeffrey Shaw

Artikel von Jeffrey Shaw

'Structure Gonflables et Participation.' – *RHOBO*, No. 3, Spring 1968.

'Concepts for an Operational Art.' – *Art and Artists*, No. 10, January 1969, pp. 47–49.

'Eventstructure Research Group.' – *Studio International*, Vol. 178, No. 916, November 1969, p. 183.

'Events.' – *Architectural Design*, May 1970, p. 226.

'Tube over the Maschsee.' – *Studio International*, Vol. 180, No. 928, December 1970, p. 253.

'Eventstructures.' – *Proceedings: International Symposium on Pneumatic Structures*, Ed. Stichting P.D.O.B. Delft Universitity of Technology, Delft, Netherlands, 1972.

'Eventstructure Research Group.' – *The Mewspaper*, Royal College of Art, No. 22, April-May 1974, pp. 3–4.

'The Narrative Landscape.' – Museumsjournal, No. 6, Spring 1986, pp. 64–65.

'Un Musée Imaginaire de la Revolution.' – *Mediamatic*, Vol. 2, No. 4, 1988.

'Le Musée Virtuel.' – *art press spécial: Nouvelles Technologies un Art sans Modèle?*, No. 12, 1991, p. 175.

'Virtual Reality: A new medium for the artist?' – *Virtual Reality International 92, Impacts and Applications*, Ed. Tony Feldman, London, 1992, pp. 65–68.

'Modalities of Interactivity and Virtuality.' – *Scan+. Electronic Media Arts*, Vol. 4, 1993, pp. 19–20.

'Reisen in virtuelle Realitäten.' – *Cyberspace. Zum medialen Gesamtkunstwerk*, Eds. Florian Rötzer, Peter Weibel, Munich, 1993, pp. 317–332.

'Virtuelle Räume im Reich der Sinne.' – *Kultur und Technik im 21. Jahrhundert*, Eds. Gert Kaiser, Dirk Matejovski, Jutta Fedrowitz, Frankfurt o. M. / New York, 1993, pp. 329–334.

'Modalities of Interactivity and Virtuality.' – *Artistic Exchange. Akten des XXVIII. Internationalen Kongresses für Kunstgeschichte Berlin, 15.-20. Juli 1992*, Ed. Thomas W. Gaehtgens, Berlin, 1993, pp. 295–300.

'Der entkörperte und wiederverkörperte Leib.' – *Kunstforum. Die Zukunft des Körpers I*, Vol. 132, November 1995-Januar 1996, pp. 168–171.

Articles, Books, Interviews and Reviews concerning Jeffrey Shaw

Artikel in Zeitschriften und Büchern, Interviews und Besprechungen

Willoughby Sharp: 'Air Art.' – *Studio International*, Vol. 175, No. 900, May 1968, pp. 262-265.

'The Happening: Disillusionment of Striptease Films.' – *The Running Man*, Vol.1, No.1, May-June 1968, pp. 22–25.

Hans Derks: 'Blaas op die hap.' – *Wonen*, No. 3, March 1969, pp. 20-23.

'Eventstructure Research Group.' – *Art International*, Vol. 178, No. 916, November 1969, p. 203.

'Eventstructure in Amsterdam.' – *Studio International*, Vol. 178, No. 916, November 1969, pp. 183–184.

'With this bag of air you can walk on water. Inflate and Float.' – LIFE Magazine, Vol. 48, No. 8, April, 1970, pp. 42–45.

'Spaziergang auf dem Wasser.' – *Stern*, Vol. 22, May 19-25, 1970, pp. 154–157.

Stacy Waddy: 'Blow-up.' – *The Guardian*, Monday, June 8, 1970.

Holger Diezemann: 'Straßenkunst. Verrücktes an der Leine.' – *Stern*, Vol. 37, September 1–7, 1970, pp. 184–185.

Jim Burns: *Arthropods: New Design Futures*, Cologne, 1971, pp. 112–115.

Terry Smith: 'Evenstructure Research Group in Australia.' – *Studio International*, Vol 184, No. 948, October 1972, pp. 149–150.

Max Arian: 'De Eventstructure Research Group tast de alledaagse werkelijkheid aan.' – *toneel teatraal*, Vol. 95, No. 1, January 1974, pp. 13–15.

Margaret Neal: 'The Narrative Landscape.' – *IEEE Computer Graphics and Applications*, Vol. 5, No. 11, November 1985, pp. 19–22.

Joost Heesels: 'De tovenaar van interactieve kunst Jeffrey Shaw.' – *AV Audiovisueel Magazine*, Vol. 7, No. 11, December 1986-January 1987, pp. 48–49.

Leo Delfgaauw: 'Towards Instruction and Pleasure.' – *Perspektief Magazine*, No. 37, December 1989–January 1990, pp. 11–17.

Jeroen Wilhelmus: 'Het is net een drie-dimensionaal boek.' – *Computer Dimensions. Tijdschrift over visuele computertoepassingen*, No. 1, 1990, pp. 12–15.

Dorothy S. Hirokawa: 'Jeffrey Shaw. Virtual World Voyage.' (Interview) – *BT Bijutsu Techno*, Vol. 42, No. 622, April 1990, p. 117–131.

Chris Reinewald: 'Reizen door leesbare steden.' – *eos magazine*, No. 9, September 1990, pp. 47–49.

Dorothy S. Hirokawa: 'Artist Interview Jeffrey Shaw.' – *03 Tokyo Calling*, Vol. 2, No. 11, November 1990, pp. 22–27.

Ilske von Schweinitz: 'Gegen Ästhetisches Junkfood.' (Interview) – *Zyma*, No. 2, March/April 1991, pp. 52–55.

Erkki Huhtamo: 'Virtuaalisen Kuvan Arkkitehti, Jeffrey Shaw'n haastattelu.' – *Lähikuva*, No. 2-3, 1991, pp. 39–45.

Florian Rötzer: 'Jeffrey Shaw: Reisen in virtuelle Realitäten.' (Interview) – *Kunstforum*, Vol. 117, 1992, pp. 286–303.

Susanne Schuck: 'Zukunftsvision: Museum im Wohnzimmer.' (Interview) – *Mediagramm*, No. 13, October 1993, p. 5.

Johan Pijnappel: 'Jeffrey Shaw. The Centre for Art and Media, Karlsruhe.' (Interview) – *Art & Design Profile*, No. 39, 1994, pp. 70–79.

Frits Gierstberg: 'Jeffrey Shaw: Breaking through the traditional framework.' – *Perspektief Magazine*, No. 47/48, June 1994, pp. 83–90.

Carl Eugene Loeffler/Tim Anderson: *The Virtual Reality Casebook*, New York, 1994, pp. 161–162.

Cornée Jacobs: 'Met computers nieuwe werelden scheppen.' (Discussion with Jeffrey Shaw and Gert-Jan Lokhorst) – *Spiraal, tien dialogen tussen kunst en filosofie*, Ed. Centrum Beeldende Kunst, Rotterdam, 1994.

Christian W. Thomson: *Visionary Architecture. From Babylon to Virtual Reality*, Munich/New York, 1994, p. 182.

Söke Dinkla: *Vom Zuschauer zum Benutzer. Interaktive Installationen und Environments im späten 20. Jahrhundert*, unpublished thesis, University of Hamburg, 1995, pp. 101–139.

Erkki Huhtamo: 'Jeffrey Shaw's EVE and the Panoramic Tradition.' – *InterCommunication*, No. 14, Autumn 1995, pp.138-139.

Peter Weibel: 'Zur televirtuellen Archi-

tektur von Jeffrey Shaw. Trigon-Personale des Steirischen Herbstes 95 im Grazer Künstlerhaus.' – *Architektur & Bauforum*, No. 178, 1995, pp. 86–89.
Annette Hünnekens: *Der bewegte Betrachter. Theorien der Interaktiven Medienkunst*, Cologne, 1997.

Exhibition Catalogues

Ausstellungskataloge

Six Events in Amsterdam, Ed. Stedelijk Museum, Amsterdam, 1969.
Sonsbeek buiten de perken, Arnheim, 1971, pp. 40–43.
11 Weken Buitenspel. kind en leefmilieu, Ed. Stichting Nederlands Instituut voor Kinderstudie, The Hague, 1972.
9e biennale de paris, Ed. Biennale de Paris, Paris, 1975.
Actie, Werkelijkheid en Fictie in de Kunst van de Jaren '60 in Nederland, Ed. Boymans-van-Beuningen Museum, Rotterdam, 1979.
Jeffrey Shaw. Going to the Heart of the Center of the Garden of Delights, Ed. de Vleeshal, Middelburg, 1986.
'The Third Australian Video Festival Catalogue.' – *Scan+*, Vol. 1, 1988, pp. 46–47
Video-Skulptur retrospektiv und aktuell 1963-1989, Ed. Wulf Herzogenrath, Edith Decker, Cologne, 1989, pp. 281–282.
Individuele Subsidies, Ed. Stichting Fonds voor beeldende kunsten, vormgeving en bouwkunst, Amsterdam, 1989, p. 224
Wonderland of Science Art, Ed. Committee for Kanagawa International Art & Science Exhibition, Kanagawa, 1989, pp. 16–17.
'Computer art in context: Siggraph '89 Art Show Catalog.' – *Leonardo*, Supplemental Issue 1989, p. 103.
Artec '89, Ed. The Chunichi Shimbun, Nagoya, 1989, p. 46.
'tekens van verzet.' – *Beeld, Tijdschrift voor kunst, kunsttheorie en kunstgeschiedenis*, Vol. 4, No. 1/2, January 1989, p. 69.
'Im Netz der Systeme. Für eine interaktive Kunst: Ars Electronica.' – *Kunstforum*, Vol. 103, September/October 1989, pp. 204–209.
Time Space Light, Ed. Academie Minerva, Groningen, 1990, p. 24–25.
Vom Verschwinden der Ferne. Telekommunikation und Kunst, Eds. Edith Decker, Peter Weibel, Cologne, 1990.
'Imago. fin de siècle in dutch contemporary art.' – *Mediamatic*, Vol. 5, No. 1/2, 1990, pp. 70–71.
l'immagine elettronica. HI TÉX NE, Ferrara, 1990, pp.18–19.
Der Prix Ars Electronica, Ed. Hannes Leopoldseder, Linz, 1990, pp. 184–187.
artifices, Ed. Direction des affaires culturelles de la ville de Saint-Denis, Saint-Denis, 1990, pp. 42–43.
Individuele Subsidies, Ed. Stichting Fonds voor beeldende kunsten, vormgeving en bouwkunst, Amsterdam, 1990, p. 289.
MultiMediale 2, Ed. ZKM Karlsruhe, Heinrich Klotz, Karlsruhe, 1991, pp. 67–70.
Wasteland. Landscape from now on, Eds. Fotografie Biennale Rotterdam, Frits Gierstberg, Bas Vroege, Rotterdam, 1992.
Moving Image – Electronic Art, Ed. ZKM Karlsruhe, Fundació Joan Miró, Munich/Stuttgart, 1992, pp. 144–146.
Outer Space, Ed. The South Bank Centre, London, 1992, pp. 20–21.
Ars Electronica 92: The World from Within - Endo & Nano, Eds. Karl Gerbel, Peter Weibel, Linz, 1992, pp. 105–109.
The Boundary Rider. 9th Biennale of Sydney, Ed. The Biennale of Sydney Ltd., Anthony Bond, Sydney, 1992, pp. 212–213.
The Robots. Man & Machine at the End of the 20th Century, Nagoya, 1992, pp. 30–33.
Binaera: 14 Interaktionen - Kunst und Technologie, Ed. Kunsthalle Wien, Toni Stoos, Vienna, 1993.
De Kracht van Heden, Ed. Stichting Fonds voor beeldende Kunsten, vormgeving en bouwkunst, Amsterdam, 1993, pp. 245–250.
InterCommunication '93: Media Passage, Ed. InterCommunication Center, Tokyo, 1993, pp. 23–63.
Der entfesselte Blick, Ed. Gerhard Johann Lischka, Bern, 1993, pp. 48–51.
MultiMediale 3, Ed. ZKM Karlsruhe, Heinrich Klotz, Karlsruhe, 1993, pp. 54– 55, 66
Ars Electronica '94: Intelligent Environment, Eds. Karl Gerbel, Peter Weibel, Vienna, 1994, pp. 84–86.
Arte Virtual, Doce propuestas de Arte Reactivo, Ed. Rafael Lozano-Hemmer, Madrid, 1994.
'Virtual Museum: Interzone '93' – *InterCommunication*, No. 7, January 1994, p. 57.
MultiMediale 4, Ed. ZKM Karlsruhe, Heinrich Klotz, Karlsruhe, 1995, p. 28.
Arslab. I sensi del Virtuale, Eds. Faure, Maria Grazia Mattei, Franco Torriani, Milan, 1995, pp. 48–49.
3e biennale d'art contemporain de lyon. installation, cinéma, vidéo informatique, Ed. Réunion de musées nationaux/Biennale d'Art contemporain, Paris, 1995, pp. 180–181.
Photography after Photography. Memory and Representation in the Digital Age, Eds. Hubertus v. Amelunxen, Stefan Iglhaut, Florian Rötzer, Munich, 1996, pp. 260–265.
Mediascape, Ed. The Solomon R. Guggenheim Foundation, New York, 1996, pp. 46–49.
Under Capricorn. Art in the Age of Globalisation, Eds. Stedelijk Museum Amsterdam, City Gallery Wellington, Amsterdam, 1996, pp. 76–77.
Artifices 4, Ed. Direction des affaires culturelles de la ville de Saint-Denis, Saint-Denis, 1996, pp. 14–27.

Illustration Credits

Abbildungsnachweis

Cover: *The Legible City*, L'Immagine Elettronica, Ferrara, Italy, 1990. Photo: Jeffrey Shaw

Inside front cover: *MovieMovie*, 4th International Experimental Film Festival, Knokke-le-Zoute, Belgium, 1967. Photo: Pieter Boersma

Inside back cover: *Place - a user's manual*. Screenshot © Jeffrey Shaw.

61: *Continuous Sound and Image Moments*. Drawings © Jeffrey Shaw/Tjebbe van Tijen

62, 63: *Emergences of Continuous Forms*, Better Books, London UK, 1966. Photos 62 left, 63 right: Clay Perry; 62/63 middle: Pieter Boersma

64: *Disillusion of a Fish Pond*, 26 Kingly Street Gallery, London, UK, 1967. Photos: Clay Perry

65 top: *Smokescreen*, Swansea Art Festival, Wales, 1969. Photo: Eventstructure Research Group (ERG).

65 bottom: *Wind and Rain*, Sigma 5, Bordeaux, France, 1969. Photo: ERG

66, 67, 68, 69: *Corpocinema*, Amsterdam, Netherlands, 1967. Photos: Pieter Boersma

70, 71, 72, 73: *MovieMovie*, 4th International Experimental Film Festival, Knokke-le-Zoute, Belgium, 1967. Photos: Pieter Boersma

74 top: *Waterquake*, Assen, Netherlands, 1970. Photo: ERG

74 bottom: *Alpevent*, Kornhauskeller, Bern, Switzerland, 1968. Photo: Pieter Boersma

75 top: *Aqua-Airground*, Floriade, Kind en Leefmilieu Festival, Amsterdam, Netherlands, 1972. Photos: ERG

75 bottom: Airground Mattress, BBC TV, London, UK, 1970. Photo: ERG

76/77 top: *Walterwalk Tube*, Straßenkunstfestival, Hanover, Germany, 1970. Photo: ERG

76, 77 bottom: *Waterwalk Tube*, Groningen, Netherlands, 1972. Photos: Pieter Boersma

78: *Waterwalk*, Brighton Festival, Brighton, UK, 1970. Photo: ERG

79: *Waterwalk*, Six Events in Amsterdam, Amsterdam, Netherlands, 1969. Photo: ERG

80: *Cloud* (of daytime sky at night), Stedelijk Museum, Amsterdam, Netherlands, 1970. Photos: Pieter Boersma

81: *Three Pavilions* (*Auditorium Pavilion*), Sonsbeek buiten de perken, Arnheim, Netherlands, 1971. Photo top: Pieter Boersma; drawing bottom © ERG

82, 83: *Diadrama*, Universiteits Theater, Amsterdam, Netherlands, 1974. Photos: ERG

84, 85, 86, 87: *Viewpoint*, 9th Biennale de Paris, Musée d'Art Moderne de la Ville de Paris, Paris, France, 1975. Photos: ERG.

88, 89: *The Lamb Lies Down on Broadway*, Genesis world tour, 1975. Photos: ERG

90, 91: *Kinetic Light and Mirror Sculpture*, Genesis world tour, 1977. Photos: ERG

92, 93, 94, 95: *Laser installations and performances*, de Appel, Amsterdam, Netherlands, 1978. Photos 92, 93: ERG; 94 left, 94/95 middle, 95 top: Thys Schouten; 95 bottom: Salli Sachse

96: *Neon Wave Sculpture*, Koopvarderplantsoen, Amsterdam, Netherlands, 1979. Photo: ERG

97: *Architext*, Stadstheater Zoetermeer, Netherlands, 1992. Photos: Jeffrey Shaw

98, 99: *Once upon a time*, Gallery Bedeaux, Amsterdam, Netherlands, 1979. Photos: Javaphile Productions

100: *Virtual Projection Installation*, Melkweg, Amsterdam, Netherlands, 1978. Photos: ERG

101: *Virtual Projection Performance*, De Lantaren, Rotterdam, Netherlands, 1983. Photos: Jeffrey Shaw

102, 103, 104, 105: *Points of View*, Apollohuis, Eindhoven, Netherlands, 1983. Photo 102/103: Jeffrey Shaw; screenshots 104/105 © Jeffrey Shaw.

106, 107, 108, 109: *The Narrative Landscape*, Aorta, Amsterdam, Netherlands, 1985. Photos 106/107: Sjoerd Holsbergen; 108: Jeffrey Shaw; screenshots 108/109 middle, 109 right © Jeffrey Shaw.

110, 111: *Going to the Heart of the Center of The Garden of Delights*, de Vleeshal, Middelburg, Netherlands, 1986. Photos 110 right, 111 right: Jeffrey Shaw. Screenshots 110 left, 111 left © Jeffrey Shaw.

112, 113, 114, 115: *Inventer la Terre*, La Villette, Cité des Sciences et de l'Industrie, Paris, France, 1986. Photo 112/113: Jeffrey Shaw; screenshots 114/115 © Jeffrey Shaw.

116, 117: *Heavens Gate*, Trigon Personale '95, Neue Galerie am Landesmuseum Joanneum, Graz, Austria, 1995. Photo 116/117 middle: Croce & WIR; screenshots 117 bottom © Jeffrey Shaw.

118, 119: *Infinity Divided by Sixteen*, Manifestation for the Unstable Media, V2, Den Bosch, Netherlands, 1987. Photos: Pieter Boersma

120: *Anamorphoses of Memory*, Kunst Over de Vloer, Amsterdam, Netherlands, 1986. Photos: Jeffrey Shaw

121: *Video Narcissus*, Lo Specchio e Il Doppio, Mole Antonelliana, Turin, Italy, 1987. Photo left: Gideon May; right: Jeffrey Shaw

122, 123: *An Imaginary Museum of Revolutions*, Amsterdam, Netherlands, 1988. Photos 122: Pieter Boersma; screenshots 123 © Jeffrey Shaw/Tjebbe van Tijen

124, 125: *Revolution*, Imago, Kunst RAI, Amsterdam, Netherlands, 1990. Photos: Jeffrey Shaw

126, 127, 128, 129: *The Legible City*, L'Immagine Elettronica, Ferrara, Italy, 1990. Photos 126 left, 126/127 middle: Jeffrey Shaw; screenshots 128, 129 © Jeffrey Shaw.

130, 131: *Alice's Room*, Kanagawa International Art & Science Exhibition, Kanagawa Science Centre, Kawasaki-shi, Japan, 1989. Photos 130 left, 130/131 middle: Jeffrey Shaw; 131 right: Gideon May.

132, 133: *The Virtual Museum*, Ars Electronica, Brucknerhaus, Linz, Austria, 1992. Photos: Jeffrey Shaw

134, 135: *Televirtual Chit Chat*, Imagina '93, Monte Carlo, Monaco, 1993. Photo 134 left (Karlsruhe): Derek Hauffen; 135 right (Monte Carlo): Jeffrey Shaw; screenshot 134/135 middle © Jeffrey Shaw.

136, 137: *Disappearance*, Binaera, Kunsthalle, Vienna, Austria, 1993. Photos: Jeffrey Shaw

138, 139: *EVE (Extended Virtual Environment)*, MultiMediale 3, ZKM Karlsruhe, Karlsruhe, Germany, 1993. Photos 138 left, 138/139 middle: Jeffrey Shaw; 139 right: Ralph Gruber.

140, 141: *The Golden Calf*, Ars Electronica '94, Linz, Austria, 1994. Photos: Jeffrey Shaw

142, 143, 144, 145: *Place – a user's manual*, Trigon Personale '95, Neue Galerie am Landesmuseum Joanneum, Graz, Austria, 1995. Photo 142/143: Croce & WIR; screenshots 144, 145 © Jeffrey Shaw.

162, (1): *The Dante Cupboard*, Centro Culturale, San Fedele, Milan, Italy, 1966. Photo: Enrice Cattaneo

162, (2): *Disillusionary Homage to Clovis Trouille*, Kasteelhoeve Beek en Donk, Netherlands, 1966. Photo: Jeffrey Shaw

162, (3): *This is No Thing - This is a Situation of Opportunity*, 1967. Drawing © Jeffrey Shaw/Tjebbe van Tijen
162, (4): *Glove Screen*, 26 Kingly Street Gallery, London, UK, 1967. Photo: Jeffrey Shaw
162, (5): *Book Plumbing*, Better Books, London, UK, 1967. Photo: Jeffrey Shaw
163, (6): *Airground*, City of London Festival, London, UK, 1968. Photo: Pieter Boersma
163, (7): *Octopus*, Stedelijk Museum, Amsterdam, Netherlands, 1968. Photo: Pieter Boersma
163, (8): *Pneutube*, Six Events in Amsterdam, Amsterdam, Netherlands, 1968. Photo: Pieter Boersma
163, (9): *Black Airground*, Museum of Modern Art, Oxford, UK, 1968. Photo: ERG
164, (10): *Supertube*, Ouderkerk a/d Amstel, Netherlands, 1968. Photo: Pieter Boersma
164, (11): *Artificial Landscapes*, 1969. Photographic collage © ERG
164, (12): *Grassroll*, Six Events in Amsterdam, Amsterdam, Netherlands, 1969. Photo: Pieter Boersma
164, (13): *Cushion*, Six Events in Amsterdam, Amsterdam, Netherlands, 1969. Photo: Pieter Boersma
165 ,(14): *Brickhill*, Six Events in Amsterdam, Amsterdam, Netherlands, 1969. Photo: ERG
165, (15): *Waterwalk Tube*, Groningen, Netherlands, 1972. Photo: Pieter Boersma
165, (16): *No Thing*, 1970. Photographic collage © ERG
165, (17): *Televents*, V.P.R.O. Television, Amsterdam, Netherlands, 1970. Photo: ERG
166, (18): *Scottish Sorrow* , Edinburgh Festival, Edinburgh, UK, 1971. Photo: ERG
166, (19): *Three Pavilions* (*Video Pavilion*), Sonsbeek buiten de perken, Arnheim, Netherlands, 1971. Photo: Pieter Boersma
166, (20): *Three Pavilions* (*Information Pavilion*), Sonsbeek buiten de perken, Arnheim, Netherlands, 1971. Photo: Pieter Boersma
166, (21): *Homage to Bladen*, Sonsbeek buiten de perken, Arnheim, Netherlands, 1971. Photo: ERG
167, (22): *Centipede*, Moomba Festival, Melbourne, Australia, 1972. Photo: ERG
167, (23): *More & Less*, Gallery House, London, UK, 1972. Photo: ERG
167, (24): *Rainbow*, National Gallery of Victoria, Melbourne, Australia, 1972. Photo: ERG
167, (25): *Projections*, Pinacotheca and Tolarno Galleries, Melbourne, Australia, 1973. Photo: ERG
168, (26): *Staircase*, Stedelijk Museum, Amsterdam, Netherlands, 1974. Photo: ERG
168, (27): *Pig*, Battersea Park, London, UK, 1972. Photo: ERG
168, (28): *Suncycle*, Lucht, Stedelijk Museum, Amsterdam, 1978. Photo: Javaphile Productions
168, (29): *Bubble Wall*, Swimmingpool de Hoogeberg, Velsen, Netherlands, 1979. Photo: ERG
169, (30): *Video Ball Sculpture*, Scholengemeenschap Quirijn, Tilburg, Netherlands, 1980. Photo: ERG
169, (31): *Corrida – Logique de la Perception*, 1982. Screenshot © Jeffrey Shaw
169, (32): *Points of View II – Babel*, 1983. Drawing © Jeffrey Shaw
169, (33): *Jules Vernes*, Stadsschouwburg Groningen, Netherlands, 1985. Photo: Jeffrey Shaw
170, (34), (35): *Sonus Lux*, Felix Meritis 1787–1987 Festival, Shaffy Theater, Amsterdam, Netherlands, 1987. Photo: Jeffrey Shaw
170, (36): *An Imaginary Museum of Revolutions*, 1988. Model of the installation © Jeffrey Shaw/ Tjebbe van Tijen
170, (37): *Propagation of the Luminous Word*, LBC Landelijk Bibliotheekcentrale, Almere, Netherlands, 1988. Photo: Jeffrey Shaw
171, (38), (39): *The Legible City* (prototype), Bonnefanten Museum, Maastricht, Belgium, 1988. Screenshot (38) © Jeffrey Shaw; photo (39): Jeffrey Shaw
171, (40): *Word Play*, Schouwburg, Arnheim, Netherlands, 1989. Photo: Jeffrey Shaw
171, (41): *Architext*, Europaweg, Zoetermeer, Netherlands, 1992. Photo: Jeffrey Shaw

Sollten ohne unsere Absicht Bildrechte nicht angeführt sein, bitten wir um Mitteilung.

In the event of any unintentional failure to credit the proprietor of a picture copyright, please notify:

ZKM Karlsruhe
Postfach 69 09
D-76049 Karlsruhe

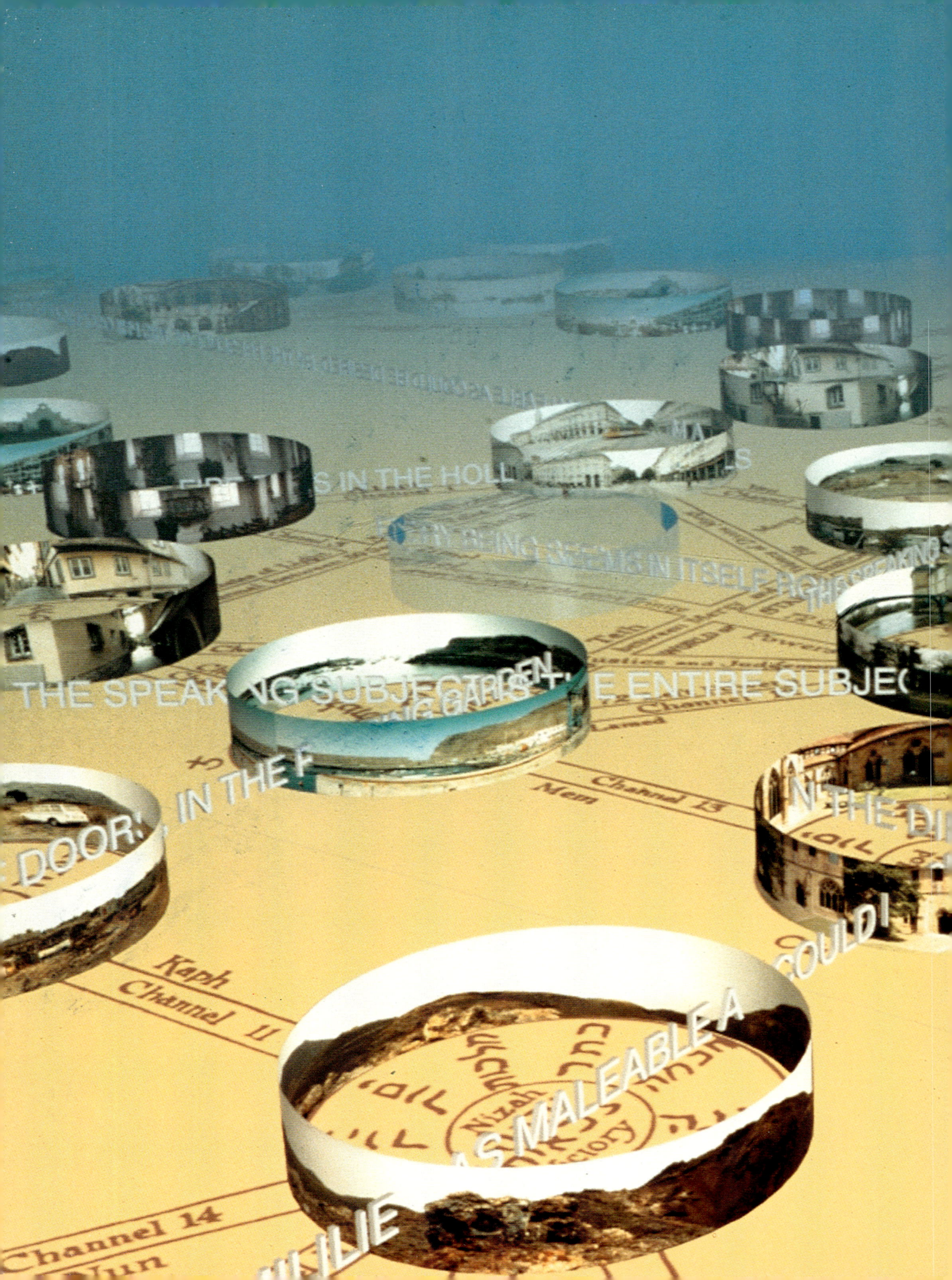
IN THE HOLL
THE SPEAK
THE ENTIRE SUBJE
DOOR
IN THE
AS MALEABLE A
COULD
Channel 13
Men
Kaph
Channel 11
Channel 14